An Introduction to Agent-Based Modeling

An Introduction to Agent-Based Modeling

Modeling Natural, Social, and Engineered Complex Systems with NetLogo

Uri Wilensky and William Rand

The MIT Press
Cambridge, Massachusetts
London, England

MIT Press books may be purchased at special quantity discounts for business or sales promotional use. For information, please email special_sales@mitpress.mit.edu.

This book was set in Times LT Std 10/13pt by Toppan Best-set Premedia Limited, Hong Kong. Printed and bound in the United States of America.

Library of Congress Cataloging-in-Publication Data
Wilensky, Uri, 1955–
An introduction to agent-based modeling : modeling natural, social, and engineered complex systems with NetLogo / Uri Wilensky and William Rand.
    pages cm
Includes bibliographical references and index.
ISBN 978-0-262-73189-8 (pbk. : alk. paper) 1. System analysis—Data processing. 2. Computer simulation.
 3. Multiagent systems. 4. NetLogo (Computer program language) I. Rand, William, 1976– II. Title.
T57.62.W54 2015
003'.3—dc23
                                        2014023747

10 9 8 7 6 5 4 3 2 1

Contents

Preface

Fortune favors the prepared mind.

—Louis Pasteur

A beginning is the time for taking the most delicate care that the balances are correct.

—Frank Herbert

As the world becomes more interconnected and complex, our ability to understand it must also. Simple models no longer suffice to answer many of our questions. The advent of widespread fast computation has enabled us to work on more complex problems and to build and analyze more complex models. This has generated a new field of knowledge called "complex systems." This book is an introduction to one of the primary methodologies that has arisen from complex systems research. This methodology, called agent-based modeling, is a new way of doing science by conducting computer-based experiments.

The rise of computation has also led to an explosion in new data. The amount of new knowledge and data about our world is growing exponentially. This is true regardless of the subject area. From physics to chemistry, from biology to ecology, from political science to economics, from management science to marketing, scientists and researchers are routinely gathering data at a rate that far outstrips that of scientists in the past. As this new data is captured, we can begin to ask questions about complex systems that hitherto could not be meaningfully asked with an expectation of data-driven answers. For example, "How do multiple species interact and compete to form a stable ecosystem?" "How do political institutions affect individual decisions, especially when those individuals have the ability to manipulate political institutions?" or "How can we engineer robots that can work and interact with complex social processes?"

As these complex questions are asked, future scientists, researchers, engineers, business entrepreneurs, politicians, and practitioners will be called on to answer them. The toolkit of complex systems methods will become a necessity for these individuals, and agent-based modeling (ABM) will play a central role in that toolkit.[1] Through this book, we will provide an introduction to ABM for anyone interested in answering questions about the complex systems that are embedded in natural, social, and engineered contexts.

Our book will draw on applications in a wide variety of fields to help illustrate the power of ABM methodology. Along the way, we will guide you through a series of hands-on examples that will help you to understand how you can use this tool in your own work. The guiding principle we used while writing this textbook (and also for NetLogo, the language we will be using) is, "Low Threshold, No Ceiling."[2] By that, we mean that there is very little prerequisite knowledge to start using the material, but at the same time there is no limit to what can be accomplished once it is mastered.

ABM is a powerful tool in helping us to understand complex systems. Our textbook, though titled "An Introduction," provides the tools necessary to enable you to build and use agent-based models to investigate your own questions.

Who We Wrote This For

Because the field of ABM is applicable to so many domains, this textbook can be used in a wide variety of contexts. It can serve as a main text for an interdisciplinary undergraduate course on complex systems or a computer-science class on agent-based modeling. It can be used as a supplementary text in a very wide range of undergraduate classes, including any class where agent-based modeling can be profitably applied. This can be quite a broad list of content areas. The material described in this textbook has been used in natural science classes such as physics, chemistry, and biology; social science classes such as psychology, sociology, and linguistics; and engineering classes such as materials science, industrial engineering, and civil engineering. We have strived to balance the examples across content areas, in order for at least one example to hit squarely on the content area of a given course. Naturally, to achieve this goal, we must sacrifice depth in any one content area. As the field of ABM progresses, we expect that in-depth domain-specific textbooks will appear.

Though we have targeted a high-level undergraduate or entry-level graduate audience, we expect that the book will be useful to other audiences as well. The prerequisite knowledge is not great; a motivated individual learner in a wide range of academic settings could use this text. Similarly, since ABM methods may be new to many graduate students, we expect that our book could be quite useful as a supplementary text to graduate classes in a wide range of subject domains. ABM methods are increasingly used in research labs, in the business community, and in policy circles. We anticipate that professionals in these areas can benefit from the methods and examples herein. The material for this textbook

---

1. If ABM is used in a plural sense (ABMs) or with an article (an ABM) then ABM stands for agent-based model and not agent-based modeling.

2. In the appendix, we discuss the history of the Logo programming language from which this slogan originated. It can also be rendered as "Low Threshold, High Ceiling."

has arisen from and has been tested for over two decades of both undergraduate and graduate classes taught in Computer Science and in Learning Sciences by Uri Wilensky and additional classes taught by William Rand, as well as hundreds of workshops, seminars, and summer school courses conducted by both authors.

In the title, we specifically highlight "natural, social, and engineered complex systems." Natural systems are studied in fields such as biology and physics: complex systems that are naturally occurring. Social systems consist of individuals interacting with each other. Social systems can be natural and/or engineered. Engineered systems are those that have been designed by humans to achieve a particular goal.

There are few prerequisites for this book. We do not assume any mathematical knowledge beyond basic algebra, and we do not assume any prior programming knowledge. For chapters 6, 7, and 8, we do assume that you have a very basic knowledge of statistics—for example, that you understand what a normal distribution is. Moreover, as we discuss later, we expect you to start with a rudimentary familiarity with NetLogo, and **we suggest that you work through the first three tutorials included in the NetLogo user manual of the NetLogo software.** The NetLogo software can be downloaded from ccl.northwestern .edu/netlogo/.[3]

Working through this book will require reading and writing of computer code. This may be quite unfamiliar to some readers. Though many people believe that computer programming is too hard for them to learn, research by Constructionist educators and decades of experience has shown the authors that virtually all students can learn to program in NetLogo. We hope that you won't be scared off by all the code in the textbook, and that you will take the time to learn to read and write the code. We are very confident that you can do it and that taking the time to learn it will pay rich dividends.

NetLogo and the Textbook

Many different agent-based modeling languages exist. As of this writing, NetLogo remains the most widely used. Of the others currently in use, Swarm, developed at the Santa Fe Institute, Repast, developed at Argonne National Laboratory, and MASON, developed at George Mason University, are the next most pervasive among scientists and researchers. Most ABM toolkits (including NetLogo) are open source and freely available. AnyLogic is a commercial package that has also been successful. Other software packages for building ABMs in current use include Ascape, Breve, Cormas, MASS, PS-I, and SeSam. It is also possible to write an agent-based model in any language. When building your own model in a standard non-agent-based programming language, the time to run the model may be faster, but often the time for the lifecycle of development will be considerably slower.

3. This textbook uses the desktop application version of the NetLogo software. At the time of publication of this book, a browser-based version of NetLogo will also be available. Most examples used in the book will work in the browser-based version, though some will require adaptation for that version.

We make use of NetLogo examples throughout this textbook, both to provide hands-on illustrations of the principles being discussed and also as a form of "pseudo-code."[4] However, this textbook is not a NetLogo manual. Before reading much farther, we suggest you **download the NetLogo software,** open source and available for free from **http:// ccl.northwestern.edu/netlogo,** and work through the introductory material in the NetLogo manual (available through the Help menu of the NetLogo software), including the three tutorials that introduce the user to basic model development and syntax. This is a necessary prerequisite to comprehending the material in the book beyond chapter 1. The NetLogo user manual (found under the NetLogo Help menu) is the authoritative reference for NetLogo and it is regularly updated and improved. It will often be advisable to consult the manual, the interface and programming guides, the dictionary and FAQ throughout this textbook. NetLogo comes with an extensive library of models from which you can learn common code patterns. The "Code Examples" models are meant to be simple models intended to show you common code patterns. There are many online resources for help with NetLogo (see http://ccl.northwestern.edu/netlogo/resources.shtml). The NetLogo users group (reachable through the NetLogo HELP menu) is a forum where people post NetLogo questions. The community is quite responsive, and if you post a question there you will likely receive a prompt response. It is a good idea to subscribe to this group early on in working through this textbook. Another resource for asking and answering NetLogo programming questions is Stack Overflow (http://stackoverflow.com/questions/ tagged/netlogo), where you will find many questions and answers about NetLogo programming.

We use the NetLogo examples in order to concretize the concepts of agent-based modeling that we present. By presenting computer code side-by-side with conceptual discussions, we hope to provide both a larger picture of the use of agent-based models as well as a specific illustration.

We have selected NetLogo as our ABM language for this text for several reasons. Before explaining the specifics, it is important to say that we believe our book will be just as useful for those using other ABM languages. Even if we had written a completely language-agnostic book, we would still have needed to include pseudo-code to illustrate our points. Since NetLogo was designed to be easily readable, we believe that NetLogo code is about as easy to read as any pseudo-code we could have used. NetLogo also has the big advantage over pseudo-code of being executable, so the user can run and test the examples. Moreover, there are a large number of agent-based models written in NetLogo in a wide variety of domains, so a literate agent-based modeler requires at least a passing understanding of NetLogo.

---

4. Pseudo-code is an intermediate form between text and computer code that is often used to describe computational algorithms.

We have several other significant reasons for choosing NetLogo as the language for our book. Uri Wilensky, the first author of this textbook, is also the author and developer of NetLogo and has conducted agent-based modeling research, development and teaching with NetLogo (and its precursors) for over two decades. He has taught NetLogo in his classes and in workshops for that same period. The second author has years of experience teaching NetLogo workshops and conducting agent-based modeling research with NetLogo. As such, we are intimately familiar with the language nuances and details. More important, NetLogo was designed with great attention to learnability. As we said, its core design principle is "low threshold, no ceiling."

Achieving both of these goals completely is not possible and to some degree, they trade-off against each other, but NetLogo has gone a considerable distance in achieving both. No other extant ABM language is close to NetLogo's low threshold. As such, it is an ideal language for learning ABM and is used widely in classrooms all over the world. Yet, NetLogo also achieves a high ceiling. NetLogo is in use by a large number of scientists and professionals and is regularly employed in cutting edge research (see http://ccl.northwestern.edu/netlogo/references.shtml for a partial list of research papers employing NetLogo). So after completing this text, you should be well prepared to use NetLogo in your research, teaching, and/or professional life. Learning NetLogo will make you a better ABM modeler/researcher regardless of the language that you may eventually use.

Learning Objectives

There are ten main objectives of our textbook, which roughly parallel the nine chapters and the appendix of the textbook. We will phrase these objectives in terms of questions a reader should be able to answer at the end of our textbook:

0. Why does agent-based modeling provide us with a unique and powerful insight into complex systems?
1. What is agent-based modeling and how is it used?
2. What are some simple agent-based models that we can create?
3. How do I extend an agent-based model that was created by someone else?
4. How do I create my own agent-based model?
5. What are the basic components of agent-based modeling?
6. How can I analyze the results of an agent-based model?
7. How can I tell if the implemented agent-based model corresponds to the concept of the model that I developed in words? How can I tell if the results of my agent-based model tell me anything about the real world? How can I make sure that someone else can repeat my results?

8. What are some advanced ways of including data and using output from agent-based models? What are some of the open research questions in agent-based modeling?
9. From what computational scientific roots did agent-based modeling arise?

Features

There are four main features that are present in nearly every chapter of the book: in-line development, textboxes, explorations, and references. In-line development is what we call the approach of developing a model or an extension to a model in the main text of the book instead of asking the reader to do it later offline. It is expected for some of these chapters (2, 3, 4, 5, 6, and 7 especially) that the reader will read the textbook while sitting at their computer, entering the code from the textbook and manipulating the models as they read along. **All models developed in the textbook can be found in their entirety in the IABM Textbook folder of the NetLogo models library.** This folder is organized by chapters of the textbook. These completed models are provided as a resource, but we encourage students to follow along with the textbook, developing the models themselves before opening the models in the IABM folder. Most other models referred to in the textbook reside in the NetLogo models library, which can be accessed through the "models library" menu item from NetLogo's "file" menu. The models library is itself comprised of subfolders. The principal subfolder is "sample models," which is organized by subject, such as biology, mathematics, social science, and others. **All models used in the book and supplementary materials can be found on the website for the book, www.intro-to-abm.com, updated regularly.**

The textboxes serve to provide additional information and concepts. There are three kinds of textboxes: (1) definitional, (2) exploration, and (3) advanced concept. *Definitional* textboxes (set in blue) define words and terms critical to the discussion. *Exploration* textboxes (set in green) provide additional explorations that are relevant to the material being discussed at that point. *Advanced concept* textboxes (set in orange) highlight concepts that are beyond the scope of the book but that might be of interest to the reader.

At the end of every chapter (except chapter 0), there are explorations. An instructor may want to draw on these explorations for student homework. These explorations are roughly in order of difficulty. Some of them are quite open-ended, while others are more constrained.

At the end of the book there is a references section, the text references organized alphabetically, and the software/model references organized by chapter. To distinguish the text from the software references, the software references are italicized in the text.

Organization

We will present the basics of ABM in nine chapters and an appendix. The nine chapters and the appendix can be thought of as three sections: (1) What ABMs are, (2) How to build ABMs, and (3) How to utilize ABMs to answer complex questions. The first two chapters (0 and 1) and the appendix describe why ABMs are interesting and useful (chapter 0), what they are (chapter 1), and where they came from (the appendix). Together this material defines and describes the field of ABM. The next four chapters (2, 3, 4, and 5) cover how to create simple ABMs (chapter 2), extend an ABM (chapter 3), and build your own ABM (chapter 4), identifying the basic components of an ABM are (chapter 5). These four chapters form a unit on the methods for building ABMs. The final three chapters describe how to analyze ABMs (chapter 6), how to verify, validate, and replicate ABMs (chapter 7), and how to use advanced features of ABMS including using external data sources (chapter 8). Together, these cover the experimental methodology of ABMs.

We believe that all of these chapters are important for someone who is interested in gaining a comprehensive knowledge of ABM. However, if you have a particular interest, there may be a subset of chapters that is more appealing. For people who are interested in what can be done with ABM but who do not need a hands-on knowledge of how to construct ABM, we recommend reading chapter 0 (for an overview of why to use ABM), chapter 1 (for a discussion of how an ABM can be used), the appendix (for an overview of the computational origins of ABM), chapter 7 (to understand how to analyze ABMs), and chapter 8 (to learn about advanced uses of ABM). For readers who simply want a practical hands-on introduction to building ABM, we recommend reading chapter 0 (for an understanding of why to use ABM), chapter 1 (to learn how to pose questions suitable for ABM), chapter 2 (to learn how to create simple ABMs), chapter 3 (to learn how to extend another user's ABM), and chapter 4 (for an introduction to designing and authoring an ABM). These readers might then move on to chapter 5 (for a discussion of the basic ABM components). For other readers, the more detailed chapter overview below may help you choose the chapters that are the most appropriate for you.

Chapters 0 and 1 and the Appendix: What Are ABMs?

In Chapter 0, we discuss the motivations for using ABM. We note the ubiquity of emergence in the world and review the literature that shows how difficult it has been for people to understand emergent phenomena. We also explore how ABM can help us to make sense of phenomena that are nondeterministic and/or have distributed mechanisms and control. Agent-based modeling is powerful because its basic ontology is parallel to the ontology of the world around us. As a result, we can define and describe complex systems using ABMs in quite naturalistic ways. We do not have to define in advance the emergent, global properties; instead, we can observe these properties as they arise from a simulation of multiple distributed interacting agents. This enables us to provide very different descriptions of the world around us, and to understand complex processes in fundamentally new ways. Even for phenomena that we may understand well such as basic physics, chemistry and biology, ABM provides a "restructuration" (Wilensky & Papert, 2005, 2010) of these disciplines, making them easier to understand for novices and enabling experts to develop new insights.

In chapter 1, we begin with a description of ant behavior and discuss how an ABM of an ant colony could be created. The practice of ABM is the use of multiple interacting, heterogeneous agents to create models of complex systems. ABM enables us to create models straight from empirical observations of behavior. We can build mechanisms that we conjecture might explain the behavior and examine how these mechanisms interact. On the basis of this examination, we can at least ascertain if our models are sufficiently generative that they *could* account for the phenomenon being observed. Using a model of ant behavior, we show how scientists might examine several different mechanisms and use models in concert with empirical observations to ascertain which of these mechanisms could explain the behavior observed.

The appendix describes the historical development of the research, people, and ideas that resulted in the creation of the field of agent-based modeling from a computational perspective. ABM, unlike some other discipline-specific methods, did not arise out of any one particular domain or field. Instead, it arose contemporaneously in many different fields, some of which were aware of each other and some of which were not. The history of ABM, like many of the applications of ABM, can itself be told in terms of complex systems with many distributed actors and nonlinear interactions that occurred. An understanding of the origins of ABM and the historical development of canonical ABM models is helpful in deciding whether an ABM approach will be productive and in selecting a design for an ABM of a target phenomenon.

Together, this material covers why ABM is useful, what it is, and who developed it. The two chapters plus the appendix provide the fundamental motivation, concepts and history of ABM.

Chapters 2, 3, 4, and 5: How to Build ABMs

In chapter 2, we develop some very simple ABMs that have powerful features. We begin with Life Simple, which is a version of the game of Life. This model illustrates how very simple rules can create interesting and emergent patterns. We then move on to Heroes and Cowards, a model that illustrates how just changing one rule can dramatically alter the results of a model. Finally, we conclude with the Simple Economy model, which demonstrates how very simple ABMs can help us think through real-world problems.

In chapter 3, we go through the process of taking an ABM that someone else has constructed and modifying it. These modifications could be as simple as adding new visual characteristics to clarify a particularly interesting set of agents or interactions in the model, or to look at a completely new phenomenon using the previous model as a basis for the new design. We will use these extensions to illustrate four characteristics of agent-based modeling: (1) simple rules can be used to generate complex phenomena, (2) randomness in individual behavior can result in deterministic global behavior, (3) complex patterns can "self-organize" without a central leader, and (4) the same phenomenon can be modeled in many different ways, depending on which aspect of it you want to emphasize.

Chapter 4 takes us to the next step of starting to develop models from scratch. We develop a model, named Wolf Sheep Simple, in five distinct stages. The model that we develop illustrates many of the basic concepts that go into ABM creation and design, and it includes many core features of ABMs, such as different agent types, environmental and agent interactions, and competition for resources. Central to this chapter is the delineation and elaboration of the key design principle of ABM.

In chapter 5, we zoom out to take a look at the broader picture, cataloguing and describing the constituent parts of an ABM. After classifying these components into the five categories of Agents, Environments, Interactions, User Interface/Observer, and Schedule, we examine each of these component classes in turn. Within each of these classes, we discuss common issues that should be considered before and while building an agent-based model. For example, what kind of topology should the environment have? Or what properties and actions do the agents in the model have? It can be quite useful to make a plan for each component class and their interactions at an early point in the design plan, and to revisit that plan throughout the design process.

Together, these four chapters provide an in-depth treatment of how to construct agent-based models and provide the basic tools needed to design, construct, and select the components that will go into a model. After reading these four chapters, you should have sufficient knowledge to design and construct basic agent-based models.

Chapters 6, 7, and 8: How to Analyze and Use ABMs
One feature of many ABMs is that they create large amounts of data. Chapter 6 discusses how to examine these data to find meaningful relationships and conduct analyses that are useful for understanding the behavior of the model. We discuss how to explore and describe model results using statistics, graphs, and geographic and network methods. We also discuss the importance of multiple model runs and how to sweep a parameter space to determine the range of behaviors exhibited by a model.

In chapter 7, we examine three key concepts in modeling: verification, validation, and replication. Verification is the process of comparing an implemented model to its associated conceptual model and investigating whether the implemented model is faithful to the conceptual model. By verifying a model, we show that the model implementer has comprehended the intended micro-level rules and mechanisms and has correctly implemented them in the model code. This is true even if the model author may have intended different emergent behavior or predicted different emergent results from those that arise in the implemented model. Validation is a comparison of an implemented model to the real world, to see if the results of the implemented model give us insight into the corresponding real world phenomenon. Validation enables us to use the model to make statements about the real world. Replication is the reproduction of a model result published by one scientist or model developer by another scientist or model developer. Replication is a central process in the creation of scientific knowledge, and replication procedures for agent-based models are explained. Overall, this chapter discusses how implemented ABMs relate to both other models and the real world.

In chapter 8, we address advanced topics with regard to agent-based modeling and how the methods that we have described in the first eight chapters can be further refined. We focus on ways to incorporate data into ABMs from advanced sources such as social network analysis, geographic information systems, and real-time sensors. We also discuss how to make ABMs more powerful, by incorporating techniques such as machine learning, system dynamics modeling, and participatory simulation. We conclude this chapter with a discussion of future challenges for ABM.

In these last three chapters we discuss how to analyze ABMs, how to verify and validate the results of ABMs, and how to use advanced techniques in ABM. These are the important practices of ABM after creating your model and for examining models authored by others.

Acknowledgments

Many people have contributed greatly to this book. Wilensky would like to first and foremost thank Seymour Papert, his dissertation advisor and colleague, who, in many ways, invented the idea of an "agent," who first created a Logo turtle, and who was inspirational regarding the power of computation to transform science and learning. Wilensky is also deeply grateful to Seth Tisue, lead developer of NetLogo for over a decade. Seth's dedication to high quality and elegant code, and his passion and dedication to parsimony, have made NetLogo a much better product. Isaac Asimov, a neighbor of Wilensky's in childhood, was inspirational in describing psychohistory and in catalyzing early notions of emergence. Walter Stroup was an invaluable colleague and joint developer of the HubNet participatory simulation module. Stroup and Corey Brady were influential in advocating for the importance of combining ABM with networked participation.

Rand would like to acknowledge his dissertation chairs, Rick Riolo and John Holland, who encouraged him to pursue his interests in agent-based modeling and helped him to develop many of his formative thoughts on complex systems and ABM. Rand would also like to thank Scott Page, who was not only a member of his dissertation committee but also a continual support to his work in ABM, not the least of which was providing him with a chance to try out the textbook with a sophomore level class at the University of Michigan. In addition, the graduate workshop hosted by Scott Page and John Miller at the Santa Fe Institute was instrumental in helping Rand discover how to teach ABM. Roland Rust had the critical insight to realize that ABM would become increasingly useful for business and worked with Rand to found the Center for Complexity in Business. Finally, and most important, Rand would also like to thank his coauthor for his wonderful support and for having the courage to allow a postdoctoral fellow to embark on such an unusual project as writing a textbook.

In addition, we received valuable feedback from a number of internal and external reviewers over the course of the writing of this textbook. Chief among them are the teaching assistants for Wilensky's agent-based modeling class at Northwestern University, in which these materials were tested over several years: Forrest Stonedahl, Josh Unterman, David Weintrop, Aleata Hubbard, Bryan Head, Arthur Hjorth, and Winston Chang carefully reviewed the materials, observed the students using the materials, and gave extensive helpful comments for improving the text, the model code, and the explorations. Many other members of the Northwestern Center for Connected Learning and Computer-Based Modeling also gave very helpful feedback, including Seth Tisue, Corey Brady, Spiro Maroulis, Sharona Levy, and Nicolas Payette. Dor Abrahamson, Paulo Blikstein, Damon Centola, Paul Deeds, Rob Froemke, Ed Hazzard, Eamon Mckenzie, Melanie Mitchell, Michael Novak, Ken Reisman, Eric Russell, Pratim Sengupta, Michael Stieff, Forrest Stonedahl, Stacey Vahey, Aditi Wagh, Michelle Wilkerson-Jerde, and Christine Yang contributed illuminating examples. Forrest Stonedahl, Corey Brady, Bryan Head, David Weintrop, Nicolas Payette, and Arthur Hjorth suggested useful explorations for the chapters that have enriched student experience. Wilensky's students at Tufts University, Ken Reisman, Ed Hazzard, Rob Froemke, Eamon McKenzie, Stacey Vahey, and Damon Centola, shared their abundant enthusiasm, generated interesting applications, and furthered the educational uses. Northwestern's dean of engineering, Julio Ottino, was always supportive and encouraging, and confident in the importance of an ABM textbook.

Many colleagues engaged us in many stimulating conversation that influenced our thinking and writing. Danny Hillis provided the context for the nascent beginnings of massively parallel simulations at Thinking Machines Corporation. Luis Amaral, Aaron Brandes, Dirk Brockman, Joanna Bryson, Dan Dennett, Gary Drescher, Michael Eisenberg, Rob Goldstone, Ken Kahn, John Miller, Marvin Minsky, Josh Mitteldorf, Richard Noss, Scott Page, Rick Riolo, Roland Rust, Anamaria Berea, and Bruce Sherin are colleagues with whom we have had ongoing stimulating conversations that helped further the ideas in this book. Mitchel Resnick was an important colleague and collaborator in developing the idea of ABM for education, antecedent software development, and the role of levels and emergence.

The development of NetLogo was supported by more than fifteen years of funding from the National Science Foundation. Additional support came from the Spencer Foundation, Texas Instruments, the Brady Fund, the Murphy Society, the Johns Hopkins Center for Advanced Modeling in the Social, Behavioral and Health Sciences, and the Northwestern Institute on Complex Systems. We are especially grateful to NSF program officers Nora Sabelli and Janet Kolodner for their years of advice and support. We are greatly indebted to the NetLogo development team at the CCL led by Seth Tisue, who worked meticulously to guarantee the quality of the NetLogo software. Spiro Maroulis and Nicolas Payette contributed greatly to expanding NetLogo's network capabilities. Ben Shargel and Seth Tisue led the design of BehaviorSpace, and James Newell led design of NetLogo 3D, assisted by Esther Verreau and Seth Tisue. Paulo Blikstein, Corey Brady, and Bob Tinker were influential in advocating for combining ABM with physical computing devices. Many members of the CCL made significant contributions to the NetLogo models library.

Many of the materials in this textbook had previously been used in Wilensky's agent-based modeling class in the Computer Science Department at Northwestern University. Early versions of the textbook were used as the basis for a summer workshop taught by Rand as part of the Summer CommuniCy (under the leadership of Klaus Liepelt) at Mittweida University in Germany, and in various classes at the University of Michigan and University of Maryland. We have also piloted these materials in hundreds of NetLogo workshops in the United States and abroad. We would like to thank the students who have been involved in these classes over the years for their feedback and support.

We are indebted to several undergraduate students for proofreading the manuscript, including Ziwe Fumodoh, Nickolas Kaplan, Claire Maby, Elisa Sutherland, Cristina Polenica, and Kendall Speer. We thank them for their many corrections. Of course, all mistakes that remain in the manuscript are our responsibility.

We are deeply grateful to our spouses, Donna Woods and Margaret Rand, for their patience and support during the many days and nights that we were busy writing and were away from family. Wilensky also thanks his children, Daniel and Ethan, for their patience when their dad was too busy writing to play. Rand also thanks his children, Beatrice and Eleanor, who were born during the writing of this book.

We would like to acknowledge the support of the Northwestern Institute on Complex Systems (NICO), which encouraged this project and supported William Rand during the early writing of this textbook. The University of Maryland Robert H. Smith School of Business Center for Complexity in Business supported William Rand during the second half of the writing of this textbook.

0 Why Agent-Based Modeling?

Some look at things that are, and ask why? I dream of things that never were and ask why not?

— John F. Kennedy

I think the next century will be the century of complexity.

—Stephen Hawking

We shape our tools and then our tools shape us.

—Marshall McLuhan

This book is an introduction to the methodology of agent-based modeling (ABM) and how it can help us more deeply understand the natural and social worlds and engineer solutions to societal problems. Before we discuss why agent-based modeling is important, we briefly describe what agent-based modeling is. An *agent* is an autonomous computational individual or object with particular properties and actions. *Agent-based modeling* is a form of computational modeling whereby a phenomenon is modeled in terms of agents and their interactions. We will describe ABM more comprehensively in chapter 1. As you will see in this textbook, ABM is a methodology that can be promiscuously applied—there are few, if any, content areas where ABM is not applicable. It can enable us to explore, make sense of, and analyze phenomena and scenarios across a wide variety of contexts and content domains. In the past two decades, scientists have increasingly used agent-based modeling methods to conduct their research.

The main argument of this introductory chapter is that ABM is a transformative representational technology that enables us to better understand familiar topics, and at younger ages; make sense of and analyze hitherto unexplored topics; and enable a democratization of access to computational tools for making sense of complexity and change. As such, we believe that developing ABM literacy is a powerful professional and life skill for students, and we should strive for universal ABM literacy for all, from young students to professionals.

This textbook is a foray in the direction of such ABM literacy, aimed at undergraduate and graduate students in virtually any domain of study. To achieve universal ABM literacy, we foresee a need for many complementary such textbooks and materials aimed at a wide variety of people, topics, and social niches.

ABM is a species of computation, growing up alongside the maturation of computer technology. The advent of powerful computation has brought about dramatic change in many areas of life, including significant changes in the practice and content of science. As access to powerful computation increases (and its cost deceases), scientists are able to perform calculations and simulations that simply were not possible in the past. The increase in computational power and connectivity has also enabled the collection and analysis of very large data sets. These data sets often include data at micro-scale levels, enabling us to extract more insight as to how individuals in society behave, animals in an ecosystem survive, or elements of an engineered system affect each other. The combination of large data, cheap computation, and high connectivity allows agent-based models to be constructed with millions of individual agents whose properties and behaviors have been validated. Moreover, computational representations are dynamic and executable, allowing for greater interactivity between the user and representation. Perhaps, even more important, agent-based representations have particular advantages in that they are easy for people to understand.

Agent-based representations are easier to understand than mathematical representations of the same phenomenon. This is because agent-based models are constructed out of individual objects and simple rules for their movement of behavior, as opposed to equational models that are constructed from mathematical symbols. In our natural discourse, we commonly describe our experience in terms of the interactions of individuals, as opposed to in terms of the rates of change of aggregates as in differential equations. In thinking about individual agents, we can make sense of them by projecting our bodily experience onto the agents. Thus, the language and concepts we use in agent-based modeling is much closer to natural language and our natural thinking.

But, to a great extent, these dramatic changes in representation and in the practice of science have not resulted in significant change in the world of education. There are many reasons for the slow pace of change in "technology transfer" to the education system. One obstacle is the lack of widespread understanding of the benefits of such a transfer. In this chapter, we develop a conceptualization of this enterprise in historical and epistemological terms that we hope will situate ABM with respect to other representational advances and increase understanding of the benefits of widespread adoption.

As a first step to presenting this conceptualization, we look back historically at changes to representational tools and practices used in science and the significant benefits they had for both scientists and learners. The example that we have found most useful in presenting our idea is the shift from Roman to Hindu-Arabic numerals in arithmetic. We believe it is important to study more systematically changes of this kind, to examine the history of science in search of cases with similar consequences for the dramatic advancement of science. By studying this transformation, we can better understand how other transformations, such as the development of ABM, can be accelerated to cultivate new insights and understandings of the world around us. We begin by looking more closely at the Roman to Hindu-Arabic numeracy transition through a thought experiment developed by Wilensky and Papert (2010).

A Thought Experiment

Imagine a country (let's call it Foo) where people represented numbers as the Romans did, using symbols such as MCMXLVIII. Fooian scientists worked laboriously to quantify and more accurately calculate basic science such as planetary motion and dynamical forces. Businesspeople had great difficulties with their financial calculations, tradespeople struggled with their measurements, and consumers labored to assess their purchases. Educational researchers and policymakers in this imaginary country were very concerned with the difficulty of learning to handle numbers, and they worked hard to make these skills accessible to more of their citizens. They engaged in a number of different approaches. Some researchers studied the misconceptions and mistakes typically made by children. They might have discovered that some children believed that since CX is ten more than one hundred, then CIX must be ten more than CI. Others constructed and studied computer programs that allowed students to practice numerical operations. Still others developed physical representations—wooden blocks marked with the symbols C, X, V, and I— to help students learn. Members of the Fooian ministry of education called for more rigorous testing on Roman arithmetic. Yet another group tried to elucidate the problem by framing it in evolutionary terms, speculating that perhaps humans were not wired to do multiplication and division, or that such tasks were only feasible for a small subset of highly trained experts.

It is not hard to imagine, in our thought experiment, that many of these approaches brought about substantial improvements in numeracy. But let us now imagine that, at some point, the scientists of this country invented Hindu-Arabic numerals. This invention then opened up a new way to handle and think about numbers. Resulting gains toward a functional numeracy due to this representational shift would likely far outstrip any of the benefits that would have accrued from any of the improved techniques for working with the Roman numeral system. Before, the knowledge gap in arithmetic was immense; only a small number of trained people could do multiplication. After, multiplication became part of what we can expect everyone to learn.

The sort of transformation exemplified here has no name in the standard scientific or educational discourse. A first step is to name the sort of innovation associated with the shift from Roman to Hindu-Arabic representations of number. It is not sufficient, for example, to say that we have a new approach to learning and working with numbers. Even in this simple case, things fundamentally change. The algorithms that are taught after this transformation are different. People's mental representation will alter, as will their sense of systematicity in the field. Psychologically important landmark values (i.e., V vs. 0) will be different. Even social embedding, such as "who can do what," changes (e.g., scribes or special human calculators for the emperor vs. modern carpenters or business people doing their own calculations). In our terminology, we will say that we have a new structuration of a discipline (Wilensky & Papert, 2010; Wilensky et al., 2005). We will proceed to flesh out this term through concrete examples. But, for now, we introduce a preliminary formal definition: By *structuration* we mean the encoding of the knowledge in a domain as a function of the representational infrastructure used to express the knowledge. A change from one structuration of a domain to another resulting from such a change in representational infrastructure we call a *restructuration*.

There have been many examples of restructurations in human history. Of course, our thought experiment is based on a historical reality. Before the transition from the use of Roman to Hindu Arabic numerals in Europe around the turn of the first millennium, most Europeans were able to use Roman numerals fluently. However, because Roman numerals were not very well suited to large numbers and to multiplication and division of such numbers, people went to special "experts" to perform multiplication and division for them. European mathematicians first started employing Hindu-Arabic numerals at the end of the tenth century, quickly realizing its advantages in working with large numbers. In 1202, the mathematician Fibonacci wrote a text outlining the Hindu-Arabic system that resulted in gradual adoption by scientists. Still, "universal" adoption of Hindu-Arabic numerals in Europe was not achieved until the sixteenth century—a restructuration that took more than half a millennium! Why did it take so long for a representational infrastructure quickly recognized as superior to gain widespread adoption? The case of Italian shopkeepers may help explain this quandary. Medieval Italian shopkeepers kept two sets of books for their accounting: one set, in which they did their real calculations, was kept in Hindu-Arabic; the other set, which was presented to the inspecting authorities, was kept in Roman, since a Roman representation was required by the government. The shopkeepers had to laboriously translate the first set into the second. That they deemed such translation worthwhile is a testimony to the value of the restructuration. The fact that the authorities did not officially recognize the Hindu-Arabic books was a major obstacle to the structuration's more rapid spread. We call this resistance to the spread of structurations "structurational inertia" (Wilensky & Papert, 2010). Just as an object's inertia keeps it from changing its motion, so structurational inertia keeps structurations from changing, impeding the spread of restructuration.

Our Roman-to-Arabic numeracy example is just one of many that we could have chosen. In his book *Changing Minds* (2001), DiSessa describes the historical restructuration of simple kinematics from a text-based to an algebraic representation. He illustrates this restructuration through a story of the seventeenth-century scientist Galileo. In his book

Dialogues Concerning Two New Sciences (1638), Galileo struggles to handle a problem involving the relationship between distance, time and velocity. He laboriously describes four theorems relating these three quantities. The reader is invited to peruse and decipher these theorems. The surprising realization is that all four of these theorems are in fact variations of the single equation $D=VT$, or distance equals velocity times time. How could it be that Galileo, inventor of the telescope, and one of the great "fathers of modern science," struggled so mightily with an equation with which most middle-schoolers are facile? The explanation is both simple and profound: Galileo did not have algebraic representation. He had to write these theorems in Italian, and natural language is not a well-suited medium for conveying these kinds of mathematical relationships. Thus, the restructuration of kinematics from the representational system of natural language to that of algebra transformed what was a complex and difficult idea for as powerful an intellect as Galileo's into a form that is within the intellectual grasp of every competent secondary student.

The development of Arabic numerals and the transformation of kinematics via algebra were empowering and democratizing, enabling significant progress in science and widening the range of people who could make sense of previously formidable topics and skills. The vista opened to the imagination is dramatic: If the problems with which we struggle today could be so transformed, think of the new domains we could enter and conquer. If algebra could make accessible to students what was hard for Galileo, what domains that are hard for us today to understand could we restructurate to make more accessible?

Complex Systems and Emergence

What might be the analogy today? What areas are widely thought to be difficult for people to comprehend and potentially ripe for restructuration? One such area is complex systems. Its very name suggests that it is a difficult area for comprehension.

What we perceive as difficult has cognitive dimensions, but difficulty is also greatly affected by our current needs. As commerce developed in the Middle Ages, there arose an increasing need for arithmetic with large numbers, so the difficulty of doing it with Roman numerals became more salient. As science developed the need to account more precisely for heavenly bodies, the difficulty of describing their motions became more transparent. In the current day, the world we live in has become increasingly complex, in part because, in earlier periods of history, we did not have to pay as much attention to complex interactions; we could get by with understanding simple systems and local effects. Yet, as technology and science have advanced, we have become more affected by complex interactions. We are now aware that changes to the rain forest in Brazil can have dramatic effects on the climate of faraway countries; that unwise financial decisions in one country can have significant economic impact on the rest of the world; that a single case of a new disease in China can spread around the globe in short order; or that a four-minute video uploaded by a Korean pop star can turn him into a worldwide sensation in a matter of days. As such, the difficulty of making sense of complex systems has become more salient.

However, even if the level of complexity in our life remained constant over the ages, our continual quest for knowledge would ultimately lead us to study complex systems. As we gain facility and more complete understanding of simple systems, we naturally progress to trying to make sense of increasingly complex systems. Simple population dynamics models, for example, make the implicit assumption that all members of a species are the same, but later, it becomes important to explore the manifold complexity of the food web and how each individual interacts with every other individual. Thus, our need to understand more complex systems is also a natural result of the growth of human knowledge.

As we gain knowledge, we create more sophisticated tools and these tools enable us to ask and answer new questions. As described earlier, the advent of powerful computation enables us to model, simulate, and more deeply probe complex systems.

For the reasons stated, the field of complex systems has arisen and grown. Complex systems theory develops principles and tools for making sense of the world's complexity and defines complex systems as systems that are composed of multiple individual elements that interact with each other yet whose aggregate properties or behavior is not predictable from the elements themselves. Through the interaction of the multiple distributed elements an "emergent phenomenon" arises. The phenomenon of *emergence* is characteristic of complex systems. The term "emergent" was coined by the British philosopher and psychologist G. H. Lewes, who wrote:

Every resultant is either a sum or a difference of the co-operant forces; their sum, when their directions are the same—their difference, when their directions are contrary. Further, every resultant is clearly traceable in its components, because these are homogeneous and commensurable. It is otherwise with emergents, when, instead of adding measurable motion to measurable motion, or things of one kind to other individuals of their kind, there is a co-operation of things of unlike kinds. The emergent is unlike its components insofar as these are incommensurable, and it cannot be reduced to their sum or their difference. (Lewes 1875)

Since Lewes's time, scholars have struggled with how to best define emergence—some definitions succinct, others more involved. For our purposes, we define emergence as *the arising of novel and coherent structures, patterns, and properties through the interactions of multiple distributed elements.* Emergent structures cannot be deduced solely from the properties of the elements, but rather, also arise from interactions of the elements. Such emergent structures are system properties yet they often feedback to the very individual elements of which they are composed.

Important features of emergence include the global pattern's spontaneous arising from the interaction of elements, and the absence of an orchestrator or centralized coordinator—the system "self-organizes." Structure (or rules) at the micro-level leads to ordered pattern at the macro-level. Because the macrostructures are emergent, composed of many elements, they are dynamic, and perturbing them often results in them dynamically reforming. Another way of thinking about such structures is to view them not as entities, but rather, as processes holding the structure in place, which are often invisible until the structure is disturbed. However, a reformed structure, while recognizably the same structure, will not be identical, since for most emergent structures, randomness plays a role in each reformation. From a micro-level perspective, this suggests that the formation rules need not be deterministic. Indeed, in many complex systems, probabilistic and random processes contribute to, and are even essential to, the creation of order.

In complex systems, order can emerge without any design or designer. The idea of order without design has been controversial throughout the history of science and religion. In modern times, the supposed impossibility of order without design has been a linchpin of the intelligent design movement against naturalistic evolution, as supporters argue that life's manifold and irreducible complexity could not arise "by chance" without a designer. Yet, complex systems theory is ever finding more complex systems that may at first seem irreducible but are found to be self-organized or evolved rather than intelligently designed by a designer.

Understanding Complex Systems and Emergence

We have said that understanding complex systems and emergence is hard for people. Emergence, in particular, presents two fundamental and distinct challenges. The first difficulty lies in trying to figure out the aggregate pattern when one knows how individual elements behave. We sometimes call this *integrative* understanding, as it parallels the cumulative integration of small differences in calculus. A second difficulty arises when the aggregate pattern is known and one is trying to find the behavior of the elements that could generate the pattern. We sometimes call this *differential* understanding (aka *compositional* understanding), as it parallels the search in calculus for the small elements that produce an aggregate graph when accumulated. Let's now consider two examples that illustrate these concepts.

Example 1: Integrative Understanding
Figure 0.1 presents a system composed of a few identical elements following one rule. Each element is a small arrow. We imagine a clock ticking and at each tick of the clock the arrows follow their rule. We initialize the system so that each individual arrow starts on a circle (of radius 20 units). We start them all facing clockwise on the circle. Now, we give them one movement behavior (or rule). At every tick of the clock, they move forward 0.35 units then turn right one degree. As the clock ticks, they continue to move and turn, move and turn, moving clockwise along the circle.

Now suppose that we slightly alter these rules. Instead of moving forward 0.35 units, we have them move 0.5 units while still turning one degree. What will be the aggregate

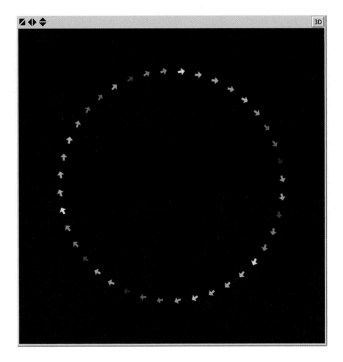

Figure 0.1
Some arrows moving clockwise around a circle of radius 20.

pattern that we see? Before reading further, take a moment to imagine what the pattern will be.

Most people do not predict the resulting pattern. We have heard people predict that the arrows will move onto a larger circle, a smaller circle, a flower shape, and many others. In fact, the pattern that emerges is a pulsating circle. All the arrows stay in a circle, but the circle changes its radius, first expanding, then contracting and repeating this cycle forever.

Example 2: Differential Understanding

Now let's consider the flip side of these difficulties. There are many coherent, powerful, and beautiful patterns we observe in the world. What accounts for their prevalence? How do they originate?

The secret to understanding the formation of these patterns is to understand that they are emergent, arising from the interactions of distributed individual elements.

One such prevalent (and often beautiful) pattern is the flocking of birds. Birds fly together in many different formations, from the classic V formation of goose flocks to the

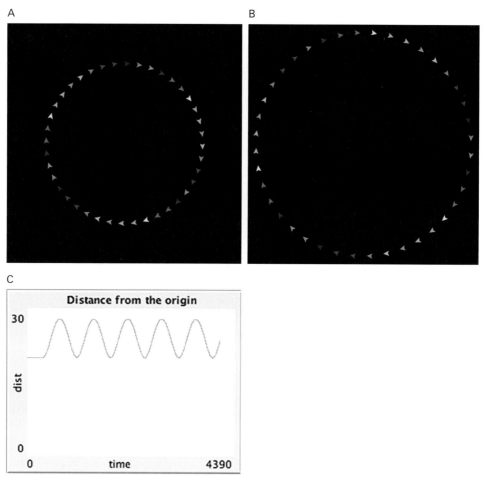

A

B

C

Distance from the origin

30

dist

0

0   time   4390

Figure 0.2
Pulsating circle, moving between large and small radius.

large, very dense flocks of starlings that resemble insect swarms. How and why do these flocks emerge?

Another more common (though less beautiful) pattern—this time, from the social rather than the natural world—is the traffic jam. In most industrial societies with individually driven vehicles, we see traffic jams. We tend to think of traffic jams as being composed of thousands of individual cars, but seen from a bird's-eye view, traffic jams appear as a single object moving backward against the flow of traffic.[1] What causes these jams to form?

---

1. See (*Wilensky, 1997a*) for a NetLogo model of a traffic jam.

Figure 0.3
Flock of geese flying in a classic V formation.

In the 1980s and early '90s, Wilensky and Resnick interviewed people from a wide range of backgrounds, asking them to explain how such patterns arise. The results suggested a phenomenon, or cognitive pattern, called the deterministic-centralized mindset, or DC mindset. The pattern stemmed from two main empirical findings: (1) Most subjects did not see any role for randomness in creating these structures, randomness was seen as destructive of pattern, not a force for creating pattern (the D component); and (2) Most subjects described these patterns as arising from the actions of a centralized controller or orchestrator (the C component).

When asked by the interviewer how geese get into V-formations, subjects typically responded that "it's the leader bird in the front and he is followed by his lieutenants" or "it's the mother bird up front and she is followed by her children" or "the biggest bird is up front pushing the air back and the next strongest follow." Similarly, when asked to explain why there is a traffic jam ahead, they hypothesized that there was an accident ahead or a radar trap.

All of these explanations reflect a commonly held DC mindset. Subjects imposed an orchestrated order on the elements—that they get into formation because of some social organization; some communicated social agreement, or some specific centralized cause. Furthermore, they saw such patterns as deterministic. The same bird is up front, determined

A

B

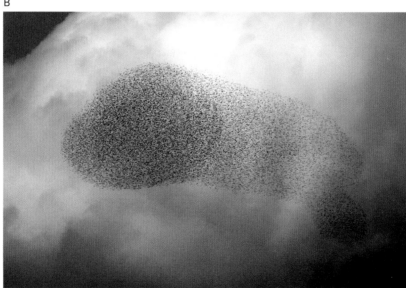

Figure 0.4
Flocks of starlings (thousands of birds) acting as a swarm.[2]

2. For beautiful video of massive starling swarms, called murmurations, see: http://www.huffingtonpost.com/
2013/02/01/starling-murmuration-bird-ballet-video_n_2593001.html, http://www.youtube.com/watch?v=Pnywh
C36UVY, http://www.youtube.com/watch?v=XH-groCeKbE, or http://www.youtube.com/watch?v=iRNqhi2ka9k.

Figure 0.5
Traffic Jam by Osvaldo Gago, 2005.

by a pecking order; the jam occurs at a specific place because the accident or radar trap was there, rather than at random locations along the road.

To be sure, accidents and radar traps cause some traffic jams. Most, however, arise from the random entry of cars into, say, a highway and the resultant statistical distribution of cars and speeds.[3] Similarly, science has established that bird flocks are not centrally organized; rather than the same bird staying at the apex of the V formation, different birds occupy that spot. The composition of the formation, hence, is not deterministic, but rather, emergent from birds' independent movements as they head in a particular direction, trying to avoid other birds and yet not get too far from their neighbor birds.[4] We will further explore models of flocking in chapter 7.

In further analyses of the interviews, Wilensky and Resnick (1999) identified a key component of the DC mindset and an obstacle to thinking about emergent phenomena: the problem of "thinking in levels." Emergent phenomena can be described as existing on at least two levels: the level of the individual elements (cars, birds, people, etc.); and the level of system or aggregate patterns (flocks, traffic jams, housing patterns, etc.). Most

---

3. For a video of a fascinating experiment to create traffic jams, see http://www.newscientist.com/article/dn13402-shockwave-traffic-jam-recreated-for-first-time.html.

4. For a NetLogo model of birds flocking, see *Wilensky (1998)*.

people fail to distinguish between these levels, instead "slipping" between levels to attribute the properties of one level to the other. Consider a V- flock, which appears to be stable and to have a consistent shape. The *appearance* of stability often leads people to conclude that the individual elements of the flock (the birds) *are* stable and have a consistent place in the flock. As we have seen, however, this is a misunderstanding based on a slippage between levels, and is an example of a failure in differential understanding. In this example, the shape of the flock is salient; the birds' behavior is less so. The natural direction of levels slippage is from aggregate to individual. We are seduced into transferring a property of the aggregate to the individual elements. With the case of traffic, we are much more familiar with the ways individual cars move then we are of aggregate traffic patterns. When we typically think about traffic, we are seated inside a car, very aware of its movements and how it responds to the movements of other cars. When we encounter a jam, we are likely to think of it as behaving like a car; we imagine it as responding to the stopping of a car in an accident and moving forward like a car, rather than moving backward as jams actually do. Here, the direction of levels slippage is opposite to that of bird flocks: the properties of the individual elements, the cars are transferred *to* the aggregate pattern, the jam. This is an example of a failure of integrative understanding.

Wilensky and Resnick also showed a host of examples where this levels slippage interfered with both integrative and differential understanding of complex phenomena in the natural and human social worlds. Furthermore, this mindset is not just a problem of the scientifically naïve. Trained scientists also fall prey to the DC mindset.[5] Wilensky and Resnick presented a host of examples across an array of content and contexts (e.g., economic markets, predator-prey relations, slime-mold behavior, human housing patterns, growth of crystals, insect foraging) where levels slippage interfered with understanding. Many of these examples (and a host of new ones) will appear in this book. Indeed, in the past two decades, researchers have found that emergent phenomena are endemic to the natural and social worlds and that using an emergent lens to make sense of complex patterns is a vital need in a twenty-first-century world.

Agent-Based Modeling as Representational Infrastructure for Restructurations

Returning to Roman-to-Arabic numerical restructuration analogy, we suggest that new computer-based representations can help restructurate our knowledge in many domains. With the aid of new computer-based modeling environments, we can simulate complex patterns and better understand how they arise in nature and society. Whereas in many areas

---

5. Keller and Segal (1985) described the scientific study of slime molds and how it was shaped by the DC Mindset. At certain stages of their life cycle, slime molds gather into clusters. Early in the study of slime molds it was assumed that there was a "founder" or "pacemaker" that controlled the aggregation process, but later it was discovered that there was no need for a specialized coordinator. Yet the centralized view was embraced and vehemently defended for more than a decade, despite strong evidence to the contrary.

of science we have relied on simplified descriptions of complexity—often using advanced mathematical techniques that are tractable and allow us to calculate answers—we can now use computation to simulate thousands of individual system elements, called "agents." This allows new, more accessible and flexible ways to study complex phenomena—we simulate to understand.

Agent-based modeling is a computational methodology that enables one to model complex systems. As the name suggests, agent-based models are composed of *agents:* computational entities that have properties, or *state variables and values* (e.g., position, velocity, age, wealth, etc.). Agents usually also have a graphical component so you can see them on the computer screen. An agent can represent any element of a system. A gas molecule agent, for instance, might have properties such as "mass" with value 30 atomic mass units, "speed" with value 10 meters per second, and "heading" with a value of the angle it is facing. A sheep agent, by contrast, might have properties such as "speed" with value 3 mph, weight with value 30 lbs., and fleece with a value of "full" (a discrete-textual rather than numerical value). In addition to their properties, agents also have rules of behavior. A gas molecule agent might have a rule to collide with another molecule; a sheep agent might have a rule to eat grass if there is grass available nearby. In an agent-based model, we imagine a universal clock. When the clock ticks, all agents invoke their rules. If the conditions of the rules are satisfied, (e.g., they are at the edge of a box, or grass is nearby), they enact the behavior (i.e., bounce or eat grass). The goal of agent-based model-ing is to create agents and rules that will generate a target behavior. Sometimes the rules are not well known, or you just want to explore the system's behavior. In that case, ABM can be used to help you better understand a phenomenon through experimentation with rules and properties.

A working hypothesis of representational theorists is that anything that is perceived as difficult to understand can be made more understandable by a suitable representation. We contend that ABM's enable restructurations of complex systems so that the (a) understand-ing of complex systems can be democratized and (b) the science of complex systems can be advanced. This hypothesis begets a design challenge: Can we design a suitable repre-sentational language that supports both parts of the claim, enabling scientists to author scientific models in this language while simultaneously enabling a wider audience to gain access to (and understand) complex systems?

The computer language used in this text, NetLogo (*Wilensky, 1999*), was developed by Uri Wilensky for these express purposes.[6] It is a general-purpose agent-based modeling language designed to be "low-threshold"—that is, novices can quickly employ it to do meaningful and useful things—but also "high-ceiling"—meaning that scientists and researchers can use it to design cutting-edge scientific models. The language borrows much of its syntax from the Logo language, which was designed to be accessible to children.

---

6. NetLogo is freely available from ccl.northwestern.edu/netlogo.

Like Logo, NetLogo calls its prototypical agent a "turtle." However, while in Logo, the user directs the turtle to draw geometric figures, in NetLogo, this is generalized to thousands of turtles. Instead of drawing with pens, they typically draw with their bodies, moving according to rules, and the configuration of their bodies presents a visualization of the modeled phenomenon. NetLogo was first developed in the late 1990s, and it is now in use by hundreds of thousands of users worldwide. Thousands of scientific papers have utilized NetLogo to construct and explore models in a wide variety of disciplines. It has also been employed by policymakers to model policy choices, business practitioners to model business decisions, and students to model subject matter in their coursework across virtually the entire curriculum. Many NetLogo-based courses have sprung up in both universities and in secondary schools.

As of yet, no textbook has been written that gives a general and systematic introduction to NetLogo in all of its features and shows how to use it to model phenomena across many different domains. It is our hope that this textbook will serve to enhance and further democratize ABM literacy. We envision it being used as a primary textbook in an agent-based modeling course, but it can also serve as a supplementary textbook in virtually any university course whose subject matter is amenable to agent-based modeling.

We further maintain that virtually every university subject can benefit from a basic familiarity with agent-based modeling. Some subject domains have embraced agent-based modeling from the start, such as chemistry, biology, and materials science. Others embraced it in a second wave, such as psychology, sociology, physics, business, and medicine. Recently, we have seen the growth of agent-based modeling in economics, anthropology, philosophy, history, and law. While different fields have different degrees of structurational inertia, there is no end to the domains of application for ABM. However, differences in structurational inertia render some fields more easily adaptable to ABM restructurations than others. To illustrate the potential power of widespread agent-based modeling literacy and restructuration, we will look briefly at two examples derived from different content domains: predator-prey interactions and the spread of forest fires.

Example: Predator-Prey Interactions
Let us start with the study of predator-prey interactions. This domain is often first introduced qualitatively in high school, then quantitatively at the university level. In its quantitative form, the population dynamics of a single predator and prey are introduced by the classic Lotka-Volterra differential equations, a pair of coupled differential equations that proceed as follows:

$$\frac{dPred}{dt} = K_1 * Pred * Prey - M * Pred$$

$$\frac{dPrey}{dt} = B * Prey - K_2 * Pred * Prey$$

The first equation says that the number of predators increases as predators interact with prey (by fixed constant K_1) and decreases by a constant mortality rate (M). The second equation says that the number of prey increase by a constant birthrate (B) and decreases in interaction with predators (by a fixed constant K_2). The solution to these equations resembles the classic sinusoidal curves that show a cycling of the predator populations with one ascendant when the other is at a trough.

These equations are fairly straightforward if you are familiar with differential equations; but, even then, the mechanisms that cause these dynamics are not readily apparent from the equations. We are still left to ponder: How do predators increase through interacting with prey? One can speculate on several chains of mechanisms for this increase, but they are not explicit, and neither is why this increase happens at a constant rate, K_1.

By contrast, an agent-based representation of predator and prey, such as the one illustrated in figure 0.6, would typically employ simple algorithmic models. They might give each predator and prey a store of energy that is depleted when they move and increased when they eat. If their energy dips too low, they die. If it is high enough, they might reproduce. And when they move, if they encounter food (which, for the predator, is the prey), they eat it. These instructions are explicitly stated in an easy-to-read language that

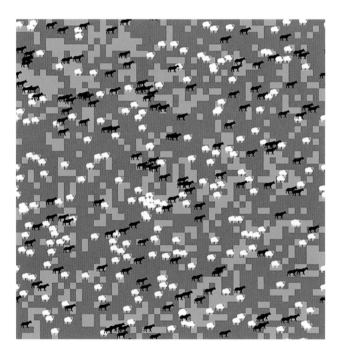

Figure 0.6
An agent-based Wolf Sheep Predation model. (See *Wilensky, 1997c*)

instructs each agent in how to behave, and accompanies the visual model. This kind of representation makes its mechanisms explicit; as such, they are usually quite understandable by even young children. They also can be challenged more easily and tested. We will explore such predator-prey models in detail in chapter 4.

There are many advantages to agent-based representations. First, it does not require knowing calculus. Requiring calculus to be able to reason about predator-prey interactions sets the entry threshold quite high. In the United States, only a small percentage of adults have ever taken calculus, and far fewer are familiar with differential equations. So calculus serves as a gatekeeper limiting access to important content to a small minority of adults and to almost all children. Yet the content of the predator-prey model can be made quite accessible to a non-calculus audience through ABM. This gatekeeper problem may seem less formidable when thinking about an audience of scientists who have likely had calculus. Even with this audience in mind, it is still often difficult to uncover the mechanisms behind the equations, to challenge them, and to propose alternate mechanisms and new equations.

Our example of the restructuration of numeracy and the example above might lead the reader to believe we are arguing for the replacement of equational representations with ABMs. That is not our intent. Agent-based models can serve as powerful complements to equation-based models. They are particularly effective entry points into scientific domains. But they also have some disadvantages as compared to equations. For an expert, an equation can more compactly represent a phenomenon than can an ABM. Moreover, when the equation is solvable, it enables the direct calculation of results without the need to run a model. When a model requires a large numbers of agents, its execution time can be so long as to be impractical as a way of calculating results. The corresponding equation-based models must often make many simplifying assumptions to gain this increase in speed. These simplifications are most justifiable when the agents are sufficiently homogenous that it can be advantageous to treat them as average quantities as opposed to the heterogeneous individuals often used in ABM. In this textbook, we will provide some guidelines as to when an ABM approach is likely to be most effective and when other approaches may be better. In general, exploring complementary approaches to a single problem provides us with deeper insight. If multiple different approaches find a similar pattern of behavior at different levels of analysis, then there is better confirmation of the underlying result.

One disadvantage of ABM representation is somewhat ironic. Many people are more prone to accept the differential equation representation at face value and can be quite critical and skeptical of the ABM representation. That is a consequence of the way ABM concretizes mechanisms and makes reasoning more accessible. For example, people might critique the simplification of having reproduction happen asexually in a predator-prey model or of the particulars of the movements of the predators and prey. This can lead critics to conclude that the ABM model is not well justified, whereas the equational model is the more valid. But the equational model is not more valid; it, too, is a model, and a highly simplified one at that. In fact, we now know from the works of biologists such as Gause (1936) that the equational model is less accurate than an ABM in the isolated predator-prey situation for which it was intended. In particular, the equational model underrepresents extinctions, since the model uses real numbers to represent the population densities. This means that the prey population, for example, can dip to 0.5, or 0.1, or 0.01 and yet still come back. In the real world, however, populations are discrete. When the model goes below one prey (or a pair), it reaches a functional point of no return.

Example: Forest Fires

Our second example is about the spread of a forest fire. This domain is not usually present in the K-12 or university curriculum, but when taught, it typically falls under the subject matter of physics, described in terms of two classic partial differential equations. The first is the classic heat equation, which describes the distribution of heat in a given region over time, where theta represents the thermal diffusivity of the material through which the heat is traveling.

$$\frac{dH(x,t)}{dt} = \theta \frac{d^2 H(x,t)}{dx^2}$$

The second equation physicists use to describe the spread of a forest fire treats the fire as if it were a potentially turbulent fluid, thus using the Reynolds equation of fluid flow.

$$\frac{dU_i}{dt} + U_j \frac{dU_i}{dx_j} = -\frac{1}{\rho} \frac{dP}{dx_i} + v \frac{d^2 U_i}{dx_j dx_j} - \frac{d}{dx_j} \overline{u_i' u_j'}$$

Needless to say, these equational representations are well beyond students in the K–12 years and, we would guess, the vast majority of undergraduate science majors. Understanding what they mean and how to compute them requires significant knowledge of higher-level physics as well as the machinery of partial differential equations.

Contrast this with the ABM approach to modeling forest fires (illustrated in figure 0.7), which would typically model the environment as a grid of cells with trees occupying certain cells. Modeling the spread of fire consists simply of giving rules to the cells that are on fire as to when to spread to neighboring tree cells. This representation is so simple, we have seen elementary school students comprehend and explore it. They can experiment to see how different densities of trees in the forest affect the fire spread and they can modify the basic model to ascertain the effects of wind, or wood type, or fire source. We will explore an ABM of a forest fire in chapter 3 and consider such extensions. Of course, a very simple ABM of forest fire spread would not correctly model a particular fire, but it does give insight into the dynamics of any fire and once we know the details of a particular fire, we can add in whatever data or rules that apply to the situation. This enables

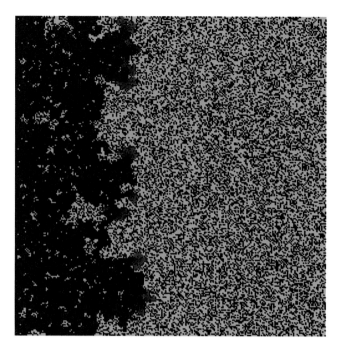

Figure 0.7
An agent-based model of a forest fire. (See *Wilensky, 1997b*)

even scientists to experiment much more fluidly with different models of spread, iteratively refining their models. ABM methods are starting to be used to model and fight real forest fires (see, e.g., www.simtable.com for a company that does agent-based modeling of emergency management including wildfires).

The restructuration of these systems using ABM provides several representational benefits. They make use of discrete rather than continuous representations, which are more easily comprehensible, more closely match real-world situations and require much less formal mathematics to employ. They are easier to explore and much easier to modify. They present immediate feedback with visualizations that allow researchers and practitioners to understand and critique them at two levels, the level of the overall aggregate pattern, such as the fire spread or predator population levels, but also the level of the behavior of the individual animals, and the fire spread to particular trees. Though these two examples highlight some of the advantages of agent-based restructurations, the full potential of ABM restructuration is not yet evident either in these examples, or in science as a whole.

The two examples we have given here come from the natural sciences. We believe the potential of ABM restructurations may be even more important in the social sciences. This is because the core representational infrastructure in the social sciences consists of words and texts. Words and texts do not as easily specify the precision of an idea and can thus be interpreted in fundamentally different ways by different people. Moreover, words and texts are not dynamic representations, so they cannot give you immediate feedback as to the consequences of the assumptions embedded in them. By capturing social science theories in dynamic ABM representations, we make their assumptions explicit, and they become demonstrations of the consequences of their assumptions. If someone wants to disagree with your model, he or she must show how either an assumption is incorrect or missing or show how the logic of the interactions is flawed. The model serves as an object-to-think-with and a test bed for alternate assumptions. This can be particularly powerful when it comes to issues of policy where one can rapidly test many different alternative potential scenarios and examine their consequences. As such, ABMs serve as powerful complements to text-based explanations.

Over the past twenty years, the authors of this textbook have been working on improving the infrastructure, NetLogo, and also on restructurating domains. We have been involved with agent-based restructurations at all levels of schooling, in a wide variety of domains including most of the natural and social sciences and engineering. Restructurations have been performed in a range of fields so diverse as to include cognitive and social psychology, linguistics, biology, chemistry, physics, and many more. Agent-based models are now used in the professions to do research in medicine and law and by policymakers to help them explore effects of alternative policies.

There is still much work to do to establish the representational infrastructure and the science of ABM. What is needed is widespread literacy in agent-based modeling. We are hopeful that this textbook will move us forward and enable a large number of students to learn about and master this new representational infrastructure. We envision a series of textbooks that use agent-based modeling to restructurate many specific subjects. It is our hope that this textbook will help to spread literacy in agent-based modeling, to catalyze these restructurations, and that the widespread use of agent-based representations will take considerably less than five hundred years.

1 What Is Agent-Based Modeling?

Ants

The ant opens her eyes and looks around. There are many of her siblings nearby, but there is no food. The ant is hungry, so she heads out from the ant colony and starts to wander around. She sniffs a little to the left and a little to the right, and still she cannot smell any food. So she keeps wandering. She passes by several of her sisters, but they do not interest her right now; she has food on her mind. She keeps wandering. Sniff! Sniff! Mmmm … good! She gets a whiff of some of that delightful pheromone stuff. She heads in the direction of the strongest pheromone scent; in the past there has been food at the end of that trail. Sure enough, as the ant proceeds along the trail, she arrives at some delicious food. She grabs some food and heads back to the colony, making sure to drop some pheromone along the way. On the way back, she runs into many of her sisters, each sniffing her way along pheromone trails, repeating the same process they will carry out all day.

What we have just fancifully described is an ant foraging for food. The opening paragraph of this section is in itself a model of ant behavior. By a *model*, we mean an abstracted description of a process, object, or event. Models can take many distinct forms. However, certain forms of models are easier to manipulate than other forms. The textual description in our first paragraph cannot easily be manipulated to answer questions about the ant colony's behavior—for example, what would we see if all the ants in the colony followed the behavior we described? It is difficult to extrapolate from the textual description of one ant to a description of an ant colony. The textual model is not sufficiently generative to answer such questions. It is a fixed description—always "behaving" the same, thus not bestowing any insight into the range of variation in behaviors. And it is not combinatorial—we cannot use the description to understand the interaction of the ants with each other or with the environment.

One way to make the preceding model more generalizable and gain insight into the behavior of an ant colony would be to implement the model in a computational form. A *computational model* is a model that takes certain input values, manipulates those inputs in an algorithmic way, and generates outputs. In computational form, it would be easy to run the "Ants" model with large numbers of ants and to observe the model's outputs given many possible different inputs. We use the term *model implementation* to refer to this process of transforming a textual model[1] into a working computational simulation (written in some form of computer "code"). Besides textual models, there are other forms of *conceptual models* that describe processes, objects, or events but are not computational; conceptual models can also be diagrammatic or pictorial.

This description lends itself particularly well to being implemented, since it results from a particular standpoint, that of an individual ant, or ant *agent*. By the word *agent*, we mean an autonomous individual element of a computer simulation. These individual elements have properties, states, and behaviors.

The ant is an agent. It has properties such as its appearance and its rate of movement. It has characteristic behaviors such as moving, sniffing, picking up food, and dropping pheromone. It has states such as whether or not it is carrying food (a binary state) and whether it can sense how much pheromone is in the environment around it (a multi-valued state).

Agent-based modeling (ABM) is a computational modeling paradigm that enables us to describe how any agent will behave.[2] The methodology of ABM encodes the behavior of individual agents in simple rules so that we can observe the results of these agents' interactions. This technique can be used to model and describe a wide variety of processes, phenomena, and situations, but it is most useful when describing these phenomena as *complex systems*. Our aim in this textbook is to facilitate your creating, modifying, and analyzing the outputs of agent-based models. We begin by describing the genesis of the ant foraging conceptual model and how it was implemented as an agent-based model.

Creating the Ant Foraging Model

Many biologists and entomologists have observed ants in the wild (Hölldobler & Wilson, 1998; Wilson, 1974) and have described how ants seemed to form trails to and from food sources and their nest. In the next few paragraphs we will describe some hypotheses about how the ants accomplish this behavior and what mechanisms are at work that enable ants to find food in this way.[3] Perhaps the trails form as follows: After an ant finds food, it goes

---

1. Or, more generally, a conceptual model in any form.

2. We will use the acronym ABM in several ways in this textbook. Sometimes we will use it to refer to the practice of agent-based modeling. Other times, we will use an ABM to refer to an agent-based model, or ABMs to refer to agent-based models. We rely on context to disambiguate our use of the term.

3. Our account of ant behavior is inspired by the actual history of the scientific study of ants. It has been simplified here for the sake of exposition. For a more detailed account, see Theraulaz and Bonabeau (1999).

Box 1.1
Complexity and Complex Systems

The study of complex systems has become an important scientific frontier. By the term *complex system* we mean *a system composed of many distributed interacting parts*. The field of complex systems or complexity science arose in the mid-1980s and was born out of a variety of disparate fields from economics to physics to ecology. Complex systems science provides a set of tools and frameworks for viewing phenomena. Any phenomenon can be viewed as a complex system, and choosing when to do so depends on assessing when it is most useful to use the lens and/or methodologies of complex systems. One important methodology of complexity science is agent-based modeling. The history of agent-based modeling and complex systems is explored in greater depth in subsequent chapters, and its roots in computer science are described in the appendix.

back to the nest, drops the food off, and communicates to the queen ant, and this queen ant tells the other ants where the food is and sends them off to collect it. Suppose a researcher notices that the food-finding ant never communicates with any kind of "boss" ant before leaving the nest again, so the researcher might reason that food gathering was not working through a centralized leader or controller but rather through distributed control (Bonabeau et al., 1999; Deneubourg et al., 1990; Dorigo & Stützle, 2004).

Another hypothesis that could be advanced is that perhaps the ant did not communicate with a central leader, but rather simply communicated with other ants, and those other ants were able to "diffuse" the information about the food source throughout the nest. There is reason to believe such a hypothesis might be true, since bees work in a similar way; when a bee finds a food source, it returns to the hive and conducts a complicated dance that tells the other bees where to find the food (Gould & Gould, 1988). However, though ants do have some methods of communicating information directly (Hölldobler & Wilson, 1998) most species do not communicate the exact route to a food source in this way. In fact, scientists rarely observe any difference in behavior between an ant returning to the nest with food and an ant returning without food. Most ants returning without food simply leave the nest again and recommence their search for food; the ants act almost exactly like they had before they found food. From this it is possible to reason that there must be some communication method between the ants or the colony could not efficiently gather food. In the mid-twentieth century, biologists such as Wilson (1974) found that ants with food do act slightly differently from ants without food. Ants with food drop a chemical pheromone onto the ground as they are carrying their food. This pheromone interacts with the environment by diffusing and evaporating.

Maybe this pheromone is the key to ant communication? An ant that finds food communicates where the food is by depositing a pheromone into the environment, and the

A   B

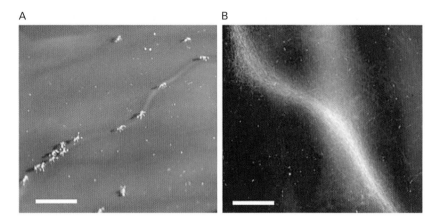

Figure 1.1
Ant trails. Pheromone trail networks of pharaoh ants on a smoked glass surface. (A) Part of a network showing bifurcations to smaller trails (scale bar: 1 cm). (B) Close-up of a single bifurcation (scale bar: 0.5 cm).[4]

other ants follow the gradient of this pheromone trail back to the original food source.[5] This would explain not only the trails that the ants form but also additional phenomena that can be observed. For instance, if ants communicated directly about food sources (as in the first two hypotheses), then any ant would have to communicate with the ant that had discovered the food source, or communicate with an ant that had communicated with that ant. However, the pheromone hypothesis does not require such a complex network of communication. Essentially, the new ant simply picks up the pheromone trail in midstream and is able to follow it correctly to the food source. No direct communication between ants is required. It also explains why the ants do not go directly to the food source (i.e., they do not make a *bee line* as bees do, where they fly directly toward the food source); instead, ants tend to follow roughly along the trail. This is because the pheromone trail can get weaker and stronger in different places as it is placed on different surfaces and in different exposures. (See figure 1.1.)

All of these descriptions require that the ants have knowledge of how to return to their nest directly regardless of how much they have wandered away from it. A combination of both experimental evidence and computational models have confirmed that ants can determine the most direct route back to their nest guided by the sun, outlines of the sky, or magnetic north (Wittlinger et al., 2006; Hartmann & Wehner, 1995; Lent, Graham & Collett, 2010).

4. Jackson et al., 2004. Adapted by permission from Macmillan Publishers Ltd: NATURE.

5. The process of communication where information is transmitted by altering the local environment is called *stigmergy* (Grasse, 1959).

Now that we have a basic hypothesis (in the form of a textual model) that describes the behavior of the ant, how do we implement the model so that we can test out this hypothesis and see if our computational model adequately accounts for what we observe in nature?[6] The first step is to create a more algorithmic description of the preceding textual model. This is just another model itself, but one that is more easily translated into an implemented model. Here is one set of rules that an individual ant could follow in order to operate in accordance with the model described earlier. We describe the rules from the point of view of an individual ant.

1. If I am not carrying food, I check if there is food where I am; if there is, I pick it up; if there isn't food right here, I try to sense a pheromone trail nearby; if I find one, then I face "uphill" along the pheromone gradient toward its strongest source.
2. If I am carrying food, I turn back toward the nest and drop pheromone on the ground below me.
3. I turn randomly a small amount and move forward a step.

These rules are easily implemented in a computer language. There are many computer languages in use for many purposes, but only a few are especially tailored to work with agent-based modeling. One of these is NetLogo (Wilensky, 1999a). NetLogo is both a modeling language and an integrated environment designed to make agent-based models easy to build. In fact, NetLogo is so easy to use that, rather than describe algorithms and models in pseudo-code,[7] throughout this textbook we will use NetLogo instead. Describing the preceding rules in the NetLogo language is straightforward. Here, for example, is one translation of rules 1–3 into NetLogo code:

```
If not carrying-food? [ look-for-food ]      ;; if not carrying food, look for it
if carrying-food? [ move-towards-nest ]      ;; if carrying food turn back towards the nest
wander                                        ;; turn a small random amount and move forward
```

This code snippet is not the complete implemented model but it does describe the core components that go into the Ants model. To complete the model we need to describe each of the subcomponents (such as "move-towards-nest," and "look-for-food," and "wander" and "look-for-food" will need to describe the ant's sniffing for pheromone). Each of which is a small amount of code. The result will be a fully implemented computational model. (See figure 1.2.)

Let us quickly try to "read" the code snippet and understand what it is doing. The "if" primitive takes as input a predicate (i.e., a statement that is either true or false) and takes

---

6. The process of comparing data from a computational model to real-world data is called *validation*. It will be discussed in depth in chapter 7.

7. Pseudo-code is an intermediate form between text and computer code that is often used to describe computational algorithms.

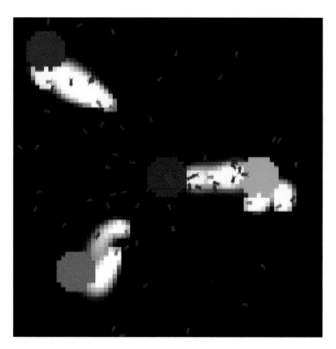

Figure 1.2
NetLogo "Ants" model of foraging behavior.[8]

one action if the predicate is true and another if it is false. The first "if" in the preceding code asks if the ant is carrying food. If she is not carrying food, then she takes the first action, that is, to look for food. She does this by checking to see if there is food where she is standing, and if there is not she looks around to see if there is a pheromone trail nearby that she can follow to find food (this is all described in the "look-for-food" procedure). If she is carrying food, then she takes the second action, which is to turn back toward the nest. To head back to the nest, she first determines if she is at the nest, if she is, then she drops her food, otherwise she turns so as to follow the trail back to the nest, dropping some pheromone along the way, since she just came from a food source. Regardless of whether she is looking for food or returning to her nest, the ant wanders a little bit along the direction she is heading. This is to simulate that ants, as with almost all animals, do not usually follow a straight line, but instead take small steps in other directions along the way.

By the end of chapter 3, you will be able to make substantive modifications to this model, and by chapter 4, you will be able to construct such a model on your own.

8. http://ccl.northwestern.edu/netlogo/models/Ants (*Wilensky, 1997*).

Box 1.2

Exploring the Ant Foraging Model

To explore this model in more depth, open the Ants model (Wilensky, 1997) (found in the Biology section of the NetLogo models library). Once you open this model, you will see a set of controls that you can manipulate to change the parameters of the model. Try varying some of the parameters (e.g., POPULATION, DIFFUSION-RATE, EVAPORATION-RATE), and explore the accompanying material that discusses this model and the real-world experiments it is based upon. As you manipulate the model, consider the following questions:

1. How does the evaporation rate affect the ability of the ants to form trails to the food? What happens if there is no evaporation?

2. How does the rate of diffusion affect the kind of trails the ants form?

3. How does the number of ants affect the colony's ability to consume the food?

Results and Observations from the Ant Model

When running the Ants model, the results are initially surprising for someone who has only seen the rules for the individual ants. The "aggregate" or "macro" behavior of the model shows apparently systematic food gathering behavior. It is as if the ant colony has a clear plan for how to gather the food. Yet, we have seen that the Ants model rules do not contain any systematic foraging plan. If we look closely at the model running, we observe that initially the ants wander around at random. Then some ants will wander into a nearby food source. Once they find that food source, they will start to bring food back to the nest, laying a pheromone trail beneath them. If just one lone ant finds the food source, the pheromone trail will not be strong enough for other ants to follow it; but as more and more ants find the food source, the trail will become stronger and stronger. Eventually, the actions of many ants will create a strong pheromone trail from the nest to the food source, and so any ant can easily find the trail to the food source.

The ants as a group appear to exploit food sources in an optimal manner. That is, they first gather food from the nearest food source, then the second nearest, and so on. This appears to be a conscious plan of the ant colony; but as we know from the ant rules, this is not the case. In fact, as you observe the model closely, you will note that sometimes ants operate almost at cross-purposes with other ants, creating additional pheromone trails to farther food sources and distracting some of the ants that are currently harvesting the closer food source. The ants do not have a centralized controller; instead, the nearest food sources are the most likely to be found first by the ants randomly wandering from the nest. The nearest food sources also require the least amount of pheromone since the pheromone only has to cover the shortest path from the nest to the food. Once a sufficient number of ants have found a particular food source, the pheromone trail to it stabilizes and thus attracts more ants to it.[9] When the food source has been completely consumed, the ants no longer lay pheromone; hence, the trail dissipates, and the ants are released to search for other food sources.

This optimal exploitation of food sources could be placed within a larger context. In many ways, the colony of ants seems to balance exploration and exploitation (Dubins & Savage, 1976. In any situation in which an entity is operating in an unknown environment, the entity must spend some time exploring the environment to understand how its actions affect its rewards, and some time exploiting the environment, that is taking actions that it knows have produced the best rewards in the past. By allocating a large number of ants to exploit the current nearest food source while other ants continue to explore, the ant colony as a whole successfully balances exploration and exploitation.

However, these "trails" that the ants build to the food source, the "optimal" behavior that they exhibit, and the "balance" between exploration and exploitation are not coded into any one ant. There is nothing that tells the ant to build a trail; there is nothing that tells the ant to go to the nearest food source first; there is nothing that tells some ants to explore while others exploit. The "trails," "optimal," and "balance" behavior of the ants is not coded into any of the ants but is instead an *emergent* phenomenon of the model (Holland, 1998; Anderson, 1972; Wilensky & Resnick, 1999). Having run and used the model, it may seem obvious that these low-level rules can create these rich and optimal global patterns. But the history of science is full of wrong turns in which scientists believed that a complex phenomenon needed a complex organizational structure and a leader (Resnick, 1994; Wilensky & Reisman, 2006; Wilensky & Resnick, 1999). In contrast, through ABM we understand that this complexity can self-organize without a leader.

What Good Is an Ant Model?

The Ant model is our first example of an agent-based model. Now that we have gone through the process of understanding how a model of ant foraging works, what knowledge have we gained from that process and how can we profitably use the model? It may seem at first that the only thing the model does is provide a visualization of one particular textual model. We describe eight main uses for agent-based models: (1) description, (2) explanation, (3) experimentation, (4) providing sources of analogy, (5) communication/education, (6) providing focal objects or centerpieces for scientific dialogue, (7) as thought experiments, and (8) prediction.

A model is *descriptive* of a real-world system. Granted, it is a simplification of the real world and does not contain all of the details and inconsistencies that are present in the real

---

9. The increase in pheromone attracts an increasing number of ants to the vicinity of the pheromone, which in turn increases the amount of pheromone. This process exhibits positive feedback, which will be discussed further in chapter 7.

Box 1.3
Emergence and Emergent Phenomena

Emergence is a property classically exhibited by many agent-based models, and it occurs when an attribute that can be described at a system level is not specifically encoded at the individual level. This can lead to surprises when behaviors encoded at an individual level result in unexpected behavior of the system at a macro level. Indeed, when most people encounter an emergent phenomenon, they tend not to see the emergence, and they usually explain the phenomenon as the result of deterministic, centralized control. Complex systems are characterized by emergent phenomena—patterns that appear to be quite complex can often be generated by simple rules. When exploring agent-based models, you may be surprised at the simplicity of the agent rules; a key to building agent-based models is to harness emergence by finding the simple rules that can generate the phenomenon.

world. But all models are coarse-grained descriptions of reality; and, in fact, models that are not coarse-grained descriptions are useless as descriptions because they are indistinguishable from the real world and therefore do not assist in our understanding of complex systems[10] (Korzybski, 1990). If your model includes all aspects of the real phenomenon, it is more efficient to simply observe reality, since it saves you the time of building the model. The function of a model is to help us to understand and examine phenomena that exist in the real world in more tractable and efficient ways than by simply observing reality. Even if you have never observed a real ant colony, the Ants model helps—it can help you know what to look for and generate hypotheses that you can confirm or disconfirm by observation.

Models are *explanatory* in that they point out the essential mechanisms underlying a phenomenon. They can function as a proof that hypothesized mechanisms are sufficient to account for an observation. Models provide us with a proof of concept that something is possible. For example, once we built the Ants model and observed the results, we proved that an ant colony could exhibit characteristics such as "trails," "optimality," and "balance" without a centralized controller (Resnick & Wilensky, 1993; Resnick, 1994; Wilensky & Resnick, 1999). These characteristics are all emergent outcomes of low-level mechanisms. A key function of ABMs is to explicate the power of the emergence. In general, it is difficult for people to understand how such simple rules can lead to complex observed phenomena, and ABMs make this connection explicit. Even if this were not the way ants actually worked, the model illustrates that this is one mechanism that could be used. We can also compare and contrast alternative hypotheses. We could, for example, build the other food-gathering hypotheses discussed earlier as computational models and compare

---

10. The Argentine author Borges has a fanciful short story (1946) based on the premise of a map as big as the terrain it maps.

their results to the Ants model and to real-world observations to determine the most plausible explanation.

Models facilitate *experimentation*. Models can be run repeatedly to note variations in their dynamics and in their outputs. Some models have very little variation from run to run. Others exhibit *path dependency* (see chapters 7 and 8) and can therefore vary tremendously from run to run. Model parameters can be varied to see their effect on model behavior and outputs. For example, in the Ants model, we could change the evaporation rate of the pheromone and see what effect that has on the performance of the ants. Alternatively, we could model the return to nest behavior in more detail, by placing a sun in the environment and have the ants calculate their path back based on the sun. From there we could start to explore some of the modern research on ant behavior that says that ants know the length of their legs and use that to calculate how to return to the nest (Wittlinger et al., 2006). We could then reproduce results from real experiments using our modified ants. Thus agent-based models enable us to easily examine different mechanisms and attributes of a system and see what effect those modifications have on the overall behavior of the system. By varying these different attributes or parameters and observing their effect on the behavior of the system, we can classify model behavior into output *regimes*, or characteristic output behaviors of the model.

Models provide us with *analogies*. Since models are simplifications of reality, they enable us to find similarities with other such simplifications even if the modeled phenomena are apparently very different. In this way, we can apply reasoning gained in one domain of knowledge to other knowledge domains. For instance, in 1996, Schoonderwoerd, extending Dorigo's work on ant colonies as optimization devices, found that the problem of ants efficiently finding food sources is similar to the problem of packets on networks efficiently seeking out their destinations (Schoonderwoerd et al., 1996). Once this analogy was created it was possible to study the ant colonies in more depth and use the results gathered from those observations to create better algorithms for controlling packet behavior. The application of algorithms based on ant colonies has become a separate field within computer science known as ant colony optimization (Dorigo & Stützle, 2004).

Agent-based models can be used as a vehicle for *communication* and *education*. We can show the model to people who have never seen an ant colony before and they can explore how ant colonies behave. Models provide us with an educational tool that encapsulates knowledge that may not be readily available from real world observation. Moreover, an agent-based model allows us to expand beyond static knowledge, enabling learners to conduct experiments much as scientists do. If someone has a hypothesis as to how a particular mechanism works, they can implement that mechanism and see whether it can account for observed behavior. Wilensky and colleagues (Blikstein & Wilensky, 2009; Levy & Wilensky, 2009; Sengupta & Wilensky, 2009; Wilensky, 1999b; Wilensky & Reisman, 2006) have demonstrated the power of using ABMs for these purposes, enabling students to more deeply understand and engage with science.

The Ants model provides the scientific community with a *focal object* (in Seymour Papert's words: "an object to think with" [1980]) that enables us to discuss the behavior of ants. It forces us to specify the important mechanisms that generate ant behavior. We can discuss which mechanisms are most important for generating the behavior and how removing or adding mechanisms would change the colony-level behavior. Then we can test alternative hypotheses by specifying the mechanisms in code and running the revised model. Since we are using a computational model, we eliminate the ambiguities that usually exist in textual models where some people may read or interpret descriptions differently from others. The agent-based model of an ant colony provides us with a "glass box" (as opposed to a "black box"), through which we can examine and observe the operations of the ants and discuss and test whether or not hypothesized mechanisms are valid. More generally, the glass box of agent-based models provides us with an unambiguous representation of the problem that we are examining, and thus is useful not only within the scientific community but also in other realms such as policy analysis.

Models can sometimes present new phenomena that are not necessarily about some real-world phenomenon, but are *thought experiments* on possible computations. Some might not use the word "model" for this kind of computational artifact, but many scientists do refer to them as models. Some classic examples of these kinds of models are cellular automata, fractals, and particle swarms. We will be examining such models as well in this textbook, and indeed we start the next chapter with a classic cellular automaton.

A common conception of computer modeling is that its major purpose is *prediction*. It is true that we often use modeling to think about possible future scenarios, and to the extent that any modeling tool can be used for discussing the future, agent-based modeling can be used in this way. However, like any modeling tool, an agent-based model's predictions depend on the accuracy of its input data. This is especially true when the events we are interested in are the results of complex systems, for which small changes in inputs can often lead to very different results. It is always difficult to assess the accuracy of a model's predictions of events when those events have not yet occurred. Many times, while modelers may claim to want to use a model to predict the outcome of a system, such as an ant colony, they actually use the model to *describe* past patterns of behavior, such as what food source was first eaten, and to *explain* future patterns that might arise, such as how ants might move around on the landscape. Sometimes modelers start off motivated by generating predictions but end up finding greater power for explanation and description. Agent-based models, in particular, are distinctive from other modeling approaches in that they were designed in order to understand and explain complex phenomena that otherwise could not be explained though traditional approaches.

We have been discussing the Ants model and its results for some time now. This model is one example of an agent-based model. But there is a wide diversity of models that are called agent-based models—from biological models to models of political systems to models of particle interactions. So what are the key components of agent-based models that make them agent-based models? Now that we have described the process of designing one particular model, let us take a step back and describe more formally what agent-based modeling is and how it can be used.

What Is Agent-Based Modeling?

The profitable uses of the Ants model that we described earlier are not particular to that one model. These are generally applicable affordances of the methodology used to develop the model, which is agent-based modeling. The core idea of *Agent-Based Modeling* is that many (if not most) phenomena in the world can be effectively modeled with agents, an environment, and a description of agent-agent and agent-environment interactions. An *agent* is an autonomous individual or object with particular properties, actions, and possibly goals. The environment is the landscape on which agents interact and can be geometric, network-based, or drawn from real data. The interactions that occur between these agents or with the environment can be quite complex. Agents can interact with other agents or with the environment, and not only can the agent's interaction behaviors change in time, but so can the strategies used to decide what action to employ at a particular time. These interactions are constituted by the exchange of information. As a result of these interactions, agents can update their internal state or take additional actions. The goal of this textbook is to explore in detail all of the different aspects and uses of agents and their interactions.

Agent-Based Models vs. Other Modeling Forms

What makes agent-based models distinct from other models? The most common form of scientific models is the equation form. Parunak, Wilensky, and colleagues (Parunak et al., 1998; Wilensky, 1999b; Wilensky & Reisman, 2006) discuss the many differences between ABM and equation-based modeling (EBM). One distinction is that because ABM models individuals it can model a heterogeneous population, whereas equational models typically must make assumptions of homogeneity. In many models, most notably in social science models, heterogeneity plays a key role. Furthermore, when you model individuals, the interactions and results are typically discrete and not continuous. Continuous models do not always map well onto real-world situations. For instance, equation-based models of population dynamics treat populations as if they are continuous quantities when in fact they are populations of discrete individuals. When simulating population dynamics it is very important to know if you have a sustainable population. After all, a wolf population cannot continue if there are fewer than two wolves left; in reality, a millionth of a wolf cannot exist and certainly cannot reproduce, but it can result in increased wolf population in EBMs. The mismatch between the continuous nature of EBMs and the discrete nature of real populations causes this "nano-wolf" problem (Wilson, 1998). As a result, for EBMs to work correctly, they must make the assumption that the population size is large and that spatial effects are unimportant (Parunak et al., 1998; Wilensky & Reisman, 2006; Wilkerson-Jerde & Wilensky, 2010, in press).

Another advantage of ABM over EBM is that it does not require knowledge of the aggregate phenomena: One does not need to know what global pattern results from the individual behavior. When modeling an outcome variable with EBM, you need to have a good understanding of the aggregate behavior and then test out your hypothesis against the aggregate output. For example, in the wolf-sheep (predator-prey) example, to build the EBM, you need to have an understanding of the relationship between (aggregate) wolf populations and sheep populations. To encode this aggregate knowledge such as in the classic Lotka-Volterra equations (Lotka, 1925; Volterra, 1926), you must have knowledge of differential equations.[11] In contrast, ABM enables you to write simple rules for simple entities, requiring knowledge only of commonsense behaviors of individual wolves and sheep and yet still observe the aggregate result by running the model. Thus, even if you have no hypothesis as to how the aggregate variables will interact, you can still build a model and generate results.

Because agent-based models describe individuals, not aggregates, the relationship between agent-based modeling and the real world is more closely matched. It is therefore much easier to explain what a model is doing to someone who does not have training in the particular modeling paradigm. This is beneficial because it means that no special training is required to understand an agent-based model. It can be understood by all of the stakeholders in a modeling process. Moreover, with some ABM languages like NetLogo, the syntax is so readable that stakeholders without knowledge of how to build a model can often read the model code and understand what is going on. This helps improve the verifiability of the model.[12] This "glass box" approach to modeling (Tisue & Wilensky, 2004) enables all interested parties to talk about the model all the way down to its most basic components.

Finally, the results generated by ABMs are more detailed than those generated by EBMs. ABMs can provide both individual and aggregate level detail at the same time. Since ABMs operate by modeling each individual and their decisions, it is possible to examine the history and life of any one individual in the model, or aggregate individuals and observe the overall results. This "bottom-up" approach of ABMs is often in contrast with the "top-down" approach of many EBMs, which tell you only how the aggregate

11. Differential equations are often represented with another modeling approach, systems dynamics modeling, which provides discrete approximations to the equations. We discuss system dynamics modeling in more depth in chapter 8.

12. A model is considered *verified* if the implemented model matches the conceptual model. Of course, since conceptual models and implemented models are distinct entities, it is impossible to say a model is completely verified, but it is possible to say that model is verified to a certain extent.

system is behaving and do not tell you anything about individuals. Many EBMs assume that one aspect of the model directly influences, or causes, another aspect of the model, while ABMs allow indirect causation via emergence to have a larger effect on the model outcomes.

Randomness vs. Determinism

One important feature of agent-based modeling, and of computational modeling in general, is that it is easy to incorporate randomness into your models.[13] Many equation-based models and other modeling forms require that each decision in the model be made deterministically. In agent-based models this is not the case; instead, the decisions can be made based on a probability. For instance, in the Ants model, as the ants move around the landscape, their decisions are not completely determined; instead, at each time step they change their heading a small amount based on a random number. As a result, each ant follows a unique, irregular path. In reality, ants might be affected by small changes in elevation, the presence or absence of twigs and stones, and even the light of the sun. To build a complete model of all of these factors might be very tedious and would probably be very specific to a particular environment. Moreover, since our real goal in building this model is to understand how ants gather food and not how they move about the landscape, there is no guarantee that a more deterministic model will provide us with a better answer to this question. Thus, using the random number serves as an approximation that may turn out to be just as correct in answering our driving question.

The "random" Ants model is easier to describe than a deterministic one. If we are explaining the Ants model to a person who has never seen it before, we can say that at each time step the ants change their heading by a small random amount. We do not have to describe how the model takes into account all of the environmental factors that could be involved. This simplification also speeds up model development, since we do not need to spend time formalizing all of these details. If at a future time we decide that the ants do need to make more deterministic decisions about their environment, we can incorporate that knowledge at that time. Thus, though randomness in a model acts as an approximation to real world concepts, the model can later be made less approximate by the incorporation of additional knowledge.

Finally, there are often times when we simply do not know enough about how a complex system works in order to build a completely deterministic model. In many of these cases the only type of model that we can build is a model with some random elements. Agent-based modeling and other modeling forms that allow you to incorporate random features are essential to studying these kinds of systems.

---

13. Since computers are deterministic machines the randomness that they possess is not true randomness but rather "pseudo-randomness." This will be discussed further in chapter 5.

When Is ABM Most Beneficial?

Agent-based modeling has some benefits over other modeling techniques, but, as with any tool, there are contexts in which it is more useful than others. ABM can be used to model just about any natural phenomenon (e.g., you could describe any phenomenon by describing the interaction of its subatomic particles). However, there are some contexts for which the cost of building an ABM exceeds the benefits, and there are other times when the benefits are extraordinary given the costs. It is sometimes difficult to discern the difference between these two scenarios. However, there are a few general guidelines that can help to identify situations where ABM will be particularly valuable. These are meant as guidelines and not particular prescriptions or "rules" about when to use ABM. Most often, you will have to judge based on the particular situation.

Some problems with large number of homogenous agents are often better modeled (i.e., they will provide more accurate solutions to aggregate problems faster) using an aggregate solution like mean field theory or system dynamics modeling (Opper & Saad, 2001; Forrester, 1968). For instance, if you are concerned about the temperature in a room, then tracking every individual molecule and its history is not necessary. On the other hand, if a problem has only a handful of interacting agents, then you usually do not need to bring to bear the full power of ABM and instead can write detailed equations describing the interaction—two billiard balls colliding, for example, does not require ABM. As a rule of thumb, agent-based models are most useful when there are a medium number (tens to millions) of interacting agents (Casti, 1995).

Agent-based models are more useful when the agents are not homogenous. For instance, modeling all the trades and events on a stock market floor requires a more rich and detailed examination of individual-level behavior. Different stock trading agents have different risk thresholds and hence will not make the same decision given the same environmental state. Even in the Ants model, while the ants all had the same rules of behavior, they were not homogenous in location, heading, food-carrying state, and so on. ABM is very useful when agents are heterogeneous and the heterogeneity of the agents affects the overall performance of the system. Since ABM enables each individual to be tracked and described at the individual level, it is much more powerful than techniques such as systems dynamics modeling (Forrester, 1968; Sterman, 2000; *Richmond & Peterson, 1990*). System dynamics modeling requires the creation of a separate "stock" for each group of agents with different properties, and, when the space of properties is large, this becomes difficult to build, track, and integrate. ABM, on the other hand, requires you only to specify how agents' properties are defined and not to keep track of all possible agent types, which provides a more concise description of a complex system. Thus, using ABM is especially beneficial when the agents are heterogeneous.

Having heterogeneous agents also allows the interactions between agents to be quite complex. Since we can specify an almost infinite number of different agent types, we can specify just a few simple rules to describe how those agents interact with each other to create a very rich tapestry of interactions. Moreover, since ABM allows individual agents to keep a history of interactions, they can change their behaviors, and even their strategies, based on past events.[14] For example, in an ABM of the evolution of cooperation, it is possible that agents can learn and hence modify their behavior as a result of continual interaction with a particular group of agents. They may learn to distrust that group, or alternatively they may learn to act more favorably toward that group. Thus ABM is very useful when modeling complex interactions of adaptive agents.

In the same way that ABM is useful when the interaction between agents is complex, it is also useful when the agents' interaction with the environment is complex. The environment in an ABM is often itself composed of stationary agents, and thus modeling agent-environment interactions has all of the power of modeling any agent-to-agent interaction. For example, in an ABM of fish ecology, a fisherman can recognize a particular location as a place that he has fished before and decide not to fish there again. This agent-environment interaction enables geographic and location-dependent information to be included in the model, and thus we get richer data than a geographic-independent model. In the fish model, it may be known that the average fish population is steady over time for a large area, but that could mean that the average fish population is steady in all of the subareas, or that different subareas trade off with each other, resulting in a larger fish population in some places and a smaller one in others. Thus, the rich description of environment and geography entailed by ABM allows for the generation of more detailed information. This enables ABM to generate spatial patterns of results as opposed to spatially homogenous aggregate results.

Another way that ABM provides more detailed information than equation-based or many other modeling approaches is through its rich conception of time. In ABM, one models agents and their interactions with each other. These interactions occur temporally; that is, some interactions occur before or after others. ABM thus enables you to move beyond a static snapshot of the system and toward a dynamic understanding of the system's behavior. In this way, ABM provides a rich and detailed account of the process of a system's unfolding in time, and not just the final state of the system. For example, in a stock market model you can actually observe individuals buying and selling stocks over time instead of modeling only the change in the stock's price. By enabling a detailed conception of time, ABM vastly expands on the detail of the resultant model.

Trade-offs of ABM
Agent-based modeling provides some benefits over other methods of modeling, but, in any particular situation, choosing a modeling methodology is a case of choosing the

14. Strategies are distinct from behavior because they express how to behave in a particular set of circumstances. Thus, a change in strategy often results in a change of behavior, but a change in behavior is not necessarily the result of a change in strategy.

appropriate tool at the appropriate time, and sometimes agent-based modeling is not the right tool for the job.

For example, ABM can be computationally intensive. Simulating thousands or millions of individuals can require great computing power. Equation-based models, by contrast, are often very simple to run and essentially just require repetitive mathematical calculations. This is true only for simple equation-based models; numerically solving complicated equation-based models may take as much computational time as agent-based models. The computational expense of running an ABM is a price one pays for having the benefits of rich individual-level data. The additional computational power needed for running ABMs is the same power that allows the tracking and development of rich histories of individuals. For example, in the Ants model we could write a simple equation that describes the rate at which food is gathered based on its distance from the nest. However, through ABM, we are able to observe the behavior of the individual ants and understand how they form trails to the food source. This same trade-off is faced by any modeling or simulation environment: more detailed results and more detailed models inevitably require additional computational resources. However, if an ABM is built well, it is possible to reduce the amount of computational power required by "black-boxing" parts of the model. This can be done by strategically using equations to control computationally intensive parts of the model. When the results warrant a higher fidelity description, one can then open up the black box.

The more detail there is in a model, the more modeling decisions have to be made by the modeler. In the equation-based modeling (EBM) literature, variables whose values are determined by the modeler are referred to as "free parameters." For example, in the Ants model, the rate at which the pheromone evaporates can be modified. This creates an additional free parameter in the system. In contrast to EBM, in ABM, there are typically more free parameters for control of the additional levels of detail. Calibrating these free parameters and making sure that they are set correctly can be a time-intensive process. Some critics of agent-based models have argued that, since ABM uses so many free parameters, it can be used to generate any result desired. We disagree. In our view, EBMs and other aggregate models and simulations simply "hide" these free parameters by making implicit assumptions about the way the system works. Often, the mathematical equations hide the implicit free parameters, since it is not possible to incorporate them within the equation. In ABM, free parameters such as the evaporation rate are exposed. One can initially set up a model to use an idealized value for evaporation rates, but the rates can also be tuned to match true biological evaporation rates. ABM generally uses more free parameters than other types of modeling because these free parameters control assumptions of the model, and ABM explicitly exposes those assumptions at more levels of action.

In order to set or modify these low-level free parameters/modeling decisions, ABM does require that the modeler have some knowledge of how individual elements of the system operate. Without knowledge of or an educated opinion about how individual agents in a complex system operate, there is no material from which to build an agent-based model. Gaining this knowledge of individual agents requires additional levels of understanding of the system—effort that may not be necessary for building an EBM or aggregate model. For example, in the Ants model, some description of an individual ant's behavior is a requirement. It would make little sense to build an agent-based model that describes only the aggregate amount of food consumption. But the work to gain this agent-level knowledge pays off—it is these same low-level assumptions that give us a richer understanding of the phenomena being observed. ABM does require us to gain an understanding of the microbehavior of a system, but without modeling the microbehaviors, ABM would not provide as elaborate a model as it does. While ABM does require us to know or guess about the individual-level mechanisms operating, it does not require knowledge of the aggregate level mechanism. It is often useful to have a description of aggregate level system behavior so that the results of an ABM can be validated. But since ABM focuses on the individual, there is no need to have a causal description at the aggregate level. For many phenomena, especially social phenomena, it is often easier to think about the individual level than the aggregate level. For example, it is easier to think of someone spreading a rumor than to think about the rate of spread of the rumor through the population. To get started building an ABM, your knowledge of the low-level elements need not be in-depth. In fact, it can take the form of an educated guess. For instance, even if we have not studied individual ants, but only ant colonies, we can make a hypothesis as to how individual ants communicate and generate a model that represents that hypothesis. If the model produces valid results, then we can say that it represents one potential way of how the ant colony might operate. This "proof of concept" or "existence proof" use of ABM is powerful.

What Is Needed to Understand ABM?

Now that we have introduced the concept of ABM, we can outline the rest of this book, which will provide you with the tools and capabilities to understand, build, and analyze your own ABMs. In chapter 2, we will construct some very simple ABMs and start to build the knowledge necessary to construct more detailed ABMs. In chapter 3, we present three already constructed ABMs and learn how to run them and to modify their code. In chapter 4, we build our first full ABM and examine how to expand upon it to create increasingly detailed ABMs. In chapter 5, we introduce and describe the major components of an ABM and also introduce network-theoretic, environmental, and user-related concepts useful for building ABMs. In chapter 6, we discuss how to present ABM results including setting up experiments and analyzing results. We cover output-related issues such as graphing, statistical analysis, network analysis and GIS analysis as well as visual displays. In chapter 7, we examine how to compare model results to the real world and use that comparison to refine and extend a model. We show how to determine if a model is verified (the code represents the conceptual model) and validated (the model has a correspondence to the real world). We also cover issues to consider in replicating an ABM. Since validation and replication usually require statistical comparison, there is a short introduction to the necessary statistics.

In chapter 8 we tie many of these threads together to discuss how ABM is applied in real-world settings and examine advanced uses of ABM. We highlight some of the principal examples from domains such as ecology, economics, land-use planning, computer science, and political science. We discuss what ABM methodology has contributed to scientific knowledge and what it will be used for in the future. We discuss how to incorporate these richer data sources into your ABM. These sources include GIS, Social Network Analysis, and sensor data (visual and nonvisual). We address how to export data from ABMs to advanced mathematical analysis packages. We also discuss how to make ABMs more powerful, by incorporating techniques such as machine learning, system dynamics modeling, and participatory simulation. We conclude with a discussion of future research trends and challenges within ABM and upcoming areas of applications of ABM to new knowledge domains.

In the appendix, we examine the origins and history of ABM, with an emphasis on its computational roots. This is provided to set a historical context for the rest of the book enabling us to understand how a variety of fields came together to create what we now call ABM. Some readers may wish to read the appendix at this time, though it can be completely skipped for the reader focused on model building. But before we embark on our ABM journey, allow us to take one last look at the Ants model.

Conclusion

The Ants model is interesting for biologists, and we have even discussed how it can be used to reason analogically about other systems, like computer networks and path planning. But what if we wanted to transform the Ants model to be more like some other system? There are many similarities between ant colonies and human organizational systems. They both exhibit problem-solving behavior. They both are results of organized structures that have evolved over the millennia. For example, what if we tried to reconceptualize the ants in the system as humans? Then we can visualize the ant colony as the central business district of a town. With this slight shift in perspective, we can start to see how the model could resemble a human city, with individuals that go off to work every day and return in the evening.

The last description suggests a major difference between the ant and the human systems. Humans tend to leave for work around the same time in the morning and return home around the same time in the evening. So we need to modify our model slightly: Instead of having the ants (now humans) leave randomly from the nest, we have them leave at random intervals around a start time, go off to find some food, and stay near the food until a certain amount of time passes, then return to their homes. And humans do not live in a colony; they live in different locations around a city, so we need to give each human a different home that they start with, and then allow them to walk (with some randomness) to their work. But humans do not walk randomly (well, not much of the time); they instead take preplanned routes on roads. So now let us put down a road network for them to drive on their way to work. But if they are driving to work, then they will be limited by the speed of the traffic. So now we need to implement a vehicle simulation on the roads. And so it goes. … Slowly, our model of one specific ant blossoms into a model of many ants collecting food, which then metamorphoses into a model of urban commuting patterns. A powerful aspect of ABM is that it enables us to find universal patterns that characterize apparently quite different phenomena, to generate these patterns with simple rules, and to explore the effects of simple modifications to those rules.

What models will you build? What are the simple rules that describe the agents in your model? What are your agents? Are they humans, ants, cars, computers, deer, viruses, cells, coffee trees, hurricanes, air particles, electrons, snowflakes, sand grains, students, teachers, videogames, marketing strategies, innovations, or any of a vast number of objects, events, or things? Whatever it is you want to model, ABM provides you with tools and capabilities that enable you to simulate and analyze it as a complex system. As you progress through this book, you will be introduced to the tools and develop the skills that you need to explore the world around you in an agent-based way.

At this point, it is recommended that you work through the three NetLogo tutorials found in the NetLogo user manual that is available from the help menu of the NetLogo application. It will be necessary to work though the tutorials to do many of the explorations at the end of this chapter and to follow chapter 2.

Explorations

Beginner NetLogo Explorations

1. Complete the tutorials that are available in the NetLogo User Manual.

2. Look over the models in the Sample Models section of the NetLogo models library. The models are grouped by subject area. Pick out a model you find interesting and try running it in different ways. What set of parameters gives you the most interesting behavior? Is there a way to change a parameter in a small way and get a very different behavior? Explicitly describe the rules the agents are following.

3. Describe a phenomenon that you think it would be interesting to model using ABM. What are the agents in this model? What properties do they have? What kind of actions can the agents take? What kind of environment do the agents exist in? What is the order of events that occurs at each time step of the model? What types of output will this model generate? What do you expect to observe as a result of running this model?

Ants and Other Model Explorations

4. Examine the code for the NetLogo Ants model, described in the chapter. The wiggle procedure right now has the ant turn a random amount to the left and then back to the right a random amount. This approximates a random walk that is centered on moving straight ahead. If you changed the procedure so the walk was biased to the left or to the right, how would that change the results? What if the limits of how much the ant turned were changed? Make these modifications and observe the results.

5. *Termites model* Run the Termites model (found in the Biology section of the NetLogo models library). In this model there are only two objects: termites and wood chips. What are the termites doing in this model? Without looking at the code or the info window, can you describe the rules governing the termites' behavior? Hint: It might help to reduce the number of termites and wood chips and to slow down the speed slider.

6. *Daisyworld model* Some ABMs are used not as models of real-world events, but rather as thought experiments. Run the Daisyworld model (found in the Biology section of the NetLogo models library). This model defines a world in which the whole surface is covered by daisies, and it examines how different factors affect the global temperature of the world. Adjust the parameters of the model and observe how the model reacts. The standard parameters result in a temperature slightly below 50. Find a set of parameters that move the temperature closer to 12. This model rarely results in a constant temperature; it usually oscillates. Describe this oscillation.

Concept Explorations

7. *Modeling at different levels* Agent-based models can be written at different levels. For example, one model may have agents that are populations of wolves and sheep, whereas another model may have agents that are individual wolves and sheep. Write a description of how packs of wolves interact with flocks of sheep at the group level. Now write a description of how individual sheep interact with individual wolves. How are your descriptions different? What phenomena are you describing? At what times would the group level description be helpful? At what times would the individual level description be helpful?

8. *Emergence and ABM* Agent-based models often exhibit emergent properties. One characteristic of an emergent phenomenon is that the system exhibits a property that is not defined at the individual level. For instance, examine the Traffic Basic model (found in the Social Sciences section of the models library). Run the model several times and observe the results. What causes the traffic jams in the model? Does there appear to be any external event that causes them? Inspect the cars. Is there any property of these cars that describes a traffic jam? If one car moves slowly, is that enough to cause traffic jams?

9. *ABM for education and understanding* ABM provides us with a new way of understanding the world around us. ABM has many uses in research. But ABM also has great potential as a tool for education. For instance, molecules in a free gas can be thought of

as agents moving around and colliding with each other. Examine the GasLab Free Gas model (found in the Chemistry and Physics section of the models library). Do you think this model is easier to understand than a traditional equation-based approach to understanding Free Gas phenomena? What affordances does the ABM approach give us that traditional approaches lack? Are there ways that ABM can be more confusing than traditional approaches? If so how?

NetLogo Explorations

10. Create at least two different ways of distributing turtles randomly across the screen. In one method, use only turtle motion commands such as *forward*, *left*, and *right*. In another method, use *set* or *setxy*. Create buttons to launch these procedures. Compare and contrast your different methods. Is one of these more efficient? Is one of them more realistic? In what situations would each of them have advantages over the other?

11. Write a procedure to get a color to spread from patch to patch. (There are many ways to do this. Pick one you like.) Create a button to launch this procedure.

12. Write a procedure that makes the turtles chase after the mouse cursor. Create a button to launch this procedure.

13. Select a new shape for the turtles from the shapes editor, and then create a "cloud" of turtles (a bunch of turtles in the same local area) using your new shape. Create some green patches. Make the turtles follow the mouse cursor around the screen but avoid the green patches. Make the green color spread from green patches to other patches nearby. Create buttons to launch these procedures.

14. Create a "cloud" of turtles, half of them one color and half of them another color. Based on a probability have one color of turtles move up and the other color turtles move down. Label the turtles with their WHO number. Create buttons to launch these procedures. Create a monitor that keeps track of how many times one of the turtles has moved.

15. (a) Create a new model with a SETUP procedure that creates turtles. (b) Create a slider that controls the number of turtles created. (c) Write a GO procedure that makes the turtles wander around the screen randomly. (d) Change the GO procedure to make the turtles afraid of each other. (e) Make the turtles die when they reach the edge of the screen. (f) Create a plot that displays the number of turtles.

16. Write two procedures. In the SETUP procedure, turn the left side of the screen red, and the right side of the screen green and create two turtles. Give one turtle a shape from the shapes editor and make a new shape for the other turtle. In the GO procedure, make the turtles move randomly about the screen. When a turtle is in an area of one color, create a circle of patches of the other color centered on the turtle.

17. Both turtles and patches can create visual images in the NetLogo view. Create a turtle and have it draw a circle (using the PEN-DOWN command). Create the outline of a circle with patches without using a turtle pen. Write a procedure that asks a turtle to draw a square given a starting location and side length. Write a similar procedure using patches.

Compare and contrast the code for these two procedures. Which set of code is more compact? Are there advantages or disadvantages to using patches or turtles to accomplish this task?

18. Open the *random walk example* (found in the Code Examples folder in the models library). Inspect the code. What do you predict the turtle's path will look like? Run the model. Does the path look like you expected it would? Modify the model code so that the turtle's path is still random but is less "jagged," i.e., is smoother and straighter.

19. Most of this textbook addresses the use of ABM to model and scientifically explain phenomena. However, you can also use ABM to create powerful visualizations. As we have mentioned, ABM has even been used to create Academy Award–winning special effects. Examine the Particle Systems Basic model (found in the Computer Science section of the models library). This model creates interesting visual images from the manipulation of simple agents. Explore this model, and understand how the agents behave and what properties they have. Describe a non-agent-based model that would create similar results as the base model with the initial parameters. Now examine the NetLogo model again. Change the initial number of particles, the step size, and the gravity. Can you describe both an agent-based model and a non-agent-based model that creates these results? Which of these two models is easier to describe? Why?

20. *Computer modeling and chaos theory* Chaos theory was developed from traditional equation-based modeling, but one of its inspirations came from computer modeling. Edward Lorenz discovered that mathematical systems could produce very different results depending on the initial conditions that the systems have. He realized this because he tried to restart a computer model of the weather system halfway through a run with a new set of parameters that lacked a small amount of precision from his previous set of parameters. The resulting model behaved very different from his original model. Agent-based models can exhibit this same "sensitivity to initial conditions." For instance, examine the Sunflower model (found in the Biology section of the models library). This is an agent-based model of how rows of sunflower seeds are added to a sunflower. Run the model with the default settings. Now change one of the parameters. Run the model again. Repeat this process. As you keep manipulating the parameters, do you eventually get to the point where you can predict the behavior of the model with new parameters? Explain your answer. Why is this model predictable or unpredictable?

2 Creating Simple Agent-Based Models

One of my central … tenets is that the construction that takes place "in the head" often happens especially felicitously when it is supported by construction of a more public sort "in the world"—a sand castle or a cake, a Lego house or a corporation, a computer program, a poem, or a theory of the universe. Part of what I mean by "in the world" is that the product can be shown, discussed, examined, probed, and admired. It is out there.

—Seymour Papert (1991)

It can scarcely be denied that the supreme goal of all theory is to make the irreducible basic elements as simple and as few as possible without having to surrender the adequate representation of a single datum of experience.

—Albert Einstein (1933, p. 165)

In this chapter, we will learn to construct a few simple agent-based models. These simple models, sometimes referred to as "toy models," are not meant to be models of real phenomena, but instead are intended as "thought experiments." They are offered, as Seymour Papert puts it, as "objects to think with" (1980). Our purpose is to show that it is relatively easy to create simple agent-based models, yet these simple models still exhibit interesting and surprising emergent behavior. We will construct three such models: "Life," "Heroes and Cowards," and "Simple Economy." All three models can be found in the chapter 2 folder of the IABM Textbook folder in the NetLogo models library.

If you have not yet completed the NetLogo tutorials, this would be a good time to do so. Although we review some of that material in this chapter, we go through it more quickly here and do not describe all the steps in detail.

Life

In 1970, the British mathematician John Horton Conway (described in Conway, 1976) created a cellular automaton that he called the "Game of Life." Martin Gardner (1970) popularized this game in his *Scientific American* column. Subsequently, millions of readers played the game.

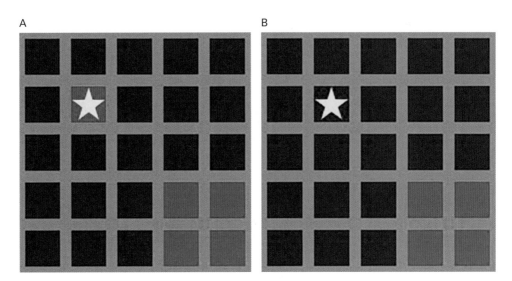

Figure 2.1
(A) Before. (B) After.

The game is played on a large grid, such as a checkerboard or graph paper. Let's say we are playing on a square grid with 51 squares[1] (or "cells") on a side. Each cell can be either "alive" or "dead." This is called the "state" of the cell. Every cell is surrounded by eight "neighbor" cells. The grid is considered to "wrap around" so that a cell on the left edge has three (3) neighbor cells on the right edge and, similarly, a cell on the top edge has three (3) neighbor cells on the bottom edge. There is a central clock. The clock ticks establish a unit of time. In the game of Life, the unit of time is called a generation. More generally, in agent-based models, the unit of time is referred to a tick. Whenever the clock ticks, each cell updates its state according to the following rules:

Each cell checks the state of itself and its eight neighbors and then sets itself to either alive or dead. In the rule descriptions that follow, blue cells are "dead," green cells are "alive" and the yellow stars indicate the cells affected by the rule described.

(1) If the cell has less than two (2) alive neighbors, it dies (figure 2.1).
(2) If it has more than three (3) alive neighbors, it also dies (figure 2.2).
(3) If it has exactly two (2) alive neighbors, the cell remains in the state it is in (figure 2.3).
(4) If it has exactly three (3) alive neighbors, the cell becomes alive if it is dead, or stays alive if it is already alive (figure 2.4).

1. The standard setup for the NetLogo grid is to have an odd number of cells, so that there is always a center cell. Other setups are possible and are described in chapter 5.

A   B

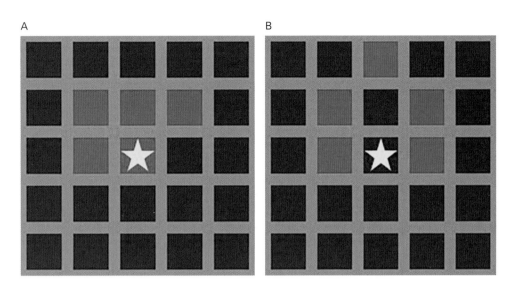

Figure 2.2
(A) Before. (B) After.

A   B

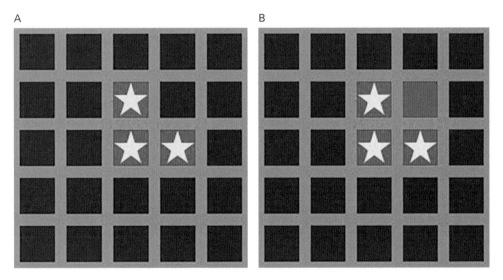

Figure 2.3
(A) Before. (B) After.

A   B

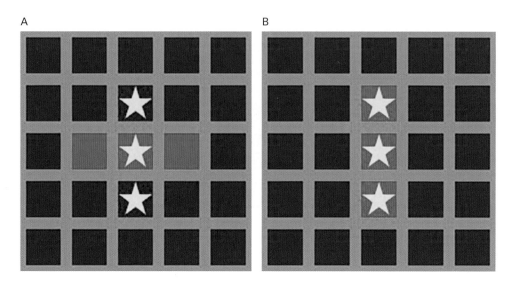

Figure 2.4
(A) Before. (B) After.

Since Gardner's publication of Conway's Game of Life, many people have explored it and have been surprised by the wide diversity of shapes and patterns that "emerge" from these simple rules. We will now use NetLogo to construct the Game of Life.

We will begin by reviewing the basic NetLogo elements. We start by opening the NetLogo application. The application opens with a blank interface with a large black square in it (see figure 2.5). The black square is the known as the "view" and is the area in which we will play the Game of Life. The surrounding white area is known as the "interface" and is where we can set up user-interface elements such as buttons and sliders. Right-click on the view and select "edit" from the drop-down menu. You will see the Model Settings dialog (figure 2.6) where we can configure some basic settings for our NetLogo model.

Every NetLogo model consists of three tabs.[2] The tab that you are looking at now is the *Interface* tab, where we work with widgets and observe model runs. Next we will work with the *Code* tab, where we write the model procedures.

A third very important tab is the *Info* tab. In this chapter, we will not work with the *Info* tab in detail, but it is an important part of any model. This is where model authors put the information about their models. Details on how the Info tab is structured can be found in the "Sections of the Info Tab" box in chapter five. The Info tab is a very useful resource for exploring a NetLogo model and we recommend that Textbook readers read them carefully when working with models and take the time to write good Info tabs for models you create.

2. In some versions of NetLogo, there is a fourth "Review" tab.

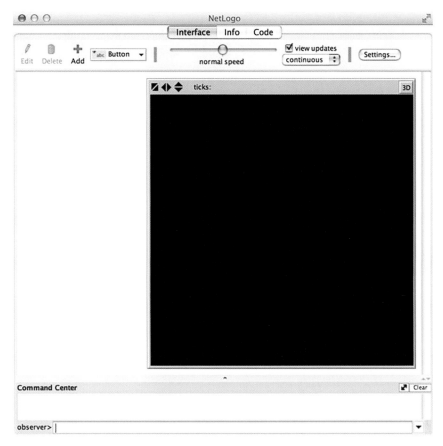

Figure 2.5
The NetLogo application at startup.

Now let us return to the Interface tab, and begin developing our Life-simple model. The view is composed of a grid of cells known, in NetLogo parlance, as patches. Click Settings in the toolbar of the Interface tab. By default, the view origin is at the center of the view and its current maximum x-coordinate and y-coordinate is 16. To begin developing our Life-simple model, we will change the values of MAX-PXCOR and MAX-PYCOR to 25, which will give us a grid of 51 by 51 patches, for a total of 2,601 patches. This creates a much larger world enabling more space to create the elements of the Game of Life. To keep the view a manageable size on the screen, we will change the default patch size from 13 to 8. As the Game of Life is played in a wrapping grid, we keep the wrapping check-boxes checked (as they are by default, we will explain these in more detail in chapter 5). We can now click OK and save these new settings. (See figure 2.7.)

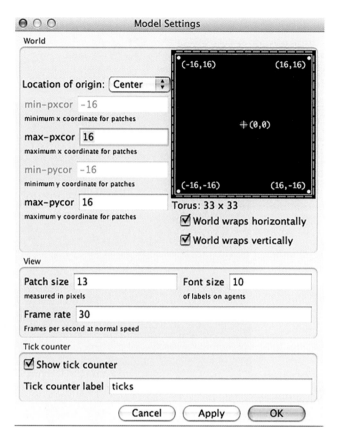

Figure 2.6
The NetLogo Model Settings dialog before adjusting the settings.

The Game of Life is played on a grid of cells, so we will consider each NetLogo patch as a different cell. Life has two kinds of cells in it, "live" cells and "dead" cells. We choose to model live cells as green patches and dead cells as blue patches. Once we have thought through what the model will look like we still need to create the model instructions. To do this, we will need to write NetLogo instructions (or code) in the Code tab. We select the Code tab and begin to write our code. NetLogo code takes the form of modules known as "procedures." Each procedure has a name and begins with the word TO and ends with the word END.

Our Life model (Life-Simple in the IABM Textbook folder of the NetLogo models library) will consist of two procedures: SETUP, which initializes the game, and GO, which advances the clock by one tick.

We create the SETUP procedure as follows:

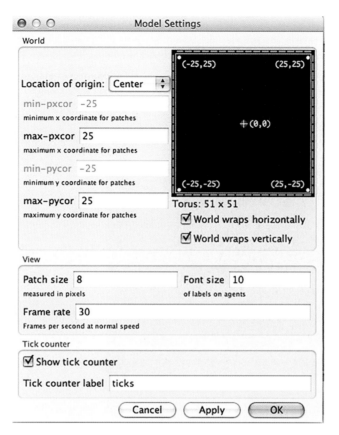

Figure 2.7
After configuring the Model Settings dialog for the Life Simple model.

```
to setup
    clear-all
    ask patches
;; create 10% alive patches
[
        set pcolor blue  ;; blue cells are dead
        if random 100 < 10
            [set pcolor green] ;; green cells are alive
    ]
    reset-ticks
end
```

This code has three sections. The first section is one line, the command CLEAR-ALL, which clears the view (setting the color of all its patches to the default color black) in case there are leftover elements from our previous play of the game. Thus, we can run multiple

Box 2.1
Wrapping

One thing to note is that the world in the Game of Life model has been set up to "wrap." In a wrapping world, a patch on the left-edge of the world is neighbor to three patches on the right edge of the world. It is often convenient to set the world to wrap "without boundary conditions," avoiding special code for patches at the edge.

A

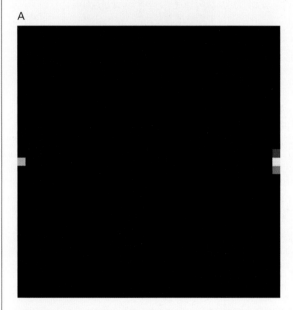

Figure 2.8
(A) With wrapping turned on, the green colored patch at the left edge of the world is a neighbor of the red, yellow, and orange colored patches at the right edge of the world. (B) The Model Settings dialog with the world set to wrap vertically and horizontally.

To set the world to wrap, select the view object and edit it. You will bring up the "Model Settings" dialog. The dialog has two checkboxes for wrapping. Checking the first one sets the world to wrap horizontally, as in the figure above. Checking the second checkbox sets the world to wrap vertically, so patches at the top of the view are neighbors with patches at the bottom. In ABM it is often useful to use a wrapping world, so NetLogo's default setting allows for the world to wrap.

Box 2.1
(continued)

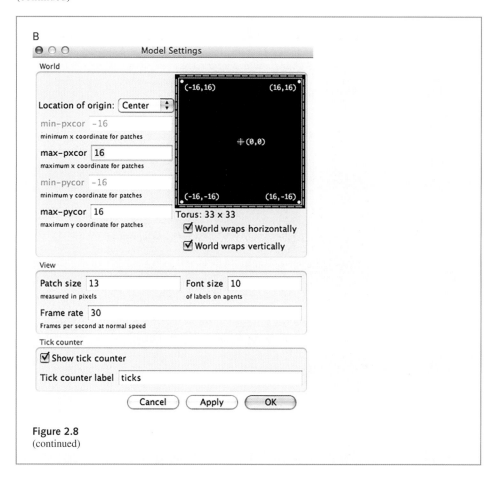

Figure 2.8
(continued)

versions of our game sequentially without having to close NetLogo and open it back up. The second section issues commands to (or makes requests of) all of the patches. In NetLogo, we are polite in our interactions with agents, so to issue commands to the patches we use the form ASK PATCHES. We then enclose our requests to the patches in brackets. However, do not mistake our politeness—the patches have no choice but to do as they are asked. As a result, you will often find that in this book, we will slip interchangeably between the language of commands and requests as synonymous. In the second section of our SETUP code, there are two commands/requests. The first asks each patch to set its color (PCOLOR which stands for patch color) to blue, making all the cells dead. When creating agent-based models, it is useful to think of commands to agents in an agent-centric way. This will help you to understand how the model works, as described in the box that follows:

Box 2.2
Agent-Centric Thinking

When asking the agents to execute some commands, it is useful to think in an agent-centric way. That is, thinking from the point of view of the agent. Instead of thinking from the perspective of telling all the agents what to do, think of each agent as individually receiving the instructions and behaving accordingly.

For example, if we issue the command:

```
ask patches [if pxcor < 0 [set pcolor blue]]
```

One way of thinking about it is that we are commanding all the patches whose x-coordinate is less than zero to turn blue. The agent-centric way to think about the same command is to think about it from the patch's perspective; each patch wakes up when it "hears" ASK PATCHES and listens for its command. In this case, the patch asks itself, "Is my x-coordinate less than zero? If it isn't, I won't do anything, if it is, I'll set my color to blue."

At first, thinking in this way may seem unnatural, but as you become more experienced at agent-based modeling, you will see the value of agent-centric thinking.

The second request is a little trickier. It asks some of the patches to turn green; that is, it seeds the game with some live cells. The way it does this is also best approached through agent-centric thinking. Each patch executes the code RANDOM 100, which can be thought of as each patch rolling a hundred-sided die.[3] If a patch rolls any number less than ten (10), it turns green. Since the dice throws are random, we cannot know exactly which patches will roll a number less than ten (10), hence do not know exactly which particular cells will turn green. However, we can expect that approximately 10 percent of the cells will turn green. NetLogo does have a way of telling exactly 10 percent of the patches to turn green. However, in designing ABMs, we often use a probabilistic procedure because most natural phenomena we model have some stochasticity or variability, so having our procedure use a randomized process is a closer model of reality.

The third section of our SETUP procedure is also just one line, RESET-TICKS. This command resets the NetLogo clock.

Returning to the Interface tab, we create a button and name it SETUP.[4] Pressing this button will now cause the SETUP procedure to run. Try it a few times. Each time you should see a different set of green cells on a blue background (see figure 2.9).

---

3. The metaphor of a die is one way we can understand the action of the "random" primitive in NetLogo. Many other metaphors are commonly used. Another useful one is a spinner, with the numbers 0 to 99 on the outside. You spin the spinner arrow and it turns till it points to one of the one hundred numbers.

4. If you don't remember how to create *Interface* elements from the tutorials, please refer to the *Interface* Guide of the NetLogo Programming Manual (http://ccl.northwestern.edu/netlogo/docs/interface.html).

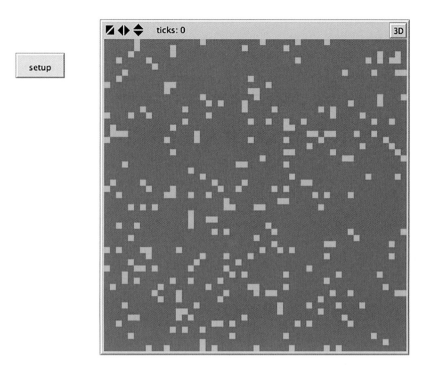

Figure 2.9
A typical random initial configuration of the Game of Life. Approximately 10 percent of the cells are alive and colored green.

Now let's take a look at the GO procedure, which advances the clock for one tick.

```
to go
    ask patches [
            ;; each patch counts its number of green neighboring patches
            ;; and stores the value in its live-neighbors variable
        set live-neighbors count neighbors with [pcolor = green]
        ]
    ask patches [
            ;; patches with 3 green neighbors, turn (or stay) green
        if live-neighbors = 3 [ set pcolor green ]
            ;; patches with 0 or 1 green neighbors turn (or stay) blue
            ;; from isolation
        if (live-neighbors = 0) or (live-neighbors = 1) [ set pcolor blue ]
            ;; patches with 4 or more green neighbors turn (or stay) blue
            ;; from overcrowding
        if live-neighbors >= 4 [set pcolor blue]
            ;; patches with exactly 2 green neighbors keep their color
    ]
    tick
end
```

Box 2.3
Neighbors

In agent-based modeling, we often model local interactions. This is accomplished by having cells in the grid talk to their neighbor cells. Most often, we are using two-dimensional grids or lattices with square cells (though later in this textbook we will see three-dimensional grids and two-dimensional grids of triangular or hexagonal lattices). In a square lattice, there are two commonly used neighborhoods: the von Neumann neighborhood and the Moore neighborhood. A cell's *von Neumann neighborhood* consists of the four cells that share an edge with it, the cells to the north, south, east and west (the green squares in the right figure that follows). A *Moore neighborhood* consists of the eight cells that touch it, adding the cells to the northeast, southeast, northwest, and southwest (the entire green area in the left figure that follows). In NetLogo, the primitive NEIGHBORS refers to a patch's Moore neighbors, and NEIGHBORS4 refers to a patch's von Neumann neighbors.

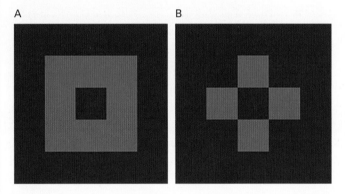

Figure 2.10
(A) Moore Neighborhood. (B) von Neumann Neighborhood. This will be further elaborated in chapter 5.

The GO procedure consists of three sections: the first two ask the patches to "behave" (i.e., they specify the rules that we described at the beginning of this section), and the third section simply advances the clock by one "tick." This third section is the standard way to end a GO procedure. First, let's examine the first two sections. The first section asks all the patches to execute one command. We assign to each patch a LIVE-NEIGHBORS variable that we will need to "declare"; that is, we will need to tell NetLogo about the existence of this patch variable. The command asks each patch to store (SET) a value in the LIVE-NEIGHBORS variable. The value to be stored is COUNT NEIGHBORS WITH [PCOLOR = GREEN]. That expression tells the patch to examine its eight neighbor patches and count

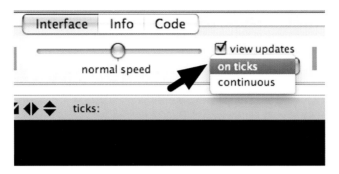

Figure 2.11
Pull-down menu to set display updating frequency.

how many are green. Thus, at the end of the first section, each patch has a variable LIVE-NEIGHBORS that has the value of the number of its live neighbors.

To declare the LIVE-NEIGHBORS variable, we add the following line to the top of the Code tab:

```
patches-own [live-neighbors]
```

The second section of the GO procedure consists of three "if" conditions.

The first asks each patch to check if its value for LIVE-NEIGHBORS is three, in other words, if it has exactly three live neighbors. If it does, then, according to the Life rules, the cell should be alive, so the patch turns green to symbolize birth (if it already was green, it remains so). If the patch's value for LIVE-NEIGHBORS is either zero or one, the patch turns blue to symbolize death from isolation. If the patch's value for LIVE-NEIGHBORS is four or more, the patch also turns blue to symbolize death from overcrowding. That is the end of the second section. Notice that the second section does not tell the patch what to do if it has exactly two (2) live neighbors. Since the patch was not asked to do anything in that case, it will not do anything, so the patch will remain the color it was before this code was executed. That ends the GO procedure.

Returning to the interface, we now create a new button called GO. We set up the GO button to call the GO procedure just like we did for the SETUP button. We also need to make sure the "view updates" pull-down is set to "on ticks"[5] (see figure 2.11). This means we see the world only after a full iteration of the GO procedure has completed.

---

5. For most NetLogo models, it is best to set this pull-down to "ticks," which will cause the view to update on each tick. But when exploring in the command center, it is often useful to set it to "continuous," so you can view behaviors that might occur between ticks. For a detailed discussion of the differences between continuous and tick-based view updates, see the VIEW UPDATES section of the PROGRAMMING GUIDE in the NetLogo users' manual, http://ccl.northwestern.edu/netlogo/docs/programming.html#updates.

Box 2.4

Variables

In most programming languages, the term *variable* is used to refer to a symbol that can have many different possible values. That is also true in NetLogo, but in NetLogo there is a distinction between a global variable and an agent variable. A *global variable* has only one value regardless of the agent that is accessing it. All agents can access that variable. In contrast, an *agent variable* can have different values for each agent of a certain type. The core agent-types in NetLogo are turtles, patches and links. Each of these agent-types can have an agent-variable, namely a turtle, patch, or link variable respectively. Each turtle has its *own* value for every turtle variable. The same goes for patches and links.

Some variables are built into NetLogo. For example, all turtles and links have a COLOR variable, and all patches have a PCOLOR variable. If you set the variable, the turtle or patch changes color. Other built-in turtle variables including XCOR, YCOR, and HEADING. Other built-in patch variables include PXCOR and PYCOR.

You can also define your own variables. You can make a global variable by adding a switch, slider, chooser, or input box to your model interface, or by using the GLOBALS keyword at the beginning of your code.

For instance, if you want to keep track of a global score for your model that all agents can access, you can create a global variable in which to store it by writing the following line at the top of your Code tab:

```
globals [score]
```

You can also define new turtle, patch, and link variables using the TURTLES-OWN, PATCHES-OWN and LINKS-OWN keywords. If you write:

```
turtles-own [speed]
```

each turtle will get a speed variable and each turtle can have a different value for speed. Similarly, if you write:

```
patches-own [friction]
```

then each patch can have a different friction with which to slow down the turtle's speed.

There are also local variables defined by the "let" primitive. We will explore their use in the next chapter.

See http://ccl.northwestern.edu/netlogo/docs/programming.html#variables in the NetLogo user's manual programming guide for more information on variables.

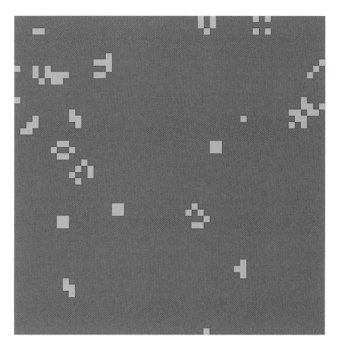

Figure 2.12
The Life-simple model view after two ticks.

When we press the GO-ONCE button once, the colors of the patches change according to the rules of the Game of Life. Each time you press it, you get another generation of the Game of Life. You'll also notice that on the gray bar above the view, the ticks counter will advance by one, recording how many times the clock has ticked. (See figure 2.12.) The initial random distribution of live cells morphs into a small set of live-cell configurations or "shapes."

When you press the GO button several times, you will notice that the original random distribution of green patches will morph into a set of structures. One reason for this is that the isolated green patches die from "loneliness" according to the first of the Life rules (cells with less than two neighbors die), leaving only clusters of cells to live on. Some of these structures remain stable over several generations.

As you can see from letting this model run, there are many different structures that can emerge in the Game of Life. Players of the Game of Life are frequently astounded by the amazing diversity and complexity of the structures that can emerge from different initial configurations. The model we have created always initializes the game to start with a random 10 percent of live cells. But this is an unnecessary constraint. Any initial configuration of live cells can be played. (See the Life model in the Computer Science section of the NetLogo models library for a version that allows you to "paint" the live cells.)

Box 2.5
Inspectors/Agent Monitors

One way to keep close track of the state of a live cell is to use an inspector, also known as an *agent monitor*. You can use an agent inspector/monitor to view the properties of any agent type. Let's look at an example of using a patch inspector. Consider the block shape we saw in figure 2.1.

We can inspect the state of any patch in the world. Let's inspect the green colored patch on the lower left. We can inspect it either by right-clicking on the patch and selecting INSPECT or by issuing the command INSPECT and specifying which patch we wish to inspect. When we inspect the lower left green colored patch, we will see an inspector window appear:

The fields in the inspector include all the built-in patch variables (PXCOR, PYCOR, PCOLOR, PLABEL, and PLABEL-COLOR) as well as any patch variables we have declared. In this case, you can see the LIVE-NEIGHBORS variable that we declared earlier. Agent monitors have many capabilities. To learn more about their capabilities, see http://ccl.northwestern.edu/netlogo/docs/interface.html#agentmonitors in the NetLogo interface guide.

Before we go further with this model, we will make one more small change to the code. Many people find the combination of the default blue and green colors that come with NetLogo to be a bit hard on the eyes. So, we will modify the color of the dead cells throughout the model to a different shade of blue, as described by the expression "blue—3." (All NetLogo colors are numbers and can be added to or subtracted from to darken or lighten their shade. For a comprehensive discussion of the NetLogo color scheme, see ccl. northwestern.edu/netlogo/docs/programming.html#colors.) After doing that, now edit the GO button and check the "forever" box in the top middle. Now when you press the GO button, it will continue advancing the clock until you press the button again.[6] In this way, you can quickly watch thousands of generations of the game. Each initial configuration leads to different life trajectories. Some trajectories quickly stabilize in just a few generations, and some go on for much longer. It is worthwhile to examine many different trajectories and see what patterns you can detect. (See figure 2.14.)

There are at least three general classes of stable Life patterns: Still Lifes, Oscillators, and Spaceships.

1. Still Lifes: *Still Life shapes* are stable unless other shapes collide with them. The most common still life shape is the block, which keeps its shape from one generation to the

---

6. If you still want a button that only executes one step at a time, then you can add another button called GO-ONCE and not click the forever button. This is what we did in the Life Simple model included in the IABM Models Folder.

Box 2.5
(continued)

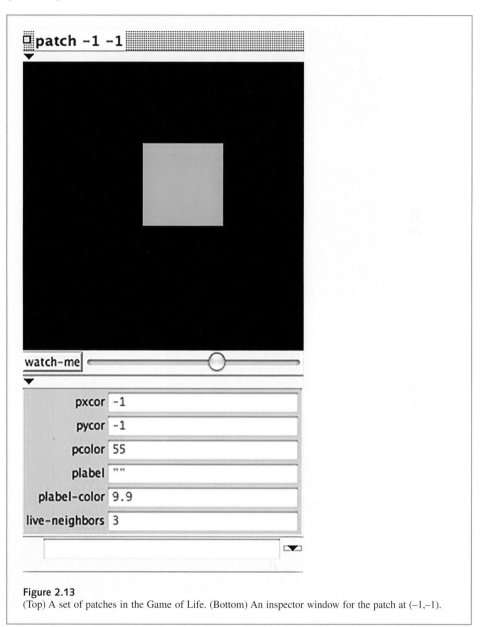

Figure 2.13
(Top) A set of patches in the Game of Life. (Bottom) An inspector window for the patch at (−1,−1).

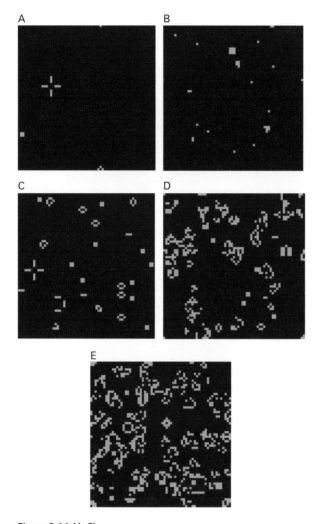

Figure 2.14 (A–E)
Some sample trajectories of the Life-Simple model (with dark red for the dead cells). Some initial conditions stabilize in just a few generations. Others take many thousands. Final states will typically include some oscillators and spaceships (see figures 2.15 and 2.16) that will continue to cycle through their different states.

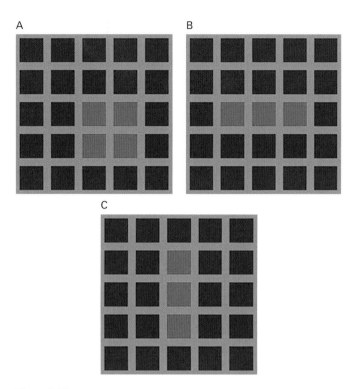

Figure 2.15
(A) A four-cell block shape is a "still-life"; it doesn't change from one Life generation to the next. Each live cell (green) has exactly three live neighbor cells, so it stays alive in the next generation. Each dead cell (blue) has one or two live neighbor cells, so it stays dead in the next generation. (B, C) The two states of the "blinker." It oscillates between these two states, alternating vertical and horizontal orientation from one generation to the next.

next (figure 2.15A). Other well-known still-lifes are the beehive, the loaf, the boat and the ship (see exploration 5).

2. Oscillators: *Oscillator patterns* repeat over time. They may have one shape in the first tick (t) and another shape in the next tick (t + 1), eventually getting back to the original shape after *n* ticks (*n* is known as the period of the oscillator). For instance, a blinker is a period two (2) oscillator. It consists of a configuration of three cells (either up and down or left and right) that rotates between horizontal and vertical orientations. (See figure 2.15B,C.)

3. Spaceships: Some Life shapes can move across the Life world. These are called *Spaceships*. For example, the "glider" is composed of five (5) cells that form a small arrowhead shape (see figure 2.16A).

At each tick, the glider moves from one state to the next. After four (4) ticks (remember, each tick represents a "generation" of the Game of Life), the glider is back to its original

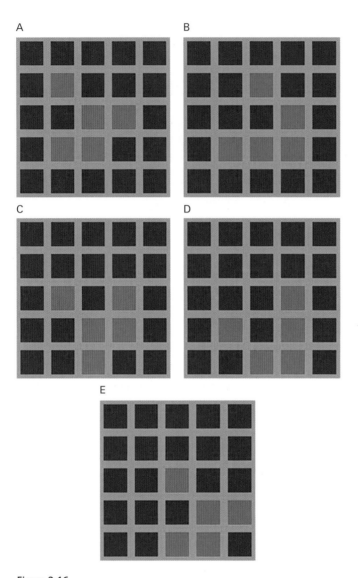

Figure 2.16
(A) The initial glider shape. (B–E) The four states of the glider. The glider changes from one state to the next. After traversing the four states, it comes back to its original shape, but has moved one step right and one step down (rightmost panel).

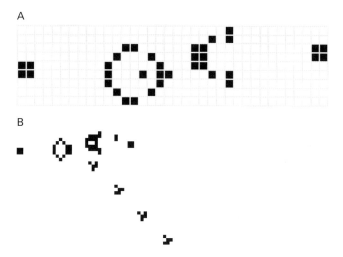

Figure 2.17
(A) Initial state of Gosper's Glider Gun. (B) The Glider Gun in action. As discussed earlier, the variety and diversity of forms that can arise in the game of Life is astonishing. See e.g., http://www.youtube.com/watch?v =C2vgICfQawE&feature=fvwp for a video of a range of forms.

shape but is moved over one cell to the right and one cell down. The glider acts as a stable shape "moving" across the grid. (See figure 2.16B–E.)

In addition to the three stable classes in the game of Life, there are also "guns." A *gun* is a pattern with a main part that repeats periodically, like an oscillator, and that also periodically emits spaceships. There are then two periods that may be considered: the period of the spaceship output, and the period of the gun itself, which must be a multiple of the spaceship output's period. It is possible to create guns that emit gliders, known as "glider guns." In 1970, the self-described "hacker" Bill Gosper discovered the first glider gun (see figure 2.17). The discovery of the glider gun eventually led to the proof that Conway's Game of Life was universal and could function as a Turing machine.[7]

Since Conway's publication of the Life model, the field of cellular automata has continued to develop and grow. Researchers have studied and simulated cellular automata in one (1), two (2), and three (3) dimensions as well as higher dimensional cellular automata. Evidence of cellular automata-like mechanisms has been abundantly found in nature, including the shapes of shells and flowers, the colorations and striations of animals, and the structure of organisms such as fibroblasts. (See figures 2.18–2.20.)

In 1969, computer pioneer Konrad Zuse published *Calculating Space*, which contained the revolutionary proposition that the physical laws of the universe are discrete, and that

7. For a fascinating video of the Game of Life simulating itself, see http://www.youtube.com/watch?v =xP5-iIeKXE8.

Figure 2.18
Textile cone and snail shell (http://en.wikipedia.org/wiki/Puka_shell).

Figure 2.19
Romanesco broccoli (http://en.wikipedia.org/wiki/File:Fractal_Broccoli.jpg).

Figure 2.20
Spotted leopard. Some patterns in nature that can be generated by a cellular automaton (http://commons
.wikimedia.org/wiki/File:Leopard_standing_in_tree_2.jpg).

the universe can be viewed as the output of a computation on a giant cellular automaton.
In writing this book, Zuse founded the field of digital physics. In the words of another
prominent digital physicist, Ed Fredkin (1990): "We hypothesize that there will be found
a single cellular automaton rule that models all of microscopic physics; and models it
exactly. We call this field DM, for digital mechanics."

The prodigal physicist and mathematical software entrepreneur Stephen Wolfram (1983)
wrote a paper that investigated a basic class of elementary cellular automata. These CAs
were the simplest possible. They were one-dimensional, and each cell could only take in
to account one neighbor on either side of it. Nevertheless, they exhibited a remarkable
amount of complexity. The unexpected complexity of the behavior of these elementary
CAs caused Wolfram, much like Zuse before him, to hypothesize that complexity in nature
may be due to simple CA-like mechanisms. Wolfram classified the 256 possible rules and
categorized them into four behavioral regimes (homogenous, periodic, chaotic and
complex). He showed that the behavior of some rules (chaotic) was indistinguishable from

randomness—that is, that when you apply the rules repeatedly the patterns they generate look like random noise.[8] He also found that other rules generated behavior that led to patterns that were intricately complex[9] and that CAs could generate many patterns found in nature as in the previous figure (Wolfram, 2002). Matthew Cook, a research assistant with Wolfram, proved that one of Wolfram's 1D CAs (rule 110) is universal—that is, any computation that can be done by any computer can also be done by that cellular automaton (Cook, 2004). In 2002 Wolfram published a voluminous and controversial book, *A New Kind of Science*, which argues that the discoveries about cellular automata have major significance for all disciplines of science.

At this time, you may want to open the Life Simple model from the chapter 1 folder of the IABM Textbook folder in the NetLogo models library. There are also several other cellular automata models in the models library that you can peruse and explore.

Heroes and Cowards

We are now going to create a model of another game, a game we call Heroes and Cowards. The origins of this game are difficult to pin down. In the 1980s and 1990s, an Italian troupe called the Fratelli theater group used the game as an improvisation activity. In the 1999 conference Embracing Complexity, held in Cambridge, Massachusetts, the Fratelli group ran this game with the conference participants, and this seems to be the first recorded public instance of the game. The game is also related to a game called "Party Planner" proposed by A. K. Dewdney in his "Computer Recreations" column in *Scientific American* (September 1987) and reprinted in the book *The Magic Machine* (1990).

To play the game you need a group of people. The game starts by asking each person to pick one other person to be their "friend" and another to be their "enemy." There are two stages to the game. In the first stage, everyone is told to act like a "coward." To act like a coward you move so as to make sure your friend is always between you and your enemy (effectively, hiding from your enemy behind your friend in a cowardly manner). When people played this stage of the game, the center of the room became empty as people "fled" from their enemy. In the second stage of the game, people were asked to behave as heroes, that is, to move in between their friend and enemy (effectively protecting your friend from your enemy in a heroic manner). When people played the second stage, the center of the room got very crowded. It was a dramatic difference and generated laughter and curiosity.

From the conference, the game spread to the nascent community of complexity scholars, since it was a nice example of surprising emergent behavior. Eric Bonabeau, the president

---

8. This proof lent more credence to some claims of Digital Mechanics, which could now show that the sources of randomness found in the universe could be generated by deterministic automata.

9. The NetLogo models library contains several models of cellular automata, including versions of Wolfram's 1D CA models. See, for example, CA 1D elementary (*Wilensky, 1998*) in the Computer Science section of the library.

of Icosystems and a well-known complexity scientist and agent-based modeler, created a version of the game while at BIOS (a company with complexity ties) in 2001. Later, Bonabeau created an agent-based model of the game that runs on the Icosystems website (Bonabeau, 2012). Stephen Guerin, the president of the Redfish group, also created an early version of the game and presented it in 2002 at the Twelfth Annual International Conference of the Society for Chaos Theory in Psychology & Life Sciences. Some images of the game being played by people (alongside the equivalent simulations) are in figure 2.21.[10]

Since then, many different versions of the game have appeared in various places within the complex systems community. Besides coding early versions, Eric Bonabeau, Stephen Guerin, and others have led people in playing it at conferences. A three-player variant of the game appears in the Systems Thinking Playbook (Sweeney & Meadows, 2010). The game does not always appear under the name "Heroes and Cowards"; in fact, it has appeared under many different names. Bonabeau calls it "Aggressors and Defenders" (Bonabeau & Meyer, 2001). We have also heard it called "Friends and Enemies" and "Swords and Shields." We prefer the name "Heroes and Cowards," since that most closely matches the agent behavior.

Building the model is fairly straightforward, so we will create a model of the game here and explore some variations of the original game. As in the LIFE model, we will create two main procedures: SETUP to initialize the model and GO to run it. This time, we will primarily use the turtle agents rather than the patches.

The SETUP procedure is as follows:

```
to setup
    clear-all
    ask patches [ set pcolor white ] ;; create a blank background
    create-turtles number [
        setxy random-xcor random-ycor

        ;; set the turtle personalities based on chooser
        if (personalities = "cowards") [ set color blue ]
        if (personalities = "heroes")  [ set color red ]

        ;; choose friend and enemy targets
        set friend one-of other turtles
        set enemy one-of other turtles
    ]
    reset-ticks
end
```

The SETUP procedure has four main sections. The first two should be familiar from the Game of Life. The view is cleared so as to start with an empty black screen area; then we

10. Pictures courtesy of Eric Bonabeau.

Figure 2.21
Three rules designed for swarms of ten agents, evolved using the IEC interface (A–C) and then given to a group
of people (D–F). Rule "circle" (A,D makes all agents run around in a circle; rule "align" (B,E) made them form
a straight line; and rule "Chinese streamer" resulted in a central cluster with a tail or "ribbon" circling behind.
(From Bonabeau et al., 2003.)

color all the patches white in order to make it easier to observe the actions of the agents. You should also recognize the fourth block, RESET-TICKS, which initializes the NetLogo clock. The new and interesting action is in the third block.

The third block is one long command. The CREATE-TURTLES command creates a number of turtles and then gives them some commands. We will use the global variable NUMBER to designate the number of turtles we start with. We will control the variable with a slider in the interface. In this case, we set the NUMBER slider to 68 turtles (the size of a party or small conference) and give them some commands.[11] The first command we give the turtles is:

```
setxy random-xcor random-ycor
```

This command sets the XCOR and YCOR values of the turtles, which has the effect of scattering the turtle agents randomly about the view. The second command is:

```
if (personalities = "cowards") [ set color blue ]
```

This command depends on a variable called PERSONALITIES, which we will create together later. PERSONALITIES tells us if we are in stage one or stage two in the game, i.e., whether the agents are playing as "heroes" or as "cowards." If it is set to the value "cowards," then we are playing stage one, where all the agents will act cowardly. To visualize the cowardly agents, we color them blue. Similarly, the third command is:

```
if (personalities = "heroes")  [ set color red ]
```

If the personalities variable is set to "heroes," then we are playing the second stage, where all the agents act like heroes. To visualize the heroic agents, we color them red.

Next the agents need to pick an agent to be their friend and another to be their enemy. To accomplish this, we use "turtle variables." We will use two such variables, FRIEND and ENEMY. We will need to "indicate" (also called "declare") in the Code tab that we have given the turtles these two variables. We do that by putting the following line at the top of the Code tab.

```
turtles-own [ friend enemy ]
```

11. You can get similar results with a large range in the number of agents, but we have tuned the sample model in the models library to work with this exact number.

This gives every turtle two variables. One variable is named FRIEND, and one is named ENEMY. Now that these variables are established, we can set them.

```
set friend one-of other turtles
set enemy one-of other turtles
```

These commands tell each turtle to choose another turtle from the set of all turtles and set the FRIEND variable to take on the value of that turtle. This is a slightly different use of variables than we have seen before. In this case, FRIEND is not a number; instead, it is a reference to another agent in the model. In NetLogo, as in many agent-based modeling languages, we can use variables to refer directly to other agents, which makes our code much easier to write.

Once the value for the FRIEND variable has been decided, the code asks the turtle to choose another turtle from the set of all turtles and set the enemy variable to be equal to the selected turtle.

The final command is reset-ticks, which, as we saw, initializes the NetLogo clock. That completes our SETUP procedure. This code is enough to set up the model as initially described. A common variation we will explore is to have a "mixed" game; that is, if PERSONALITIES = "mixed," we would like some of the agents to act bravely and others to act cowardly. To do this, we add one line to the SETUP procedure.

```
if (personalities = "mixed")     [ set color one-of [ red blue ] ]
```

The ONE-OF primitive picks a random element of a list, which in this case is the list [RED BLUE]. This command will randomly set some of the agents to be red and cowardly, others to be blue and brave. The final form for the SETUP procedure is:

```
to setup
   ca
   ask patches [ set pcolor white ] ;; create a white background
   create-turtles number [
      setxy random-xcor random-ycor

      ;; set the turtle personalities based on chooser value
      if (personalities = "brave")    [ set color blue ]
      if (personalities = "cowardly") [ set color red ]
      if (personalities = "mixed")    [ set color one-of [ red blue ] ]

      ;; choose friend and enemy targets
      set friend one-of other turtles
      set enemy one-of other turtles
   ]
   reset-ticks
end
```

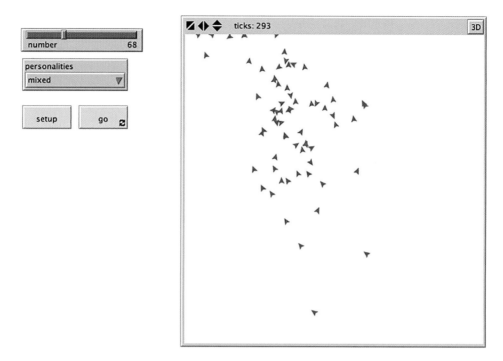

Figure 2.22
The setup for the Heroes and Cowards model. The hero agents are blue; the cowards are red.

To create the interface for the model, we go to the NetLogo *Interface* tab and create two widgets: a button that says SETUP and a chooser that has three values: HEROES, COWARDS and MIXED. The chooser variable name is the PERSONALITIES variable we have been branching on. If you press the SETUP button, you should see a screen like the one shown in figure 2.22.

Now that we have verified that our SETUP procedure seems to be working well, we are ready for our GO procedure.

Here is the GO procedure for the model.

```
to go
    ask turtles [
        if (color = blue) [ act-bravely ]
        if (color = red)  [ act-cowardly ]
    ]
    tick
end
```

Box 2.6
Turtle Monitors and Links

Similar to the patch monitors we explored in the Game of Life, we can use a turtle monitor to inspect the properties of any turtle. If we right-click on the blue turtle near the center of the view and select inspect, a turtle monitor pops up.

Looking at its properties, we see that its COLOR is 105, which is blue. We also see that it has a FRIEND property and that its FRIEND is turtle 45, and its ENEMY is turtle 41.

It may be handy to keep track of the relative position of our turtle with its FRIEND and ENEMY. One way to do that is to create a link agent linking the turtle to its FRIEND and ENEMY. Link agents are a core agent class in NetLogo, just like turtles and patches. We will go over link agents in detail in chapter 6. We can create link agents directly in the turtle monitor. We type into the command center of the turtle monitor, the command:

```
create-link-with turtle 45 [set color green]
```

This would be equivalent to writing:

```
create-link-with friend [set color green]
```

We will then see a green link connecting our focal turtle with its FRIEND.

This GO procedure simply asks the blue turtles to act bravely, the red turtles to act cowardly, and then advances the clock one tick. We will need to define the ACT-BRAVELY and ACT-COWARDLY procedures later, but first, let's take a look at the behavior of the model. If you are following along and writing this model as you go, then save your current version of the model and load the version of the Heroes and Cowards model that is in the chapter two subfolder of the IABM Textbook Folder of the NetLogo models library.

In the library model, we have added a GO button (a forever button) and set the PERSONALITIES chooser to COWARDS. We have also turned wrapping off both vertically and horizontally in the Model Settings dialog since in the real world a person cannot wander out of one door of a room and come in the other side. In the finished model with the settings in the next figure, if we press SETUP, the model creates 68 red turtles. When we press GO, we see the turtles fleeing to the boundaries of the view. They are all cowards, so they are trying to get behind their friends, which leads them to move outward (see figure 2.26).

Now, let's set the personalities chooser to HEROES. Can you predict what the agents will do? You may have correctly predicted the model's hero behavior based on what we

Box 2.6
(continued)

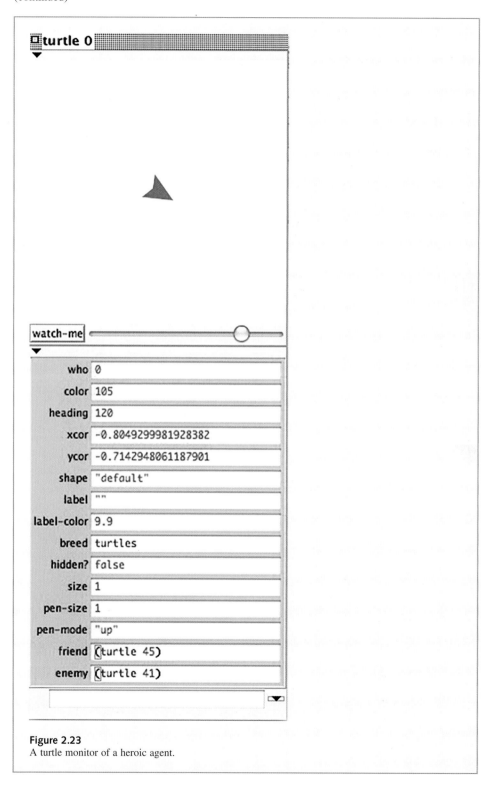

Figure 2.23
A turtle monitor of a heroic agent.

Box 2.7
Turtle Monitors and Links, Continued

Similarly, we can type:

```
create-link-with turtle 41 [set color red]
```

which is equivalent to:

```
create-link-with enemy [set color red]
```

and we will see a red link connecting our turtle with its ENEMY.

---

described at the beginning of this section. All the agents collapse into one small area (see figure 2.27).

A more complex behavior emerges when we set the personalities chooser to "mixed." Can you predict what will happen? Most people are unable to predict the behavior of the "mixed" model. In mixed mode, the model exhibits a variety of different possible behaviors. Since the behavior of the agents is deterministic, the model's behavior is completely determined by the initial setup. As we will describe, this initial setup contains enough randomness to generate several different interesting behaviors.

To examine this, we developed a special version of the model in which the buttons below the SETUP and the GO button of the interface encode two initial setups that exhibit interesting behavior. Each button sets NetLogo's random number generator to a particular "seed" state. The random numbers spewed out by the generator determine the "random" locations of the initial agents. They also determine which agents are heroes and which cowards as well as which friends and enemies they choose. Each press of these two setup buttons will generate the same exact initial setup and hence the same model behavior from then on.

You will notice that the model exhibits a variety of qualitatively different "final behaviors." Once reached these final behaviors, similar to "attractor states" in dynamical systems theory, stay qualitatively stable.[12] We will illustrate four such final behaviors for this model. In the associated model file (Heroes and Cowards.nlogo), we have setup buttons for two of these final states, "frozen" and "slinky." There are many possible states, and we leave it as an exercise to the reader to find other interesting final states.

---

12. For a good introduction to attractors and dynamical systems, please see *Nonlinear Dynamics and Chaos* by Steven Strogatz published in 1994 by Westview Press.

Box 2.7
(continued)

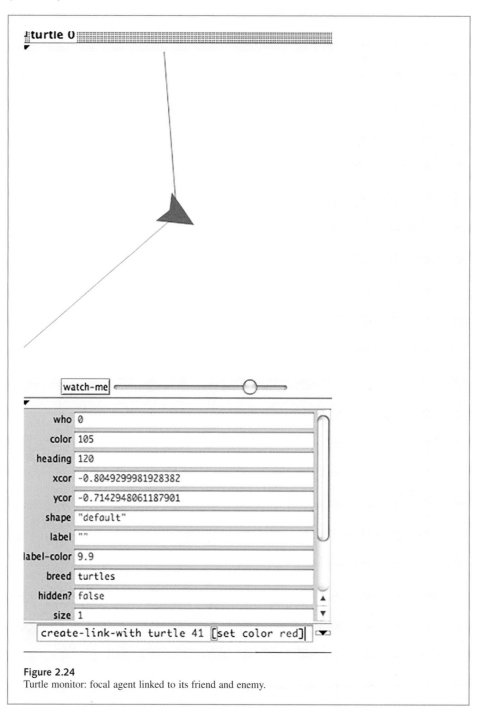

Figure 2.24
Turtle monitor: focal agent linked to its friend and enemy.

Box 2.7
(continued)

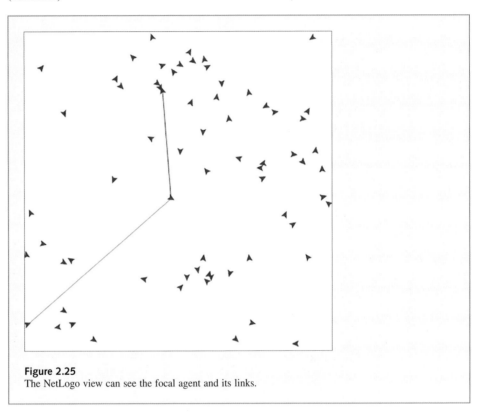

Figure 2.25
The NetLogo view can see the focal agent and its links.

1. *Frozen* The agents end up scattered on the screen, frozen at a certain location. They vibrate a little but do not stray from their location (see figure 2.28).

2. *Slinky* The agents form a line and the line slinks on the edges of the view and then jumps across the view (see figure 2.29).

3. *Dot* The agents coalesce into a small vibrating dot (see figure 2.30).

4. *Spiral* The agents coalesce into a loose rotating spiral and gradually get into a tighter spin (see figure 2.31).

Now that we have explored the behavior of the model, we can go back to looking at the model code. If you were working along with your own version before, then go ahead and reload that version. Make sure to create SETUP and GO buttons as we did before and the PERSONALITIES chooser and NUMBER slider if you have not already done so. Finally, don't forget to turn wrapping off.

Once all of that is done, we will begin creating the ACT-BRAVELY and ACT-COWARDLY procedures. Each of these makes the agent point in a direction and move a

Box 2.8
A Text-Based Pseudo-Code Format

When first working with agent-based models, it can often be useful to use a text-based form for explicitly describing the model rules. This pseudo-code format, should have two sections: "Initialize," which describes how the model's initial conditions, and "At each tick," which describes the behavior of the agents at every tick of the NetLogo clock. For agent-based models, it is recommended that you write the text from the point of view of the agents, especially in the "At each tick" section. Here is a text-based form for the Heroes and Cowards model:

```
Initialize:
    Create NUMBER turtles, where NUMBER is set by a slider in the interface
    Each turtle moves to a random location on the screen
    If the PERSONALITIES slider is set to "brave," each turtle turns blue
    If the PERSONALITIES slider is set to "cowardly," each turtle turns red
    If the PERSONALITIES slider is set to "mixed," each turtle "flips a
    coin" and depending on the outcome, it turns red or blue
    Each turtle picks one other turtle as a friend
    Each turtle picks one other turtle as an enemy
    The NetLogo clock is started

At each tick:
    Each turtle asks itself "Am I blue?" If yes, then I will act bravely by
    moving a step towards a location between my friend and my enemy
    Each turtle asks itself "Am I red?" If yes, then I will act cowardly by
    moving a step towards a location that puts my friend between my enemy
    and me
```

small step in that direction. ACT-BRAVELY points the agent to a spot midway between its friend and enemy. ACT-COWARDLY points the agent to a spot behind its friend. These procedures use a little bit of vector mathematics, so we won't review them carefully here. Readers who have a mathematical background will recognize the mathematical form of the vectors. Others may prefer to examine the two figures below each procedure, which illustrate pictorially what the code does. Essentially, the ACT-BRAVELY code points the turtle toward the midpoint between the friend and enemy, while the ACT-COWARDLY code points the turtle toward a point that is as far away from its FRIEND as the FRIEND is from the ENEMY. (See figures 2.32 and 2.33.)

```
to act-bravely
    ;; move toward the midpoint of your friend and enemy
    facexy ([xcor] of friend + [xcor] of enemy) / 2
           ([ycor] of friend + [ycor] of enemy) / 2
    fd 0.1
end
```

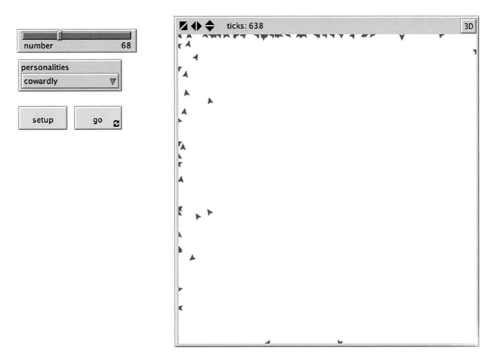

Figure 2.26
Heroes and Cowards cowardly behavior. All the agents move out to the edges.

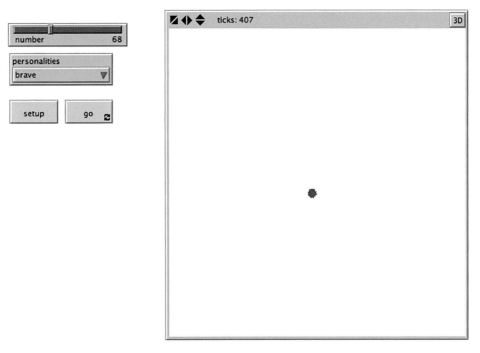

Figure 2.27
Heroes and Cowards brave behavior. All the agents move to the center.

Box 2.9
Random Number Generators

Agent-based models frequently need to make use of randomness; agents' behavior is often best modeled as a random process. In general, when programmers need to make use of randomness in computational environments, they use random numbers from a random number generator (RNG). A *random number generator* is a computational device (it can also be a physical device) designed to generate a sequence of numbers or symbols that lack any pattern and that seem to be random. However, the random numbers used by computer programs are actually "pseudo-random," so that while they appear random, they are generated deterministically. "Deterministic" means that if you start with the same random "seed" you will always get the same results. We'll explain in a minute what we mean by "seed." If you wanted to generate random numbers physically rather than pseudo-random, there are many different ways that have been developed, several of which have existed since ancient times, e.g., rolling of dice, flipping of coins, shuffling of playing cards, or using yarrow stalks in the I-Ching. As you can imagine, generating large amounts of random numbers using these techniques took a long time. As a result, books and tables of random numbers would sometimes be generated and then distributed for use by mathematicians. Nowadays, since RNGs generate numbers that are almost indistinguishable from true random numbers, they are used for everything from computer simulations to lotteries to slot machines.

In the context of scientific modeling, pseudo-random numbers are more desirable than true random numbers. This is because it's important that a scientific experiment be reproducible/replicable, so that anyone who runs the experiment will get the same result. (We will discuss this idea more in chapter 8.) Since NetLogo uses pseudo-random numbers, other researchers/scientists/modelers can reproduce the "experiments" that you conduct with it.

Here's how it works. NetLogo's random number generator can be started with a certain seed value, which is just an integer. Once the generator has been "seeded" with the random-seed command, it always generates the same sequence of random numbers from then on. For example, if you run these commands:

```
random-seed 137
show random 100
show random 100
show random 100
```

You will always get the numbers 79, 89, and 61, in that order. To create a number suitable for seeding the random number generator, use the NEW-SEED command. NEW-SEED creates a seed, evenly distributed over the space of all possible seeds, based on the current date and time. It never reports the same seed twice in a row.

If you do not set the random seed yourself, NetLogo sets it to a value based on the current date and time. There is no way to find out what random seed it chose, so if you want your model run to be reproducible, you must set the random seed yourself ahead of time.

See the Random Seed Example model from the Code Examples section of the NetLogo models library.

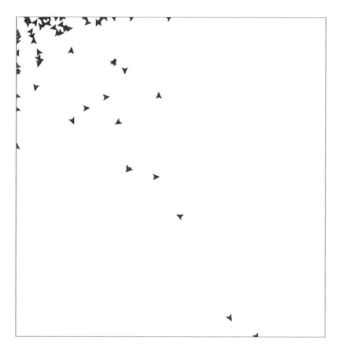

Figure 2.28
The Frozen final state of the Heroes and Cowards model.

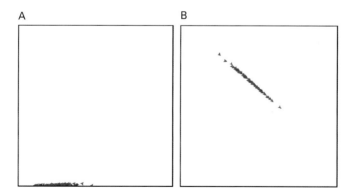

Figure 2.29
(A, B) Snapshots of the Slinky final state of the Heroes and Cowards model.

Figure 2.30
The Dot final state of the Heroes and Cowards model.

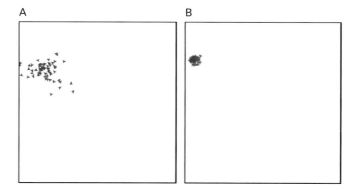

Figure 2.31
(A, B) Two snapshots of the Spiral final state of the Heroes and Cowards model.

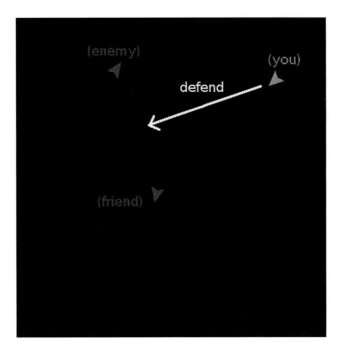

Figure 2.32
A brave agent sets it heading toward a spot midway between its friend and its enemy.

```
to act-cowardly
    ;; put your friend between you and your enemy
    facexy [xcor] of friend + ([xcor] of friend - [xcor] of enemy) / 2
           [ycor] of friend + ([ycor] of friend - [ycor] of enemy) / 2
    fd 0.1
end
```

Although the Heroes and Cowards game is in many ways a parlor game, there has been a considerable amount of follow-up research on the game, due to the surprising diversity of configurations and behaviors that can arise from its simple rules. In some ways, the game can be seen as a microworld for exploring how swarms can self-organize from distributed elements. Many researchers have been interested in finding new configurations with especially interesting behaviors. Researchers have also worked on the "reverse-engineering" of rules to make for a particular desired swarm behavior, but, as we have discussed, finding the micro-level rules that generate a macro-level pattern generally can be very difficult. Bonabeau proposes one solution to both of these problems: finding new swarms and rules that generate a particular swarm by evolving the rules for known swarms. However, this is difficult, as Bonabeau and his colleagues stated in 2003:

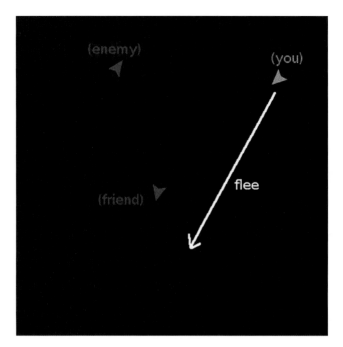

Figure 2.33
A cowardly agent sets its heading toward a spot behind its friend.

Designing the individual level rules of behavior and interaction that will produce a desired collective pattern in a group of human or non-human agents is difficult because the group's aggregate-level behavior may not be easy to predict or infer from the individuals' rules. While the forward mapping from micro-rules to macro-behavior in self-organizing systems can be reconstructed using computational modeling techniques, the inverse problem of finding micro-rules that produce interesting macro-behavior poses significant challenges, all the more as what constitutes "interesting" macro-behavior may not be known ahead of time.

Bonabeau et al. (2003) used an exploratory design method with an interactive evolutionary computation approach to find new configurations and behaviors. In this approach, users were provided with a set of original configurations. They could choose any one of these and mutate it slightly, or they could choose two and mate them. The resulting offspring are then evaluated for aesthetic interest and the best ones are kept as potential parents of the next generation.[13] In this way, users could use their aesthetic judgments to breed interesting configurations and behaviors (see figure 2.34 for some examples of offspring configurations). These final configurations can have complex dynamic behavior such as configuration (e), which Bonabeau describes as a "Chinese streamer," as in figure 2.35.

13. This is very similar to the biomorphs idea described by Richard Dawkins in *The Blind Watchmaker* (1986).

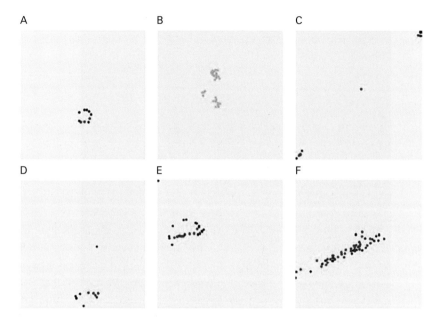

Figure 2.34
A few examples of evolved behaviors. (A) Circle: agents chase each other around in a circle. (B) Juggle: two blobs fuse and reemerge and sometimes toss a smaller blob at each other. (C) Corner-middle: two groups of agents go to opposite corners while one stays in the middle. (D) Pursuer-evaders: an agent follows a larger group that slows down, is reached by the pursuer, then escapes again. (E) Chinese streamer: a D shape that moves around. (F) Somersault: a thick line that makes a 360 degree turn, then stops, then turns back in the opposite direction. (From Bonabeau et al., 2003.)

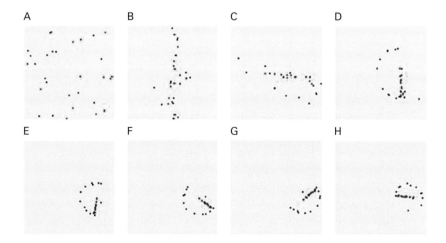

Figure 2.35
"Chinese streamer" pattern. From a random initial placement, a pattern quickly emerges (A–D) and starts turning, stabilizing in a shape with a handle and trailing ribbon, which rotates smoothly. The direction of rotation can be clockwise or counterclockwise (as here), presumably depending on the initial positions. (From Bonabeau et al., 2003.)

In this way, starting with one set of rules, we can discover new, "interesting" patterns of collective behavior when one does not know in advance what the system is capable of doing.

Simple Economy

In the past two decades, there has been increasing interest in and use of agent-based modeling in the social sciences. In fact, several of the models that we have already discussed, such as Ants, the Game of Life and Heroes, and Cowards have been applied to understanding social systems. Agent-based methods may be particularly valuable in the social sciences where agents are heterogeneous and mathematical descriptions often do not offer sufficient descriptive power. Several prominent communities have organized around using complex systems methods and agent-based modeling in the social sciences. Among these are the Complex Systems Social Sciences Association (CSSSA) and the World Congress on Social Simulation (WCSS), both of which also organize conferences. There are also a number of such events that are included as part of other meetings. In recent years, organizations such as the American Education Research Association (AERA), Marketing Science, Eastern Economics Association, and American Association of Geographers (AAG) have hosted sessions on the intersection of agent-based modeling and social science.

One area that has been receiving increasing attention from the ABM community is economics. As economies consist of heterogeneous actors such as buyers and sellers, there is a natural mapping of ABM methods to economics. In 1996, the economists, Josh Epstein and Robert Axtell published a book that depicted a world they called SugarScape, which was populated by economic agents.

In this section, we will build a very simple economics model that has some surprising results. Suppose you have a fixed number of people, say 500, each starting out with the same amount of money, say $100. At every tick, each person gives one of his or her dollars to any other person at random. What will happen to the distribution of money? An important constraint is that the total amount of money remains fixed, so no one can have less than zero money. If you run out of money, you cannot give any away until you get some back. Refining the question a little further, we ask: Is there a stable limiting distribution of the money? If so, what is it? For instance, will all the wealth be concentrated in a few hands or will it be equitably distributed?

Many people, when posed with this question, have an intuition that there is a limiting distribution and that it is relatively flat. The reasoning behind the intuition is that since no person starts off with an advantage and the selection of people to whom money is transferred is random, no person should have much of an advantage over any others. Thus, the resulting wealth distribution should be relatively flat: Everyone should wind up with roughly the same amount of money he or she started with. Other people have an intuition

Box 2.10
SugarScape and Agent-Based Economics

One of the first large-scale agent-based models was Epstein and Axtell's SugarScape from their book *Growing Artificial Societies: Social Science from the Bottom Up*. SugarScape consists of a series of models based on a population with limited vision and spatially distributed resources available (sugar and spice). Agents look around, find the closest cell filled with sugar, move, and metabolize. Agents can also leave pollution, die, reproduce, combat other agents, inherit resources, transfer information, trade or borrow sugar, or transmit diseases. Each of the models in the SugarScape series explores some of the conditions and dynamics. Sugar and Spice in the SugarScape models can be seen as a metaphor for resources in an artificial world through which we can study the effects of social dynamics such as evolution, marital status, and inheritance on populations. The SugarScape work inspired a host of generative social science models (Epstein, 2006) and invigorated the field of agent-based economics and social science in general (see also Tesfatsion & Judd 2006). Agent-based modeling is especially well suited as a methodology for behavior-based economics.

Behavior-based economists are unsatisfied with traditional approaches of economists—which have prioritized simplified approaches for the sake of soluble theoretical models over agreement with empirical data. In particular, traditional approaches have usually posited perfectly rational agents, whereas behavioral economists make use of "boundedly rational" (Simon, 1991) agents that do not have complete information and use shortcuts or heuristics to make decisions.

---

that the wealth should be normally distributed. To explore this question of wealth distribution, let us build the model we described to see if that intuition is correct.

We start with our SETUP procedure. We will need to keep track of the wealth of each agent, so we need to give the agents a WEALTH variable:

```
turtles-own [wealth]
```

Since one of our main questions of interest is what the limiting distribution of money in this model is, we will also need to create a histogram of the wealth of the agents. To do that, we create a plot widget in the NetLogo interface and give it the plot command:[14]

```
histogram [wealth] of turtles
```

---

14. This is the easiest way to create a simple plot. In chapter 4, we will discuss a slightly more complex way that has some advantages, especially for complex plots.

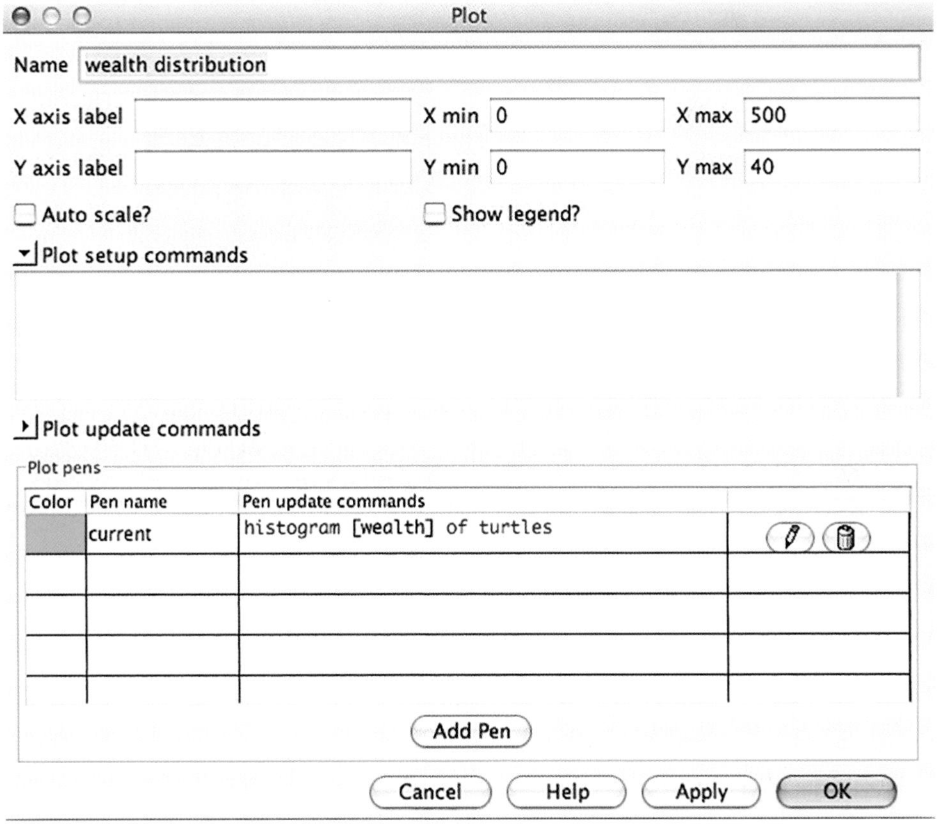

Figure 2.36
The plot widget that runs the histogram command at every clock tick.

At each clock tick the plot widget will run its plot command (see figure 2.36). To make our plot widget work with the parameters of our model, we also set the X MAX to 500 and the Y MAX to 40 and turn off AUTO SCALE? If you want to exactly match the images in the book you also need to change the pen color to green (by double-clicking on the color to the left of the pen name, and the pen mode to bar (by double-clicking on the pencil to the right of the pen update commands and selecting "bar" from the mode drop down menu).

Our SETUP procedure needs to clear the view, create 500 agents, give them some properties and then reset the tick counter. We visualize the agents as green circles and initialize every agent to start with $100. Though we have already set up a histogram to tell us about the wealth distribution, it is often useful to also visualize such distributions

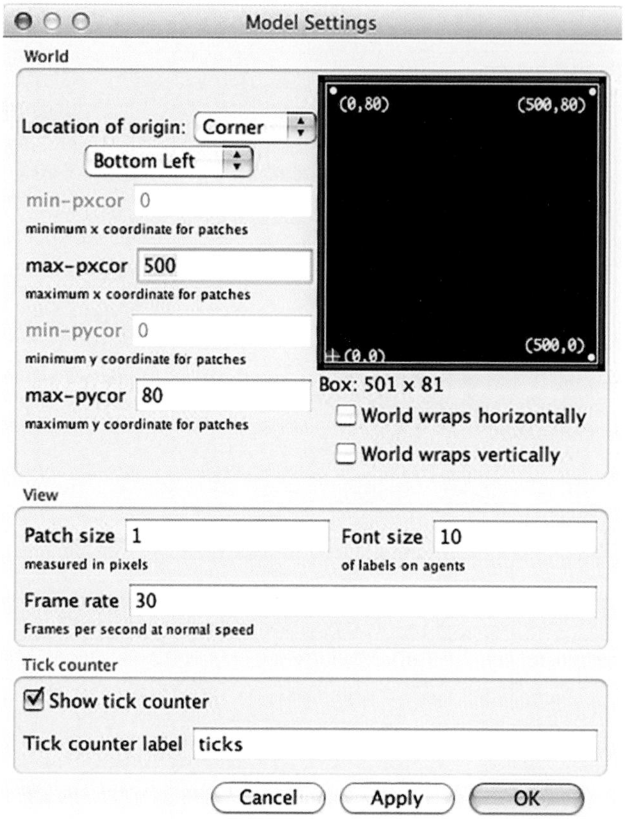

Figure 2.37
Configuring the view as a long rectangle.

in the view by changing the visualization of the agents in some way to reflect their wealth. One way to do that is to set the agent's XCOR to its wealth, so that the poorest turtles are on the left edge of the view, and as we move right, the turtles get wealthier (which some may claim may also have political consequences). To ensure that there will be plenty of space for the agents to move right, we shape the view as a long rectangle and make the patch size small.

In figure 2.37, we have set the view with an origin (coordinate 0,0) at the bottom left and a maximum x-coordinate of 500, so as to visualize agents with a wealth of up to 500 and a maximum y-coordinate of 80 so we can see a spread of agents. We also set a small patch size of 1, so the view fits well on a reasonably sized screen.

Because the patches are small, we increase the size of the agents to two (2) to better view them. Here is the code for the SETUP procedure.

Figure 2.38
The view is placed above the histogram and aligned with it. All 500 agents start out with $100 apiece.

```
to setup
    clear-all
    create-turtles 500 [
        set wealth 100
        set shape "circle"
        set color green
        set size 2

        ;; visualize the turtles from left to right in ascending order of wealth
        setxy wealth random-ycor
    ]
    reset-ticks
end
```

After running SETUP, the view and histogram will look as it does in figure 2.38.

The GO procedure for the model is very simple. At every tick, each agent will need to transact (give one dollar) with one other agent. So the main line of code is:

```
ask turtles [transact]
```

We will then need to fill in the details of the TRANSACT procedure. This line of code, however, does not take into account the agents with no money left, as they cannot give away anything. To fix that "bug," we add a restricting WITH modifier, so only turtles with at least a dollar to their name can give away their money.[15]

---

15. An alternative way to code this is to keep the line as is, asking all agents to transact, and then code the transact procedure to exclude agents with no money.

Box 2.11
Agentsets and Lists

Agentsets and lists are two of the most used data structures in NetLogo.

An agentset is much like it sounds: a set of agents. Agentsets can have turtles, patches, or links, but they cannot mix agent types. You can ask an agentset to perform some commands. NetLogo comes with three special agentsets built in: "turtles," "patches," and "links," which we have already asked to execute commands. What makes agentsets so powerful is that you can create your own agentsets—for example, an agentset of all the red turtles, or an agentset of all the patches in the upper right quadrant. Agentsets are always in random order. So if you ask an agentset, several different times, to execute some commands, each time the order in which the agents take turns executing the commands will be different.

Lists are ordered collections of data. You can have a list of numbers, a list of words, even a list of lists. You can also have a list of agents. Since they are in a list, these agents will have a particular order, so you can use the list to execute their commands in any order you might like.

We will discuss agentsets and lists more in chapter 5.

See also: http://ccl.northwestern.edu/netlogo/docs/programming.html#agentsets in the NetLogo programming guide of the NetLogo User Manual.

```
ask turtles with [wealth > 0] [transact]
```

The only other line in our GO procedure is to move the agents to an x-coordinate corresponding to their wealth. The code for the GO procedure is:

```
to go
    ;; transact and then update your location
    ask turtles with [wealth > 0] [transact]
    ask turtles [set xcor wealth ]
    tick
end
```

Now, we have to write the TRANSACT procedure. First, we decrease the agent's wealth by one (1) dollar. Then we choose a random other agent and increase its wealth by one (1) dollar. The resulting code is:

```
to transact
    ;; give a dollar to another turtle
    set wealth wealth - 1
    ask one-of other turtles [set wealth wealth + 1]
end
```

That is the entire code for the Simple-Economy model. There is, however, one small bug in our GO procedure. We have asked the turtles to set their XCOR to their wealth. If their wealth gets very large, then the resulting XCOR will be beyond the world boundaries. To correct for that bug we add a check to ensure that we only relocate turtles within the world boundaries. The resulting code is:[16]

```
to go
    ;; transact and then update your location
    ask turtles with [wealth > 0] [transact]
    ask turtles [if wealth <= max-pxcor [set xcor wealth]]
    tick
end
```

Now that we have revised the code for the GO procedure, let's pause for a moment to reflect on what we expect the behavior of the model to be. As mentioned earlier, most people have an intuition that the distribution will vary from tick to tick, but that overall, it will stay relatively flat. Surprisingly, it is not a flat distribution.

Running the model for 10,000 ticks yields the following picture (figure 2.39). We can see that the distribution is not at all flat. There are a few very wealthy individuals and many poor agents. At this time step in this model run, the wealth of the top 10 percent of the agents is a total of \$12,633, or an average of \$253 per person, whereas the total wealth of the entire bottom 50 percent is only \$10,166, or an average of \$41 per person. The crossover point at which the wealth of the top 10 percent of all agents exceeded the wealth of the bottom half, or 50 percent, of all agents was at 5,600 ticks.

If we run it for 25,000 more ticks, the gap continues to grow and now the top 10 percent have more than twice as much in total (and more than 10 times as much per individual) than the bottom 50 percent. (See figure 2.40.)

The distribution of money eventually converges to a stationary distribution. This distribution has been shown to be exponential, which means that there is great inequality in monetary wealth. The key condition that creates this stationary distribution is the conservation of money. The *conservation law of money* states that money is not allowed to be created or destroyed by any of the agents in our model, but can only be transferred between agents. Thus, the total amount of money in the system is always fixed. Indeed, any set of interacting agents that exchange a conserved quantity that cannot become negative will always result in such an exponential distribution. This is the result of a famous law from statistical mechanics, known as the *Boltzmann-Gibbs law* (see box 2.12).

---

16. There are several alternative ways to code this check as well. We leave the exploration of these ways as an exercise for the reader.

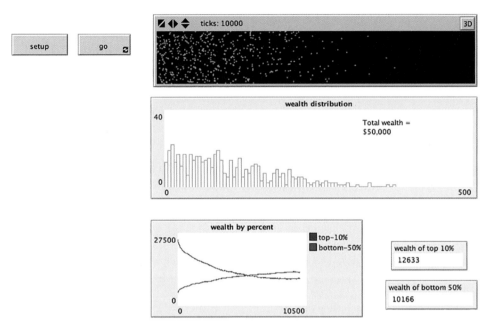

Figure 2.39
The Simple Economy model after 10,000 ticks.

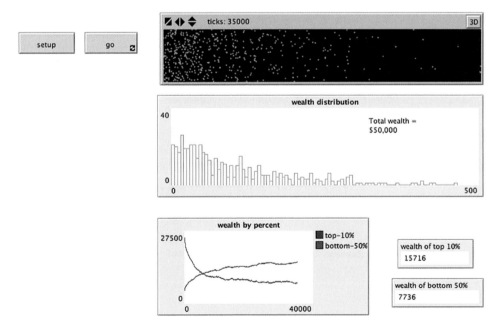

Figure 2.40
The Simple Economy model after 35,000 ticks.

Box 2.12
Boltzmann-Gibbs Law

The distribution we have just seen in the Simple Economy model is one instance of a broader class of models in which a conserved quantity is exchanged in a closed system. The great nineteenth-century Austrian physicist Ludwig Boltzmann first examined such models when he worked out the physics of gas molecules in a box. He imagined these molecules as "billiard balls" moving and colliding. When they collide, they change speed and direction, but because of the conservation of energy, the total energy after a collision remains the same. He derived an equation, now known as the *Boltzmann equation*, for the distribution of the energies of the billiard balls and solved the equation to show that their energies formed a stationary exponential distribution, known as Boltzmann distribution, the Boltzmann-Gibbs distribution, and the Maxwell-Boltzmann distribution.

  The Boltzmann distribution is a central component of statistical mechanics. Statistical mechanics uses probability theory to understand the thermodynamic behavior of systems composed of a large number of particles. Statistical mechanics provides a framework for relating the microscopic properties of individual atoms and molecules to the macroscopic bulk properties of materials that can be observed in everyday life. In physics, the methods of statistical mechanics have been used with a range of "particles" from single atoms interacting to complex molecules, and they can be used to explain macroscopic concepts such as work, heat, and entropy. Since statistical mechanics gives scientists the ability to reason from microscopic particles to macroscopic patterns, it has been extremely useful in generating a comprehensive theory of physics. In many ways, agent-based modeling can be seen as extending this perspective to content domains beyond physics.

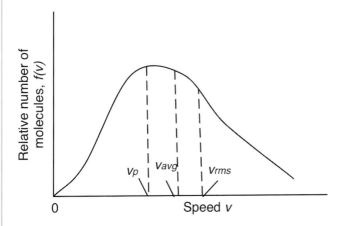

Figure 2.41
Maxwell-Boltzmann distribution of molecule speeds (illustration from Giancoli, 1984).

In recent years, theories and methods from physics have been applied to economics. The physicist Gene Stanley (1996) coined the term "econophysics" for this interdisciplinary research field.

In their 2000 paper, Dragulescu and Yakovenko describe several variants of the kind of monetary exchange we have explored in this model. They show that if agents are allowed to go into debt (subject to a fixed credit limit), there is still a stationary exponential distribution, but one that results in even greater inequality. We have referred to our agents as owning wealth. A more specific term for what we are modeling is *monetary wealth*. Dragulescu and Yakovenko caution:

It is tempting to identify the money distribution with the distribution of wealth. However, money is only one part of wealth, the other part being material wealth. Material products have no conservation law: They can be manufactured, destroyed, consumed, etc. Moreover, the monetary value of a material product (the price) is not constant. The same applies to stocks, which economics textbooks explicitly exclude from the definition of money. So, in general, we do not expect the Boltzmann-Gibbs law for the distribution of wealth.

In fact, empirical studies have shown that wealth distribution in most countries is not distributed exponentially, but rather as a power law known as the Pareto distribution (Pareto, 1964). This distribution is even more unequal than an exponential distribution. Power law distributions arise in a surprising number of contexts and are typically associated with preferential attachment processes (Barabási, 2002), in which the amount that someone receives is proportional to the amount they already have (there is more on this process in chapter 5, and more on power laws when we discuss networks). If this process governs wealth distributions it would result in an ever widening wealth gap between the rich and the poor.

Summary

In this chapter, we have shown three simple models that are easily created as agent-based models. Even though they are easy to create, they exhibit quite complex behavior. In each case, these models demonstrate that predicting the emergent behavior of even the simplest models from knowledge of the rules that generate that behavior is very difficult to do. The ability to encode these conceptual models as ABMs enables us to easily explore a range of their behaviors and to dispel incorrect deductions we might easily make.

Beyond simple exploration of the model, we will often want to systematically analyze a model's behavior. Conducting such analyses can require considerably more effort. We will discuss analysis of agent-based models and conduct some analyses in chapters 6 through 8. In the next few chapters we will learn to modify existing agent-based models, describe a methodology for carefully building agent-based models, and review the many primitives and tools that are available for building ABMs.

Explorations

Chapter Model Explorations

1. Run the Life model several times. What is the minimum number of ticks before the model stabilizes? What is the maximum number of ticks you can find before it stabilizes? Is it possible for the model to never come to a stable state?

2. Write the rules for the Life Simple model in textual pseudo-code format.

3. In the Life model, we introduced the variable, live-neighbors. In the GO code, we initially calculate live neighbors and then branch on the value of live-neighbors as follows:

```
to go
    ask patches [
        set live-neighbors count neighbors with [pcolor = green]
        ]
    ask patches [
if live-neighbors = 3 ….
```

Why do we need to use the live-neighbors variable? Would the model behave any differently if we changed the code to count the neighbors "in-line" as follows:

```
to go
    ask patches [
        if  (count neighbors with [pcolor = green]) = 3
```

Can you explain why or why not?

4. In the Life model in the Computer Science section of the NetLogo models library, find a pattern where there are no more than 10 green cells to begin with but after 10 time steps there are at least 100 green cells. Also, start with at least 100 green cells and find a pattern that ends with no green cells after no more than 10 time steps.

5. Four well-known still-lifes are the loaf, the boat, the ship, and the beehive. Explain why each of these is a still-life. Can you find another still-life? Modify the Life model in the NetLogo models library to include a button that saves your new still-life configuration.

6. In the Game of Life, a blinker is a period 2 oscillator. Can you find another period 2 oscillator? How about a period 3 oscillator? A period 15 oscillator? Save your configurations as buttons in the Life model in the NetLogo models library.

7. In the Game of Life, can you construct a glider gun of glider emission period 15? Period 20? Save your configurations as buttons in the Life model in the NetLogo models library.

8. A methuselah is a small pattern that behaves chaotically for a large number of generations before settling down into a predictable pattern. Erik de Neve found a methuselah he named Edna. It runs on a 20×20 grid and is chaotic for 31,192 ticks. Can you find a methuselah on a 31×31 grid? How many ticks does it take to settle down?

9. In the Game of Life, we can define the "speed of light" (c, just as in physics) as the maximum attainable speed of any moving object, a propagation rate of one step (horizontally, vertically, or diagonally) per tick. This is both the maximum rate at which information can travel and the upper bound on the speed of any pattern. How fast (in terms of c) does the glider move? Can you find a spaceship that moves faster than a glider?

10. Besides the Life model that we have explored, there are several other types of Cellular Automata in the NetLogo models library. For instance, examine CA 1D Elementary (found in the Computer Science section of the library). There are two main differences between this model and the Life model. The first is that the model is 1D so the y-axis illustrates each time-step. Second, the model allows you to choose the rules that govern the behavior of the system rather than using prescribed rules such as we did in the Life model. Can you find a rule that starting with a single "live" cell will result in all of the cells becoming alive? Can you find a rule that starting with a single live cell will result in all of the cells becoming dead? Of course, you can always just turn all the rules on or all the rules off, but can you find solutions to this problem where exactly half the rules are on and half the rules are off?

11. Explore the Heroes and Cowards model. Can you find some other interesting final states beyond those captured in the model's buttons? Create some additional buttons to capture those behaviors and name them.

12. In Heroes and Cowards, what happens if you change the number of agents in the model? If you increase or decrease the number of agents is the pattern predictable?

13. There is a small bug in the Heroes and Cowards model. Can you find and fix it?

14. Another model that uses similar rules to Heroes and Cowards is the Follower model in the Art section of the NetLogo models library. How do the rules of this model differ from Heroes and Cowards? Why do we occasionally get similar behavior in both models? For instance, the Follower model sometimes seems similar to the dog-chases-tail pattern.

15. Write the rules for the Simple Economy model in textual pseudo-code format.

16. The Simple Economy model results in a surprising limiting exponential distribution. Describe in words why the limiting distribution is not relatively flat or normal.

17. What rule could you add to the Simple Economy model to increase the wealth inequality? What rule could you add that would decrease the inequality?

18. Open the SugarScape 1 Immediate Growback model from the Social Science section of the NetLogo models library. Explore the model. Try varying the initial POPULATION. What effect does the initial POPULATION have on the final stable population? Does it have an effect on the distribution of agent properties, such as vision and metabolism?

19. Open the SugarScape 2 Constant Growback model from the NetLogo models library. Explore the model. How dependent is the carrying capacity on the initial population size? Is there a direct relationship?

20. Open the SugarScape 3 Wealth Distribution model from the Social Science section of the NetLogo models library. Explore this model. How does the initial population affect the wealth distribution? How long does it take for the skewed distribution to emerge? How is the wealth distribution affected when you change the initial endowments of wealth? Do the results of this model seem similar to Simple Economy? Compare and contrast the results of the two models.

NetLogo Explorations

21. The NetLogo models library contains a folder of code examples, useful examples of how to code that aren't full-fledged models. Open the random walk example from the Code Examples folder in the models library. Inspect the code. What do you predict the turtle's path will look like? Run the model. Does the path look like you expected it would? Modify the model code so that the turtle's path is still random but is less "jagged," that is, is smoother and straighter.

22. Create a model that has two buttons. The first should create twenty-five turtles and scatter them around the world. The second button, when pressed, should ask each turtle that is to the left of the origin to print its WHO value to the command center output. If you press the "report WHO value button" repeatedly, what do you notice about the list that is displayed? What is the cause of this behavior? Why might this be desirable? After coding the model, please answer these questions by adding a new section of the Info tab (you can add a new section to the Info tab by clicking the "edit" button). (Hint: the OF and PRINT primitives might be useful for this activity.)

3 Exploring and Extending Agent-Based Models

Part of the inhumanity of the computer is that, once it is competently programmed and working smoothly, it is completely honest.

—Isaac Asimov

The perfect journey is never finished, the goal is always just across the next river, round the shoulder of the next mountain. There is always one more track to follow, one more mirage to explore.

—Rosita Forbes

Sailors on a becalmed sea, we sense the stirring of a breeze.

—Carl Sagan

In this chapter you will learn how to modify and extend an agent-based model. We will do this by taking several classic models, examining how they work, and then discussing how to change and extend these models. Sometimes the modified models explore alternative scenarios, variations on the original model. Other times, the modifications may lead to models of very different phenomena.

During these explorations it is important to pay attention to four characteristic features of agent-based modeling:

1. Simple rules can be used to generate complex phenomena

Many of the models that we will look into have very simple rules that do not require complex mathematical formulas or a deep understanding of the knowledge domain that they are attempting to model. Nonetheless, they are able to reproduce complex phenomena that are observed in the real world. For instance, a model of fire spread may have only a simple rule to describe fire spread from one tree to another, but it still may have interesting things to say about how likely a fire is to spread across an entire forest.

2. Randomness in individual behavior can result in consistent patterns of population behavior

It is common for people when they see an ordered population level behavior such as a flock of birds to assume that there must be deterministic processes that govern the behavior of the individuals (Wilensky & Resnick, 1999). In the case of the birds, people tend to believe that there must be specific social rules or communications that tell each bird how to place itself in the flock. However, nature has some surprises for us: Many times the individual level rules are quite simple (see point 1) and do not necessarily tell the bird where to position itself in the flock. Instead, the rules often contain a certain amount of nondeterminism and are robust to perturbations in the initial conditions. Despite the stochastic nature of these systems, they can still result in the generation of predictable high-level behavior like the flocking of birds.

3. Complex patterns can "self-organize" without any leader orchestrating the behavior

Similarly, it is common for people when they see a flock of birds, to assume that there must be a leader who orchestrates the behavior—a leader bird who tells each follower bird what to do (Resnick & Wilensky, 1993; Resnick, 1994a; Wilensky & Resnick, 1999).[1] However, nature again surprises: a population of individuals, each following very simple rules, can "self-organize," generating complex and beautiful patterns without any orchestrator or centralized controller—these patterns are called "*emergent*" (Wilensky & Reisman, 2006).

4. Different models emphasize different aspects of the world

Even after we have completed a good working model of a particular phenomenon, we have not finished with the modeling process. Every model foregrounds certain aspects of the world and backgrounds other aspects. There can be many models of the same phenomenon, and they may each have something interesting to say about the way the world works. For instance, a model of residential location preferences may emphasize how likely a person is to move into a neighborhood based on how she likes the other people in the neighborhood. Such a model may have very interesting things to say about how urban populations develop, but it may say nothing about school districts, location of retail businesses, or development of parks, all of which are also affected by residential location preferences.

In the rest of this chapter, we will dive right into several classical agent-based models and go through the steps of modifying and extending each of the models.

---

1. Together, points 2 and 3 make up what Resnick and Wilensky have called the "deterministic-centralized mindset." This mindset is a widespread tendency for people, when observing a population-level behavioral pattern, to explain it by postulating a centralized controller and nonrandom individual-level behavior (Wilensky & Resnick, 1999).

Figure 3.1
A forest fire consuming trees in a forest.

The Fire Model

Many complex systems tend to exhibit a phenomenon known as a "critical threshold" (Stauffer & Aharony, 1994) or a "tipping point" (Gladwell, 2000).[2] Essentially, a tipping point occurs when a small change in one parameter results in a large change in an outcome. One model that clearly contains a tipping point is the early agent-based model of a forest fire. This model is easy to understand, yet exhibits some interesting behavior. Besides being interesting in its own right, the model of forest fire spread is highly relevant to other natural phenomena such as the spread of a disease, percolation of oil in rock, or diffusion of information within a population (Newman, Girvan & Farmer, 2002).

This simple model is highly sensitive to one parameter. When observing the resultant outcome of whether or not a fire will burn from one side of a forest to another (percolate), the output is mainly dependent on the percentage of the ground that is covered by trees (see figure 3.1). As this parameter increases, there will be little to no effect on the system for a long time, but then all of a sudden the fire will leap across the world. This is a "tipping point" in the system. Knowing that a system has tipping points can be useful for a variety

---

2. There are several different terms from different fields that are used to describe tipping, for example, "phase transition" in physics (Stanley, 1971). In general, all of these terms refer to a small change of an input parameter resulting in a large change in some output variable of interest.

of reasons. First, if you know a system exhibits a tipping point, you know that continuing to put effort into the system, even if you are not seeing any results yet, may yet bear fruit. Second, if you know where the tipping point is, and if you know how close you are to it, then you can determine whether or not it is worth putting additional effort into the system. If you are far away from the tipping point, then it might not be worthwhile trying to change the state of the system, whereas if you are close to the tipping point it may take only a small amount of effort to make a big change in the state of the system.

Description of the Fire Model

The Fire model arose from a number of independent efforts to understand percolation phenomena. In percolation, a substance (such as oil) moves through another material (such as rock), which has some porosity. Broadbent and Hammersley (1957) first posed this problem, and since then many mathematicians and physicists have worked on it. Influenced by cellular automata models, they introduced a percolation model using the example of a porous stone immersed in a bucket of water. The question they focused on was: What is the probability that the center of the stone becomes wet?

A fire moving through a forest can be thought of as a kind of percolation where the fire is like the oil and the forest is like the rock, with the empty places in the forest analogous to the porosity of the rock. A similar question to Broadbent and Hammersley's is: If you start with some burning trees on one edge of the forest, how likely is the fire to spread all the way to the other side of the forest? Many scientists created and studied such fire models. In 1987, the Danish physicist and complex systems theorist Per Bak and his colleagues showed that the spread of the fire depended on a critical parameter, the density of the forest. Because this parameter arises naturally, the complexity of the fire can arise spontaneously and was therefore a possible mechanism to explain the world's naturally arising complexity. Bak and his colleagues called this phenomenon "self-organizing-criticality" and demonstrated it in a number of contexts including, famously, the emergence of avalanches in sand piles.

Herein, we will explore a version of the Fire model adapted by Wilensky (1997a) that is developed in the NetLogo modeling language and is distributed in the Earth Science section of the NetLogo models library. You can find the simplified version of the Fire model in Sample Models > IABM Textbook > Chapter 3 > Fire Extensions > Fire Simple .nlogo. This version of the Fire model contains only patches, no turtles. The patches can have four distinct states. They can be (1) green, indicating an unburned tree, (2) red, indicating a burning tree, (3) brown, indicating a burned tree, or (4) black, indicating empty space (illustrated in figure 3.2). When the model is first set up the left edge of the world is all red, indicating that it is "on fire." When the model starts running, the fire will ignite any "neighboring" tree—that is, a tree to its right, left, below, or above it that is not already burned and not already on fire. This will continue until the fire runs out of trees that it can ignite. The only "control parameter" in this model is the density of trees in the world. This

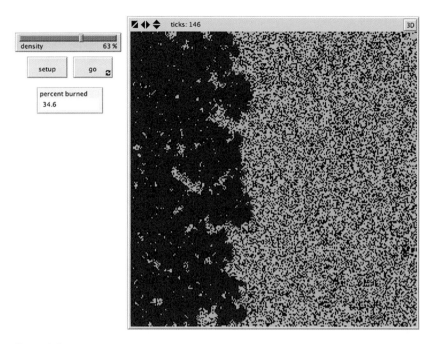

Figure 3.2
NetLogo Fire Simple Model. Based on NetLogo Fire model (Wilensky, 1997). http://ccl.northwestern.edu/netlogo/models/Fire.

density parameter is not an exact measure of the number of trees in the world. Rather, it is a probability that determines whether or not each patch in the world contains a tree. Because the density is probabilistic and not deterministic, even if you run the model multiple times with the same density setting, you will get different results.

Let us examine the simple rules that govern the Fire model. The code that initializes the model is as follows:

```
to setup
    clear-all
      ;; make some green trees
    ask patches [
      if (random 100) < density
          [ set pcolor green ]
      ;; make a column of burning trees at the left-edge
      if pxcor = min-pxcor
          [ set pcolor red ]
    ]
    ;; keep track of how many trees there are
    set initial-trees count patches with [pcolor = green]
    reset-ticks
end
```

Box 3.1
Modeling Choices

> This way of setting up the trees is only one of many possible ways to do it. Can you write
> rules so that the same number of trees will be created on each run of the model? Can you
> think of other ways of initializing the trees?

Just as in the Life Simple model we saw in chapter 2, the Fire Simple model will use only
stationary agents, patches, and no moving agents, turtles. Besides these basic types of
agents, agent-based models can have many other types, including user created agent types.
We will discuss these different types of agents in detail in chapter 5.

The first line of the procedure is a command, CLEAR-ALL (or CA for short in the
NetLogo language), which resets the world to its initial state—it resets the model's clock,
kills all moving agents, and restores the default values to the stationary agents. The rest
of this code issues commands to the patches. First, it populates the world with trees, and
second, it makes a column of burning trees (by setting their color to red, the indication
that they are on fire) at the left edge of the world. We have made many modeling choices
here. Foremost among these are (1) modeling empty space in the forest as black patches,
(2) modeling nonburning trees in the forest as green patches, and (3) modeling fire as
burning trees, which are represented as red patches.

Once these modeling choices are made, we can write the code to populate the model.
To set up the trees, we have asked the patches to perform:

```
if (random 100) < density
   [ set pcolor green ]
```

To help us in understanding the setup code, suppose that the density is set to 50.
This code tells each patch to roll a hundred-sided "die" (or, an alternative metaphor,
spin a spinner with 100 equal sectors). Let us take the point of view of a patch. If I'm
a patch, I throw the die. If that die comes up less than 50, then "I become a tree,"
otherwise "I don't do anything." So, half of the time I will become a tree (turn green)
and the other half of the time I'll remain black. Note that each patch throws its own
independent die so theoretically all of them (or none of them) could become trees. But,
on average, half will become trees. If the density were higher or lower, the same code
would work to populate the model with roughly the appropriate tree density. This trick
of taking the point of view of the agent, what we called agent-centric thinking in the
last chapter, is one we will employ frequently and is a good habit to form for facility
with ABM.

The fact that the behavior of an agent-based model can vary from run to run is an important aspect of agent-based modeling. It means that one run is never enough to truly capture the behavior of most ABMs—instead, you have to perform multiple runs and aggregate the results. How to perform this aggregation will be discussed in greater depth in future chapters.

Once the model is set up or initialized, we must define what the model does at each "tick" of the clock. This is typically done in a procedure named GO.

The core of the GO procedure for the Fire Simple model is:

```
to go
    ;; ask the burning trees to set fire to any
    ;; neighboring (in the 4 cardinal directions) non-burning trees
    ;; the "with" primitive restricts the set of agents to
    ;; those that satisfy the predicate in the brackets
    ask patches with [ pcolor = red ] [
       ask neighbors4 with [ pcolor = green ] [
          set pcolor red
       ]
    ]
    ;; advance the clock by one "tick"
    tick
end
```

The code is short. It asks all the fire agents (which are the red patches) to ignite their neighboring unburned tree (green) patches by setting their color to red. (The neighbors4 primitive specifies those neighbors in the cardinal directions, i.e., north, south, east and west). Finally, it tells the clock to advance one tick.

Running this GO procedure repeatedly (as described earlier) will produce a working fire model. For visualization purposes it is useful to distinguish trees that have just caught fire from trees that are all burned up. We therefore add one more line to the model:

```
set pcolor red - 3.5
```

which, as we saw with the Life Simple model in chapter 2, darkens the color of the burned trees.

As currently written the GO procedure will never stop running. To fix that, we add a stopping condition so that the model stops when all of the fires are burned out. This is added to the beginning of the GO procedure:

```
if all? patches [pcolor != red]
    [ stop ]
```

The code for the GO procedure is then as follows:

```
to go
    ;; stop the model when done
    if all? patches [pcolor != red]
      [ stop ]

    ;; ask the burning trees to set fire to any neighboring non-burning trees
    ask patches with [pcolor = red] [ ;; ask the burning trees
      ask neighbors4 with [pcolor = green] [ ;; ask their non-burning neighbor trees
      set pcolor red ]   ;; to catch on fire
    set pcolor red - 3.5    ;; once the tree is burned, darken its color
]
tick  ;; advance the clock by one "tick"
end
```

This model is now functionally complete. The Fire Simple model included in the IABM Textbook folder in the models library also sets up some variables so as to display the percentage of the trees that have been burned.

In the following box, we describe the two basic types of primitives and procedures in NetLogo, commands and reporters. It is often handy to write reporter procedures to shorten code. For example, we might want to shorten the code calculating the patches that are on fire. We can create a reporter, called e.g., fire-patches, that calculates these. To do, we use the special NetLogo primitives, "report" and "to-report."

```
to-report fire-patches
    report patches with [pcolor = red]
end
```

Now we can change the code from the GO procedure above:

```
ask patches with [pcolor = red] [
```

to

```
ask fire-patches [
```

In this case, creating the reporter only slightly reduced the length of the code, but in more complex cases, encapsulating code as reporters can both shorten and clarify the code. There are many other good reasons to use reporters.

Box 3.2
Commands and Reporters

In NetLogo, *commands* and *reporters* tell agents what to do. A command is an action for an agent to carry out, resulting in some effect. A reporter is instructions for computing a value, which the agent then "reports" to whoever asked it.

Typically, a command name begins with a verb, such as "create," "die," "jump," "inspect," or "clear." Most reporter names are nouns or noun phrases.

For example, "forward" is a command, it tells a turtle agent to carry out a movement. But "heading" is a reporter, it tells the agent to report the angle it is facing.

Many commands and reporters are built into NetLogo, and you can create new ones in the Code tab. Commands and reporters built into NetLogo are called primitives. The NetLogo Dictionary has a complete list of built-in commands and reporters.

You can create your own commands and reporters by defining them in procedures. Each procedure has a name, preceded by the keyword to or to-report, depending on whether it is a command procedure or a reporter procedure. The keyword end marks the end of the procedure. It can be useful to notice that reporters are colored purple and commands are colored blue in NetLogo's automatic syntax highlighting.

Sometimes an input to a primitive is a *command block* (zero or more commands inside square brackets, e.g., [forward 10 set color red]) or a *reporter block* (a single reporter expression inside square brackets, e.g., the Boolean reporter [color = red]).

For more information on commands and reporters, see http://ccl.northwestern.edu/netlogo/docs/programming.html#procedures/.

• By creating a reporter that we can reuse, we avoid repetition of the code and therefore minimize the risks of inconsistency.
• The name of the reporter procedure can serve as self-documentation; a good procedure name clarifies intent.
• Isolate complexity: allows reasoning about, e.g., a GO procedure without being burdened by details of what goes on inside the reporter code.

We examine the use of reporters a little further in the explorations for this chapter.

Now run the Fire Simple model several times. If we run it with a low density of trees, we will see, as expected, very little spread of the fire. If we run it with a very high density of trees, we will see, as expected, the forest being decimated by the inexorable march of the fire. What should we expect at medium densities? Many people surmise that if the density is set to 50 percent, then the fire will have a 50 percent probability of reaching the right edge of the forest. If we try it, however, we see that at 50 percent density, the fire does not spread much. If we raise it to 57 percent, the fire burns more, but still doesn't usually reach the other side of the forest (see figure 3.3). However, if we raise the density to 61 percent, just 2 percent more density, the fire inevitably reaches the other side (see figure 3.4). This is unexpected. We would expect a small change in density to have a

A   B

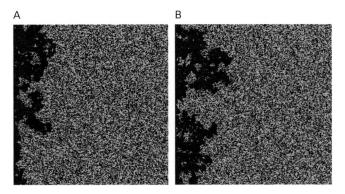

Figure 3.3
Two typical runs of the Fire Simple model with density set to 57 percent.

A   B

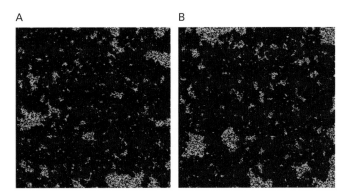

Figure 3.4
Two typical runs of the Fire Simple model with density set to 61 percent.

relatively small effect on the spread of the fire. But, it turns out, the Fire model has a "critical parameter" of 59 percent density. Below 59 percent density the fire does not spread that much; above it, it spreads dramatically farther. This is an important and prevalent property of complex systems: They exhibit nonlinear behavior where a small change in input can lead to a very large change in output.

In the next three sections, we will be creating variants/extensions to the Fire Simple model. These extensions can be found in the NetLogo models library, in the IABM folder, in the subfolder Chapter Three > Fire Extensions.

First Extension: Probabilistic Transitions
The Fire Simple model, like any model, makes many simplifying assumptions about the way the world works. In particular, fire in the real world does not spread deterministically

from one tree to another tree, but rather it jumps to another tree based on a variety of factors such as wind, the type of wood, even how close the branches are to each other. Often when there are many factors that affect a process like this one, we simplify the mechanism by using random numbers. We know that it is not certain that the fire will spread from one tree to another, but we do not know exactly what the probability of the spread is. We can model the mechanism by which fire spreads from one tree to another via a probability, and we can make this probability a parameter of the system. By experimenting with different values of the probability we can explore what effect the probability has on the overall spread of the fire.

To do this we first create a slider in the NetLogo model called PROBABILITY-OF-SPREAD. We set up this slider to go from 0 to 100. This is the variable that will control how frequently the fire spreads from one tree to another. Simply adding the slider is not enough—we need to modify the code itself to take this parameter into account. To do that we must first decide how we want this parameter to affect the model. Every time the model "spreads" the fire, we want it to create a random number between 0 and 100, if that number is less than the PROBABILITY-OF-SPREAD then we spread the fire as before. If it is not, then the fire does not spread in that direction. Let's examine the GO procedure in the original model. The fire spread occurs when all the fire agents (which are the red patches) ignite their neighboring tree patches by setting their color to red. This seems like the logical place to insert our new variable. The old code looks like this:

```
ask patches with [pcolor = red] [
    ask neighbors4 with [pcolor = green] [
        set pcolor red
    ]
    …
```

To modify this model to take our new parameter into account, all we have to do is add one additional check:

```
ask patches with [pcolor = red] [
                ask neighbors4 with [pcolor = green] [

        ;; only burn if a random draw is greater than the probability of spread
                        if random 100 < probability-of-spread [ set pcolor red ]
                ]
    …
```

As before the fire agents look to their four neighbors and pick out those that are unburned trees. But this time, instead of just burning those trees, each tree executes RANDOM 100 which will generate an integer between 0 and 99; if that number is less than the value of PROBABILITY-OF-SPREAD the model proceeds as before. If not, then the fire does not spread to that tree. It is important to note that even if one of these probabilities "fails" it is still possible that the tree in question may be burned down by one of its other burning neighbors.

Try setting both the DENSITY and the PROBABILITY-OF-SPREAD parameters to a variety of values. You can reproduce the results of the original model by setting the PROBABILITY-OF-SPREAD slider to 100 percent. It is a good rule of thumb to extend your model so you can reproduce previous results. By doing so, you can check to see if your new model is consistent with your old model and verify that you did not introduce any coding errors into the new model. You will often want to be able to generate the old results in order to compare them to the new results—ensuring that the new model can replicate the old mechanisms means you do not have to keep multiple versions of the model around.

Change these parameters and let the model run a few times. What happens to the model? If you set the tree densities to values that, in the original model, would have allowed the fire to burn through the forest, and set the PROBABILITY-OF-SPREAD at 50 percent, the fire rarely burns through the forest. In fact, with a 50 percent spread probability, it takes a very high density for the fire to burn completely through the forest. While experimenting, you might now notice that the density parameter has an upper bound of 99 percent. In the original model, this made sense as 100 percent density was uninteresting, but now, since fire spread between trees is probabilistic, 100 percent density is also interesting. Modify the upper bound of the slider, set the density to 100 percent and observe the fire spread. Our new parameter has dramatically altered the numerical results of the model. A screenshot of the Fire Simple model after completing this first extension is shown in figure 3.5.

Second Extension: Adding Wind

Sometimes we can take an ABM for which we used a probability to model a suite of mechanisms and refine it so that some of those mechanisms are modeled in a more physical way. Our first extension hides a host of possible mechanisms in the PROBABILITY-OF-SPREAD. We can pull out one of those mechanisms and model it in a more refined way. Wind is a good example of a process that we can model more specifically. We can think of the effect of wind on a fire as increasing the chance of fire spread in the direction it is blowing, decreasing the chance of fire spread in the direction it is not blowing, and having little effect on fire spread that occurs perpendicular to the direction of its movement. Of course, this too is an oversimplification—there are often local effects of wind, such as turbulence. As we have seen, all models are simplifications, and playing the modeling game means we will accept this one for now.

To implement wind in our model, we will create two sliders. One will control the speed of the wind from the south (a negative value will indicate a wind from the north)

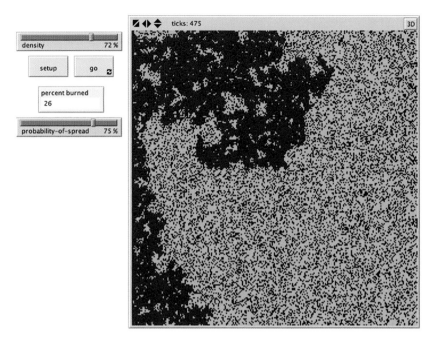

Figure 3.5
NetLogo Fire Simple model after first extension.

and one will control the speed of the wind from the west (a negative value will indicate a wind from the east). We create these two sliders and set them up to go from –25 to 25. How do we use these new parameters in the code? If we think back to our first modification, we want these new parameters to affect the PROBABILITY-OF-SPREAD. This effect will be based on the direction that the fire is attempting to spread. Since we have set the wind speed to vary from –25 to 25, we could conceive of those numbers as percentages by which to modify the probability of spread which is expressed as a percent. In order to do this, let us first create a local variable called PROBABIL-ITY that will initially be set to PROBABILITY-OF-SPREAD. A local variable is one that has a value only within a limited context, usually inside the procedure in which it is defined. If we only need to reference a variable in one procedure, then it is best to use a local variable. But, remember, you will not be able to see the value of the variable elsewhere in your program or in the command center. We define a local variable with the "let" primitive and can modify it with the "set" primitive. We can modify PROBABILITY to take into account WIND-SPEED by increasing or decreasing it by the WIND-SPEED in the direction the fire is burning. When we put this all together, we get the following code:

```
to go

    if all? patches [pcolor = red]
        [ stop ]

    ;; each burning tree (red patch) checks its 4 neighbors.
    ;; If any are unburned trees (green patches), change their probability
    ;; of igniting based on the wind direction
    ask patches with [pcolor = red] [
        ;; ask the unburned trees neighboring the burning tree
        ask neighbors4 with [pcolor = green] [
            let probability probability-of-spread        ;; define a local variable

            ;; compute the direction you (the green tree) are from the burning tree
            ;; (NOTE: "myself" is the burning tree (the red patch) that asked you
            ;; to execute commands)
            let direction towards myself
            ;; the burning tree is north of you
            ;; so the south wind impedes the fire spreading to you
            ;; so reduce the probability of spread
            if (direction = 0 ) [
                set probability probability - south-wind-speed ]

            ;; the burning tree is east of you
            ;; so the west wind impedes the fire spreading to you
            ;; so reduce the probability of spread
            if (direction = 90 ) [
                set probability probability - west-wind-speed ]

            ;; the burning tree is south of you
            ;; so the south wind aids the fire spreading to you
            ;; so increase the probability of spread
            if (direction = 180 ) [
                set probability probability + south-wind-speed ]

            ;; the burning tree is west of you
            ;; so the west wind aids the fire spreading to you
            ;; so increase the probability of spread
            if (direction = 270 ) [
                set probability probability + west-wind-speed ]
            if random 100 < probability [ set pcolor red ]
        ]
        set pcolor red - 3.5
    ]
    tick
end
```

This code is a little tricky. Essentially, what it does is modify the probability of spread, increasing it in the direction of the wind and decreasing it in the opposite direction. It calculates the change in the probability by first determining which direction the fire is trying to spread and then determining which of the winds will affect it. Once this probability is calculated, it is then used to determine whether or not the fire spreads to the neighboring tree.

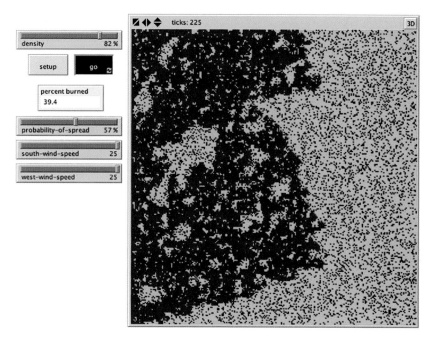

Figure 3.6
NetLogo Fire model after second extension.

This modification can lead to quite interesting patterns of spread. For example, set the density at 100 percent, and make the wind blow strong from the south and west. At the same time, set the PROBABILITY-OF-SPREAD fairly low, say around 38 percent. This creates a triangular spread, and, all else being equal, the fire should spread to the northeast. (See figure 3.6.)

Third Extension: Allow Long-Distance Transmission

We have modeled the effect of wind as pushing the fire to spread in one direction. Another possible effect of wind is to enable the fire to jump over long distances and start fires where there are no surrounding burning trees. That might be an interesting process to model. In order to make sure the revised model can replicate our old results, we add a switch to control the jumping. We add a Boolean (TRUE or FALSE) switch labeled BIG-JUMPS? Switches in NetLogo provide a way to have direct control over variables that can only be true or false. This particular switch allows us to turn on and off the jumping behavior. With the switch off, the revised model should produce the same results as Fire Simple Extension 2. One way to model fire jumping due to wind would be to ignite a new fire at some distance in the direction of the wind. We can do this by modifying the code inside our earlier GO procedure as follows picking up after we do all of the changes in probability based on wind:

```
...
if random 100 < probability [
                    set pcolor red

                ;; if big-jumps is on, then sparks can fly farther
                if big-jumps? [
                        let target patch-at ( west-wind-speed / 5 ) ( south-
                        wind-speed / 5 )
                        if target != nobody and [pcolor] of target = green [
                        ask target [
                            set pcolor red ;; ignite the target patch
                        ]
                        ]
                ]
        ]
...
```

The first part of this code turns the current patch to red, which is the same as the previous version, but the second part after IF BIG-JUMPS? is what has changed. If BIG-JUMPS? is true then it looks for a target patch that is some distance away in the direction of the wind. If there is an unburned (green) tree at that location, then that tree is also set on fire (due to the spark having landed there). A more detailed model could include explicit spark agents, which travel according to the wind, and catch trees on fire when they land, but in this case we just model the effects of flying sparks without modeling the sparks themselves.

Insert this code and see what effect it has on the model. You start to see lines in the direction of the wind as it jumps across gaps in the forest (as shown in figure 3.7). This extension can have visually dramatic effects. Explore different sets of parameters and observe the different patterns of spread you can get. This modification increases the probability that the fire will reach the right edge of the world (our measure), but the resultant pattern is no longer the same; there are big chunks of the world that are not burned anymore. As new patterns emerge we may need to reevaluate the questions that drove us to create the model, which may change the measures we collect about the model.

Each extension can lead to many more questions, which in turn call for new extensions. In our third fire extension, it is of course also possible to have big jumps be probabilistic in the same way that the neighboring spreads are, or to have the sparks from the big jumps land in a random rather than a determined location. Both of these modifications are left as exercises to the reader.

Summary of the Fire Model

We have made three different changes to the model, which have affected our tipping point in three different ways. The final change to the model points out that the measure we were observing (whether or not the fire made it to the right edge of the world) might not even be the measure we want to observe. As we change the fire spread mechanisms, other measures such as "percent burned" may become more important. These new measures

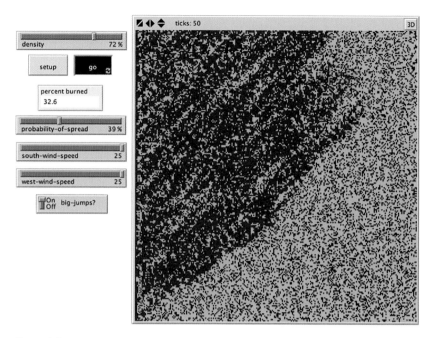

Figure 3.7
NetLogo Fire model after third extension.

may or may not have tipping points. This illustrates an important feature of tipping points. They are defined by an input and an output measure. A model does not have a tipping point in and of itself—the tipping point is relative to the choice of inputs and output measures.

Advanced Modeling Applications

As we mentioned, the Fire model can be generalized into a model of percolation, which is a well-studied problem in geology and physics (Grimmett, 1999). The generalized percolation form is: Given a structure with probabilistic transitions between locations, how likely is it that an entity entering that structure will make it from one side of the structure to the other? (See figure 3.8.) This form of the question has obvious ramifications in the area of oil drilling (Sahimi, 1994). Yet these generalized percolation forms can be useful well outside of traditional percolation contexts, such as studying the diffusion of innovation. Percolation bears a resemblance to innovation diffusion (Mort, 1991) and can be used to model it. Many things can spread in communities. Communities can often spread diseases and, in this way, percolation can be relevant to epidemiology (Moore & Newman, 2000). Newman, Girvan, & Farmer (2002) have studied so-called highly optimized tolerant system such as forests that are robust in the face of fires. They use the degree of

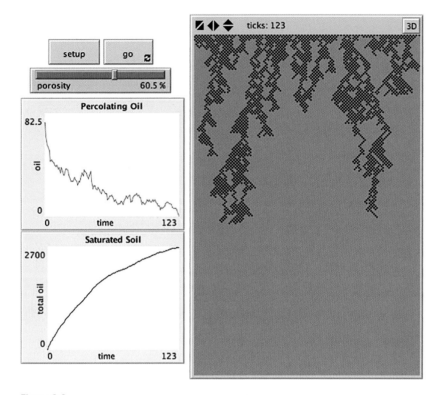

Figure 3.8
NetLogo Percolation model. http://ccl.northwestern.edu/netlogo/models/Percolation (*Wilensky 1998*).

percolation as a measure of the robustness of the system. These are but a few examples of the percolation of percolation models into other domains. Starting with the simple Fire model that we have examined, it is possible to model and gain insight into a wide variety of different phenomena.

The Diffusion-Limited Aggregation (DLA) Model

As we discussed in chapter 0, the ABM perspective enables a new and different understanding of complex systems. As demonstrated with the Fire Simple model, it is possible to think about inanimate objects (such as trees) as agents. By reconceptualizing atoms and molecules as agents, and then developing procedural rules to describe how these agents interact we can gain a deeper understanding of many different types of physical phenomena.

For instance, the formation of complex beautiful patterns in nature has mystified and amazed humans for many years (see figure 3.9), yet many of these patterns can be

Figure 3.9
A DLA copper aggregate formed from a copper sulfate solution in an electrode position cell (Kevin R. Johnson, 2006, http://commons.wikimedia.org/wiki/File:DLA_Cluster.JPG).

generated using simple rules. Often in ABMs we will see that the complexity of a resulting pattern bears little direct relationship to the complexity of the underlying rules. In fact, in some cases the results will seem to be exactly the opposite; simpler rules will often create more complex patterns. The focus of our interest should not necessarily be on the complexity of the rules, but instead on the interaction those rules produce. Many agent-based models are interesting not because of what each agent does, but because of what the agents do together.

In this section, we will look at a very simple model where all that the agents do is move randomly around the world, and eventually stop moving when a basic condition is met; despite the simplicity of the rules, interesting complex phenomena can emerge.

Description of Diffusion-Limited Aggregation

In many physical processes from the creation of clouds, to snowflakes, to soot, smoke, and dust, particles aggregate in interesting ways. Diffusion-limited aggregation (DLA) is an idealization of this process, and was first examined as a computational model in the early eighties (Witten & Sander, 1981, 1983). DLA models were able to generate patterns that resemble many found in nature, such as crystals, coral, fungi, lightning, and growth of human lungs, as well as social patterns such as growth of cities (Garcia-Ruiz et al., 1993; Bentley & Humphreys, 1962; Batty & Longley, 1994).

A NetLogo version of diffusion-limited aggregation was one of the first models written for the NetLogo models library (*Wilensky, 1997b*). You can find a simplified DLA model in the NetLogo models library under Sample Models > IABM Textbook > Chapter Three > DLA Extensions > DLA Simple.nlogo. This model starts with a large number of red particle agents and one green patch in the center. The green patch at the center of the screen is stationary, but when you press GO, all of the red particles move randomly by "wiggling" left and right (resulting in a small random turn) and then moving forward one step. After a particle moves, if any of its neighbors (i.e., nearby patches) are green, the particle dies, turning the patch it is on green (the particle can do so because all turtles have direct access to the variables of the patch they are on). If you let the model run long enough, you will get an interesting fractal-like pattern forming from the green patches (see figure 3.10).

Here is the NetLogo code for the GO procedure for DLA Simple. WIGGLE-ANGLE is a global variable, the value of which is set by a slider in the interface.

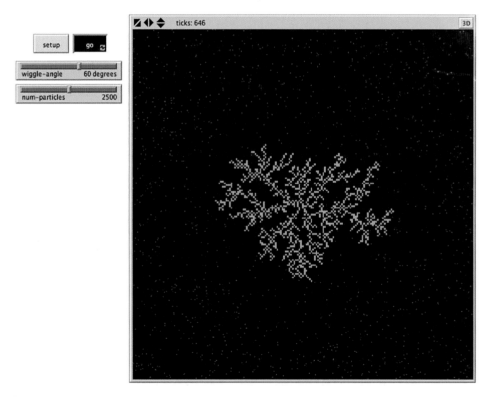

Figure 3.10
NetLogo model of diffusion limited aggregation. http://ccl.northwestern.edu/netlogo/models/DLA (based on *Wilensky, 1997b*).

```
to go
   ask turtles
      ;; turn a random amount right and left
      [ right random wiggle-angle
         left random wiggle-angle
         forward 1
         ;; if you are touching a green patch, turn your own patch green and
         ;; then die
         if ( any? neighbors with [pcolor = green] )
            [ set pcolor green
               die ] ]
   tick
end
```

As the code shows, if any of the neighbors are green the particle stops moving, changes the color of the patch that it is on to green and dies. Turtles have direct access to the variables of the patch they are on—that is how the turtle can set the color of the patch it is on (the PCOLOR in NetLogo).

We will now create three extensions of the DLA Simple model. They are available in the folder Sample Models > IABM Textbook > Chapter Three > DLA Extensions.

First Extension: Probabilistic Sticking

The DLA Simple model has very simple rules. The code consists of only two procedures, and both of them are very small, yet these two procedures can generate many interesting results. In these extensions we will examine how adding a few more simple rules can enable us to generate more interesting patterns.

After you run the model for a while, you will realize that it always produces thin and wispy types of structures. Often the "stems" and "trunks" of the structures are only a single patch wide. This is because as soon as a particle touches anything green it will stop moving. It is much more likely that it will touch something toward the edge of the structure rather than near the interior of the structure.

However, we can change this. One way to think of this system is that if a particle comes into contact with a stationary object, then it becomes stationary itself with 100 percent probability. What if we decrease this probability? That is exactly what we will do in this extension. We will allow the user to control the probability of a particle becoming stationary.

In the original code, if any of the neighbors are green, the particle stops moving, changes the color of the patch that it is on to green, and dies. What we need to do is add another test to this rule, but we also have to make one other change to the code at the same time. Since stopping will be probabilistic, it is now possible that a particle could be on top of another green particle, and, in that case, we do not want the particle to stop. So we also need to make sure we are not on a green particle before we stop, which involves adding an additional condition to the model:

```
to go
    ask turtles
      [ right random wiggle-angle
          left random wiggle-angle
          forward 1
          if (pcolor = black) and ( any? neighbors with [pcolor = green] )
    and ( random-float 1.0 < probability-of-sticking )
              [ set pcolor green
                                      die ] ]
      tick
end
```

Now, a particle will only stick if a random number it generates is less than a given probability, but where is this probability defined? If you add this code into the GO procedure and then move to the Interface tab, NetLogo will generate an error because we have not defined this parameter yet. So we will do that now. We go back to the Interface tab and create a slider called PROBABILITY-OF-STICKING, and we give it a minimum value of 0.0, a maximum value of 1.0 and an increment of 0.01.[3] Now we are finished with this extension, and we can run the model with a PROBABILITY-OF-STICKING of 0.5, as seen in figure 3.11.

You will notice that the branches of the structure become thicker when the probability is 0.5. This is because particles have a smaller probability of getting stuck on the outside of the structure and can wander deeper in to the structure before stopping. If you want you can still generate the original results by setting the probability to 1.0. As with the extensions to the Fire Simple model, it is often helpful to make sure that when extending a model you can still generate the previous results. Not only does this allow you to inspect whether any errors were introduced by your code change, but also, as you continue to add new parameters and mechanisms, you will often want to go back to your original results for comparison.

Second Extension: Neighbor Influence

The addition of our probability parameter enables us to explore a whole new range of structures, while not interfering with our ability to add additional simple rules to this model. One commonly explored extension to the DLA model is to explore how the probability of sticking is related to the number of neighbors that are already stationary (the green patches) (Witten & Sander, 1983). If a particle is moving, it is more likely that it will stick somewhere if two or three of its neighbors are at rest than if just one of its neighbors is at rest. Thus, we want the probability of stopping to increase as the number of stopped neighbors increases.

Let us begin this extension by adding a switch to our interface, which we will call NEIGHBOR-INFLUENCE? This switch will determine whether or not we are taking the

---

3. Whereas the "random" primitive generates random whole number, here we use the "random-float" primitive so we can get probability values between 0 and 1.

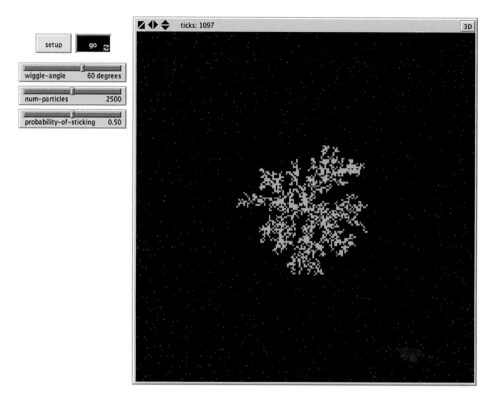

Figure 3.11
DLA model after first extension.

number of neighbors in to account when determining if a particle should stop moving. NEIGHBOR-INFLUENCE? is a Boolean variable, that is, it has one of two values, TRUE or FALSE. It is conventional to append a question mark character to the end of the variable name to point out to the reader that the variable is Boolean. After we add this switch we can go back and look at our GO procedure. We left the GO procedure looking like this:

```
to go
   ask turtles
      [ right random wiggle-angle
         left random wiggle-angle
         forward 1
         if ( pcolor = black ) and ( any? neighbors with [pcolor = green] ) and
             ( random-float 1.0 < probability-of-sticking )
             [ set pcolor green
               die ] ]
   tick
end
```

We need to modify the PROBABILITY-OF-STICKING based on the NEIGHBOR-INFLUENCE? switch. To accomplish this we must first create a variable, which we will call LOCAL-PROB If NEIGHBOR-INFLUENCE? is turned off then LOCAL-PROB will be the same as PROBABILITY-OF-STICKING. However, if NEIGHBOR-INFLUENCE? is turned on, then we will reduce the probability of sticking for small numbers of green neighbors. We accomplish this by multiplying the PROBABILITY-OF-STICKING by the fraction of its eight neighbors that are green. For example, if PROBABILITY-OF-STICKING is set to 0.5 and if a particle encounters a neighborhood with four green neighbors, then we multiply PROBABILITY-OF-STICKING by 4/8 to get a sticking probability for that encounter of 0.25. We do this in order to create a relationship such that if many neighbors are green the probability approaches the PROBABILITY-OF-STICKING and if few neighbors are green the probability approaches zero.[4] As a further exploration, try some other functions and see how it affects this result; to facilitate this, you may want to make the number of neighbors that affect a particle a parameter. The new code looks like this:

```
    to go
              ask turtles
[ right random wiggle-angle
    left random wiggle-angle
    forward 1
    let local-prob probability-of-sticking

    ;; if neighbor-influence is TRUE then make the probability proportionate
    ;; to the number of green neighbors, otherwise use the slider as before
    if neighbor-influence? [
    ;; increase the probability of sticking the more green neighbors there are
                      set local-prob probability-of-sticking *
(count neighbors with [pcolor = green] / 8)
    ]

    if (pcolor = black) and ( any? neighbors with [pcolor = green] )
and ( random-float 1.0 < local-prob )
    [ set pcolor green
          die ] ]
    tick
end
```

When we run the model with this change in the code, we notice (1) that it takes much longer to form a structure because there is a much lower probability of a mobile particle stopping, and (2) the structures that emerge are very thick and almost bloblike. In addition there are many fewer one patch-wide branches, because the probability of stopping when in contact with only one other stationary patch is very small. You can see the results in figure 3.12.

4. Note that, in doing so, we limit the probability of sticking with only one green neighbor to one-eighth of the probability set in the slider.

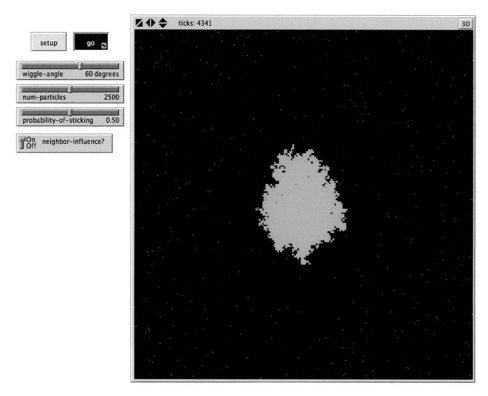

Figure 3.12
DLA model after second extension.

Third Extension: Different Aggregates

The previous two extensions have concentrated on deciding how a particle should stop
when it is moving—there is another way that we can control how a particle stops. We can
simply give it more places to stop at the beginning. If we look at the SETUP procedure
in the previous version of the model, we can see that it creates one green patch in the
middle of the world:

```
to setup
   clear-all
   ;; ask the middle patch to turn green
   ask patch 0 0
     [ set pcolor green ]
   create-turtles num-particles
     [ set color red
         set size 1.5   ;; make the particle bigger so it's easier to see
         setxy random-xcor random-ycor ]
end
```

Patch 0 0 is the unique name for the patch that is at x-coordinate 0, and y-coordinate 0, which is at the center of the NetLogo world by default. However, what if we want to create multiple green patches at the start? If there are multiple green patches, then there will be more places for the moving particles to come to rest, and we can generate different patterns of aggregation. To begin with, we need to create a slider so we can control the number of different aggregates that we create; we will call this slider NUM-SEEDS. We give this slider a minimum of 1 (since we need at least one seed), a maximum of 10, and an increment of 1.

Once we have this slider, we can ask NUM-SEEDS patches to turn green in the setup:

```
to setup
    clear-all
    ;; start with NUM-SEEDS green patches as "seeds"
    ask n-of num-seeds patches
        [ set pcolor green ]
    create-turtles num-particles
        [ set color red
            set size 1.5
            setxy random-xcor random-ycor ]
    reset-ticks
end
```

The N-OF reporter selects a random set of NUM-SEEDS patches. We then ask these randomly chosen patches to turn green, making them seeds for the aggregates. This is different from what we did in the Fire model; in that model, we asked each of the patches to determine if they should become a tree (a seed) using a random variable. The Fire model method will generate roughly the fraction of trees specified by the slider; the N-OF method will always generate exactly the number of seeds specified by the slider. In agent-based modeling, the probabilistic method used in the Fire model is often considered more realistic since nature does not specify exact numbers. However, the N-OF method gives us more precise control over the model's behavior.

This code works, but note that it no longer re-creates the exact results of the original model. Even if we set NUM-SEEDS to 1, we will no longer always create a seed at the center of the world. Instead, the seed will be randomly placed somewhere in the world. In this case it is simpler to deviate from the original version and not much is lost by doing so. There is really nothing special about the center of the world, and having the seed start anywhere randomly will be sufficiently similar to the original result for testing and exploration purposes. If we really desire to have the seed start at the center of the world, we could add another parameter; this is left as an exercise for the reader. The final version of the simple DLA model, after all three extensions, is shown in figure 3.13. With multiple seeds, the patterns look somewhat like frost forming on a cold window.

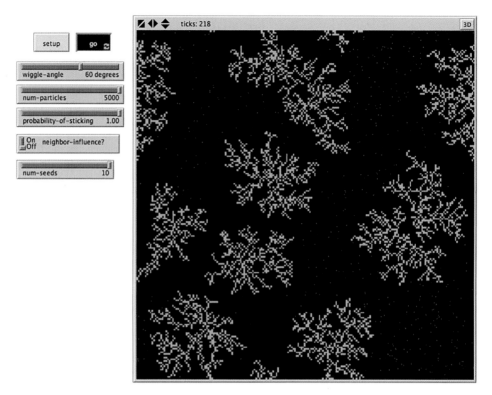

Figure 3.13
DLA model after third extension.

Summary of the DLA Model

In this section, we created three versions of the DLA model that enable us to generate different interesting patterns from very simple rules. Despite the complex and intricate nature of these patterns, the rules can be described in just a few words. The first two extensions modified how the particles "decide" when to stop moving. These are classical extensions and can result in thicker and more substantial patterns. The final extension added the idea of starting from multiple seeds, which enables the generation of different patterns by the same model and these different patterns can then be compared and contrasted side by side. The DLA model is a classic example of simplicity at a micro level creating complexity at a macro level.

Advanced Modeling Applications

The DLA model is one simple example of how ABM can be used to examine phenomena from classical chemistry and physics. There are many more examples in the NetLogo models library. For example, the Connected Chemistry (Wilensky, Levy & Novak, 2004)

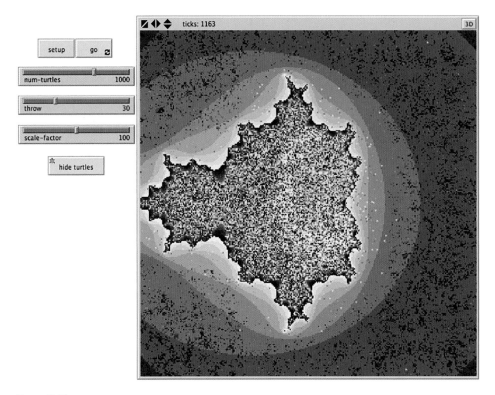

Figure 3.14
NetLogo Mandelbrot model. http://ccl.northwestern.edu/netlogo/models/Mandelbrot (*Wilensky, 1997c*).

model package models many standard chemistry principles using NetLogo, while NIELS (Sengupta & Wilensky, 2005) does the same for electromagnetism. The DLA model straddles the line between agent-based modeling and the mathematics of fractals. There are many other models in the NetLogo models library that involve the mathematics of fractals (see the Mathematics section of the models library in the subsection Fractals). Since many fractal systems are actually created using conditional rules, agent-based modeling is a natural way to describe these systems, and the results can be quite beautiful (see figure 3.14).

The Segregation Model

There are two fundamental approaches to starting to build an agent-based model. The first approach, more common in science contexts, is to start with a known phenomenon to be modeled. This approach is called *phenomena-based modeling*. Usually when engaged in phenomena-based modeling, we have an aggregate pattern, termed a *reference pattern* that we are trying to generate with agent rules. Another way to begin is to start with some simple rules and play them out to see what patterns develop. This approach is sometimes referred to as *exploratory modeling*. Frequently in pursuing ABM, we take some combination of these two approaches. In his investigations into the nature of nature of segregation, Thomas Schelling took a more exploratory modeling approach with his Neighborhood Tipping model (1971). Schelling wondered what would happen if you assume that everyone in the world wanted to live in a place where at least a reasonable fraction of their neighbors were like themselves, i.e., they have an aversion to being an extreme minority (which he called weakly prejudiced; see Anas, 2002). He explored this model using a checkerboard as a grid, with pennies to represent one race and dimes to represent another. He counted by hand the number of pennies surrounding each dime and divide by the number of neighbors surrounding that dime. If this value exceeded a certain threshold value, he would move the dime to a random empty location on the board. He repeated this process hundreds of times and observed the outcome. (See figure 3.15.)

For high levels of the threshold, the model confirmed what he predicted. The checkerboard would quickly segregate into areas of all pennies and all dimes. What surprised Schelling about this model (and many other people at the time) was that even at low levels of the threshold, he would still see groups of pennies and groups of dimes together in dense clusters. This global segregation occurred despite the relative tolerance of each individual. There was no single individual in the Schelling model who wanted a segregated neighborhood, but the group as a whole moved toward segregation. Schelling described this as "macrobehavior" derived from "micromotives" (1978).

At the time when Schelling introduced this model, it was very controversial for several reasons. First, it was widely believed at the time that housing segregation was caused by individuals being prejudiced. Schelling's work seemed to be "excusing" people from prejudice, saying that prejudice itself is not the cause of segregation. The cause of segregation is an emergent effect of the aggregation of people's weak prejudice. But Schelling's point was not to excuse people for their prejudice, his model demonstrates that prejudice is not a "leverage point" of the housing system. Unless you can reduce prejudice to close to zero, so that everyone is perfectly comfortable being the sole member of their race in their neighborhood, this segregation dynamic will emerge. So, if your goal is to reduce housing segregation, it may not be effective to work directly on reducing individual's prejudice.

Another controversial aspect of Schelling's model is that it modeled the people as behaving with very simple rules. Critics argued that "people are not ants"; they have complex cognition and social arrangements, and you cannot model them with such simple rules. To be sure, Schelling's model was highly oversimplified model of people's housing choices. Nevertheless, it did reveal a hitherto unknown important dynamic. Eventually, Schelling carried the day. For his large body of work on exploring the relations of

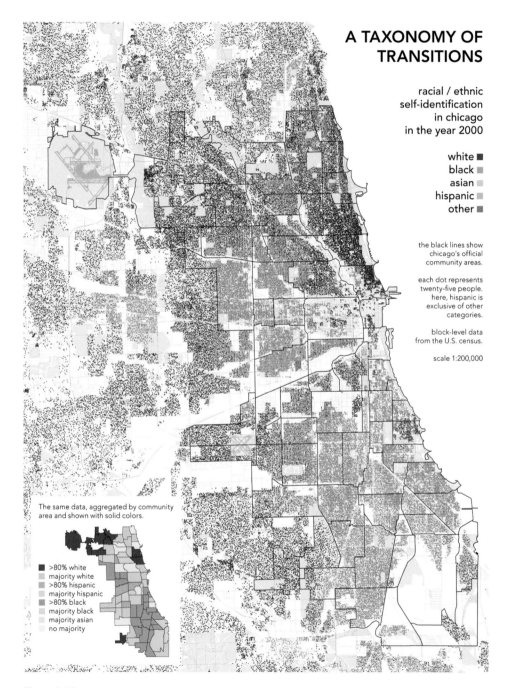

Figure 3.15

A map of Chicago with each dot representing twenty-five people. By representing the data at this finer level than traditional maps that aggregate demographics are mapped at a high level, Rankin illustrates nuances of segregation much like ABM enables us to explore nuances of individual-level behavior.

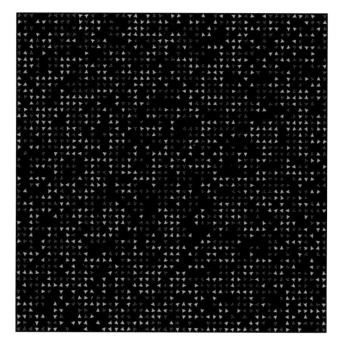

Figure 3.16
Initial state of the NetLogo Segregation model. Red and green turtles are distributed at random. http://ccl.north-western.edu/netlogo/models/Segregation (*Wilensky, 1997d*).

micromotives and macrobehavior and his work on conducting game-theory analyses of conflict and cooperation, Schelling was awarded the Nobel Prize in economics in 2005. To this day, it remains controversial how much of human behavior can be modeled with simple rules. We will explore this further in later chapters of this textbook.

Description of the Segregation Model

A NetLogo version of the segregation model is distributed in the IABM Textbook section of the models library. You can find it in Sample Models > IABM Textbook > Chapter Three > Segregation Extensions > Segregation Simple.nlogo. This model is shown in figure 3.16. When you press the SETUP button, an approximately equal number of red and green turtles will appear at random locations in the world.

Each turtle will determine if it is happy or not, based on whether the percentage of neighbors that are the same color as itself meets the %-SIMILAR-WANTED threshold. When you press the GO button, the model will check if there are any unhappy turtles. Each unhappy turtle will move to a new location. It moves by turning a random amount and moving forward a random amount from 0 to 10. If the new location is not occupied then the turtle settles down, if it is occupied, it moves again. After all the unhappy turtles

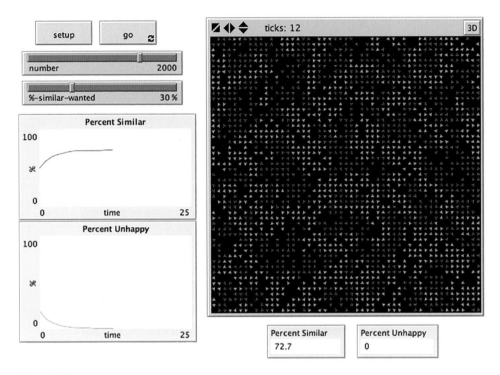

Figure 3.17
A run of the Segregation model with a "tolerance" level of 30 percent. Even though most agents are comfortable in an integrated neighborhood, the housing gets very segregated with 72.7 percent of agents surrounded by their same color agents.

have moved, every turtle again determines whether or not it is happy and the process repeats itself. (See figure 3.17.)

The SETUP procedure for this model is as follows:

```
to setup
    clear-all
    ;; create a turtle on NUMBER randomly selected patches.
    ask n-of number patches
        [ sprout 1 ]

    ask turtles [
        ;; make approximately half the turtles red and the other half green
        set color one-of [red green]
    ]

    update-variables ;; update the turtles and the global variables
    reset-ticks
end
```

The code asks a random set of patches to each sprout a red turtle. The size of the patch set is determined by the NUMBER slider, so after sprouting, the number of turtles is exactly the value on the NUMBER slider, each turtle on its own patch. The code then asks the turtles to turn red or green with equal probability, resulting in an approximately equal number of red and green turtles.

The GO procedure is:

```
to go
    if all? turtles [happy?] [ stop ]
    move-unhappy-turtles
    update-variables
tick
end
```

This code stops the simulation when all the turtles are happy. If there are any unhappy turtles, it asks them to move, and then all turtles recalculate their happiness.

The happiness calculation takes place in the update-turtles procedure, which follows:

```
to update-turtles
    ask turtles [
        ;; in next two lines, we use "neighbors" to test the eight patches
        ;; surrounding the current patch

        ;; count the number of my neighbors that are the same color as me
        set similar-nearby count (turtles-on neighbors)
            with [color = [color] of myself]

        ;; count the total number of neighbors
        set total-nearby count (turtles-on neighbors)

        ;; I'm happy if there are at least the minimal number of
        ;;    same-colored neighbors
        set happy? similar-nearby >= ( %-similar-wanted * total-nearby / 100 )
    ]
end
```

This code asks each turtle to count how many of its neighbors are same-colored turtles and how many are differently colored turtles. It then sets its "happy?" variable to TRUE if the percentage of same-colored neighboring turtles is at least equal to the value set by the %-SIMILAR-WANTED slider.

The PERCENT SIMILAR monitor displays what percentage of a turtle's neighbors are the same color as it, on average, while the PERCENT UNHAPPY monitor display what percentage of all turtles are unhappy.

First Extension: Adding Multiple Ethnicities

One simple extension to this model is to add a third, fourth, and even fifth ethnicity. This can be done by modifying the SETUP code. Currently the model sets all the turtles to red initially, then asks half of them to become green. Recall the code that sets up the turtles:

```
;; create turtles on random patches
ask n-of number patches
   [ sprout 1 ]
ask turtles [
   ;; make half the turtles red and the other half green
   set color one-of [red green]
]
```

We need to figure out how to modify this code so that it works with more than two ethnicities. Since we are now allowing the number of colors to vary we need to go beyond red and green turtles, sometimes we will need blue, yellow, and orange turtles as well. Therefore, we begin by defining the colors we will allow the turtles to have. We do this by establishing a global variable *colors*:

```
globals [
percent-similar     ;; on average, what percent of a turtle's neighbors
                                    ;; are the same color as that turtle?
   percent-unhappy  ;; the percent of the turtles that are unhappy
   colors                           ;; a list of colors we use to color the turtles
]
```

The last line, "colors," is the only new global variable. Now we need to define what the value of this global is. We can do this in the SETUP procedure:

```
set colors [red green yellow blue orange ]
```

This line of code initializes the global variable *colors* to be a list of the five colors. Next, we would like to allow the model user to control of the number of ethnicities in the system, and we can do this by adding a NUMBER-OF-ETHNICITIES slider. We will initially set the bounds of this slider from 2 to 5. Now we have to make the code use this slider. We do this by modifying the turtle coloring code. We replace all of the SETUP code above with the following:

```
;; create a turtle on NUMBER randomly selected patches.
      ask n-of number patches
                  [ sprout 1 ]
```

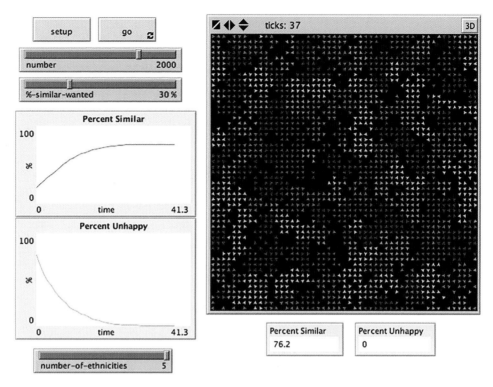

Figure 3.18
NetLogo Segregation model after first extension.

```
;; assign a color to each turtle from the list of our colors
        ask turtles
        [ set color (item (random number-of-ethnicities) colors) ]
```

This code tells a number (equal to the interface slider NUMBER) of random patches to sprout a turtle. Each turtle picks its color randomly from the list of colors we just initialized. But the turtles can only pick the colors in the list up to the number of ethnicities. For example, if the NUMBER-OF-ETHNICITIES is 3, only the first three colors in the list are used.

Now that we have code that allows multiple ethnicities, try running the model with different numbers of ethnicities and observe what effect this has on the segregation of the system. You will notice that as you increase the NUMBER-OF-ETHNICITIES, it takes longer for the system to settle—that is, for all the turtles to be happy. (See figure 3.18.) However, once the system has settled, the final PERCENT SIMILAR displayed in the monitor remains pretty much the same regardless of how many ethnicities there are. Can you explain why this might be?

Second Extension: Allowing Diverse Thresholds

In the original version of Schelling's model, every agent in the world had exactly the same similarity threshold. This meant that every agent had the same level of tolerance for having other ethnicities in its neighborhood. Although relaxing this assumption might have been difficult to enact with a checkerboard, it is straightforward to do using an ABM language. It's likely that different individuals in a real population would have different levels of tolerance. And with an ABM language we can easily give each individual agent its own personal characteristics. Agents can act on these personal characteristics and make decisions based on them. This means that even when agents in an ABM are running the exact same code, their behavior can be quite different.

So how can we make the individuals in the Segregation model more diverse? One way would be to give them a range of similarity thresholds rather than requiring them all to have the same value for that threshold. To do this, we need to first give the turtles the ability to have their own %-SIMILAR-WANTED. We do this by modifying the *turtles-own* properties. As we showed in chapter 2, any variable in a turtles-own declaration is a variable that is a property of every turtle, that means every turtle can have a different value for that variable.

```
turtles-own [
    happy?              ;; for each turtle, indicates whether at least
    ;; %-SIMILAR-WANTED percent of that turtle's neighbors
    ;; are the same color as the turtle
    similar-nearby   ;; how many neighboring patches have a turtle with
            ;; my color?
    total-nearby   ;; sum of previous two variables
    my-%-similar-wanted        ;; the threshold for this particular turtle
]
```

Now, in addition to the other properties that the turtles have, they each have a MY-%-SIMILAR-WANTED property, but as of right now this value is not set. We need to modify the SETUP procedure in order to initialize the turtles with their own MY-%-SIMILAR-WANTED values.

```
;; assign a color to each turtle from the list of our colors using number-of-
;; ethnicities to maximize the number of colors and assign an
;; individual level of %-similar-wanted
    ask turtles
        [ set color (item (random number-of-ethnicities) colors)
            set my-%-similar-wanted random %-similar-wanted⁵ ]
```

5. Note that by making this modeling choice, we have made it impossible to reproduce the model behavior before the extension. In general, when extending models, it is inadvisable to eliminate previous behaviors. In this case, we did it for clarity of exposition. To make this extension "backward compatible," you could use the "random-normal primitive, and then to reproduce the previous behavior, you would give it a standard deviation of 0.

We insert this new code directly after specifying the color that we changed in the first extension. This value is set to a random value between 0 and the value from the %-SIMILAR-WANTED slider. This means that the %-SIMILIAR-WANTED variable no longer specifies the tolerance of each agent, but rather it specifies a maximum value that any agent can have for its tolerance.

However, the code that determines whether or not a turtle is happy has not yet changed, and so all of these individual tolerance values will be ignored. Let us change the UPDATE-TURTLES code to use these new values. This requires only one small change to the code:

```
set happy? similar-nearby >= ( my-%-similar-wanted * total-nearby / 100 )
```

All we do is replace %-SIMILAR-WANTED with MY-%-SIMILAR-WANTED to tell the turtle to use its own agent variable instead of the global variable.

Now that we have all of the code for the agents to use their own thresholds, run the model several times with different values of %-SIMILAR-WANTED. Do you see any different results? If you play with the model enough, you will notice that the PERCENT SIMILAR monitor ends up with a lower value at the end of the run then it did after the first extension. This result is logical, since no individual can be less tolerant in this extension than before, but some individuals will be more tolerant allowing them to find locations where they are happy even though there are more ethnically different individuals around them. In fact, the average of the MY-%-SIMILAR-WANTED values of the turtles will be approximately half of the global %-SIMILAR-WANTED slider. Comparing the original Segregation model with this extension of the model using twice the %-SIMILAR-WANTED value is left as further exploration for interested readers. (See figure 3.19.)

Third Extension: Adding Diversity-Seeking Individuals

Another simplification that the original segregation model makes about the world is that individuals are concerned about too much diversity but that no agents actively seek diversity in their neighborhoods. An easy way to overcome this simplification is to allow individuals to have a %-DIFFERENT-WANTED property just as they have a %-SIMILAR-WANTED property. We begin by creating a slider for %-DIFFERENT-WANTED that is just like the %-SIMILAR-WANTED slider. After that we only need to make one additional change to the code. We've already been calculating the number of ethnically different turtles in the neighborhood and so we only have to modify the update-turtles procedure to make use of the new parameter:

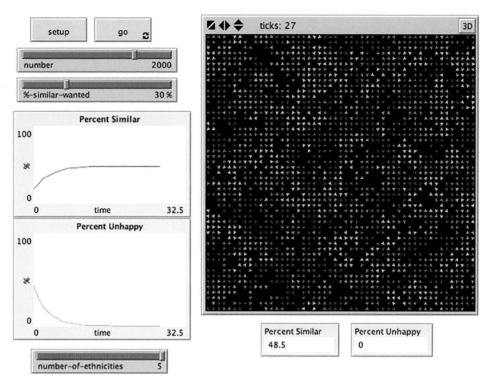

Figure 3.19
NetLogo Segregation model after second extension.

```
;; count the number of my neighbors that are a different color than me
let other-nearby count (turtles-on neighbors)
          with [color != [color] of myself]

set happy? similar-nearby >= ( my-%-similar-wanted * total-nearby / 100 )
                and other-nearby >= ( %-different-wanted * total-nearby / 100 )
```

With the addition of the new clause (shown in bold), the new happiness calculation tells the agents that they are only happy if the number of similar agents nearby is greater than their %-SIMILAR-WANTED threshold *and* the number of other agents nearby is greater than the %-DIFFERENT-WANTED threshold. So for an agent to be happy it cannot be too much in a minority or too great a majority. Now that we have added this code to the model, run it a few times and observe the results.

As you play around with these sliders, it becomes quickly clear that it is much easier for the PERCENT SIMILAR results to decrease after this extension has been implemented. The reason is that all of the agents actually seek out diversity now, so they are deliberately taking actions that decrease the PERCENT SIMILAR results. Moreover, as you manipulate the sliders, you can easily find states of the parameters where the system never settles down. For instance, if you put both the %-SIMILAR-WANTED and %-DIFFERENT-WANTED sliders over 50 percent, the model will probably never reach equilibrium. This is because some agents (those with MY-%-SIMILAR-WANTED greater than 50) will be trying to satisfy impossible demands; they will never find a location where more than half the agents around them are similar to themselves and more than half the agents around them are different than themselves.[6] In general you will find that it takes this new system much longer to settle down to an equilibrium state. This is because the agents are now pickier in terms of where they are happy. They are seeking both diversity and similarity. (See figure 3.20.)

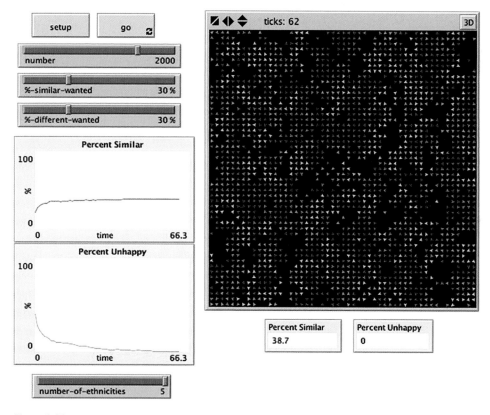

Figure 3.20
NetLogo Segregation model after third extension.

6. Contrary to the traditional assumptions in economics of a rational *Homo economicus*, people sometimes *do* have inconsistent preferences, and ABMs are well suited for modeling these inconsistencies.

There are two quick modifications that could be built to further expand on this model. First, the current %-DIFFERENT-WANTED slider specifies a global variable. It could easily be modified to give agents varying thresholds like we did for the %-SIMILAR-WANTED slider in the second extension. This would involve adding a MY-%-DIFFERENT-WANTED for each turtle, the same way we added MY-%-SIMILAR-WANTED. Second, we could modify the model so that some agents sought only diversity and some agents sought only similarity. How would you go about doing this? What effect would these two modifications have on the results?

Summary of the Segregation Model

One of the major aspects of ABM to take away from the Segregation model is that different models emphasize different aspects of the world. In the original model, Schelling made a particular set of assumptions about people's preferences and behavior. In the first extension we decided to place more emphasis on the multiplicity of ethnicities in the world than Schelling did. In the second extension, we shifted emphasis from uniform agents to heterogeneous agents who had different thresholds. This enables us to focus more on individual differences and diversity rather than on individual similarities and universality. Finally, in the third extension, we removed the emphasis on ethnocentric behavior that existed in Schelling's original model and instead started to examine agents that actually seek out diversity. Typically, ABMs can be built to emphasize particular features of the world or particular mechanisms of interaction. Choosing which features and mechanisms to select and trying out alternative selections is a part of the art of modeling complex systems.

Advanced Urban Modeling Applications

Agent-based modeling has frequently been used for the modeling of urban landscapes. The Segregation model described earlier can be seen as one particular example of what are generally called "residential preference" models, which are a major component of urban modeling systems. These models can be combined with commercial, industrial, and governmental models of urban policy to create an integrated model of a city. One such example is the CITIES project (see figure 3.21) carried out by the Center for Connected Learning and Computer-Based Modeling at Northwestern University. The goal of the CITIES project was to procedurally develop realistic cities that could be used as tools in education and exploration (Lechner et al., 2006). Another goal of urban modeling is to explore the ecological impact of cities and their footprint on the environment. The SLUCE project at the University of Michigan built several models of residential and tract development to explore land-use policies and their effect on the surrounding environs in southeastern Michigan (Brown et al., 2005; Rand et al., 2003). Both of these projects can be seen as a subset of the larger category of land-use modeling. For a detailed review of agent-based models of land use, see Parker et al. (2003) and Batty (2005).

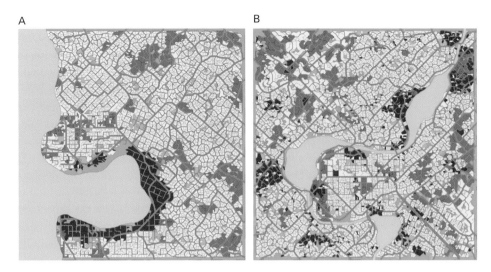

Figure 3.21
Some runs of the CITIES model in NetLogo (Lechner et al., 2006).

The El Farol Model

Occasionally, when working on agent-based models, you will find a model that reproduces phenomena that you are interested in but does not quite provide the output or data that you want. In this section we will take a model of an economic scenario, the El Farol model, and we will add additional reporters to this model. In this way we can gain new information from the model that was not previously available. This is possible because data collection in agent-based models is fairly simple, and the capabilities of ABMs for visually displaying information are diverse.

This section is a good example of how you do not need to understand every part of an agent-based model in order to work with it. The El Farol model uses "lists" and mathematical regression, but the modifications we will make to this model do not require knowledge of how these particular methods work. Although it is almost always desirable to understand the basic rules of the model, for the purposes of a particular extension, it may be sufficient to develop that understanding from reading the Info tab rather than trying to puzzle out the details of the code. When extending models, it is useful, though not easy, to develop the skill of understanding only the code you will need to modify and know which code is safe to ignore. Our extensions to this model will not require much understanding of the mechanics of the model.

Description of the El Farol Model

W. Brian Arthur was an Irish economist who, at age thirty-seven, became the youngest holder of an endowed chair at Stanford University. He was a pioneer of using complexity methods in economics and is on the founders' board of the Santa Fe Institute. In 1991, Arthur posed the El Farol Bar problem as an exploration of bounded rationality and inductive reasoning. Traditional neoclassical economics presupposes that humans are completely rational: that is, they have access to perfect information and maximize their utility in every situation (Arthur, 1994). When each agent behaves this way the aggregate can achieve an "optimal" equilibrium. But this is an idealization and people do not really conform to this normative description. Therefore, Arthur suggested the El Farol Bar problem as an example of a system where agents do not perfectly optimize, yet a classical economic equilibrium is achieved. Arthur's example is even more striking, because it is a situation in which it would be difficult for the "ideal" economic model to achieve equilibrium.

On Canyon Road in Santa Fe, New Mexico, there is a bar called the El Farol. This bar was popular with researchers from the Santa Fe Institute, including Arthur. One night each week, the El Farol had live Irish music, and Arthur enjoyed going on these nights, but occasionally it got crowded, and he did not enjoy it on those nights. Arthur wondered, how do people decide if they should go to the bar or not? He imagined that there were one hundred citizens of Santa Fe who liked Irish music, and that each week they each tried to predict if the El Farol would be crowded. If they thought it was going to be crowded, specifically that more than sixty people would go to the bar, then they would stay at home, but if they thought it was not going to be crowded, then they would go to the El Farol. Assuming that the attendance information at the bar each week was readily available, but that each citizen could only remember a limited number of weeks of the attendance, Arthur hypothesized that one way to model this situation would be to give each agent a bag of strategies. Each of these strategies would be some rule of thumb about what the attendance was that week, e.g., "twice last week's attendance," "half the attendance of two weeks ago," or "an average of the last three weeks attendance." Each agent had a group of these strategies, and he would see how well these strategies would work had he used them in the previous weeks. The agents would use whichever strategy would have worked the best to predict this coming week's attendance, and they would decide whether to attend the bar based on this prediction. When Arthur wrote this up as an agent-based model and examined the results, he found that the average attendance at the bar was around 60. So despite all of the agents using different strategies and not having perfect information, they managed to optimally utilize the bar as a resource.

This model is available in the NetLogo models library under Sample Models > IABM Textbook > Chapter Three > El Farol (*Rand & Wilensky, 2007*; http://ccl.northwestern.edu/netlogo/models/ELFarol). This model has a few controls. You can adjust the MEMORY-SIZE of the agents, which controls how many weeks of attendance they remember. You can also change the NUMBER-STRATEGIES, which is the number of strategies each agent has in its bag of strategies. Finally, you can adjust the OVERCROWDING-THRESHOLD, which is the number of agents needed to make the bar crowded. If you

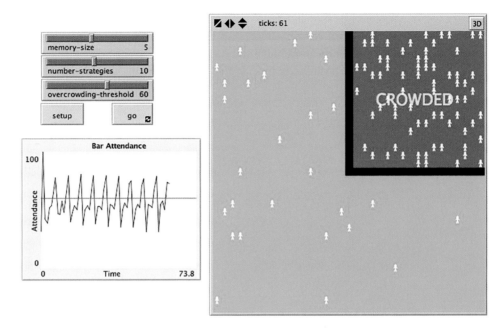

Figure 3.22
The El Farol model. Rand & Wilensky (2007). http://ccl.northwestern.edu/netlogo/models/ElFarol.

run the model as is, you will see the agents moving back and forth from the bar (the blue area) to their homes (green area), and the attendance is plotted on the left. The Interface tab of the model can be seen in figure 3.22.

First Extension: Color Agents That Are More Successful Predictors
The original model tells you how many agents are attending the bar, and you can get the visual reference of them moving to and from the bar, but there is nothing in this model to indicate which agents are better at choosing good times to attend the bar. Are some agents better at deciding when the bar will not be crowded than others? In order to find this out, we first need each agent to keep track of how often they go to the bar when it is not crowded; to do this, we add a property to each agent. We will modify the turtles' properties to add one additional item, REWARD:

```
turtles-own [
    strategies        ;; list of strategies
    best-strategy ;; index of the current best strategy
    attend?               ;; true if the agent currently plans to attend the bar
    prediction        ;; current prediction of the bar attendance
    reward                ;; the amount that each agent has been rewarded
]
```

We are calling this new property REWARD, since the agents get rewarded if they attend the bar when it is not crowded. Now we have to initialize this property, since each agent will start with reward of 0. To do this we modify the create turtles part of the SETUP procedure, to initialize the REWARD to 0:

```
;; create the agents and give them random strategies
create-turtles 100 [
    set color white
    move-to-empty-one-of home-patches
    set strategies n-values number-strategies [random-strategy]
    set best-strategy first strategies
    set reward 0
    update-strategies
]
```

We also need to update the reward whenever the agent goes to the bar and it is not crowded. If we look at the GO procedure there is some code that determines if the bar is overcrowded or not and, if it is, the word CROWDED is displayed on a patch in the bar:

```
if attendance > overcrowding-threshold [
    ask crowded-patch [ set plabel "CROWDED" ] ;; label the bar as crowded
]
```

We want to update the reward of turtles who attend the bar when this condition is not true, so we can make this IF statement, an IFELSE statement, and then in the ELSE part of the IFELSE we can ask all the turtles who attended the bar to increase their reward:

```
ifelse attendance > overcrowding-threshold [
    ask crowded-patch [ set plabel "CROWDED" ]
]
[   ;; if the bar is not overcrowded, reward the turtles that are attending
    ask turtles with [ attend? ] [
        set reward reward + 1
    ]
]
```

Now that we have given rewards to agents attending the bar when it is uncrowded, the final step is to modify the visualization to display these rewards appropriately. One way to do that is to give each agent a different color based on how much reward it has accumulated. To make sure that we can keep track of relative differences in the model, we are going to color the agents relative to the maximum reward obtained. This means that we need to recolor every agent not just the ones that have gathered new rewards this time step.

If you look farther up in the GO procedure you will find some code where we ask each agent to predict the attendance that week. This is a good place to have the agents update their color. NetLogo has a command called SCALE-COLOR that allow you to do this, we can set each agent's color to a shade of a color based on their reward. The SCALE-COLOR primitive takes four inputs: (1) a base color, which we will make red, (2) the variable that we are linking the color to, REWARD in this case, (3) a first range value, in this case we set it to slightly more than the maximum reward so far, and (4) a second range value, which we set to 0. If the first range value for SCALE-COLOR is less than the second one, then the larger the number of the linked variable the lighter the color will be. If the second range value is less than the first one (as it is in this case), then the large the number of the linked variable, the darker the color will be. In this model, we set the first value to be the larger of the two so that everyone starts as white, and then turns a darker color as they accumulate rewards. This makes the model more consistent with the basic version, where all the agents are white:

```
ask turtles [
      set prediction predict-attendance best-strategy sublist history 0 memory-size
      ;; set the Boolean variable
      set attend? (prediction <= overcrowding-threshold)
      set color scale-color red reward (max [ reward ] of turtles + 1) 0
   ]
```

In this case, the darkest agents will be the one with the lowest reward, and the lightest agents will be the ones with the most reward (see figure 3.23).

Second Extension: Average, Min, and Max Rewards

The first extension enables us to visually see which agents are doing better at going to the bar when it is not crowded. However, we do not have any hard numbers for the agents. We could simply inspect each agent by right clicking on it and selecting inspect agent. This would enable us to see the reward for each agent, but a better way might be to constantly display some information about the agents. We can do this by using monitors, which display values about the agent-based models.

To begin with we add a monitor to the Interface tab. In the first monitor, we can calculate the maximum reward collected by any agent. In the reporter area of the monitor editing window, we can put the following code snippet:

```
max [ reward ] of turtles
```

We can also give this monitor the name "Max Reward." After this we can add another monitor for the minimum reward with the following code:

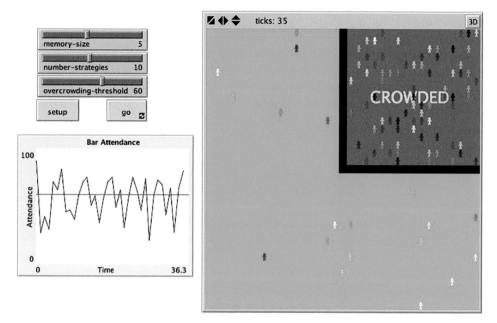

Figure 3.23
El Farol model: first extension.

```
min [ reward ] of turtles
```

And give this monitor the name "Min Reward." Finally, we can create a third monitor and calculate the average or mean reward using the following code:

```
mean [ reward ] of turtles
```

We can give this monitor the name "Avg. Reward." The model interface window now should look like figure 3.24. When we run this model we now get data on the average, maximum, and minimum rewards over time. It quickly becomes apparent that though both the average and maximum reward increase over time, the max reward grows faster than the average reward meaning that some agents do better and better as time goes on. Though this extension did not take much coding, it gives you information and insight into what is going on in the model that was not available before.

Third Extension: Histogram Reward Values
The second extension provides more data about how the agents in the model are doing, but this data has been aggregated so it is not obvious how many agents occupy each reward

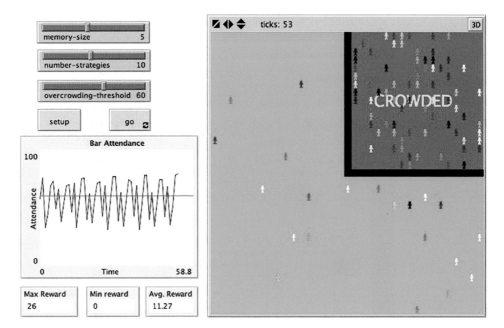

Figure 3.24
El Farol model: second extension.

level. For example, are the agents distributed uniformly across reward levels or are many agents at the minimum value and many agents at the maximum value with few agents in between? To find out an answer to this question, we are going to add another plot to the El Farol model. This plot will be a histogram of the distribution of rewards. This is similar to the plot we created in chapter 2 for the Simple Economy model, but in this model we will need to use the plot widget's "Plot update commands" feature.

To do this we first need to create a new plot in the Interface tab. In the configuration for this plot, we can give the plot the name "Reward Distribution," and change the Mode of the pen to "Bar" by clicking on the pencil in the first row of the Plot pens table. We tell the pen to display a histogram of the distribution by putting the following code in "Pen update commands."

```
histogram [ reward ] of turtles
```

This tells the pen to display a histogram of the REWARDs of the turtles. If we ran the model in this state, we would see a histogram drawn. However, the axes of the plot would not update correctly. Thus, we must enter the following under "Plot setup commands."

Figure 3.25
El Farol model: reward plot properties.

```
set-plot-y-range 0 1
set-plot-x-range 0 (max [ reward ] of turtles + 1)
```

These commands are run every time the plot is updated. They set the X and the Y range of the plot window to reflect the current values that we are plotting. By setting the Y-range to 1, we are letting NetLogo automatically decide how to increase this range if it needs to in order to show all the data. (See figure 3.25.)

As you run the model over time, you will see it start out similar to a normal distribution, but the distribution will quickly change with a few groups of individuals maintaining large rewards and many more having a lower reward. This lends credence to the hypothesis that there are a few agents that achieve a high reward level, but then there is a large gap between

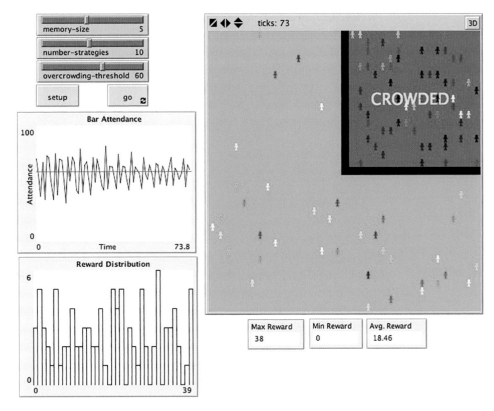

Figure 3.26
El Farol model: third extension.

these high achieving agents, and the majority of agents, which achieve more average reward levels. (See figure 3.26.)

Summary of the El Farol Model

In this section, we have discussed how we can modify the El Farol model so that it provides more data than the original version. In the first extension we provided an agent visualization that helped us to visualize the diversity in the success of the agents. In the second extension, we provided numerical output of the minimum, maximum and average reward values of the agent via monitors. Finally, in the third extension we created a histogram of that data which gives us a richer understanding of the underlying distribution if rewards per agent. These three output methods provide a richer view of how the El Farol Bar model works. If we had just been looking at the average attendance over time, it would not have become clear that some agents are doing very well and other agents are not.

A natural next question would be, "Why are some agents doing much better than others?" One thought would be that the agents that are doing well have a set of strategies that allow them to routinely outperform the other agents. We could look at these strategies and see how different they are from the strategies of agents that are not doing well. It may also be the case that agents who are doing extremely well are switching strategies more often or less often than agents who are not doing well, so that is another hypothesis that could be investigated. These further extensions are left as an exercise for the reader.

Advanced Modeling Applications

The El Farol model has been investigated in many different ways. Partially because it is an exciting model in that it combines both ABM and machine learning (Rand, 2006; Rand & Stonedahl, 2007). Machine learning enables the creation of powerful agent-based models where the agents not only change their actions over time, but also their strategies, i.e., the agents change the way they decide to take actions. We will discuss machine learning in more depth in chapter 5. The El Farol model has also been idealized into the Minority Game (Challet, Marsili & Zhang, 2004), which has been studied by physicists and economists because it provides insights into complex systems. For instance, both El Farol and the Minority Game can be seen as a crude approximation for financial markets. In some sense, if everyone else in a financial market is selling, you want to be buying, and if everyone else is buying then you want to sell; being in the minority is usually a good way to make money.

The El Farol model is also one example of an economic model. Another early agent-based economic model was the Artificial Stock Market developed by a group of Santa Fe Institute researchers (Arthur et al., 1997). This model attempted to simulate the stock market and allowed researchers to investigate how investors affect phenomena like booms and busts in the market. There are several other economic models in the NetLogo models library, such as the Oil Cartel model and the Root Beer Supply Chain (see figure 3.27).[7] Both of these models are interesting because they make use of the HubNet facility that is also provided with NetLogo. HubNet (*Wilensky & Stroup, 1999c*) is a NetLogo feature that enables Participatory Simulations, which is a simulation method where humans control agents in an agent-based model (see chapter 8 for more information on participatory simulations). This gives humans the ability to mix with nonhuman agents and to gain a deeper understanding of how their decisions affect and are constrained by a complex system.

After extending four NetLogo models, you should have the tools to extend many other NetLogo models. In the Fire model extensions and in the DLA extensions, we have seen that it is often useful to extend a model by replacing deterministic rules by probabilistic rules. Conversely, as we saw in modeling wind and long distance transmission in the Fire model, it is sometimes useful to replace a probabilistic rule with an agent-based mechanism that generates the probabilities. And with each change to the model, we need to consider

---

7. *Maroulis & Wilensky (2004).* http://ccl.northwestern.edu/netlogo/models/HubNetOilCartel.

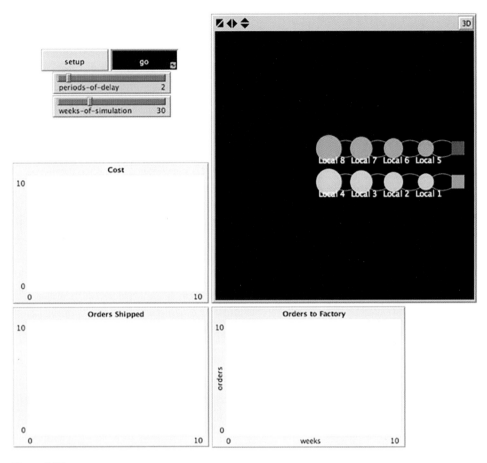

Figure 3.27
NetLogo HubNet Root Beer Game model. (*Wilensky & Stroup 2003*). http://ccl.northwestern.edu/netlogo/models/
HubNetRootBeerGame.

whether we also need to design a new metric for measuring model performance. In the DLA model we saw that it can be useful to explore the effect of different rules. We also explored the effect of different starting and stopping conditions for that model. In the Segregation model, we explored changing global parameters, such as %-SIMILAR-WANTED to heterogeneous agent-level properties, and different possible numerations of the agent-classes, starting with Schelling's two ethnicities to multiple ethnicities. In addition, we looked at heterogeneity not just in agent properties, but also in agent-rules as some agents actively seek diversity. In the El Farol model we extended the model by having it provide us with more data, in the form of richer visualizations, numerical values, and information about the distribution of agent properties in the populations.

Conclusion

We have illustrated how to extend four different models, each in three different ways, and we have explored how these models relate to some of the key concepts of ABM. At this point you should have the tools and capabilities to start modifying models that you are interested in exploring on your own. You can go a long way in agent-based modeling using this approach. However, you may become interested in building a model that differs significantly from any extant model, and, in this case, the best solution will be to build your own new model from scratch. This is what we will discuss in the next chapter.

Explorations

1. Modify the Fire Simple model to use the fire-patches reporter.
2. Modify the Segregation Simple model to use two new reporters.
3. Write a reporter procedure for the Segregation model that reports the agentset of unhappy turtles. Write a second reporter that reports a statistic from the first reporter.
4. Write a reporter procedure that reports an agentset of all unhappy turtles. Then write another reporter that reports the average of number of similar neighbors for unhappy turtles. Can you use the first reporter as part of the code in your second reporter?
5. Write a reporter for the Simple Economy model from chapter 2 that reports when the wealth distribution reaches a stationary distribution.
6. We have seen that the Fire Simple model is based on a theory known as percolation that explains how less dense substances are able to make progress through more dense substances. One particular case where this is both interesting and potentially profitable is oil percolation. How can you change the Fire Simple model to be a model of oil percolation?
7. The Segregation model is overly simplified, partially because of the modeling resources that Schelling had access to at the time. Nonetheless, the model offers some strong lessons even though there are many mechanisms of housing selection that are left out. List three additional mechanisms/factors that could be included in the Segregation model, and give pros/cons for their inclusion. How do you think Schelling might have decided to include in the model and what not to include? When is it better to leave parts of a real world system out in order to emphasize other aspects?
8. *Ants with multiple pheromones* As mentioned in its Info tab, the Ants model focuses on the problem of food foraging, and assumes that ants can always find their own way directly back to the nest using a perfectly distributed predefined nest-scent gradient, once they have found the food. To make the model more physically plausible, change it so that the nest-scent is a new kind of pheromone that is released by ants for some limited time period after they have left the nest. This nest-scent pheromone should diffuse and evaporate just like the food-carrying pheromone does.

9. *Adding agent types* In the Disease Solo model in the Biology section of the NetLogo models library there is no way for an agent to recover after they have become infected with a disease. Add doctors to the model that wander around and cure the sick patients. How does this affect the results?

10. *Docking percolation and fire* Often when looking at the Fire model we ask what density of trees is necessary to reach the right side of the screen. We can ask the same question about the porosity value in the Percolation model and whether or not the oil in that model reaches the bottom of the screen. Modify the size of the world in the Percolation model so that it is similar to the Fire Simple model. What values of porosity do you need to get to the bottom of the screen? What values of tree density do you need to get to the right side of the screen in Fire? Are these values the same? If not can you explain why they might be different? If they are the same can you explain why that is?

11. *Making sparks probabilistic* Right now in the Fire Simple model as we extended it, sparks from fires always occur when a new fire is started. Modify this so that whether sparks are generated is probabilistic in the same way that the fire spread was made probabilistic in the first extension. How does this modify the behavior of the model?

12. *Random location of sparks* After the third extension in the Fire model, sparks are generated deterministically in the same place every time. This does not seem realistic, since real sparks probably jump to random nearby locations. Modify the Fire model so this is the case. How does this change the behavior of the model? Modify your model further by representing the sparks as turtles that can be visualized.

13. *Phase transitions and tipping points* Phase transitions and the related idea of tipping points occur in many different systems, where a small change in one parameter causes a large change in an output variable. The Fire Simple model (and percolation models in general) is an example of this. Name some other phenomena where phase transitions occur. Choose one of these phenomena and describe how you would build an agent-based model of this phenomenon.

14. In the original Fire Simple model, when the density is set to 50 percent, there are roughly an equal number of green patches (trees) and black patches (empty space). Many people guess that at that density the fire would have a good chance of spreading a lot. What stops the fire from spreading at this density?

15. In extension 1 of the Fire Simple model, there are two parameters governed by sliders, DENSITY and PROBABILITY-OF-SPREAD. How do these two interact with regard to a critical spread of the fire?

16. The original Fire Simple model has each patch check its four neighbors in the cardinal directions. Modify it so that it checks all eight of its Moore neighbors. How does this affect the spread of the fire? Is there still a critical density for the forest fire spread? If so, what is it?

17. In the Fire Simple model, the fire is initialized on the left edge of the view. Modify it so that it starts at a single random location. Can you redefine criticality under these

conditions? What is the critical threshold for spread under these conditions and with your definition of criticality?

18. Open the Sandpile model from the Chemistry and Physics section of the NetLogo models library. This model, originally developed by Bak, Teng, and Weisenfeld (1987), was the first model in which self-organizing criticality was presented. The white flashes help you distinguish successive avalanches. They also give you an idea of how big each avalanche was. Most avalanches are small. Occasionally a much larger one happens. Describe how it is possible that adding one grain of sand at a time can cause so many squares to be affected. Can you predict when a big avalanche is about to happen? What do you look for?

19. In the Sandpile model, the sand grains are distributed, one to each neighbor. Modify the model so that grains are distributed to neighbors randomly. How does this change the model behavior?

20. The Sandpile model exhibits characteristics commonly observed in complex natural systems, such as self-organized criticality, fractal geometry, 1/f noise, and power laws. These concepts are explained in more detail in Per Bak's book (1996). Add code to the model to measure these characteristics.

21. In the Sandpile model, try coloring each patch based on how big the avalanche would be if you dropped another grain on it. To do this, make use of the *push-n* and *pop-n* procedures so that you can get back to the distribution of grains before calculating the size of the avalanche.

22. In the last extension to the Segregation model we added a %-DIFFERENT-WANTED parameter that was a global variable for all agents. Modify this parameter so that each agent can have a different %-DIFFERENT-WANTED, similar to how we modified the %-SIMILAR-WANTED in the second extension. How does this change the results of the model?

23. In the Segregation model, the agents look to their neighborhood composition to decide if they are happy. Can you make the size of shape of the neighborhood a parameter? How does this change the results of the model?

24. In the Segregation model as we have extended it, agents can have different levels of %-SIMILAR-WANTED, and they also have a %-DIFFERENT-WANTED parameter, but these variables control all of the agents in similar ways. What if there are two kinds of agents, some who only seek diversity and some who only seek similarity? Modify this model so that this is the case. How does this change affect the results of the model?

25. *Modeling urban form* We have discussed how the Segregation model is one approach to modeling urban form. There are many different ABMs that capture various aspects of the creation of urban patterns. In NetLogo, the Urban Suite of models has several examples of this. Open the Path Dependence model in the Urban Suite and examine it. Modify the Path Dependence model to include elements of Schelling's segregation model. Give each

agent in the Path Dependence model a threshold of similarity and different colors in addition to its other properties. Have the agents move if they get unhappy with the distribution of colors in their current patch. How does this change the results of the original Path Dependence model?

26. The DLA Simple model often winds up with long, tendril-like particle traces. Why does this occur? Why does this pattern change when you make the decision to stick or not to stick probabilistically as we did in the second extension?

27. Modify the DLA Simple model so that it can have multiple colors of particles.

28. In the second extension of DLA Simple, we make the probability of sticking dependent on the number of neighbors. We accomplished this by multiplying the probability of sticking by the fraction of neighbors that are green. Is this modeling choice realistic for DLAs? Propose and defend another way of modeling the changing probability.

29. In El Farol Extension 1, we modify the color based on reward with the agents starting as white and becoming darker as they accumulate rewards. Can you modify this code to use a different color? Or can you modify it so the agents start out dark and become lighter over time? Is there some other visual way to indicate this reward?

30. In El Farol Extension 2, we display the Min./Max./Avg. Rewards, but these statistics are mainly used for a normal distribution. What should you display if you expected the rewards were not normally distributed? Modify the model to display some additional statistics about the reward distribution.

31. In El Farol Extension 3, we now graph the actual award distribution using a histogram. Another common way of displaying wealth distributions like this is to use a cumulative distribution function, where the y-value at any point is equal to the accumulation of the number of individuals with an x-value less than or equal to the current x-value. In other words, this graph would display how many agents have less than or equal to that much reward. Can you modify the model to add this graph instead of the histogram?

32. In the El Farol model, the weights that determine each strategy are randomly generated. Try altering the weights so that they only reflect a mix of the following agent strategies:

  (a) always predict the same as last week's attendance
  (b) an average of the last several week's attendance
  (c) the same as two weeks ago
  Can you think of other simple strategies that the agents could use?

33. Open the Rope model from the Chemistry and Physics section of the NetLogo models library. This model simulates a wave moving along a rope. The right end of the rope (shown in blue) is fixed to a wall. The left end of the rope (shown in green) provides an input, moving up and down in a sinusoidal motion. This creates a wave that travels along the rope. Change the right end of the rope so that it moves freely, rather than being fixed. How does that change the behavior of waves in the rope?

34. Open the Wandering Letters model from the Computer Science section of the NetLogo models library. This model illustrates how to build a word processor where each of the letters acts independently. Each letter knows only which letter comes before it and how long its word is. When the letters or margins are moved, the letters find their own ways back to their proper locations. Can you extend the model so the user can type his/her own message? You might want to use the user-input primitive for this.

35. Open the NetLogo Flocking model from the Biology section of the models library, which shows emergent rules for generating bird flocks. Can you add a predator bird that changes the other birds' behavior?

36. Choose any model from the Sample Models section of the models library and modify the rules for its agents. Please avoid the Games folder, the Optical Illusions folder, and the System Dynamics folder when you choose. If you choose Fire, DLA or Segregation, make sure your modifications are substantially different than any in the textbook. This should be a more substantial modification than the modifications we did in this chapter. Make sure that the modified model shows some interesting new emergent behavior. Write a short description of the rule changes and include a justification for why this model extension makes sense, and add it as a new section (EXTENSION JUSTIFICATION) to the model's Info tab. Describe how the behavior of the modified model differs from the original.

37. Create a simple model that includes some agents, a rule for birth of agents (see *hatch* primitive) and a rule for death of agents (see *die* primitive). It is often useful to include a rule for agent movement. The agents can be anything—animals, particles, organizations, etc. Can you find rules that have interesting behavior? Create a SETUP button to initialize your model and a GO button to run it. In your write-up of the model, make sure to *explicitly* describe the rules the agents are following. Try running the model in different ways. What set of parameters gives you the most interesting behavior? Use a text-based pseudo-code format to describe the rules.

38. In chapter 2, we looked at the cellular automata models Life Simple and Sample Models > Computer Science > Cellular Automata CA 1D Elementary. The first of these shows a simple 2D CA. The second shows a one-dimensional CA with its time evolution displayed in the second dimension. Create your own cellular automaton model. Decide on a dimension of the CA (If you like, you can use NetLogo 3D and explore a 3D CA). Decide on the radius of the CA neighborhood. Decide on either a synchronous or asynchronous update scheme. Give the CA at least three distinct states. Fill in a section of the info window that describes the rules for your CA. In another section of the info window, describe some interesting behavior of your CA.

4 Creating Agent-Based Models

If you didn't grow it, you didn't explain it.

—Josh Epstein (1999)

In a minute there is time for decisions and revisions which a minute will reverse.

—T. S. Eliot (from "The Love Song of J. Alfred Prufrock," 1920)

What I cannot create, I do not understand.

—Richard Feynman (as seen on his blackboard and attributed by Hawking, 2001)

In the previous two chapters, we had our first taste of working with agent-based modeling code, writing simple models, examining model code, and extending it. One can accomplish a lot by working with publicly available models and modifying and extending them. Even in the most advanced ABM models one can often find code snippets borrowed from other models. However, eventually you will want to design and build your own model from the ground up. This chapter is intended to take you from the first step of devising a question or area you want to explore, all the way through designing, and building your model, to refining your question and revising your model, to analyzing your results and answering your question. This sequence is presented here in linear order, but in reality these steps fold back on each other and are part of an iterative exploration and refinement of the model and motivating question.

We will explore all of this within the context of a particular model, but at the same time we will discuss general issues related to model authoring and model design. To facilitate this process, this chapter is broken into three main sections: (1) *Designing your model* will take you through the process of determining what elements to include in your model, (2) *Building your model* will demonstrate how to take a conceptual model and create a computational object, and (3) *Examining your model* will address how to run your model, create some results, and analyze those results to provide a useful answer to your motivating question.

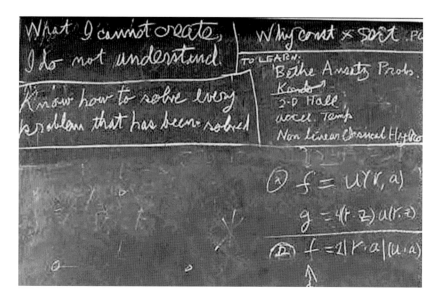

Figure 4.1
From the physicist Richard Feynman's blackboard at the time of his death.

Throughout this chapter we will be designing, building, and examining a simple model of an ecological system. The basic question that we will be addressing is: "How do the population levels of two habitat-sharing animal species change over time?" For our purposes in this chapter, we will call this model the Wolf Sheep Simple model. Though we will discuss this model in the context of two biological species, the model could be generalized to other situations such as companies competing for consumers, electoral parties competing for votes, or viruses evolving in a computer system. More important, the components that we will be developing in this model are basic components utilized in most ABMs.

Designing Your Model

There are many ways of designing an agent-based model.[1] Which you choose will depend on many factors including the type of phenomenon to be modeled, your level of knowledge of the content domain, your comfort with NetLogo coding and your personal modeling style.

---

1. As mentioned in chapter 1, a model can be either the conceptual/textual description of a process or the implemented software-based description of the model. In this chapter we will use the word *model* to describe either concept, but when it is necessary to distinguish between them we will describe the textual description as a conceptual model.

We consider two major categories of modeling: *phenomena-based modeling* and *exploratory modeling*. In *phenomena-based modeling*, you begin with a known target phenomenon. Typically, that phenomenon has a characteristic pattern, known as a *reference pattern*. Examples of reference patterns might include common housing segregation patterns in cities, spiral-shaped galaxies in space, leaf arrangement patterns on plants, or oscillating population levels in interacting species. The goal of phenomena-based modeling is to create a model that will somehow capture the reference pattern. In ABM, this translates to finding a set of agents, and rules for those agents, that will generate the known reference pattern. Once you have generated the reference pattern you have a candidate explanatory mechanism for that pattern and may also vary the model parameters to see if other patterns emerge, and perhaps try to find those patterns in data sets or by conducting experiments. You can also use phenomena-based modeling with other forms of modeling, such as equation-based modeling. In equation-based modeling, this would mean writing equations that will give rise to the reference pattern.

The second core modeling form is *exploratory modeling.* This form is perhaps less common in equational contexts than it is in ABM. In exploratory modeling with ABM, you create a set of agents, define their behavior, and explore the patterns that emerge. One might explore them solely as abstract forms, much like Conway and Wolfram did with cellular automata as we read in chapter 2. But to count as modeling, we must note similarities between the behavior of our model and some phenomena in the world (just as patterns we saw generated by cellular automata in chapter 2 resembled patterns on shells). We then refine our model in the direction of perceived similarities with these phenomena and converge toward an explanatory model of some phenomenon.

Another distinction in modeling methodology is to what degree we specify a question to be answered by a model. At one end of the spectrum, we formulate a specific research question (or set of questions) such as "How does a colony of ants forage for food?" or "How does a flock of geese fly in a V-shape?" At the other end, we may only begin with a sense of wanting to model ants or bird behavior, but without a clear question to be answered. As we explore the model design space, we will gradually refine our question to one that can be addressed by a specific model.

Yet a third dimension is the degree to which the process of designing the conceptual model is combined with coding your model. In some cases, it is advisable to work out the entire conceptual model design in advance of any coding of the model. This is referred to as *top-down* design. In a top-down design, the model designer will have worked out the types of agents in the model, the environment they reside in, and their rules of interaction before writing a single line of code. In other cases, the conceptual model design and the coding of the model will coevolve, each influencing the evolution of the other. This is often referred to as *bottom-up* design. In bottom-up design, you choose a domain or phenomenon of interest with or without specifying a formal question. Using this approach, you would then start writing code relevant to that domain, building the conceptual model from the bottom up, accumulating the necessary mechanisms, properties and entities, and perhaps formulating some formal research questions along the way. For example, in a bottom-up design, you might start with a question about how an economic market would evolve, code some behaviors of buyers and sellers and, in so doing, realize you'll need to add brokers as agents in the model.

These model design dimensions can be combined in various arrangements. You could start with a very specific research question and design all the agents and rules before coding, or you can start with some agents, play with various rules for them and only get to your modeling question near the end of the process.

In practice, model authors rarely use exclusively one style when building their models, but use some combination of the styles, and often switch back and forth between the forms and styles as their research needs and interests change. In cases where a scientist is collaborating with a programmer who will code the model, the top-down design style is usually the one employed as it separates the roles of the two team members. NetLogo was designed to make it easier for scientists to code their own models. Often, as modelers become more comfortable with coding, they use the NetLogo code as a tool to build their conceptual model. In this chapter, we will present our model building using a mixture of the approaches, but for clarity of the exposition, we will emphasize the top-down approach.

The top-down design process starts by choosing a phenomenon or situation that you want to model or coming up with a question that you want to answer, and then designing agents and rules of behavior that model the elements of the situation. You then refine that *conceptual model* and continue to revise it until it is at a fine enough level of detail that you can see how to write the code for the model.

Throughout the design process there is one major principle that we will use. We call this the *ABM design principle*: Start simple and build toward the question you want to answer.[2] There are two main components of this principle. The first is to begin with the simplest set of agents and rules of behavior that can be used to explore the system you want to model. This part of the principle is illustrated by a quote from Albert Einstein, "The supreme goal of all theory is to make the irreducible basic elements as simple and as few as possible without having to surrender the adequate representation of a single datum of experience" (1933). Or in another phrase he is reputed to have said: "Everything should be made as simple as possible, but not simpler." In the case of ABM, this means making your model as simple as possible given that it must provide you with a

---

2. This design principle is stated from a top-down perspective of model building. The bottom-up variant is not that different: Start simple and be alert to possibly interesting questions, increasing the complexity of the model to pursue these questions. In a bottom-up process, you start with a domain or phenomenon of interest and build a very simple model related to that domain or several components that might be useful for investigating the phenomenon. You then explore the simple model or model components, looking for promising directions. The bottom-up perspective does not require a driving question in advance; the question and the model coevolve, changes in one driving changes in the other.

stepping-stone toward your final destination. Second, always have your question in mind, which means not adding anything to your model that does not help you in answering your question. The statistician George Box provides a quote that illustrates this point, "All models are wrong, but some models are useful" (1979). What Box meant was that all models are by necessity incomplete because they simplify aspects of the world. However, some of them are useful because they are designed to answer particular questions and the simplifications in the model do not interfere with obtaining that answer.

This core ABM design principle is useful in several ways. First, it reminds us to examine every candidate model agent and agent-rule and eliminate it if progress can be made without it. It is not uncommon for novice modelers to build a model in which certain components have no effect whatsoever. By starting small and slowly adding elements to your model, you can make sure that these extraneous components never get developed. By examining each additional component as to whether it is needed to answer the research question you are pursuing, you reduce the temptation to, paraphrasing William of Occam, "multiply entities unnecessarily." In so doing, you reduce the chance of introducing ambiguities, redundancies, and inconsistencies into your model. Another virtue of the ABM design principle is that, by keeping the model simple, you make it both more understandable and easier to verify. *Verification* is the process of ensuring that a computational model faithfully implements its target conceptual model. A simpler conceptual model leads to a simpler model implementation, which makes it easier to verify the model. Starting simple and building up also facilitates the process of just-in-time results. At every point of the model development process, the model should be able to provide you with some answers to your research question. Not only does this help you make productive use of your model early on, but it also enables you to start questioning your model assumptions and examining its results early on in the modeling process. This can prevent you from going too far down an unproductive path. Fewer components also mean fewer combinations to test in order to develop a causal account of your results.

To apply our principle to the context of the Wolf Sheep Simple model, we need to start our design by reflecting on two habitat-sharing animal species and identifying simple agents and behaviors for our model. We will start by identifying a question we want to explore, which is required by the ABM design principle (top-down version). After that we will discuss what the agents in our models are and how they can act. Then we move on to the environment and its characteristics. As part of this process, we need to discuss what happens in an individual time step of the model. Finally, we discuss what measures we will be using to answer our question.

Choosing Your Questions

Choosing a question may seem to be a separate issue from model design. After all, the natural progression seems to be: *first* choose a question, and *second* build a model to answer that question. Sometimes, that may indeed be the procedure we follow, but in many instances we will need to refine our questions when we start to think about it in an agent-based way. Our original question for the Wolf Sheep Simple model was: "How do the population levels of two species change over time when they coexist in a shared habitat?" We will now evaluate whether this question is one that is amenable to ABM and refine our question within the ABM paradigm.

Agent-based modeling is particularly useful for making sense of systems that have a number of interacting entities, and therefore have unpredictable results. As we discussed in chapter 1, there are certain problems and questions that are more amenable to ABM solutions. If our primary question of interest violates our guidelines, it may be an indication that we should consider a different modeling method. For example, we might be interested in examining the dynamics of two very large populations under the assumption that the species are homogenous and well-mixed (no spatial component or heterogeneous properties) and that the population level of each species is simply dependent on the population level of the other species. If that is the case then we could have used an equation-based model instead of an agent-based model since EBM's work well for large homogeneous groups, and as we mentioned in chapter 0 there is a classic EBM for this situation known as the Lotka-Volterra differential equations (Lotka, 1925; Volterra, 1926). (Near the end of this chapter there will be additional discussion of the relative merits of using EBM versus ABM for ecological predation models.) ABM will be more useful to us if we are thinking of the agents as heterogeneous with spatial locations. This affects how we conceptualize the agents. One aspect of the animals that is likely to be relevant to our question is how they make use of their resources. Animals make use of food resources by converting them to energy hence we will want to make sure that our agents have different amounts of energy and different locations in the world. A third guideline is to consider whether the aggregate results are dependent on the interactions of the agents and on the interaction of the agents with their environment. For example, if one species is consuming another then the results will be dependent on agent interaction. Predator-prey interactions are usually set in rich environments. Keeping the ABM design principle in mind, we start with the simplest environment—we enrich the environment a little by going beyond just predators and prey and including resources from the environment that the lowest level prey species consume. Yet another guideline is that agent-based modeling is most useful for modeling time dependent processes. In the Wolf Sheep Simple model, our core interest lies in examining how population levels change over time. We might therefore refine our question to focus on conditions that lead to the two species coexisting together for some time. In this way our guidelines help us evaluate whether our question is well suited to ABM and, if so, to focus our question and conceptual model.

Having evaluated our question's suitability to ABM, we are now in position to state it more formally. "Can we find model parameters for two species that will sustain positive population levels in a limited geographic area when one species is a predator of the other and the second species consumes resources from the environment?" Now, keeping this question in mind, we can proceed to design the conceptual model.

A Concrete Example

Now that we have identified our research question in detail it can be useful to consider a particular context for this research question. Earlier, we discussed reference patterns as a source of phenomena-based agent-based models. Sometimes that reference pattern is the original inspiration for the model. Other times, as now, we have refined our research question enough that we seek out a reference pattern that will help us test whether our model is a valid answer to the question. In the case of the predator-prey relations, there is a famous case of cohabiting small predator-prey populations in a small geographic area. This is the case of fluctuating wolf and moose populations in Isle Royale, Michigan.

The wolves and moose of Isle Royale have been studied for more than five decades. This research represents the longest continuous study of any predator-prey system in the world. . . . Isle Royale is a remote wilderness island, isolated by the frigid waters of Lake Superior, and home to populations of wolves and moose. As predator and prey, their lives and deaths are linked in a drama that is timeless and historic. Their lives are historic because we have been documenting their lives for more than five decades. This research project is the longest continuous study of any predator-prey system in the world. (From the Wolves & Moose of Isle Royale Project Website, http://isleroyalewolf.org/)

Figure 4.2 shows the wolf and moose populations in Isle Royale from 1959 through 2009. This graph can serve as a reference pattern for our model. Our completed model

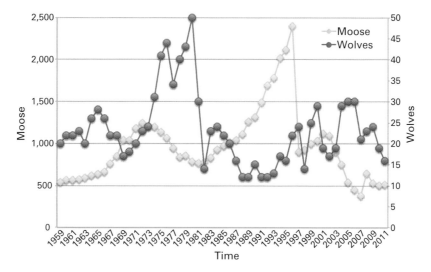

Figure 4.2
Five decades of fluctuating wolf and moose populations at Isle Royale. Note that when the wolf population peaks, the moose population is at a low point and, similarly, when the moose population peaks, the wolf population is at a low point.

will have to be able to generate a graph "similar" to this one to be a possible explanatory model of these phenomena. In general, this process is called *validation* and will be discussed in detail in chapters 7 and 8.

As we can see in the data from Isle Royale, the wolf and moose populations in Isle Royale have been sustaining themselves for more than fifty years without either species going extinct. The populations also exhibit a rough oscillation, with moose at a low when wolves peak and vice versa. This data can serve as a reference pattern for our phenomena-based modeling. It allows us to further refine our research question to this: "Can we find model parameters for two species that will sustain *oscillating* positive population levels in a limited geographic area when one species is a predator of the other and the second species consumes resources from the environment?"

In the models in this chapter, instead of modeling wolf and moose, we will model wolf and sheep. The wolf and moose data set is well established, but our goal in this chapter is not to match this particular data, but to introduce you to classic examples of predator-prey modeling and to try to reproduce the oscillating sustained pattern of population levels.

Choosing Your Agents

Now that we have identified and contextualized our driving research question, we can begin to design the components that will help us answer it. The first question we should ask ourselves is: What are the agents in the model? When designing our agents, we want to choose those components of our model that are autonomous and have properties, states, and behaviors that could possibly have bearing on our question. But we must be careful to avoid agent overload. Depending on the perspective one takes, almost any model component could be considered an agent. However, a model that is designed with an excess of agent types can quickly become unmanageable. When choosing what are to be the agents in a model, it is important to concentrate on those autonomous entities which are most relevant to our research question.

A related issue is the "granularity" of the agent. Every entity is composed of multiple smaller entities. What is the right level of entity to choose? Should our agent be molecules or atoms? Body organs or cells? Some agents can be treated as mass properties. If we want to model a field of grass, we might not want to model every blade of grass, but instead choose "clumps" of grass as our agents. It is important that the granularity of each agent be at roughly the same level. For instance in the temporal scale, if you are modeling the sheep actions at the level of days of activity, but the grass minute by minute, that can be difficult to reconcile. And in the physical scale, if there is more grass than the sheep can consume then you will not see many interesting behaviors since grass will not serve as a limiting condition.

If we suspect that, in the future, some model entities might need to become full agents, we can choose to design them as *proto-agents*. By the term proto-agent, we mean agents that do not have individual properties, states, or behaviors but instead inherit some or all of their characteristics from a global agent type. For example, in the Wolf Sheep Simple model we might desire to have a human hunter who interacts with the other two species. This hunter might simply eliminate a part of the populations every now and then. There is no need to build the hunter as a full agent at the start; instead we can create a simpler proto-agent that has the ability to kill off a random percentage of the population. Eventually, if needed, this hunter could become a full agent and have full properties and behavior just like any other agent. We discuss proto-agents further in chapter 5.

Given the preceding discussion, we start our Wolf Sheep Simple model design by choosing three agent types. We model the predators, which we will call wolves, and the prey, which we will call sheep, and the resources the sheep consume, grass. We could have added many other agents to this model. For example, we could model the hunter described above or the precipitation levels or soil nutrition. However, by choosing just wolves, sheep, and grass, we stick to the ABM design principle. We have the two simple mobile agent types, and one stationary agent type to model the environment, and those are the minimal set of agents necessary to answer our question of what parameters will allow two populations to coexist in a limited geographic area.

Choosing Agent Properties

Agents have properties that distinguish them from other agents. It is important to determine these properties in advance so we can conceptualize the agent and design the agents' interaction with each other and with the environment.

In the Wolf Sheep Simple model we give the sheep and wolves three properties each: (1) an energy level, which tracks the energy level of the agent, (2) a location, which is where in the geographic area the agent is, and (3) a heading, which indicates the direction the agent is currently moving or would be moving.[3] The energy property is not merely describing temporary energy (such as whether an animal is fresh or fatigued). Rather, "energy" incorporates some notion of the amount of "vitality" in a creature, abstracting away the messy details of metabolism, calorie storage, or starvation, and condensing it all into a single measure. We could add additional properties and some of them might be useful for future extensions. For instance, we could add a movement speed and allow different agents to move at different speeds, or an offense/defense capability that affects the ability of the individual to predate or resist predation. However, these additional properties

---

3. We also give the wolf and sheep agents shapes, and to all three agent types we give colors, which are not core to the behavioral rules for the ABM but are important for effective visualizations.

do not seem necessary to answer our simplest question, and thus we resist the temptation to include them unnecessarily.

If the sheep and the wolves have exactly the same properties, then what makes them different from each other? We will discuss this in the next section, where we talk about the behavior that each of these two agent types exhibit.

Choosing Environmental Characteristics and Stationary Agents   Now that we have the mobile agents and their behaviors defined, we can decide on the nature of the environment in which these mobile agents will live and how they can interact with that environment.

In the Wolf Sheep Simple model, the first obvious environmental attribute is the presence or absence of grass, since that is what the sheep consume. We could model many other attributes such as elevation, water, woodlands, and other features that might affect the movement of the animals or affect sheep predation. However, in keeping with our design principle, we start with an environment consisting of a large grassy field. We use the stationary patch agent types to model the grass. As mentioned, it would not make sense to model every blade of grass, so we model the grass by giving the patches a "grass amount" property that will have a numerical value. This is effectively using the patches to model clumps of grass, which is our stationary agent type. The numerical value of this property should be in proportion to the feeding behavior of the sheep, since that is how it will be used in the model. In other words, the granularity of this variable should be set appropriately as discussed above.

In order to avoid dealing with boundary conditions (such as wolves stepping beyond the bounds of the modeled world), the world will "wrap" horizontally and vertically, so a wolf stepping off the right edge of the world will appear on the left. This "torus-shaped" world topology is often convenient for ABMs, and is thus the default for new models in NetLogo. (Other topologies will be discussed in chapter 5.)

It is also worth noting that in some ABMs the environment also controls the birth and death processes of the agents. In this model birth and death will be modeled endogenously within the actions of the agents, but it is possible to simply have birth and death of agents controlled by the environment instead. This is a less "emergent" way of modeling life-cycles, but sometimes is a useful simplification.

Choosing Agent Behavior

In addition to designing the structure of the agents, it is important to determine what kind of behavior the agents can exhibit. These behaviors are necessary to describe how agents interact with each other and the environment.

In the Wolf Sheep Simple model, sheep and wolves share many common behaviors. They both have the ability to turn randomly, move forward, reproduce and die. However, sheep and wolves differ in that sheep have the ability to consume grass and wolves have the ability to consume sheep. This differentiates the two species/agent types from each other. Of course, once again there are many other behaviors we could prescribe for these agents. For instance, we could give sheep the ability to huddle in herds to defend against wolf attacks, or the ability to fight back. The wolves could have the ability to move at different speeds from a walk to a run or to chase sheep. Wolves and sheep also engage in a number of behaviors, such as sleeping, digesting food, and seeking shelter during a thunderstorm. However, again the behaviors we have described (moving, reproducing, eating, and dying) are reasonable choices for a simple model that can address our research question. For the grass clump agents, we give one simple behavior, the ability to grow.

Designing a Time Step   Now that we have established the basic components of the model, we can design the typical time step in the model. To do this we need to think through all of the behaviors that will be exhibited by the agents of our model and decide how they will perform these behaviors and in what order they should be performed. In the real world, animals behave concurrently, and time appears continuous. To build our ABM, we simplify by dividing time into discrete steps, and we further divide each step into serialized, ordered phases. By doing it this way, we are making an implicit assumption that having the agents use some order to perform their actions will not substantially affect our results. This is a working assumption and may need to be reexamined later. In general, determining the order in which agents exhibit behaviors can be tricky. We will discuss agent "scheduling" further in chapter 5.

In the Wolf Sheep Simple model, there are four basic animal behaviors (move, die, eat, reproduce) and one grass behavior (grow). Another working assumption we may make is that, given that we need an order, deciding which order the animals perform their behaviors can be arbitrary. Any order for the behaviors would be reasonable, so we arbitrarily choose an order, because it's much easier to work with (and debug) a fixed order of behaviors. We choose to order the behaviors as in the first sentence of this paragraph. We can check to make sure the order makes sense. Movement is the act of turning and then stepping forward. Since the *move* action changes the location of the agents and thus changes the local environment of each agent, it makes sense to move first. In the Wolf Sheep Simple model, movement costs energy and thus we schedule *death* next, because we should check to see if any of the agents expended so much energy while moving that they have no energy left. After that we schedule the agents to attempt to gain new energy by *eat*ing if there is something in their local environment that they can eat. Since they now have new energy the agents may be able to *reproduce* (which also requires energy). Thus, each agent checks to see if they have enough energy to create a new agent.[4] Finally,

---

4. This is a drastic simplification of biological reproduction! We have made the choice to simplify reproduction to asexual reproduction based on a working hypothesis that for the purposes of answering our question, the details of reproduction are not relevant.

since the model has done everything else, the grass agents *grow* before we cycle to the next movement step.

There are many alternative ways to set up this time step. The order that behaviors occur could be altered, and in some ABMs the order can significantly change results (Wilensky & Rand, 2007). However, in this case there is no obvious reason why changing the order would have a significant effect on the model, and the order is a logical one. We could also add additional steps to this large picture framework, for instance we could separate out the wolves and sheep and allow all the wolves to move before the sheep move. However, the order and steps presented above are logical and simple and provide a good starting point. We take note of the many working assumptions we make along the way, and, if necessary, this time step structure can be reexamined and revised in the future.

Choosing Parameters of the Model

We could decide to write one set of completely specified rules to control the behavior of all of these agents and their environmental interactions during a time step, but it makes more sense to create some parameters that enable us to control the model, so that we can easily examine different conditions. A next step is to define what attributes of the model we will be able to control through parameters.

There are several possible parameters of interest in the Wolf Sheep Simple model. For instance, we will want to be able to control the number of initial sheep and wolves. This will enable us to see how different values of the initial population levels affect the final population levels. Another factor to control is how much energy it costs an agent to move. Using this parameter, we can make the landscape more or less difficult to traverse, and thus simulate different types of terrain. Related to the cost of movement is the energy that each species gains from food. Thus, we choose to have parameters for controlling the energy gained from grass and the energy gained from sheep. Finally, since the sheep consume grass, in order to sustain the population over time we will want the grass to regrow. So we will need a parameter for the grass regrowth rate.

There are many other parameters that we could have included in this model. For instance, the parameters we chose are homogenous across the model. In other words, one sheep will gain the same from grass as any other sheep. However, we could make this model more heterogeneous by drawing the energy gain for each sheep from a normal distribution, and have two model parameters that control the mean and variance of the energy gain. We could also add parameters to control aspects that we are currently planning to specify as constant values in the code. For example, we did not create a parameter to control the speed of the agents. Having the ability to modify those speeds and (particularly the ratio between movement rates for wolves and sheep) might dramatically affect the model. However, guided by our ABM design principle, this complication does not seem necessary at this stage of the modeling process. Allowing different movement speeds for wolves and sheep is an expansion on this model that is left for the reader to explore. See the explorations listed at the end of this chapter.

Choosing Your Measures   If we had implemented all of the preceding components, then we would have a working model. However, we still would have no process for answering our question. For that purpose we need to decide what measures we will collect from the model. Creating measures can be very simple at times, but often some of the most interesting results of a model are not recognized until after the measures have been properly designed. When considering what measures to incorporate into your model it is useful to review the research question. It is advisable to include only the most relevant measures, because extraneous measures can overwhelm you with data and may also slow down model execution.

In the Wolf Sheep Simple model, the measures that are most relevant are the population counts of the wolf and sheep over time, since what we are interested in is what sets of parameters will enable us to sustain positive levels of both populations over time.

We could construct measures of much other data in this model, such as the amount of energy possessed by sheep or wolves on average. This might bear on our question, since it could indicate how likely the current populations are to persist, but it does not directly address the question so we do not include it here. Sometimes it is useful to include measures like this for debugging purposes. For example, if we saw that the energy levels of sheep were increasing even though there was no grass regrowing, then we would wonder if there was a bug in the section of the code where we converted grass to energy for the sheep.

Summary of the Wolf Sheep Simple Model Design

Now that we have gone through the major design steps, we can create a summary document that describes our model design. The Wolf Sheep Simple model can be described in the following way:

Driving Question Under what conditions do two species sustain oscillating positive population levels in a limited geographic area when one species is a predator of the other and the second species consumes limited but regenerating resources from the environment?

Agent Types Sheep, Wolves, Grass

Agent Properties Energy, Location, Heading (wolf and sheep), Grass-amount (grass)

Agent Behaviors Move, Die, Reproduce (wolf and sheep), Eat-sheep (wolf only), Eat-grass (sheep only), Regrow (grass)

Parameters Number of Sheep, Number of Wolves, Move Cost, Energy Gain From Grass, Energy Gain From Sheep, Grass Regrowth Rate
Time Step:
    1. Sheep and Wolves Move
    2. Sheep and Wolves Die
    3. Sheep and Wolves Eat
    4. Sheep and Wolves Reproduce
    5. Grass Regrows
Measures Sheep Population versus Time, Wolf Population versus Time

It is quite useful while designing a model to write notes to yourself, as we have done in this section. You will find these notes invaluable after you have left the model for a while, since you will be able to go back and recall why you made certain decisions and alternative choices that you considered. Also, for the purposes of explaining your model to others, it is very helpful to have such documentation about the model. Finally, we recommend that you date your notes as you create them so that you can track your model design process.

For instance, if you are using the top-down design process that we have just discussed, then you might look over the following set of questions and write down answers to them as a provisional guide for how to build your model:

1. What part of your phenomenon would you like to build a model of?
2. What are the principal types of agents involved in this phenomenon?
3. In what kind of environment do these agents operate? Are there environmental agents?
4. What properties do these agents have (describe by agent type)?
5. What actions (or behaviors) can these agents take (describe by agent type)?
6. How do these agents interact with this environment or each other?
7. If you had to define the phenomenon as discrete time steps, what events would occur in each time step, and in what order?
8. What do you hope to observe from this model?

A more bottom-up approach would not start with these questions. Instead, you might know only that you want to build some kind of ecological model and could begin by creating some sheep and have them spread out in the world. Next, you might think of and start implementing some behaviors for the sheep such as moving, taking steps, eating, reproducing and dying. In order for the sheep to eat, you might decide to add grass to the model. Having sheep eat grass provokes the question, "What eats sheep?" Therefore, you modify the model to include wolves, as predators for the sheep. This process allows the wolf sheep model to be designed and even implemented without first considering the final goal of the model.

Now that we have completed the initial design of the Wolf Sheep Simple model, the next step is to implement the model.

Building a Model   Having designed our conceptual model, we can begin the implementation process. In the model building process as well, we will continue to apply the ABM design principle. Even though our model as described is fairly simple, we will break this model down into a series of submodels that we will implement over five iterations. These submodels will all be capable of running on their own and will enable us to build the complete model in steps, checking our progress along the way and making sure that the model is working as we hoped it would work.

Many times, in agent-based models, the end results are not what we expect. This can be due to an error in model implementation. But often it is neither our implementation nor our conceptual model that is wrong, but rather our surprise stems from a core property of complex systems—emergent behavior, which, as we have seen, is notoriously difficult to predict. By building up our model gradually we can observe unusual behavior and more easily determine its cause than if we had built the model all at once. Thus, the ABM design principle still applies throughout the model implementation process as well.

First Version   What is the simplest form of our model that we could create that would exhibit some sort of behavior? One simplification that we can make from the total model is to only look at one species, and ignore the environment. Given these two simplifications, it seems that the simplest model would have some sheep wandering around on a landscape. To do this we create two procedures, a SETUP procedure, which creates the sheep, and a GO procedure that has them move.

The first thing we need to do is create a sheep *breed* in the NetLogo Code tab:

```
breed [ sheep a-sheep ]
```

This just says that a class of mobile agents (in NetLogo, turtles) called SHEEP exists. The plural form "sheep" is given first, followed by the singular form "a-sheep," which is a little awkward in the case of sheep. It will feel more natural when we add the "wolves"/"wolf" breed later. In your code, you will mostly need to use the plural form (SHEEP), but it is helpful to provide the optional singular form in the breed declaration as well, so that NetLogo can give you more meaningful error messages, among other things. One last thing to note is that even though we are creating SHEEP at this point, the agentset of TURTLES still exists. All mobile agents in a NetLogo model are TURTLES regardless of their breed. So if you want to ask all the moving agents to do something, i.e., both SHEEP and WOLVES, then you can ASK TURTLES. If you want to just ask the SHEEP, then you can ASK SHEEP, and if you want to just ask the WOLVES, then you can ASK WOLVES (once we create them).

After we have created the SHEEP breed, we can create the SETUP procedure:

```
;; this procedure sets up the model
to setup
    clear-all
    ask patches [ ;; color the world green
      set pcolor green
    ]
    create-sheep 100 [ ;; create the initial sheep
      setxy random-xcor random-ycor
      set color white
      set shape "sheep"
    ]
    reset-ticks
end
```

This SETUP procedure will end up being the longest procedure of the finished model, but its behavior is fairly straightforward. First, it clears the world. The *world* of the model is the representation of all the agents, including the mobile agents (e.g., turtles, sheep, wolves) as well as the stationary agents (e.g., patches, grass). As we saw in the previous chapters, the command CLEAR-ALL resets any variables in the model and readies it so that a new run can be executed. After this, all the patches are asked to set their patch color (PCOLOR) to green to represent grass. Even though our model does not yet include any grass properties nor any rules for sheep to interact with the grass, changing the color helps the visualization. Finally, we create one hundred sheep. When we create the sheep, we also give them some initial properties. We assign them a random x-coordinate and a random y-coordinate to spread them over the world. We then set their color to white and their shape to the "sheep" shape[5] so they look a little more like real sheep. The final line, RESET-TICKS, starts the NetLogo clock so the model is ready to run.

Documenting the procedures within your model (by using the semicolon to comment the code) is very useful. Any text written after a semicolon is ignored when the model is run; adding text in this way is called "commenting" your code. Without these comments, not only is it quite difficult for someone else to read your code, but it will also become more and more difficult, as time passes, for you to understand your own code. A model without comments (and other documentation) is not very useful, since it will be difficult for others to figure out what the model is trying to do.

After we have created the sheep, we go on to write a GO procedure to tell them how to behave. Looking back at our design document, one of the main behaviors the sheep exhibit is moving around, so we will have them do that. We break up the sheep movement

---

5. NetLogo has a default set of turtle shapes that is available to all models, and "sheep" is included in this. There is also an extensive library of additional shapes, which can be imported for the models use, or you can design your own custom shapes. See the "Turtle Shapes Editor" under the Tools menu.

into two parts, turning and moving forward. We create the procedures WIGGLE and
MOVE, which we define later.

```
to go
   ask sheep [
      wiggle ;; first turn a little bit in each direction
      move   ;; then step forward
   ]
   tick
end
```

This asks all of the sheep to perform a series of actions: WIGGLE, then MOVE. The
sheep will take their turns in random order, and each sheep will complete both actions
before the next sheep takes its turn. After all the sheep have finished, the TICK command
increments the model clock, indicating that one unit of time has passed. Of course, to
make the code work, we must define WIGGLE and MOVE. The sheep will execute both
of these procedures. As such, we document them as "sheep procedures," that is, procedures
that do not explicitly ask any agents but are written with the implicit assumption that the
calling procedure will ask the right set of agents to perform them.

```
;; sheep procedure, the sheep changes its heading
to wiggle
      ;; turn right then left, so the average direction is straight ahead
      right random 90
      left random 90
end

to move
      forward 1
end
```

The first procedure simply turns to the right a random amount between 0 and 90, and
then back to the left a random amount between 0 and 90. The idea behind this turning
behavior is to have the sheep change the direction they are heading, without bias toward
turning either left or right.[6] This type of randomized turning is very common in ABMs,
and could be called an ABM "idiom." In NetLogo, it is common to refer to this turning
behavior as "WIGGLE." The second procedure simply moves the sheep forward one unit.[7]

6. Technically, RIGHT 90 LEFT 90 causes the new heading of the turtle to be randomly drawn from a binomial
distribution, centered on the previous heading of the turtle. Qualitatively, this means that smaller turns (in either
direction) are more likely than large turns. A binomial distribution is similar to a normal distribution in this
respect.

7. Since the move procedure is just one command, we did not have to break it out into a separate procedure,
but because in our design we had included other effects of the movement, we anticipate the more complex move
procedure ahead by breaking it out at the outset.

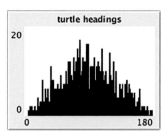

Figure 4.3
A plot of the headings of 1,000 turtles that have "wiggled." All turtles start at a heading of 90, and their headings after wiggling are distributed binomially around 90

As mentioned in the design section, the distance the sheep moves could later be controlled by a global parameter, but for now we will keep it to a constant single unit (the width of one patch). (See figure 4.3.)

You can go ahead and run this model right now. You can just type "setup" and then "go" in the command center.[8] To make this model easier to use, it helps to create GO and SETUP buttons in the model's Interface tab. In the GO button, we check the "forever" check box so that the GO procedure will indefinitely repeat. After this, your model should look like figure 4.4.

Second Version   Now that we have our sheep moving around, we have something we can see and we have a first verification that our model is working as we intended it to work. Next we need to consider what is the simplest extension that we can develop that follows our design. We have the sheep moving around but, in our first version, movement does not cost them anything. In the real world, movement does require energy. Therefore, the next step in our model development is to include a movement cost. Recall that we designed the sheep to have three properties: heading, location, and energy. The sheep in the first version of this model already have headings and locations—these properties are automatically provided to any NetLogo "turtle" agents. However, we have to define a new property (variable) for energy, which we can do by adding this code near the top of our model's procedures:

```
sheep-own [ energy ]     ;; sheep have an energy variable
```

8. As was explained in the NetLogo tutorials, the command center is where you can type single command lines to test their effects.

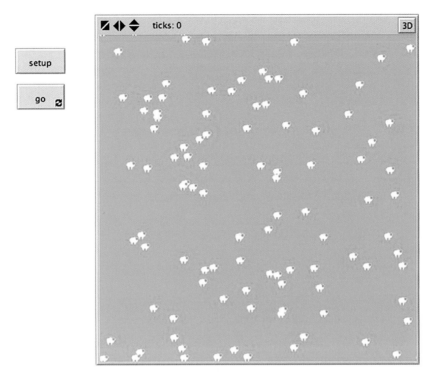

Figure 4.4
The first version of the Wolf Sheep Simple model. (See the supplementary materials.)

Just declaring that sheep have energy is not enough. We also need to initialize the energy variable and make it change when sheep move. While we are editing the code, we will also make it so that the number of sheep initially created is based on a NUMBER-OF-SHEEP slider on the model's Interface tab, rather than hard-coded to be 100. This will allow us to change the number of sheep in the model easily from the interface, because, as mentioned in the Design section earlier, the number of sheep is a model parameter that we would like to be able to manipulate. In creating the slider widget, we need to give it some properties, a minimum value for the NUMBER-OF-SHEEP initially created, a maximum number, and an increment, which is the amount the slider will change when you click on it. In this case, we can set the minimum number to 1 (since less than one sheep makes no sense), the maximum number to start with to 1,000 and the increment to 1, since it makes no sense to have e.g., 2.1 sheep. (See figure 4.5.)

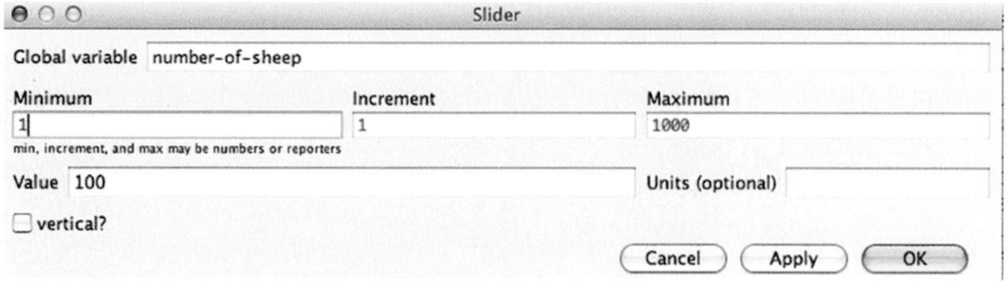

Figure 4.5
Setting up the NUMBER-OF-SHEEP slider.

The modified SETUP procedure is thus:

```
;; this procedure sets up the model
to setup
    clear-all
    ask patches [ ;; color the whole world green
        set pcolor green
    ]
;; create the initial sheep and set their initial properties
create-sheep number-of-sheep [
        setxy random-xcor random-ycor
        set color white
        set shape "sheep"
        set energy 100
    ]
    reset-ticks
end
```

We also need to add one line to the MOVE procedure to give a cost to movement:

```
;; sheep procedure, the sheep moves which costs it energy
to setup
  forward 1
  set energy energy - 1    ;; take away a unit of energy
end
```

We can start by setting the cost to one unit, knowing that as we extend the model, we will want to make the movement cost a parameter of the model. Adding a cost to movement does not mean anything if there is no penalty for expending energy. We want the sheep to die if they have too little energy. Therefore, we also need to check to see if the sheep have expended all of their energy. We can modify the GO procedure to call a sub-procedure that checks whether a sheep should die.

We write this procedure:

```
to go
ask sheep [
      wiggle ;; first turn a little bit
      move    ;; then step forward
      check-if-dead ;; checks to see if sheep dies
    ]
tick
end
```

We also need to write the check-if-dead procedure itself:

```
;; sheep procedure, if my energy is low, I die
to check-if-dead
   if energy < 0 [
      die
   ]
end
```

Now if we press SETUP and GO, the model will run for a while and then all the sheep will disappear at the same time. Unfortunately the model will keep running (you can tell because the GO button remains depressed). It would be nice if the model would stop when there were no more sheep. We can add a clause to the GO procedure to do that:

```
to go
   if not any? sheep [stop]
   ask sheep [
   wiggle
      move
      check-if-dead ;; checks to see if sheep dies
   ]
   tick
end
```

Now, if you rerun the model, when all the sheep disappear the model stops running. It might be useful to know how many sheep there are, so we can add a plot that indicates what the population of the sheep is at any point in time. If you remember, we also created a plot in chapter 2, but in that chapter we used code within the plot widget to control the updating of the plot. In NetLogo, there are two ways to handle plotting. The chapter 2 method is referred to as the *widget-based* method, since it makes use of a graphic widget. The other method is the *programmatic* or *code-based* method. In both methods, code is written to update the plots, but in the *code-based* method the code is actually located in the NetLogo Code tab. In the widget-based method that we saw in the previous chapters, the code is located inside the plot widget itself. In general, each method of plotting can do any plotting task the other can do, so it is up to the modeler to decide which method to use. They both have advantages and disadvantages. The advantage of the widget-based method is that you do not need to clutter up the Code tab with extra code for plotting, and, that for simple plots, it is quicker to set up. However, for complex plots with many pens, it can be more difficult to set up a plot with the widget-method. Furthermore, if there is buggy code in the widget plot, it can be hard to notice, since it won't show up as an error in the Code tab. The Code tab plotting method has the reverse advantages and disadvantages. We regard this choice as a stylistic choice for the modeler. Our general recommendation is to use the widget for relatively simple plots and the Code tab for complex plots with intricate setup conditions and/or many pens.

In this chapter, we will introduce the programmatic method of updating the plot using plotting code written in the Code tab. Everything we do here in the Code tab can also be done using the widget-based approach, but it is useful to know both methods so you can decide which method best suits your model. To plot using the programmatic method, we first create a plot on the interface and set its properties, then we add a call to a plotting routine in the main GO procedure:

```
to go
    if not any? sheep [
        stop
    ]
    ask sheep [
        wiggle
        move
        check-if-dead ;; checks to see if sheep dies
    ]
    tick
    my-update-plots ;; plot the population counts
end
```

Then we need to define the procedure MY-UPDATE-PLOTS (the "update-plots" primitive does something similar for widget-based plotting):

```
;; update the plots in the interface tab
to my-update-plots
    plot count sheep
end
```

We could have used "plot count sheep" directly at the end of the GO procedure. But we know it is likely that we will have to plot other population counts, so we can look ahead and create the "my-update-plots" procedure. We can then use this procedure later on for other plots as well. Now, if we run the model, the plot shows us that there was a full population of sheep up until the end of the run, when they all died out. The death of all of the sheep in the 101st time step is a result of the initial energy and the movement cost that we have assigned to the sheep (set to 1 energy unit per movement step). Recall that we wanted the movement cost to be a parameter of the model. We need to add another slider to control the movement cost and then modify the MOVE procedure to take this in to account:

```
to move
    forward 1
    ;; reduce the energy by the cost of movement
    set energy energy - movement-cost
end
```

At the end of the run, your model should look like figure 4.6.

Third Version   At present, the model exhibits a very predictable behavior. Every time the model runs for 100/MOVEMENT-COST time steps (ticks), then all of the sheep disappear and the model stops. The reason is because the sheep currently expend energy

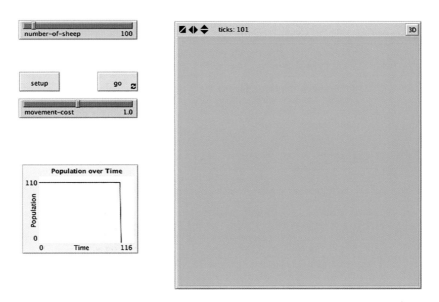

Figure 4.6
The second version of the Wolf Sheep Simple model at the end of a run. (See Wolf Sheep Simple 2 model in the supplementary materials.)

(by moving) but have no way of gaining energy. Therefore, we need to give the sheep the ability to eat grass and gain energy. However, first we must create the grass. To do this, we tell NetLogo that the patches (which serve as the grass clumps for this model) have a GRASS-AMOUNT property, which measures how much grass is currently available on that patch by adding the following line after the SHEEP-OWN line we already have:

```
patches-own [ grass-amount ]    ;; patches have an amount of grass
```

Then we need to set up this grass, and, while we are at it, we will modify the color of the patches so that they indicate how much grass is available. We do this by setting the initial amount of grass to a random (floating-point) number between 0.0 and 10.0.[9] We use a floating-point number for grass, since unlike sheep, which are individuals, each patch contains a "clump" of grass, not an individual blade. This ensures some variability in the amount of grass and creates some agent heterogeneity. Then we set the color of the grass to a shade of green such that if there is no grass at all the patch will be black and if there is a lot of grass it will be bright green:[10]

```
to setup
    clear-all
    ask patches [
        ;; patches get a random amount of grass
        set grass-amount random-float 10.0
        ;; color it shades of green
        set pcolor scale-color green grass-amount 0 20
    ]
    create-sheep number-of-sheep [
        setxy random-xcor random-ycor
        set color white
        set shape "sheep"
        set energy 100
    ]
    reset-ticks
end
```

9. "Floating-point" technically refers to the representation used by the computer to store a number in memory, with a floating decimal (binary) point. However, for most practical purposes, what you need to know is that RANDOM N reports a random nonnegative integer less than N, whereas RANDOM-FLOAT X reports a random real number less than X, such as 0.9997 or 3.14159.

10. As we saw in the El Farol model extensions, SCALE-COLOR takes four inputs, a color that we are scaling, the variable that determines how bright or dark to make the color, a lower value of the variable and an upper value of the variable. Here we set the upper value of the variable to 20 even though the most it can be is 10. This means that SCALE-COLOR will only use half the range of GREEN. If we allowed it to use the full range then patches with lots of grass would be white and not bright green.

Now we need to modify the GO procedure so that the sheep can eat the grass. As we mentioned in designing a time step, we put this procedure after the check for death:

```
to go
    if not any? sheep [
        stop
    ]
    ask sheep [
        wiggle
        move
    check-if-dead
    eat
    ]
tick
    my-update-plots
end
```

Then we write the EAT procedure:

```
;; sheep procedure, sheep eat grass
to eat
    ;; check to make sure there is grass here
    if ( grass-amount >= 1 ) [
        ;; increment the sheep's energy
        set energy energy + 1
        ;; decrement the grass
        set grass-amount grass-amount - 1
        set pcolor scale-color green grass-amount 0 20
    ]
end
```

This procedure just checks to see if there is enough grass in the patch below the sheep. If there is enough there to eat, then the sheep converts the grass into added energy, and we decrement the amount of grass in the patch. At the same time we recolor the patch to reflect the new amount of grass in the location.

The model behavior is still not very interesting. The sheep wander around, eat as much grass as they can, and eventually all die out. The only variation in the model is the level of the grass in the patches. Due to the random distribution of grass originally and due to the fact that the sheep move randomly around the landscape, there will be some areas of grass that are completely consumed by the sheep and other areas that will be only partially consumed.

To make the model a little more interesting we add in a procedure to make the grass agents regrow. By allowing the grass to regrow it should be possible to maintain the sheep population over time since there will be a renewable source of energy for them. We begin by modifying the GO procedure:

```
to go
    if not any? sheep [
        stop
    ]
    ask sheep [
        wiggle
        move
        check-if-dead
        eat
    ]
    regrow-grass ;; the grass grows back
    tick
    my-update-plots ;; plot the population counts
end
```

Then we define the REGROW-GRASS procedure:

```
;; regrow the grass
to regrow-grass
    ask patches [
        set grass-amount grass-amount + 0.1
        if grass-amount > 10 [
            set grass-amount 10
        ]
        set pcolor scale-color green grass 0 20
    ]
end
```

This procedure simply tells all of the grass clump agents to increase the amount of grass that they have by one tenth of one unit. We also make sure that the grass never exceeds 10, which represents the fact that there is a maximum amount of grass that can exist in any one clump. It then changes the color of the grass to match the new value. With this small change the sheep persist throughout a run of the model. We now have the grass recolor code at three different places in the model, so it would also be nice to place that in its own procedure. Often when we start to duplicate code, it is worth placing it in a separate procedure; that way we have to modify the code in only one location if we need to change it later (for instance, if we want grass to be colored yellow instead of green). Keeping the code more concise, and placing useful pieces of code in appropriately named subprocedures, will also help make your code more readable for others. So we define a RECOLOR-GRASS procedure:

```
;; recolor the grass to indicate how much has been eaten
to recolor-grass
   set pcolor scale-color green grass-amount 0 20
end
```

Now we just replace the coloring code in SETUP, REGROW-GRASS, and EAT with RECOLOR-GRASS, and the model works the same as before.

Running the model several times with one hundred initial sheep, it becomes clear that one hundred sheep cannot consume all the grass, and thus eventually the whole world becomes a solid shade of green. However, if you increase the number of initial sheep to a larger number, say seven hundred, and then run the model, the sheep will consume almost all the grass in the model, and then many of them will die off. However, a few of them that had a large amount of energy before all the grass disappeared will survive, and eventually the grass will regrow permitting them to persist since they are no longer competing with as many sheep for the grass.

Another parameter that we want to introduce, which may affect the dynamics of the model as much as the initial number of sheep, is the rate at which grass regrows. To do this we add a slider called GRASS-REGROWTH-RATE, give it boundary values of 0 and 2 and an increment of 0.1, and then we modify the REGROW-GRASS procedure to reflect the use of this new parameter:

```
;; regrow the grass
to regrow-grass
   ask patches [
      set grass-amount grass-amount + grass-regrowth-rate
   if grass-amount > 10 [
      set grass-amount 10
]
      recolor-grass
]
end
```

Now if we set the GRASS-REGROWTH-RATE to a high enough value (try 2.0), then even with seven hundred sheep in the model, the full sheep population can be sustained. This is because the sheep are able to gain a full unit of energy from the grass, which regrows that energy in one time step. The sheep then expend that energy in the next time step moving, but that energy is immediately replaced. However, if you change the MOVEMENT-COST slider to be greater than 1.0, then the sheep will eventually die off. This is because they are expending energy faster than they can gather it from the environment, even if there is no shortage of grass. In order to make our model more flexible, we can add yet another parameter, ENERGY-GAIN-FROM-GRASS, which will control the amount of energy the sheep can gain from eating the grass. As in the previous sliders, we will need to set reasonable bounds and an increment for this slider as well. To use this new slider, we need to modify the EAT procedure:

```
;; sheep procedure, sheep eat grass
to eat
    ;; check to make sure there is grass here
    if ( grass-amount >= energy-gain-from-grass ) [
        ;; increment the sheep's energy
        set energy energy + energy-gain-from-grass
        ;; decrement the grass
        set grass-amount grass-amount - energy-gain-from-grass
        recolor-grass
    ]
end
```

Note that we used the energy-gain-from-grass parameter both to increment the sheep's energy gain from eating as well as to decrement the grass's value. We could have used two different parameters for these two functions, but we can think of the sheep/grass system as energy conversion, so that the energy in the grass flows to the sheep. Now we can get some interesting dynamics. For instance, in figure 4.7, you can see an instance of the run where we started out with seven hundred sheep, and they lasted for around three hundred time steps. But then there was a mass starvation, which became more gradual, until after around

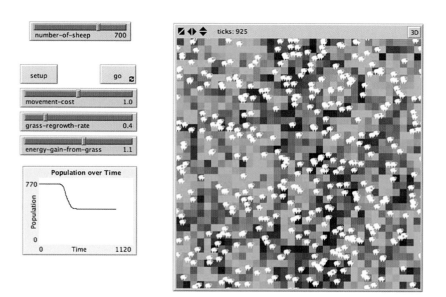

Figure 4.7
Third version of the model, having reached an equilibrium. (See Wolf Sheep Simple 3 model in the supplementary materials.)

five hundred ticks, the population held steady with a little over four hundred sheep. After enough sheep have died out, the grass can continually regenerate and support the living sheep and the system has reached a state of equilibrium. Since sheep movement is random, it is possible that a large number of sheep might happen to cluster together on the same few patches for a long time, and thus starve, but this is not likely. Depending on your choices for the model parameters, many other outcomes are also possible. Feel free to experiment and explore before moving on to the next version of the model.

Fourth Version   So now the model has sheep moving around on a landscape, consuming resources, and dying. However, there is no way for the sheep population to go back up; currently it can only go down. Thus to get it to go back up, we will add reproduction to the model.

To build a full reproductive model with sexual pairings and to have a pregnant sheep would take a long time, and it is not clear that it would be worth the effort to answer the question we posed at the outset of making our model. Instead, we will make two simplifying assumptions. First, single sheep can produce new sheep. You can view this as either asexual reproduction or you can think of each sheep as representing a life-bonded pair of sheep. This assumption may seem strange at first and is certainly obviously contrary to reality. This is a good time to recall George Box's words: "all models are wrong, but some are useful." It is OK to make our model wrong about such a basic fact of reproduction if the simplified model is still useful. If later we see that this simplification lost us some usefulness of the model, we can always add sexual reproduction later. The second simplifying assumption is this: Rather than worry about gestation, we will assume that sheep immediately give birth to a new lamb when they reach a certain energy level. This energy level can be seen as a proxy for having the ability to gather enough resources to make it all the way through the gestation period.

To implement this we begin by adding code to the GO procedure:

```
;; make the model run
to go
   if not any? sheep [
      stop
   ]
   ask sheep [
      wiggle ;; first turn a little bit
      move   ;; then step forward
      check-if-dead   ;; check to see if sheep dies
      eat                      ;; sheep eat grass
      reproduce      ;;sheep reproduce
]
   regrow-grass ;; the grass grows back
   tick
   my-update-plots ;; plot the population counts
end
```

Then we need to write the REPRODUCE procedure:

```
;; check to see if this sheep has enough energy to reproduce
to reproduce
    if energy > 200 [
        set energy energy - 100    ;; reproduction transfers energy
        hatch 1 [ set energy 100 ] ;; to the new sheep
    ]
end
```

This code checks to see if the current sheep has enough energy to reproduce (twice the original amount of energy). If the sheep does then it decrements its energy by 100, and creates a new child sheep (HATCH makes a clone of the parent agent on the same patch) and sets its energy to 100.

Now if we run the model with a low energy movement cost compared to the rate of energy gain from grass, starting from 700 sheep, the population increases over time, and eventually levels off near 1,300 sheep, as shown in figure 4.8.

Fifth Version Now we essentially have the sheep working the way we described in our conceptual model but our original goal was to have two species. So now we need to add

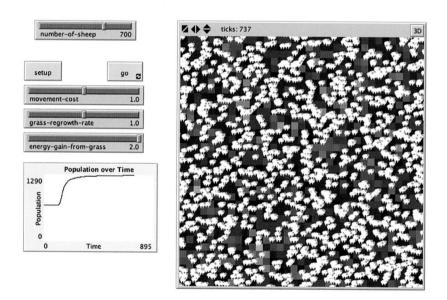

Figure 4.8
The fourth version of Wolf Sheep Simple model (includes reproduction). (See Wolf Sheep Simple 4 model in the supplementary materials.)

in the wolves. The first thing we need to do is tell NetLogo that there is now a second breed of turtles that we are calling wolves. At the same time we need to give wolves ENERGY as well. We could do this by adding a WOLVES-OWN like our SHEEP-OWN statement, but since the only turtle agents in the model are sheep and wolves, we can make ENERGY a generic property of all turtles. We do this by changing our SHEEP-OWN statement to a TURTLES-OWN statement:

```
breed [sheep a-sheep]
breed [wolves wolf]

turtles-own [ energy ]     ;; agents own energy
```

After that we need to create the wolves, just like we did the sheep. First, we add a NUMBER-OF-WOLVES slider, and then we modify the setup procedure:

```
;; this procedures sets up the model
to setup
    clear-all
    ask patches [
        set grass random-float 10.0 ;; give grass to the patches
        recolor-grass ;; change the world to green
    ]
    create-sheep number-of-sheep [ ;; create the initial sheep
        setxy random-xcor random-ycor
        set color white
        set shape "sheep"
        set energy 100 ;; set the initial energy to 100
    ]
    create-wolves number-of-wolves [ ;; create the initial wolves
        setxy random-xcor random-ycor
        set color brown
        set shape "wolf"
        set size 1.5  ;; increase their size so they are a little easier to see
        set energy 100   ;; set the initial energy to 100
    ]
    reset-ticks
end
```

Now that we have added wolves to the model, we need to add in their behaviors as well. We note that all of the behaviors are common to both the wolves and sheep, even if the exact details differ (e.g., wolves eat sheep, while sheep eat grass, but both "eat"). So we replace "sheep" in our GO procedure with "turtles," since all of our moving agents will execute these behaviors.

```
;; make the model run
to go
    if not any? turtles [ ;; this time check for any turtles
       stop
    ]
    ask turtles [
       wiggle ;; first turn a little bit
       move  ;; then step forward
       check-if-dead    ;; check to see if agent should die
       eat        ;; wolves eat sheep, sheep eat grass
       reproduce  ;; wolves and sheep reproduce
    ]
    regrow-grass ;; regrow the grass
    tick
    my-update-plots ;; plot the population counts
end
```

We note that all of the behaviors that we gave to sheep apply equally well to wolves, so the model will run as is. However, the eating behavior for the wolves is different from the eating behavior for the sheep, so we will need to modify our "eat" procedure.

```
;; sheep eat grass, wolves eat sheep
to eat
    ifelse breed = sheep [
       eat-grass
    ]
    [
       eat-sheep
    ]
end
```

Now our eat behavior will be different for sheep and wolves. The sheep will eat grass and the wolves will eat sheep. We rename our old "eat" procedure to "eat-grass" as that is the behavior we defined. We now must define the "eat-sheep" behavior. We start doing this by adding a slider for ENERGY-GAIN-FROM-SHEEP, just like the ENERGY-GAIN-FROM-GRASS slider we added earlier, and we write the EAT-SHEEP procedure:

```
;; wolves eat sheep
to eat-sheep
    if any? sheep-here [ ;; if there are sheep here then eat one
       let target one-of sheep-here  ;; select a random sheep on my patch
       ask target [ ;; eat the selected sheep
          die
       ]
       ;; increase the energy by the parameter setting
       set energy energy + energy-gain-from-sheep
    ]
end
```

In this procedure the wolf first checks to see if there are any sheep available to eat on the patch it is on. If there are, then it kills one of them (chooses one randomly from the sheep on the patch) and gets an energy increase according to the energy gain parameter.

Now our model has all of the agents, behaviors, and interactions that we had set out to create. However, our graph does not contain all the information yet. It would be helpful if it also displayed the wolf population, and at the same time we can add a display of the amount of grass in the world. To do this we first add two additional pens to the population plot, WOLVES and GRASS. We also rename the default plot pen to SHEEP. Then we modify the MY-UPDATE-PLOTS procedure:

```
to my-update-plots
    set-current-plot-pen "sheep"
    plot count sheep

    set-current-plot-pen "wolves"
    plot count wolves * 10 ;; scaling factor so plot looks nice

    set-current-plot-pen "grass"
    plot sum [grass] of patches / 50  ;; scaling factor so plot looks nice
end
```

This code is fairly straightforward. The "* 10" and "/ 50" are just scaling factors so that the plot is readable when all of the data is plotted on the same axis. (But keep in mind, when reading the number of wolves off of the plot, the actual population count is ten times smaller.)[11] It is often useful to add monitors for these variables as well to be able to read off exact values. We can now experiment with a variety of parameter settings for the Wolf Sheep Simple model. Many parameter settings will result in extinction of one or both species. But we can find parameters that result in a self-sustaining ecosystem where the species' population levels vary in a cyclic fashion. One such set of parameters is shown in figure 4.9. With those parameters, the wolf and sheep populations are sustained and oscillate.

Examining a Model

We have found one set of parameters that exhibits the behavior of our reference pattern. We note that these particular values for the parameters do not correspond to any real predator and prey populations. We did not calibrate our model from real-world data, so the parameter values themselves are not important. But, discovering that there exist model

11. Note that all of this plotting could also be done within the widget-based method.

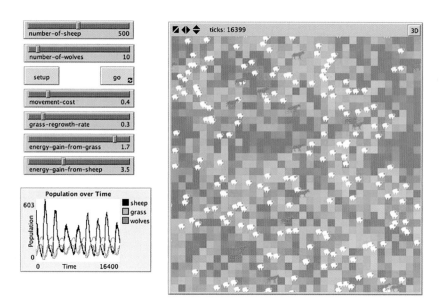

Figure 4.9
The Wolf Sheep Simple model, now including wolves. (See Wolf Sheep Simple model 5 in the supplementary materials.)

parameters that exhibit our reference pattern gives us insight into the natural phenomenon we were trying to model. Now that we have built our model, and we have found a set of parameters that allow the wolf and sheep populations to coexist and to oscillate, we have partially answered our research question: What parameters of two species will sustain oscillating positive population levels in a limited geographic area when one species is a predator of the other and the second species consumes limited but regrowing resources from the environment? We now know that it is possible for the rules we set up to produce the target reference pattern and therefore they could be a possible generative explanation for that pattern. However, just observing the behavior of this model once does not provide us with a robust answer. First, because many components of our model are stochastic in nature, there is no guarantee that the model when run again with the exact same parameters will exhibit the same behavior. Second, we have found one set of parameters that allow wolves and sheep to exist, but are there other parameter settings? A more general answer would allow us to make statements about ranges of parameters, and relationships between parameters, that allow both the wolves and the sheep to survive. However, if we run the model many times with a variety of parameter settings, this will create a lot of data. Thus, to give us even a simple answer to our question, we really need to examine multiple runs across multiple different parameter settings and summarize this data in a useful way. We will explore data analysis in greater detail in chapter 6, but before we leave the Wolf Sheep

Simple model, we will perform a basic analysis, in order to develop a preliminary answer to our question. With this analysis, we will have taken a model from the very beginning stages of its design to a first set of actual results. Chapter 6 will revisit many of these topics in greater detail.

Multiple Runs

Whenever you have a model that has stochastic components, it is important to run the model several times so that you can be certain you have correctly characterized the behavior of the model. If the model is run only once, you might happen to see anomalous behavior that is not what the model usually produces. For instance, in the Wolf Sheep Simple model it might be possible to run the model and arrive at a state in which there is simply one wolf and one sheep, and the sheep produces a second sheep often enough to keep the wolf fed, but not often enough to produce three sheep. However, due to the way the wolves and the sheep wander around the landscape, such an outcome is extremely unlikely, and it would not be typical of the model. Thus, it is important to run the model multiple times so that you can characterize the normal/average behavior of the model and not the aberrant behavior of the model.[12] On the other hand, there are times when the anomalous/aberrant model behavior *is* what you are interested in investigating, in which case you will need to run the model many times in order to find it and characterize it.

Most ABM platforms provide a way to do this. NetLogo provides you with the BehaviorSpace tool (*Wilensky & Shargel, 2002*) that enables you to run a model for several iterations with the same (or different) parameter settings and collect the results. We will learn to use the BehaviorSpace tool in chapter 6.

One additional consideration when performing multiple runs is how many time steps to run the model for. Since we want to be able to compare the results across different random number seeds, it is useful to hold the number of time steps we run the model constant. How long to run the model, how many times to run the model, and how to average the model results are nontrivial questions when you are attempting to describe the behavior of a model. These questions will be explored in chapter 6, but for now let us take the Wolf Sheep Simple model and run it with the parameter settings mentioned before for a thousand time steps ten times, and let us output the wolf, sheep, and grass population at the end of the model run.

Parameter Sweeping and Collection of Results   As we mentioned in the introduction, just because you have found one set of parameters that seem to answer your question does not

---

12. This is true not just of ABM but also of stochastic modeling in general. To learn more about the history and methods of stochastic simulation (sometimes known as Monte Carlo methods), see Hammersley & Handscomb, 1964; Kalos & Whitlock, 1986; Metropolis & Ulam, 1949.

mean that you are done. Often there are other sets of parameters that will also result in a similar behavior. On the other hand, maybe these particular parameter settings are unique and other parameter settings, even ones that are close to the current settings, will result in very different behavior. Thus, it is important to examine critical parameters in the model to explore the robustness of the model behavior and to understand how sensitive the model is to changes in parameters.

Robustness and sensitivity analysis will be explored more in chapter 6, but for now we can concentrate on one important factor. In the Wolf Sheep Simple model, one parameter that seems to affect the behavior at times is the initial number of wolves. If there are too many wolves, then they will eat all the sheep, and then they will die for lack of a food source. If there are too few wolves, then the population may not survive until the sheep have increased their population enough to sustain them. To examine this effect let us run the model ten times for each of the eleven different values of the initial number of wolves parameter from 5 to 15.

Analysis of Data   Summarizing data can be done in a variety of ways. Not only does data analysis enable us to describe complex data results in a much more compact form, but it also gives us a uniform way of looking at data so we can compare and contrast data sets.

Having lots of data is nice, but it is difficult to make claims about three (3) different variables with ten (10) different random number seeds and eleven (11) different initial parameter settings. Altogether that combination produces 330 different values. Thus, we need to summarize and analyze this data in some way, so that it is comprehensible. One typical way to summarize the data is to average it across the runs. This turns ten values into two values if we express the results in terms of the average and standard deviation. Another method for summarizing data is to plot it on a graph. Thus, we plot the initial parameter values on the x-axis and the values themselves on the y-axes. Given these two simplifications we have reduced our 330 different values into three plot lines. This data is now much easier to understand, and is observable in figure 4.10 (the results have been scaled by the same scaling factors we used in the Wolf Sheep Simple model plot). Of course, it is possible to examine all of the data that the model produces, and we will discuss ways of doing so later in the book.

Now we have designed a model, implemented it, and conducted a basic analysis in order to answer a question of interest. Since in many cases there are oscillatory patterns in the wolves, sheep, and grass counts, the final numbers are not always relevant, but they can be useful as a starting point for investigation. For instance, though all that is plotted in what follows is the average of the final numbers, if you were to examine the variance of those numbers you might have more insight into how oscillatory the patterns were at the end of a run. In chapter 6, we will go into much more detail about how to do model analysis.

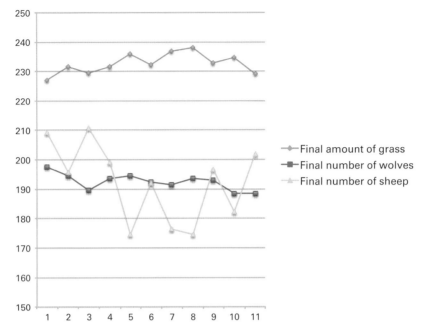

Figure 4.10
Results of Wolf Sheep Simple model analysis.

Predator-Prey Models: Additional Context

One of the first uses of agent-based modeling was for modeling of ecosystems, where it was often called individual-based modeling (see the appendix for a brief discussion of the historical role of individual-based modeling). Modeling of ecological systems has been of interest to biologists and environmentalists for quite some time. If we can better understand how ecologies operate and what the effects of successful ecosystems on the global environment are, then we may be able to better intervene to assist in the sustenance of these systems. For more information on this topic, refer to Grimm and Railsback (2005).

As discussed briefly in chapter 0, one of the first attempts to study ecologies and population dynamics in a concrete way was the work of Lotka (1925) and Volterra (1926). They developed a system of equations to describe a two species predator-prey interaction. These simple equations showed that you could meaningfully model ecological systems with just a few parameters. And once you have a model of a system you can start to explore options for perturbing the system into favorable states. The general result of the Lotka-Volterra equations is that predators and prey populations move in cycles. This is seen in figure 4.11.

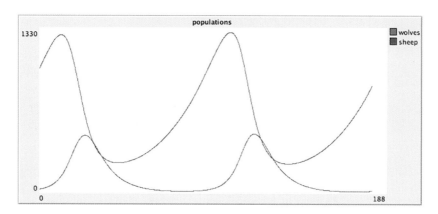

Figure 4.11
Lotka-Volterra relationship (Wolf Sheep Predation System Dynamics model) (*Wilensky, 2005*).

Depending on the parameter settings, if the two populations are equal at the start, then the predators will begin consuming the prey; this will result in a decrease of the prey population. Eventually, the prey will die off to the point where predators cannot find any more prey to eat. This will in turn cause predators to die off because they have no prey to feed on. At this point the prey will be able to reproduce before the predators eat them, and the prey population will increase. As the prey population increases it will become easier for the predator population to find them and the predator population will increase as well. This, in turn, results in the prey population's decreasing trend, and the whole process begins again.

The Lotka-Volterra equations have been a standard way of describing the fluctuations in predator and prey populations. Because they are differential equations (see figure 4.12), they represent a continuous model of population change. But populations are not continuous; they are discrete. Sometimes a continuous approximation of a discrete process is fine, but in this case it may be an oversimplification. The general problem is that as the population of a species becomes very small, standard differential equation models do not allow the population to actually go to 0, which means that there is always a positive probability that the population will rebound. However, this is not what happens in the real world. There is no rebounding from 0.1 prey. If a species goes extinct, it goes extinct, and there is no probability that it will rebound. This phenomenon is so common in differential equation-based modeling that it is sometimes referred to as the "nano-sheep problem" in specific reference to the wolf-sheep/predator-prey model (Wilson, 1998). The problem is that nano-sheep (i.e., a millionth of a sheep) do not exist: Sheep either exist or do not exist, and therefore modeling them with a continuous distribution can be problematic.

To rectify the nano-sheep problem, biologists have created agent-based (or to use the term biologists favor, individual-based) models of predator-prey relationships, similar to

$$\frac{dx}{dt} = \alpha x - \beta xy$$

$$\frac{dy}{dt} = \delta xy - \gamma y$$

Figure 4.12
Classic Lotka Volterra differential equations. x is the number of prey, y is the number of predators, and α, β, γ, and δ are parameters describing the interactions of the two species.

the model that was built in this chapter. Under certain conditions these models have been shown to replicate the Lotka-Volterra results, but without the nano-sheep problem. They also predict that this system is in fact highly susceptible to extinctions, something that the Lotka-Volterra equations fail to capture (Wilson et al., 1993; Wilson, 1998). In 1934, Gause showed that indeed for isolated predator and prey (with no other competing species) the agent-based model was more accurate in its predictions—indeed, extinctions happen much more frequently than the Lotka-Volterra equations predict. The simple agent-based model we have created in this chapter shows similar results. For many parameter values, either wolves or both sheep and wolves go extinct, but for some sets of parameter values, the population levels are sustained and oscillate.

Advanced Modeling Applications
More broadly, the modeling of environmental and ecological systems has a long and rich history, representing some of the first applications of an agent-based modeling paradigm (DeAngelis & Gross, 1992). It also continues to be an exciting area for current research. One use of agent-based models in ecological systems is the modeling of food webs (Yoon et al., 2004). This combines ABM with another new complex systems methodology, network analysis (Schmitz & Booth, 1997). By understanding both the structure of ecological interactions via network analysis and the process of animal interactions via ABM, researchers gain a deeper insight into overall ecological systems (See, e.g., figure 4.13). Another particularly interesting application of ABM and ecological modeling has been in doing prescriptive design of engineered systems to ameliorate human interventions in the environment. For instance, Weber and his colleagues have done significant modeling of fish populations, and then examined the effect of various fish ladders near dams on salmon populations (Weber et al., 2006).

Ecological models can also be underpinnings of models of evolution. Agent-based modeling has been frequently used to model evolution of organisms (Aktipis, 2004; Gluckmann & Bryson, 2011; Hillis, 1991; Wilensky & Novak, 2010). Evolution lends itself well to the ABM approach as natural selection and other evolutionary mechanisms can be thought of as computational algorithms. Models can be used to try to understand adaptation and speciation in the historical record. Figure 4.14 shows two examples of such

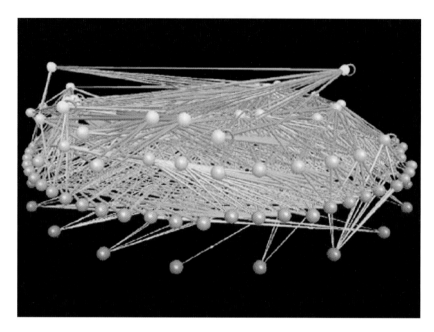

Figure 4.13
Little Rock Lake food web (foodwebs.org, 2006).

models of evolution from the NetLogo models library. In the field of Artificial Life, scientists sometimes evolve artificial organisms *in silico*. Moreover, as we will see in chapter
8, mechanisms inspired by evolution can be employed as methods of machine learning.

Conclusion

The Wolf Sheep Simple model was designed using the ABM design principle: Start simple
and build toward the question you want to answer. We showed how this principle guided
us not only in the design of the model, but also in its implementation and analysis. To
design ABMs requires a new way of thinking about modeling, but it is more natural in
some ways because it simply asks us to think like an agent (Wilensky & Reisman, 2006).
Thus, we do not need to guess at the causal relationship between our model and the real
world. Instead, by thinking as an agent and encoding the decisions that those agents make
in the real world, we construct our model from the bottom up. This is true both when
designing our ABM but also when implementing it. Finally, once our ABM has been
constructed, we observe its behavior and analyze the results. This analysis may cause us
to rethink some of our decisions about the ABM design and revisit our original design.

The Wolf Sheep Simple model is not only meant to be a basis for understanding the
concepts and principles of constructing your own agent-based model, but it is also meant

A   B

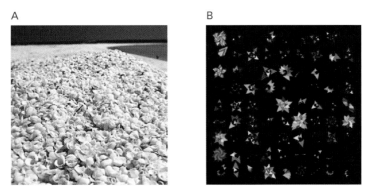

Figure 4.14
Agent-based models of evolution. (A) Evolution of camouflage of insects on a landscape. Different landscapes lead to the bugs evolving colorations that camouflage them in that landscape. (http://ccl.northwestern.edu/netlogo/models/BugHuntCamouflage.) (B) Evolution of computational biomorphs. Artificial flowers evolve through mating and blending their characteristics. (http://ccl.northwestern.edu/netlogo/models/Sunflower Biomorphs.)

to be generalizable enough to be used as the basis for other models that you are interested in developing on your own. For instance, for someone interested in exploring economics, this model could resemble a model of companies (the wolves) competing for consumers (the sheep) constrained by their budgets (grass). If a model author were interested in politics, then the model might be reminiscent of politicians (the wolves) competing for voters (the sheep), and the location of the agents could represent their feelings on particular issues. Of course, this model, in its present form, should not be directly used in these contexts—some of the mechanisms would need to be changed and the parameters or outputs of interest might be very different. These examples illustrate how the ABM methodology can be applied to a broad set of phenomena, and moreover that seemingly unrelated phenomena can be viewed as similar from an agent-based perspective as, even though the agents themselves might be quite different, they follow a similar set of rules.

Explorations

1. *Adding new parameters* When we added reproduction to the Wolf Sheep Simple model, we set two constants in the code. First, reproduction can occur only if the animal has more than 100 units of energy, and second, reproduction costs 100 units of energy. Create sliders for these parameters. How does varying these parameters affect the behavior of the model?
2. The Wolf Sheep Simple model only plots the counts of the animals, but the energy of the animals is almost as important as how many animals there are. Add a new plot to the model that plots the energy of the animals over time.
3. Right now all of the turtle agents in the Wolf Sheep Simple model move at the same speed. How would you expand the model so that they could move at different speeds?

How would you change the model so that the sheep and wolves could move at different speeds from each other? What effect would this have on the model? In particular, how does the ratio of the wolf speed to sheep speed affect the model dynamics?

4. The ability to move faster might come at the cost of a higher rate of energy expenditure. How would you change the model so that the speed of an agent affected its movement cost?

5. In this chapter we used the programmatic, as opposed to widget-based, method of updating the plots. However, what we did could be done using widget-based plots instead. Rewrite the model so plots are widget-based instead of programmatic/code-based.

6. In the Wolf Sheep Simple model, the wolves and sheep move randomly. In the real world, predators chase prey and prey try to escape. Can you modify the movement mechanism so the wolves chase the sheep? Again, how does the ratio of the wolf speed to sheep speed affect the model dynamics?

7. The Wolf Sheep Simple model explores two animal species interacting, but most ecologies have many more animal species. Create a third species in the model. One interesting way to do this would be to create a species that competes with the wolves for sheep, and can also eat wolves and be eaten by wolves. Can you get this three species ecosystem to stabilize?

8. Extend the Wolf Sheep Simple model by making the grass grow probabilistically, instead of at a constant rate.

9. The Wolf Sheep Simple model as written has the animals reproduce asexually. Modify the model so that it more realistically models the reproductive process. Possible avenues include: requiring two agents of the same breed to be on the same patch for reproduction to occur; giving the agents gender; and implementing a gestation period between when two agents are on the same patch and when the new agent is created. Does it change the dynamics of the model in any significant way?

10. We have talked a lot about designing models, but we have assumed so far that you know what the level of complexity of your model will be. Is there always an appropriate level of complexity of an agent-based model? Discuss your thoughts about the comparative benefits of making a simple model with the benefits of making a more elaborated and realistic model.

11. *Deterministic and random behavior* It is human nature to assume that there is a causal force behind everything that we observe, but some times this is not the case. However, even when we have a perfect understanding of a phenomenon, that is we know how all the underlying processes work, we might still want to use nondeterminism in our model. Can you explain some reasons why you would want to include random behavior in a model that could be completely deterministic? Is it possible to have deterministic macrobehavior even though the microbehavior is nondeterministic? Build a model of agents moving such that they always result in the same pattern even though they take random steps and random turns to get there.

12. *Designing a model* Assume that you have been asked by the city council to build an agent-based model of transportation patterns in the city. In particular they are interested in seeing where they should spend money with the goal of minimizing the time it takes for the average inhabitant to get to work. Design two models that would help them answer this question. In the first model, concentrate on the scale of a single neighborhood or political ward in the city. In the second model, concentrate on the level of the whole city. What are the agents in your model? Are they different in the two different scenarios? What data would you need if you were to actually build these models? How would you simulate the different policy choices, namely, the allocation of funds to minimize commuter time? What measures would you collect to answer the council's question?

13. *Evolution* In the Wolf Sheep model that we have built during this chapter, the wolf and sheep are exactly the same in every generation, but real wolves and sheep evolve over time. For instance, wolves might get faster or have better eyesight (though both of these traits might also incur a higher metabolism cost). Sheep might also get faster and might learn to avoid wolves (though again this might have a cost). Add an evolutionary mechanism to the wolf-sheep model. Does this make it more or less difficult to maintain a population?

14. *Modeling food webs* We mentioned how ABM can be used to describe food webs. However, these models are often written as an aggregate description. Imagine a model where instead of individual wolf and sheep there is simply a description of how wolf populations and sheep populations increase and decrease. In addition, imagine that there are many more species described, like the grass, insects, and birds. The description of how all these animals predate on each other is called a food web. Is this still an agent-based model? Please explain your answer.

15. *Crossing disciplines* At the end of the chapter, we speculated on how the Wolf Sheep Simple model might be construed as, or converted into, a model of companies moving around in a marketplace searching for resources. Develop this parallel and describe how you would use the Wolf Sheep Simple model as the basis for a model of economic competition.

16. *Building one model from another* Related to exploration 15, more generally, another way to build a model of a phenomenon you wish to model is to take a model that you already have that uses a similar mechanism to the model you want to build, and repurpose that model to transform it into a model of what you wish to model. Can you repurpose the Wolf Sheep Simple model along any of the lines suggested in the conclusion of the chapter?

17. Suppose a professional sports team approaches you. They are interested in understanding how their workers collect trash after a game. They want you to build a model where individuals pick up trash and then deposit it in garbage cans that are located around the stadium. This reminds you of the Termites model in the NetLogo models library. Modify

the Termites model to reflect this scenario, so that the termites are humans and they deposit the garbage (wood chips) in garbage cans.

18. *Building a simple model from a textual description* Now that you know how to build a simple model, can you build one that someone else has described? For instance, imagine you read the following in a scientific paper: "Agents are placed randomly throughout the world. Each agent has a status of either being healthy or sick. At the start of the model all agents are healthy except for one. Each time step agents move locally to a new random location. If, after they move, there are any agents that are sick nearby then they become sick." Build this model. Is it specified with sufficient detail that you believe your model is the same as the model built by the authors of the scientific paper?

19. *Types of agents* Look at the Termites model in the models library. In this model, the termites gather wood in piles. This model only has one type of termite, a wood-piler termite. Now imagine that there is a second type, or breed, of termite, a wood-unpiler termite. Add this second type to the model. How does this second type affect the results? Compare and contrast the patterns generated by the two models.

20. *Cyclic cellular automata* Create a cyclic cellular automaton. In a 2D cyclic CA, each cell can take on one of k states. But unlike a traditional CA, if a cell is in state i, it can only advance to state $i + 1$, and if state $i = k$, then it advances to state 0. A cell changes its state if some threshold of its neighbors is currently in the state that the cell is considering advancing to. Build this model. Change the number of states and the threshold how do these two parameters affect the resulting patterns of the model? How does changing the size of the world affect the model? Can you think of any real-world phenomena that might have similar behavior to a cyclic CA?

21. *Adding humans to the model* Take the Wolf Sheep Simple model that we have built in this chapter. Add humans to the model. Humans kill the wolves, but they do not gain energy from the wolves because they do not eat them. Humans will also kill the sheep, but they do gain energy from the sheep. How does the addition of humans affect the behavior of the model?

22. *Spatial location and grass* In the Wolf Sheep Simple model, the grass is randomly distributed across the space. However it is more realistic that areas of grass are spatially collocated, that is, areas with more grass are likely to be near each other, and areas low in grass are near each other. Change the SETUP and/or GO procedure for the grass to reflect this. How does this change affect the model? How does it affect the sheep?

23. *Changing mechanisms* In the Wolf Sheep Simple model, the grass grows linearly every time step an increment of grass is added to the patch. This is not realistic. Real grass will grow quicker if there is more of it around since there are more plants to produce seeds. Change the way grass grows so that it is dependent on the density of grass already present in the local area. Eventually the grass will hit a limit of physical space and be adversely affected by overcrowding and competition for water, nutrients, and sunlight. How would

you model that? How does this change in the grass mechanism affect the behavior of the model?

24. *Different types of distributions* In this model we used a mean and discussed how to use variance to characterize the results of multiple runs. This characterization assumes that the distribution of data can be described using these statistics. However, for some data, these statistics can be unhelpful or misleading. Describe a scenario where model output data are not well described by mean and variances. Why is it not possible to describe such a data set using these descriptive statistics? How would you describe this data set?

25. *ABM and OOP* Agent-based modeling shares many features with object-oriented programming (OOP). In some ways ABM and OOP are very different from each other. OOP describes a class of potential programming languages, whereas ABM also describes a perspective on thinking about the world. With that in mind, compare and contrast OOP and ABM. In what ways are agents like objects in OOP? How are agents different from objects?

5 The Components of Agent-Based Modeling

Divide each difficulty into as many parts as is feasible and necessary to resolve it.

—Rene Descartes

The whole is more than the sum of its parts.

—Aristotle

It's turtles all the way down.

—Author unknown

Now that we have had some experience with extending agent-based models and building ABMs on our own, we can take a step back and more comprehensively examine the individual components of such models. This gives us a chance to reflect on some issues that arise when implementing new ABMs. We begin this chapter by laying out an overview of the components of an ABM; in some cases, this will be a review of features discussed in previous chapters. We will then discuss each of the components in turn. At the end of the chapter, we will discuss how all of these components come together to create a full set of tools for the construction of ABMs.

Overview

As we have described in chapter 1, the raison d'être of agent-based modeling is the idea that complex systems can be productively modeled and explained by creating agents and environment, describing their behavior through agent rules, and specifying agent-agent and agent-environment interactions. This description of an ABM is itself a simplified picture, a model of agent-based modeling, if you will. The main components of any ABM are *agents*, *environment*, and *interactions*. Agents are the basic ontological units of the model, while the environment is the world in which the agent lives. The distinction between agents and environment can be fluid, as the environment can sometimes be modeled as agents. Interactions can occur either between agents or between agents and the environment. Agent actions can also occur internally, directly affecting only the agent's internal state. Such is the case when an agent is trying to determine which action to take, as when the residents in the Segregation model are deciding whether or not they are unhappy. The environment is not merely passive; it can also act autonomously. For instance, in the models we discussed in chapter 4, the grass regrows on its own.

To this list of three basic components, we will also add two additional components. The first is called the Observer/User Interface. The observer is an agent itself,[1] but one that has access to all of the other agents and the environment. The observer *asks* agents to carry out specific tasks. Users of agent-based models can interact with the agents by way of the User Interface, which enables the user to tell the observer what the model should do. The second component, the Schedule, is what the observer uses to tell the agents when to act. The Schedule often involves user interaction as well. In NetLogo models, the interface typically includes SETUP and GO buttons. The user presses SETUP and then GO to schedule these events to occur.

We will now describe each of these five components in further depth. Throughout this chapter, we will use a variety of models from the NetLogo models library to illustrate our examples. We start by examining the Traffic Basic model, a simple model of traffic flow (found in the Social Science section of the library). An early version of this model was designed by two high school students (Resnick, 1996; Wilensky & Resnick, 1999) to explore how traffic jams form. The students thought that they would have to include traffic accidents, radar traps, or some other form of traffic diversion to create a traffic jam, but they built an initial model without any such hindrances. To their surprise, traffic jams still formed despite the lack of impediments. This happens because as cars speed up and approach the cars in front of them, they eventually have to slow down, causing the cars behind them to slow down creating a ripple effect backward. Eventually, the car at the front of the jam will be able to move again, but by that time, there are many cars behind that car that cannot move, causing the traffic jam to move backward even as the traffic jam moves forward.[2] This simple model (figure 5.1) again illustrates that emergent phenomena often do not correspond to our intuitions. As we discussed in chapter 0, one common pitfall in making sense of emergent phenomena is the tendency toward levels confusion. In this case, it is easy to misattribute the properties of the individual agents (the cars) to the jam. Hence, it seems paradoxical to us that the cars would move forward while the jam moves backward.

---

1. In NetLogo, the observer is conceptualized as an agent with a point of view. In some other ABM packages, it is conceptualized as a "disembodied" controller.

2. This is an example of how levels affect perception, as we discussed in chapter 0.

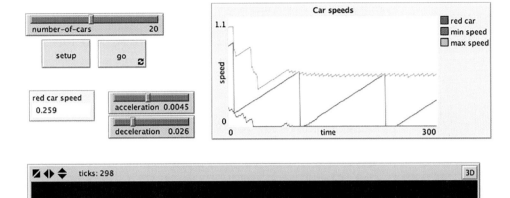

Figure 5.1
Traffic Basic model (Wilensky, 1997b).

Agents

Agents are the basic units of agent-based modeling. As such, it is important to choose the design of your agents carefully. The two main aspects that define agents are the *properties* that they have and the *actions* (sometimes called behaviors or methods) that they can execute. *Agent properties* are the internal and external state of the agents—their data and description. *Agent behaviors or actions* are what the agents can do.

Besides these two main agent attributes, there are also several issues that are related to agent design. First is the issue of agent "grain-size": which is most effective for the chosen model? For example, if you are modeling a political system, do want to model the individual actors or, instead, the political institutions or even each nation's government as a single entity? A second factor to consider is agent cognition. How much capability do the agents have to observe the world around them and make a decision? Do they act in a stimulus-response fashion? Or do they plan out their actions? Finally, we discuss some special types of agents: proto-agents, which are not fully specified agents; and meta-agents, composed of other agents.

Properties

Agent properties describe an agent's current state, the items that you see when you inspect an agent. In chapter 2, we briefly described how to use a patch monitor to see the current state of a patch, but you can also use monitors to inspect turtles and other types of agents as well. In this example, we are going to explore agent properties using a turtle monitor, but in NetLogo, you can monitor links and patches as well.

If you inspect one of the cars in Traffic Basic, you see (under the graphical image of the agent's local environment) the list of properties described in figure 5.2.[3] This list contains two sets of properties. The first set is a standard set of properties of every turtle created in NetLogo: WHO, COLOR, HEADING, XCOR, YCOR, SHAPE, LABEL, LABEL-COLOR, BREED, HIDDEN?, SIZE, PEN-SIZE, and PEN-MODE. Patches and links also have a default set of properties. For patches, these are PXCOR, PYCOR, PCOLOR, PLABEL, and PLABEL-COLOR, while for links, these are END1, END2, COLOR, LABEL, LABEL-COLOR, HIDDEN?, BREED, THICKNESS, SHAPE, and TIE-MODE. (All of these properties are described in more detail in the NetLogo User Manual.)

In NetLogo, turtles and links have COLOR as a property, while patches have PCOLOR as a property. Likewise, turtles have XCOR and YCOR as properties, while patches have PXCOR and PYCOR. To make things simpler, turtles can directly access the underlying properties of their current patch. For instance, for a turtle to set its color to the color of the underlying patch (effectively making it invisible), the turtle can just execute SET COLOR PCOLOR. If the patch property had the same name as the turtle property, this would not work, since there would be a confusion over which COLOR the code was describing. Only turtles can access patch properties directly, since a turtle can only be on one and exactly one patch. Links can span multiple patches and are always connected to multiple turtles, so you have to specify which patch you are referring to if you want to use a patch property in a link procedure. Similarly, you have to specify which link you are referring to when you want to use a link property in a turtle or patch procedure. Moreover, patches cannot directly access turtle or link properties, because a patch could have 0, 1 or many links or turtles on it. Therefore, you must specify which turtle or link you are referring to when accessing their properties.

In the inspector window, the default properties of the agent appear first. These are followed by the properties that the model author has specifically added to the agents for the model (e.g., in figure 5.2, SPEED, SPEED-LIMIT, SPEED-MIN). These author-defined properties should be described in the Info Tab associated with the model as well as in the comments in the Code Tab. For this model, SPEED describes the current speed of the car, SPEED-LIMIT is the maximum speed of the car and SPEED-MIN, its minimum speed.

When the Traffic Basic model starts up, all of these properties are set in the SETUP-CARS procedure:

---

3. You can inspect an agent by right-clicking on it or by using the NetLogo INSPECT primitive.

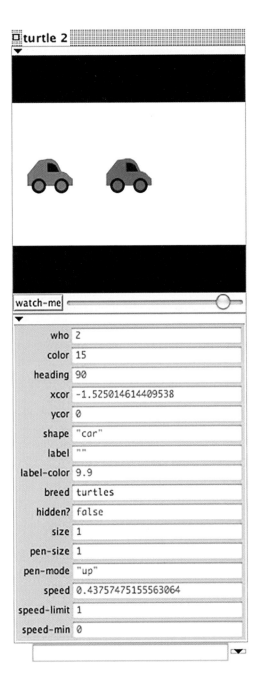

Figure 5.2
Agent properties for the Traffic Basic model.

```
set speed 0.1 + random-float .9
set speed-limit 1
set speed-min 0
```

The SPEED-LIMIT and SPEED-MIN are set to constant values, which means that all of the cars in this model will have the same SPEED-LIMIT and SPEED-MIN. However, the SPEED is set to a constant value plus a randomly drawn value. This will cause all of the cars to have at least a speed of 0.1 and at most a speed of just less than 1.0, but each car will (probably) have a different speed. It is possible for two cars to have the exact same speed, but that would require both of them to generate the same random floating-point number, and that is very unlikely.

The current method for initializing the speed of the cars uses a uniform distribution. As a result, it is just as likely that there will be as many cars with a speed of 0.2 as there will be cars with a speed of 0.9. However, often we want all the agents to all have roughly the same value for a property, but with some variation. A common way to achieve this result is by setting the property with a *normally* distributed random variable instead of a uniformly distributed random variable. For instance, in the Traffic Basic model, we could rewrite the example of setting the speed to work like this:

```
set speed random-normal .5 .1
```

Box 5.1
Basic Properties of Agents

In NetLogo, there is a standard set of properties that all agents have, some of which are common across toolkits and are essential properties for ABM. Here are some basic properties of NetLogo's turtle agents (for a complete list of properties, refer to the NetLogo documentation):

WHO   Calling this property a "who number" is unique to NetLogo, but all ABM toolkits have some unique identification number or string that is used to track each agent over time.

XCOR and YCOR   These are the coordinates of the agent in the world. They are useful for determining where the agent is in the world, and how the agent relates to other agents.

HEADING   The heading of an agent—the direction it is facing—is an intrinsic property of NetLogo agents. In some toolkits agents have no heading built-in, but if the model includes motion then it is often useful for the agents to have a heading property.

COLOR   The color used to display the agent in the ABM visualization. In NetLogo, both turtles and links have COLOR, and patches have a PCOLOR property. (In some ABM toolkits color is not a standard agent property, when model visualization is less closely tied to model mechanics.)

RANDOM-NORMAL takes the mean of the distribution you want to draw from and the standard deviation. This code will give each car a different speed, but it will be close to 0.5. The 0.1 specifies how distributed the speed is around the mean value of 0.5. If we change the standard deviation from 0.1 to 0.2, then there is a higher probability that one of the agents will have a speed much greater or less than 0.5. With 0.1, 67 percent of the cars will have a speed between 0.4 and 0.6; 97 percent will have a speed between 0.3 and 0.7; and 99 percent of the cars will have a speed between 0.2 and 0.8.

So far, we have initialized agent properties by setting them to constant values or to statistical distributions. Other ways to initialize agent properties are to set the values from a list or from a data file. If, for example, we were trying to replicate a particular instance of a traffic pattern, then we might know the initial speeds of all the cars that were involved. We could store this in a list and then initialize each agent from this list. This method enables us to recreate particular empirical examples and applications.

We can also change agent properties during the running of the model. For instance, in Traffic Basic, the speed parameter mentioned before gets modified throughout the running of the model to increase and decrease the speed as the car is able to move. In the SPEED-UP-CAR procedure, the speed is increased:

```
set speed speed + acceleration
```

Thus properties define an agent's current state, but they can also change to reflect how the state changes as the model progresses.

Behaviors (Actions)

Besides items that define the state of an agent (properties), it is also necessary to define how the agent can behave (the actions it can take). An agent's *actions* or *behaviors* are the ways in which the agent can change the state of the environment, other agents, or itself. In NetLogo, there are many behaviors that are predefined for the agents. The list of all these predefined behaviors is too large to iterate through here, but it includes actions like FORWARD, RIGHT, LEFT, HATCH, DIE, and MOVE-TO. (For a complete list of the predefined behaviors in NetLogo, you can look in the NetLogo Dictionary under the categories Turtle, Patch, and Link.) Unlike properties, which can be viewed through the inspector, this is the only way to find out what predefined behaviors an agent possesses.

It is also possible to define new behaviors for agents to carry out within a particular model. For example, in the Traffic Basic model, the agents have two additional behaviors that they can carry out—SPEED-UP-CAR and SLOW-DOWN-CAR—both of which modify the agents' speed:[4]

---

4. In NetLogo, it is customary to note that an action applies to a particular agent type by adding a comment that describes the action as a "turtle procedure."

```
;; turtle procedure
to slow-down-car
  set speed speed - deceleration
end

;; turtle procedure
to speed-up-car
set speed speed + acceleration

end
```

In addition to accelerating or decelerating, each car adjusts its speed based on the speed limits and always moves forward according to its speed. In the Traffic Basic model, the code for that action is in the main GO procedure:

```
    let car-ahead one-of turtles-on patch-ahead 1
    ifelse car-ahead != nobody
[slow-down-car ]
    ;; otherwise, speed up
    [ speed-up-car ]
    ;; don't slow down below speed minimum or speed up beyond speed limit
  if speed < speed-min [ set speed speed-min ]
  if speed > speed-limit [ set speed speed-limit ]
  fd speed ]
```

Each car first checks to see if there is another car/turtle ahead of it. If there is, it then slows down to a speed below the car ahead, making sure that it does not run into the car ahead of it. Otherwise, it speeds up (but never exceeds the speed limit). This agent action is an *interaction*, as a car interacts with another car by sensing that car's speed and changing its own state based on the other car. Conversely, if a car slows down, this will then

Box 5.2
Basic Behaviors/Actions of Turtle Agents

Most ABM toolkits have a standard set of actions that agents have. Many of these are common across toolkits and are essential properties of any ABM. Here are some common actions that NetLogo's turtle agents can take:

FORWARD/BACKWARD   Enables the agent to move forward and backward within the world.

RIGHT/LEFT   Enables the agent to change its heading within the world.

DIE   Tells an agent to destroy itself and removes the agent from all appropriate agent sets.

HATCH   Creates a new agent that is a copy of the current agent with all of the same properties as the current agent.

force the cars behind it to slow down as well. The action of each agent affects the actions of other agents.

So far, we have seen cars changing their own internal state and affecting the state of other cars. You might also imagine how cars might affect the road that they are driving on, thereby affecting the environment of the model. For example, the more traffic there is on a road, the more worn down the road might become, so we could add a WEAR property to the patches of the road and then add a WEAR-DOWN procedure in which the cars wear down the road over time. This, in turn, might affect the top speed that the cars can reach on that section of road.

Behaviors are the basic way for agents to interact with the world. We will discuss some traditional interaction mechanisms later on in this chapter.

Collections of Agents

Types of Agents   Agents are typically divided into three main types: mobile agents that can move about the landscape; stationary agents that cannot move at all; and connecting agents that link two or more other agents. In NetLogo, turtles are mobile agents, patches are stationary agents, and links are connecting agents. From a geometric standpoint, turtles are generally treated as shapeless area-less points, although they may be visualized with various shapes and sizes). Thus, even if a turtle appears to be large enough to be on several patches at the same time, it is only contained by the patch at the turtle's center (given by XCOR and YCOR). Patches are sometimes used to represent a passive environment and are acted upon by the mobile agents; other times, they can take actions and perform operations. A primary difference between patches and turtles is that patches cannot move. Patches also take up a defined space/area in the world; thus, a single patch can contain multiple turtle agents on it. Links are also unable to move themselves. They connect two turtles that are the "end nodes" of the link, but the visual representations of the links do move when their end nodes move. Links are often used to represent the relationship between turtles. They can also represent the environment—e.g., by defining transportation routes that agents can move along, or by representing friendship/communication channels. Despite these differences, all three share the ability to behave, that is, to take actions and perform operations on themselves.

In some ABM toolkits, the environment is passive and does not have the full capabilities of an agent. Giving the environment, the ability to directly perform operations and actions allows an easier representation of many of the autonomous environmental processes. For instance, in the Wolf Sheep Simple model in chapter 4, we could have the grass regrow by just adding to the grass variable instead of asking all the patches in the environment to execute a grass-growth behavior. Though computationally this may not be that different, representing the environment as a collection of agents allows users to reason spatially locally—e.g., they can take the viewpoint of a patch of grass, which can make the model easier to understand.

Breeds of Agents Besides these three predefined agent-types, modelers can also create their own types of agent called breeds. The breed of an agent designates the category or class to which the agent belongs. In the Traffic Basic model, all of the agents are of the same type, so it is not necessary to distinguish between different agent breeds. Instead, we used agents of the "turtles" breed, the default breed in NetLogo. Different breeds of agents are required if different agents have different properties or actions.

In chapter 4, we had two breeds of agents, the "wolf" the "sheep" breeds. Even though these two breeds had the same set of properties, it was useful to create two breeds because each had different characteristic actions—wolves eat sheep, while sheep eat grass. We defined the breeds at the beginning of the model:

```
breed [sheep a-sheep]
breed [wolves wolf]
```

At the same time, we can define the properties that breeds have:

```
turtles-own [energy]
```

In this case, both the wolves and the sheep have the same property of "energy," but we could also give them separate properties. For instance, we could give the wolves a "fang-strength" property and the sheep a "wooliness" property. The fang-strength could be used to determine how successful a wolf is at killing sheep. Wooliness, by contrast, could be an indication of how well the sheep was able to fend off the wolves' attack, if we assume that the wolves sometimes get a mouthful of wool instead of flesh. If this were the case, we would add two additional lines:

```
sheep-own [ wooliness ]
wolves-own [ fang-strength ]
```

These properties are in addition to the properties that all agents have, so that the sheep would have "wooliness" and "energy" just as the wolves have "fang-strength" and "energy."

Sets of Agents Breeds are particular collections of agents where the collections are defined by the kinds of properties and actions of their agents. We can also define collections of agents in other ways. NetLogo uses the term *agentset* to designate an unordered collection of agents, and we will also use this term/definition throughout this textbook. Usually we construct agentsets either by collecting agents that have something in common (e.g., agent location or other properties) or by randomly selecting a subset of another agentset.

In the Traffic Basic model, we could create a set of all the agents that have a speed over 0.5. In NetLogo, this is usually done with the WITH primitive. Here is an example of how we could create such an agentset that we could insert into the GO procedure in this model:

```
let fast-cars turtles with [speed > 0.5]
```

However, we usually want to ask these turtles to do something specific. For instance, we can ask all of the turtles that have a high speed to set their size bigger so they are easier to see.

```
let fast-cars turtles with [speed > 0.5]
ask fast-cars [
  set size 2.0
]
```

The "let" statement above collects the fast cars into an agentset. If we don't plan to "talk to" this agentset again, we can do without the LET and instead construct the agentset "on the fly" and ask the turtles directly:

```
ask turtles with [speed > 0.5] [
    set size 2.0
]
```

If you insert this code into the model, you will soon see that all of the cars are big. This is because we never told the turtles to set their size to small again, once their speed has dropped below 0.5. To do that we would need to add some more code. One way to accomplish this would be to use another ask.

```
ask turtles with [speed > 0.5] [
    set size 2.0
]
ask turtles with [speed <= 0.5] [
    set size 1.0
]
```

Another way to accomplish the same goal, without creating agentsets, is to ask all the turtles to do something, but choose what actions they take based on their properties. In the previous example, all of the faster turtles took their actions before any of the slower turtles took their actions. In the following example, all of the agents are asked with the same ASK command, so the order in which the turtles take actions will be random. In this case the result of running the code will be the same, but depending on what actions the agents take (for instance, if they were to change their speed, instead of their size), the results could be different.

```
ask turtles [
    ifelse speed > 0.5 [
set size 2.0
]
[
    set size 1.0
    ]
]
```

Another method for creating agentsets is on the basis of their location. The Traffic Basic model does this in the GO procedure:

```
let car-ahead one-of turtles-on patch-ahead 1
        ifelse car-ahead != nobody
            [ slow-down-car ]
```

TURTLES-ON PATCH-AHEAD 1 creates an agentset of all of the cars in the patch in front of the current car. It there is at least one such car, it then selects one of these cars at random, using the ONE-OF primitive, and sets the speed of the current car to a little less than the speed of that car ahead. There are many other ways to access a collection of agents based on their location, such as using NEIGHBORS, TURTLES-AT, TURTLES-HERE, and IN-RADIUS.

It is also often useful to create a randomly selected set of agents. These agents are not related in any particular way, but rather, are a collection of agents that we want performing some action. In NetLogo, the primary procedure for doing this is N-OF. For example, the Segregation model that we talked about in chapter 3 used N-OF to ask a random set of patches to create a set of red turtles and then asked all of those turtles to turn green or red randomly:

```
;; create turtles on random patches
ask n-of number patches
    [ sprout 1
        [ set color one-of [red green] ]
```

Agentsets and Lists   Throughout our examples, we have used both agentsets and lists, sometimes explicitly and sometimes implicitly. This may be a good time to stop and clarify what they are, how they work, how they differ, and under what circumstances we would use one over the other. Agentsets and lists are both variables that can contain one or many other variables. We can specify that a variable is an agentset or a list when we create them, by using their respective constructor reporters. If we want to create an empty list, we can write

```
let a-list []
```

If we want, we can then add numbers, strings, and even turtles to the list.

```
;; we put items at the start of the list
set a-list fput 1 a-list
set a-list fput "and" a-list
set alist fput turtle 0 a-list
show a-list
;; prints [(turtle 0) "and" 1
```

In contrast to lists, which can hold any type of item, an agentset can hold only agents. Moreover, it can hold only agents of the same type, such as turtles, patches, or links. NetLogo has special reporters for empty agentsets, no-turtles, no-patches, and no-links.

```
;; this creates an empty agentset of turtles
let an-agentset no-turtles
```

no-turtles is an empty turtle agentset (i.e., an agentset containing no turtles), so by setting an-variable to no-turtles, we specify that this variable is of the type agentset. Now that we have an empty agentset, we can then add turtles to it by using the turtle-set reporter:

```
;; this adds turtle 0 to the agentset
set an-agentset (turtle-set turtle 0)
;; this adds turtle 1 and turtle 2 to the agentset
set an-agentset (turtle-set an-agentset turtle 1 turtle 2)
show an-agentset
;; prints (agentset, 3 turtles)
```

We can only put agents (turtle-breeds, patches and links) in agentsets, but we can put anything we want, including agents, in lists. There are two important properties that set agentsets and lists apart from each other.

First, we can "ask" agentsets to do things, but we cannot ask lists to do things. So for instance, when we use

```
ask turtles [] ;; do stuff
```

what we are really doing is first creating an agentset of all turtles, and then asking all those turtles, in a random order, to do whatever we put in the brackets. If we try this with lists, we will simply get an error.

Second, agentsets are unordered. This means that whenever we invoke them, they will output a list of agents in a random order. Notice how showing a list shows both what is inside the list and the order in which it appears, but showing an agentset shows only what is inside the agentset.

So when we want to interact with turtles, when would we use one or the other? Unless we have a very good reason to, we always use agentsets. The primary reason is that we usually want our turtles to do things in a random order. That is because there could be threats to model validity if the agents always execute in the same order. For instance, in the Wolf Sheep Predation model, some sheep would have an unfair advantage if they are always first to check if there is grass on their patches.

But sometimes we do want to determine the order in which turtles do things. For instance, it could be that we *want* some turtles to have an advantage. In that case we would need to create an ordered list, and order them by whatever parameter we think determines their advantage. If turtles have different information, we might, for example, want the turtles with more information to take their turns later.

```
turtles-own [information] ;; information determines how late they get their turn
;; (later is better because then they will know what everyone else did
;; before making their decision)

;; create an empty list
let a-list []
;; sort-on reports a list containing turtles sorted by the parameter specified
;; in the brackets
set a-list sort-on [information] turtles
```

a-list now contains all turtles sorted by information in ascending order. But, as we just discussed, we cannot ask lists of agents to do things. Rather, we must iterate through the lists, and ask each agent in the list to do what we ask. For this we can use the foreach command:

```
foreach a-list [
    ask ? [ ] ;; do stuff here
]
```

The "?" is a special variable that takes on the value of each element of the list. So this code will iterate through each turtle in the list, and ask each in that particular order, to do what we specify in the brackets. We will further discuss the "?" variable later in this chapter.

Similarly we can create lists of patches. Suppose we want to label the patches with numbers in left-to-right, top-to-bottom order. We can create a sorted list of patches and then label them using the code below:

```
;; patches are labeled with numbers in left-to-right,
;; top-to-bottom order
let n 0
foreach sort patches [
    ask ? [
        set plabel n
        set n n + 1
    ]
]
```

Agentsets and Computation   Before we end our discussion of agentsets, it should be noted that once you ask an agentset to perform an action, all the agents collected at that moment (and only those agents) will perform the action. If one agent's (agent A) action causes another agent (agent B) in the agentset to no longer satisfy the collection criteria, B will

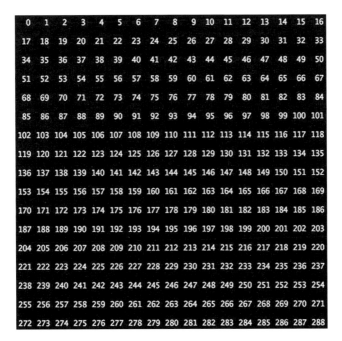

Figure 5.3
Patches labeled in ascending order.

still perform the action. Likewise, if A's action causes agent C, which is not in the agentset, to meet the collection criteria, C will still not perform the action.

As an illustration, let's consider this code snippet from the Agentset Ordering model in the chapter 5 subfolder of the IABM Textbook folder in the models library:

```
to setup
    clear-all
    create-turtles 100 [
        set size random-float 2.0
        forward10
    ]
end

to go
    ask turtles [
        set color blue
        ]
    ask turtles with [ size < 1.0 ] [
        ask one-of turtles with [size > 1.0] [
            set size size - 0.5
        ]
        set color red
    ]
    print count turtles with [ color = red ]
    print count turtles with [ size < 1.0 ]
end
```

The bolded code has the potential to change the set of agents with size < 1.0 by making some agents smaller, thereby changing the agentset defined in the first ASK. For example, if we started with a total of ten agents, with eight of those having a size less than 1, and the other two, are size 1.2, then any big turtle that was selected by at least one small turtle would shrink to a size below 1.0. However, this newly small turtle will not execute the inner ask, since the first agentset, with 8 members, is held constant as soon as it is created; therefore, the agents taking actions will not change until the next time you execute the GO loop and recreate the agentset. The net result is that, at the end of the execution of the GO procedure, it is possible to have a turtle that has a SIZE less than 1.0 and is still blue. The print statements confirm that these two values, the counts of red turtles and small turtles, are not equal. This can be confusing when first thinking about agentsets, but really, this is a variant of the same issue you run into whenever you take action based on the condition of a variable and that action affects the value of the same variable.

Another problem that often comes up when working with agentsets pertains to computational efficiency. Sometimes it is more efficient to compute an agentset before performing a set of operations that involve the agentset. For instance, look at the GO-1 procedure below from the Agentset Efficiency model in the chapter 5 subfolder of the IABM Textbook folder of the models library:

```
;; GO-1 sets red patch labels to a small random number and
;; green patch labels to a larger random number
to go-1
    if any? patches with [ pcolor = red] [
       ask patches with [ pcolor = red] [
              set plabel random 5 ;; red patches are labeled 0-4
       ]
    ]
    if any? patches with [ pcolor = green] [
       ask patches with [ pcolor = green] [
              set plabel 5 + random 5 ;; green patches are labeled 5-9
       ]
    ]
    tick
end
```

This code computes each of the two agentsets PATCHES WITH [PCOLOR = RED] and PATCHES WITH [PCOLOR = GREEN] twice.

The procedure GO-2 below has the same behavior as GO-1, but it is more efficient in that it computes each of those agentsets only once. Computing agentsets can be an expensive operation, so it is often advisable to compute them first and then ask them to behave.

```
;; GO-2 has the same behavior as go-1 above. But it is more efficient as it
computes each of the patch agentsets only once.
to go-2
 let red-patches patches with [ pcolor = red ]
 let green-patches patches with [ pcolor = green ]
 if any? red-patches [
    ask red-patches [
    set plabel random 5
    ]
]
if any? green-patches [
    ask green-patches [
    set plabel 5 + random 5
    ]
]
 tick
end
```

In the code above, GO-2 is twice as efficient as GO-1. The efficiency problem can get even worse and the gain correspondingly bigger when the duplicated agentset construction is inside an ASK PATCHES. For example, if the GO loop, asked each patch to check and construct a neighbors agentset, then each patch would be executing code that is half as efficient as possible, and so computing the agentset ahead of time would provide an even larger gain in performance.

However, it is important that your code be readable, so others can understand it. In the end, computer time is cheap compared to human time. Therefore, it should be noted that,

Box 5.3
Computational Complexity

Agent-based models can be computationally intensive. It is often necessary to make sure that model code is as efficient as possible. Computing agentsets before iterating over them is one example of how you can make your computation more efficient, but there are many other ways as well. A standard way of describing the efficiency of an algorithm is Big-O notation. Big-O notation indicates how much time must be spent on an algorithm as a function of its inputs. For instance, the time it takes to complete a function that is $O(n)$ is linear in the size of its inputs, while the time it takes to complete a function that is $O(n^2)$ grows as the square of its inputs. If the number of inputs is large, then an $O(n^2)$ algorithm will take much longer to run than an $O(n)$ algorithm. For instance, if we compute the distance between each agent and the center of the world, that will only take $O(n)$ time, since we only need to examine each agent once. However, if we want to find the distance between each agent and every other agent in the world, that will take $n \cdot (n - 1)$ operations, which means it will run in $O(n^2)$ time. There is a whole field of computer science called computational complexity devoted to creating more efficient algorithms (Papadimitriou, 1994). In practice, Big-O notation is used for conveniently comparing two algorithms: if one algorithm runs in $O(n^2)$, and another operates in $O(n)$ time, then the $O(n)$ algorithm is faster and will usually be used.

whenever there is a possibility of trade-off, clarity of code should be preferred over efficiency.

A more pernicious issue arises if we change just one line of GO-1 and GO-2:

```
;; GO-3 shows what happens if patch colors are changed "on the fly"
to go-3
    if any? patches with [ pcolor = red] [
      ask patches with [ pcolor = red] [
            set pcolor green
      ]
    ]
    if any? patches with [ pcolor = green] [
      ask patches with [ pcolor = green] [
            set pcolor red
      ]
    ]
    tick
end
```

If you run this code, you might expect to get a picture that looks like figure 5.4; that is, you expect red patches to turn green and vice versa. In fact, this is not what happens. Instead, this code will result in a picture like figure 5.5, where all the patches are red. Why does this unexpected behavior happen? This is another example of the ordering issue we just discussed above. The first "if statement" turns the patches green, so by the time the

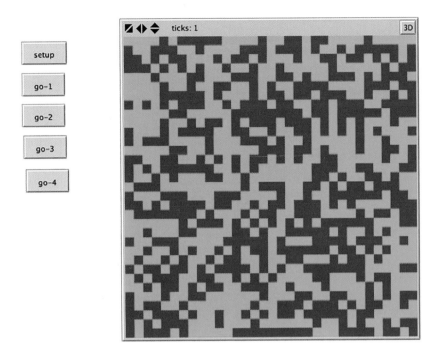

Figure 5.4
Constructing agentsets at the outset results in expected behavior.

second "if statement" is executed, all the patches are green and therefore then turn red. By computing the agentsets ahead of time, as in GO-4, you are not only using more efficient code but are also ensuring that the green-patches agentsets you ask to execute the instructions are the same green-patches agentsets as at the start of the procedure and not the set of green patches that result from the first "if-statement," resulting in the expected picture of figure 5.4.

```
;; GO-4 shows what happens if you keep track, at the outset, of which patches
;; are red and which are green
to go-4
        let red-patches patches with [pcolor = red]
        let green-patches patches with [pcolor = green]
        if any? red-patches [
            ask red-patches [
                set pcolor green
            ]
        ]
        if any? green-patches [
            ask green-patches [
                set pcolor red
            ]
        ]
    tick
end
```

setup

go-1

go-2

go-3

go-4

Figure 5.5
Constructing agentsets after the model state has changed, results in unintended outcome.

The Granularity of an Agent

One of the first considerations when designing an agent-based model is at what granularity should you create your agent—at what level of complexity is the agent you are modeling. In chapter 0, we discussed one prominent hierarchy of levels of complexity, e.g., atoms, molecules, cells, humans, organizations, and governments. Thus, what we mean by granularity of the agent is the point in such a hierarchy that we select the agents in the model. This point may seem obvious if you characteristically think of agents in an agent-based model as people, i.e., that there should be an agent for every individual person in the model. But that "obvious" answer is often not the best choice. For example, if you are modeling the interactions of national governments, you probably do not want to model each individual in each of the governments. Instead of the individuals within a government, it often makes more sense to model each government as an agent.

So how do you choose the level of complexity for the agents in your model? The guideline is to choose agents such that they represent the fundamental level of interaction that pertains to your question about the phenomenon. For instance, if you look at the Tumor model (shown in figure 5.6) in the Biology section of the NetLogo models library, the agents are cells within the human body, since the research question the model examines

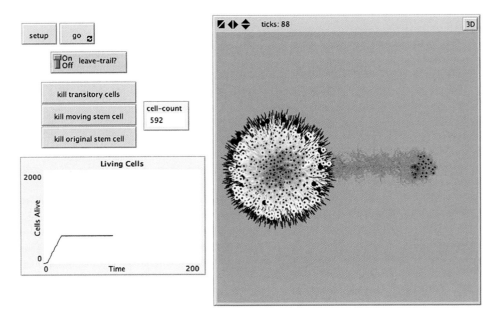

Figure 5.6
NetLogo Tumor model. http://ccl.northwestern.edu/netlogo/models/Tumor (*Wilensky, 1998b*).

is how tumor cells spread. However, even though the AIDS model in the Biology section of the NetLogo models library (see figure 5.7) is also concerned with disease, the basic agents are humans instead of cells. This is because the AIDS model is more concerned with how the disease spreads between humans instead of how it spreads within the human body. In the Tumor model, the question of concern is how cells interact to create cancer. Thus, the most important interactions happen at the cell level, and this makes cells a good choice for agents In the AIDS model, the question of concern is how humans interact to spread disease, with humans as the agents being the most appropriate choice. These two models highlight the relationship between the question being investigated, the interactions being modeled, and the resulting choices of granularity for the agents.

It is not always as easy to determine the most productive granularity for your agents, as these two cases might suggest. In some other cases, there may be more than one appropriate grain-size for the agents. For instance, in the Tumor model, it may be appropriate to move up to a larger level of aggregation. Besides looking at cells, it may also be useful to have agents represent organs so that the tumor's effect throughout the body can be examined. Within such models, it is often possible to view a group of cells as operating homogenously, meaning that you can view a few dozen cells as your core agent. This has the advantage of decreasing the computational requirements for your model. However, this has the trade-off of losing detail about the interactions that occur within this new grouping

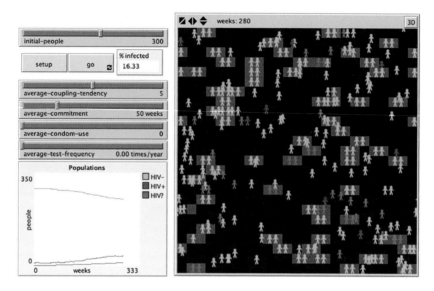

Figure 5.7
NetLogo AIDS model. http://ccl.northwestern.edu/netlogo/models/AIDS (*Wilensky, 1997a*).

of agents. Both individual cells and groups of cells can be valid choices for the level of complexity of these agents, and deciding between them will depend on details of the question you are asking as well as considerations of computational complexity.

Choosing the appropriate granularity for your agents can make your models much easier to create, as it allows you to ignore unnecessary aspects of the phenomena being modeled and instead focus on the interactions of interest. For instance, in the AIDS model, by not representing the actual AIDS virus, we can assess the spread of the disease through a population rather than its development within a single human. By contrast, by looking at cells in the Tumor model we are able to examine cellular interactions at a greater resolution than we could if we tried to use molecules as our agents. Selecting an appropriate grain-size for your agents is a critical early step in the development of a successful ABM.

It is also important that the granularity of your agents is comparable relative to each other within the model. This is sometimes known as the scale of the model. In other words, agents should operate on roughly the same time scales, and should have roughly the same physical presence within the model. If agents are not at the same scale it is still possible to include them within the same model, but it requires adjusting the model behavior so that they can interact appropriately.

Agent Cognition
As we have described, agents have different properties and behaviors. Still, how do agents examine their properties and the world around them to decide what actions to take? This

question is resolved by a decision-making process called agent cognition. We will discuss several types of agent cognition: *reflexive agents*, *utility-based agents*, *goal-based agents*, and *adaptive agents* (Russell & Norvig, 1995). Often, these types of cognition are thought of in increasing order of complexity, with reflexive agents being the simplest, and adaptive agents the most complex. In reality, though this is not a strict hierarchy of complexity. Instead, these are descriptive terms that help us talk about agent cognition and can be mixed and matched; for instance, it is possible to have a utility-based adaptive agent.

Reflexive agents are built around very simple rules. They use if-then rules to react to inputs and take actions (Russell & Norvig, 1995). For instance, the cars in the Traffic Basic model are reflexive agents. If you look at the code that controls their actions, it looks like this:

```
let car-ahead one-of turtles-on patch-ahead 1  ;;choose a car on the patch ahead
ifelse car-ahead != nobody [  ;; if there is a car ahead
    slow-down-car car-ahead ;; set car speed to be slower than car ahead
]
[   ;; otherwise, speed up
    speed-up-car ;; increase speed variable by the acceleration
]
;; ….
fd speed
```

Put in words, this code says that if there are cars ahead, then slow down below the speed of the car in front; if there are not any cars ahead, then speed up. This is a reflexive action based on the state of the program, hence the name *reflexive agent*. This is the most basic form of agent cognition (and often a good starting point), but it is possible to make the agent cognition more sophisticated. For instance, we could elaborate this model by giving the cars gas tanks and fuel efficiencies based on the speed they are going. We could then have the cars change their speeds in order to improve their fuel efficiencies. As a result, the agents might have to speed up and slow down at different times than they currently do to minimize their gas usage while still not causing accidents. Giving the agents this type of decision-making process would give them a *utility-based* form of agent cognition in which they attempt to maximize a utility function—namely, their fuel efficiency (Russell & Norvig, 1995). To implement this model of agent cognition, we need to start by replacing our SPEED-UP-CAR procedure with a new procedure that accounts for the car's fuel efficiency.

```
;; choose a car on the patch ahead
let car-ahead one-of turtles-on patch-ahead 1
ifelse car-ahead != nobody [ ;; if there is a car ahead
    slow-down-car car-ahead  ;; set car speed to be slower than car ahead
]
[ ;; otherwise, adjust speed to find ideal fuel efficiency
    adjust-speed-for-efficiency ]
```

We want the ADJUST-SPEED-FOR-EFFICIENCY procedure to maintain the same speed if the car is at the maximally fuel efficient speed. If it is not at its most efficient speed, the logic in this procedure should have the car speed up if it is moving too slow and slow down if the car is moving too fast. Additionally, the car would still need to slow down if it was about to crash into the car in front of it. As such, the true utility function includes an exception that gives a utility of 0 to any action that results in a crash. As a result, we can leave the first part of the code that slows the car before it crashes and just add ADJUST-SPEED-FOR_EFFICIENCY when there is no car directly ahead, as illustrated in the code below from the Traffic Basic Utility model, which is also in the chapter 5 subfolder of the IABM Textbook folder of the NetLogo models library.

```
;; car procedure
to adjust-speed-for-efficiency
  if (speed != efficient-speed) [ ;; if car is at efficient speed, do nothing
        if (speed + acceleration < efficient-speed) [
;; if accelerating will still put you below the efficient speed then accelerate
            set speed speed + acceleration
        ]                                      ;;
;; if decelerating will still put you above the efficient speed then decelerate
        if (speed - deceleration > efficient-speed) [
            set speed speed - deceleration
        ]
    ]
end
```

In the language of utility functions, each car agent is minimizing a function f, defined by:

$$f(v) = |v - v^*|$$

where v is the current velocity of the car and v* is the most efficient velocity. The constraint that is described in the code is that the v cannot be adjusted arbitrarily, but instead, can only be changed by a limited increment every time step. By trying different values for EFFICIENT-SPEED, you can obtain quite different traffic patterns from the original model. For low values of EFFICIENT-SPEED, the system can achieve a free-flow state (with no jams) on a consistent basis.

Note that the original model code can be viewed also as maximizing a utility function—the simple utility function of the car's speed subject to the speed limit. However, this is such a simple utility function that we do not categorize the agent as a utility-based agent but rather as a reflexive agent. Such judgments can be subjective. While this second implementation of the car agent's cognition is more sophisticated than our initial design, it is still built on an underlying assumption that can be further refined. The modified code is also simplified in that it assumes we have predefined EFFICIENT-SPEED. But what if we

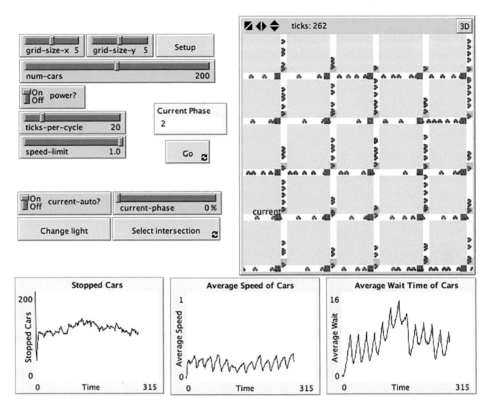

Figure 5.8
Traffic Grid model. http://ccl.northwestern.edu/netlogo/models/TrafficGrid (*Wilensky, 2002b*).

did not know what the most efficient speed for a car to travel at was? If we had access to the instantaneous gas mileage of the car, then we could actually learn these values over time. This addition would make our cars into simple *adaptive agents*.

The third type of agent cognition we will discuss is goal-based cognition. Imagine that each car in the Traffic Grid model (see figure 5.8) from the social sciences section of the NetLogo models library has a home and a place of work, with the goal of moving from home to work in a reasonable amount of time. Now, not only do the agents have to be able to speed up and slow down, but they also have to be able to turn left and right. In this version of the model, the cars are *goal-based agents*, since they have a goal (getting to and from work) that they are using to dictate their actions.

We will need to modify the Traffic Grid model so that each car has a house and a work location. We will want both of these locations to be off-road, but adjacent to the road. As the background of the grid is a shade of brown (color 38), we first create an agentset of all brown patches adjacent to a road (roads are white). These patches are the possible houses and work locations of the agents.

```
let goal-candidates patches with [pcolor = 38 and any?
neighbors with [pcolor = white]]
```

Then when we create the cars, each car sets its house to a random patch in that agentset and its work location to be any other patch in the agentset.

```
set house one-of goal-candidates
set work one-of goal-candidates with [ self != [ house ] of myself ]
```

The part of the GO procedure that is relevant to the cars looks like this:

```
;;set the cars' speed this tick, cars move forward an amount equal to their speed
;; record data for plotting, and set the color of the cars to either dark blue or cyan
;; based on their speed
ask turtles [
    set-car-speed
    fd speed
    record-data       ;; Record data for plotting
    set-car-color  ;; Set color to indicate speed
  ]
```

To implement the goal-based version of the model, we start by defining the procedure that the cars will use to navigate between their two desired destinations. Instead of just moving straight all the time, as with the cars in the original model, the new model should have the car at each step deciding which of its neighboring road patches is the closest to its destination, subsequently proceeding in that direction. We do this in the procedure called NEXT-PATCH. First, each car checks if it has arrived at its goal, and if so, switches its goal:

```
;; if I am going home and I am on the patch that is my home
;; I turn around and head towards work (my goal is set to "work")
    if goal = house and patch-here = house [
      set goal work
    ]
;; if I am going to work and I am on the patch that is my work
;; I turn around and head towards home (my goal is set to "home")
    if goal = work and patch-here = work [
      set goal house
    ]
```

The code above doesn't quite work. That's because the house and work are off-road and the cars remain on the road, so the condition "patch-here = house" or "patch-here = work" will never be satisfied. As we placed the house and work adjacent to the road, we can fix this by having the car check if it is right next to its goal.

```
;; if I am going home and I am next to the patch that is my home
;; I turn around and head towards work (my goal is set to "work")
if goal = house and (member? patch-here [neighbors4] of house) [
      stay set goal work
    ]
;; if I am going to work and I am next to the patch that is my work
;; I turn around and head towards home (my goal is set to "home")
   if goal = work and (member? patch-here [neighbors4] of work) [
       stay set goal house
    ]
```

Having established a goal, each car then chooses an adjacent patch to move to that is the closest to its goal. It does this by choosing candidate patches to move to (adjacent patches on the road) and then selecting the candidate closest to its goal.

The resultant NEXT-PATCH procedure is:

```
;; establish goal of driver
to-report next-patch
;; if I am going home and I am next to the patch that is my home
;; I turn around and head towards work (my goal is set to "work")
if goal = house and (member? patch-here [neighbors4] of house) [
      stay set goal work
    ]
;; if I am going to work and I am next to the patch that is my work
;; I turn around and head towards home (my goal is set to "home")
   if goal = work and (member? patch-here [neighbors4] of work) [
       stay set goal house
    ]
;; CHOICES is an agentset of the candidate patches which the car can
;; move to (white patches are roads, green and red patches are lights)
let choices neighbors with [pcolor = white or pcolor = red or pcolor = green]
         ;; choose the patch closest to the goal, this is the patch the car will move to
   let choice min-one-of choices [distance [goal] of myself]
;; report the chosen patch
    report choice
end
```

With this procedure in place, we can modify the GO procedure to ask each of the cars to now move between their homes and their work.

```
ask turtles
    [
;; head towards the patch that is closest to your goal
        face next-patch
        set-car-speed
        fd speed
        set-car-color
    ]
```

Now, we have goal-directed car agents in the grid. However, the agents' approach is rather naïve and ineffective, since agents are measuring the nearness to their goal by direct distance (as the bird flies) as opposed to the distance by following the road. Thus, the cars will often get stuck going back and forth on the same stretch of road, instead of going around a block. In the explorations at the end of this chapter, we challenge the reader to come up with more intelligent, sophisticated planning so that the agents can more reliably reach their goals.

One of the powerful advantages of agent-based modeling is that agents can change not only their decisions but also their strategies (Holland, 1996). An agent that can change its strategy based on prior experience is an *adaptive agent*. Unlike conventional agents, which will also do the same thing when presented with the same circumstance, adaptive agents can make different decisions if given the same set of inputs. In the Traffic Basic model, cars do not always take the same action; they operate differently based on the cars around them by either slowing down or speeding up. However, regardless of what has happened to the cars in the past (i.e., whether they got stuck in traffic jams or not) they will continue to take the same actions in the same conditions in the future. To be truly adaptive, agents need to be able to change not only their actions in time, but also their strategies. They must be able to change how they act because they have encountered a similar situation in the past and can react differently this time based on their past experience. In other words, the agents learn from their past experience and change their behavior in the future to account for this learning. For instance, the agent could have observed that in the past that, when there was a car five patches ahead of it, it braked too quickly, even though it could have waited longer to brake without hitting the other car. In the future, it could change its rule for braking to brake only when a car is four patches ahead. This agent is now an *adaptive agent* because it not only modifies its *actions*, but also, its *strategies*.

Another example of adaptive cognition in our traffic model would be to have the agents learn the best rate of acceleration to maintain the highest velocity. We can implement this form of agent cognition by changing the code in the GO procedure in Traffic Basic as follows. (To get this code to work we would also have to change the SETUP procedure and some global properties but that is left as an exercise for the reader.) This code is also in the Traffic Basic Adaptive model in the chapter 5 subfolder of the IABM Textbook folder of the NetLogo models library:

```
to adaptive-go
    ;; check to see if we should test a new value for acceleration this tick
    let testing? false
    if ticks mod ticks-between-exploration = 0 [
        set testing? true
;; choose new value for acceleration, slightly different from current acceleration
        set acceleration acceleration + (random-float 0.0010) - 0.0005
    ]

  ;; run the old go code
    go

;; check to see if our new speed of turtles is better than the previous speeds
;; if so, then adopt the new acceleration
    ifelse mean [ speed ] of turtles > best-speed-so-far and testing? [
        set best-acceleration-so-far acceleration
        set best-speed-so-far mean [ speed ] of turtles
    ]
    [
        set acceleration best-acceleration-so-far
    ]
    if not testing? [
;; you don't want to take one data point as a measure of the speed. Instead you
;; calculate a weighted average of past observed speed and the current speed.
        set best-speed-so-far (0.1 * mean [speed] of turtles) + (0.9 * best-speed-so-far)
    ]
end
```

Though this code may appear complicated, it is straightforward. Essentially, cars use the best acceleration they have found so far unless they are in a tick where they are exploring a new acceleration value, as specified by TICKS-BETWEEN-EXPLORATION. Over time, the cars keep a weighted average of the speed they are able to maintain at the best acceleration; if the new acceleration allows for a faster speed, the cars will then switch to using that new acceleration. This average for the best acceleration weighs the past historical speeds higher (0.9) than the present speed (0.1), accounting for the fact that you can occasionally get spurious results (noise). Thus, it is better to rely on a large amount of data than one particular data point. However, the code still allows the best acceleration to change, which means even if the environment were to change (e.g., more cars on the road, longer road, etc.) the car could adapt to the new situation.

If you run the Traffic Basic Adaptive model, you will notice the cars eventually stop forming traffic jams, though it may take them quite some time to arrive at the free-flow state. Eventually, the model "learns" that a high rate of acceleration results in the best speed overall. In this case, the model learns one acceleration value for all agents. Another change we could make to this model would be to allow the individual agents to learn different best accelerations for themselves. (This is left as an exercise for the reader.) Since

Box 5.4
Machine Learning

Machine learning is the study of computer algorithms that use previous experience to improve their performance. For example, in the 1980s, American Express had a procedure that would classify credit applications into three states: applications that (1) should be immediately approved, (2) should be immediately denied, and (3) need to be examined by a loan officer (Langley & Simon, 1995). However, it turned out that the loan officers were able to correctly determine whether the borderline applicants would default on their loan only 50 percent of the time. Michie (1989) used a machine-learning algorithm to examine these borderline cases. This algorithm was able to correctly classify 70 percent of these cases, and American Express decided to use this algorithm instead of human loan officers.

In this example, the algorithm was trained on a group of test cases. These test cases consisted of inputs based on the credit application and an output based on whether or not the applicant defaulted on the loan. The algorithm was then tested on cases that it had not been shown during the training period, with the algorithm correctly predicting 70 percent of these cases. Because the algorithm is continuously learning, the algorithm continues to improve itself with use. This is just one example of the many possible uses of machine learning. For a general overview, see Mitchell (1997).

the model now learns acceleration, another exercise would be to learn the deceleration values as well.

Besides the basic types of cognition that we have discussed, there are also more advanced methods of giving cognition to agents. One of the best ways to do this is by combining agent-based modeling with *machine learning*. Machine learning is an area of artificial intelligence that is concerned with giving computers the ability to adapt to the world around them and learn what actions to take in response to a given set of inputs. By giving agents the ability to use various machine-learning techniques such as neural nets, genetic algorithms, and Bayesian classifiers, they can change their actions to take into account new information (Rand, 2006; Rand & Stonedahl, 2007; Holland, 1996; Vohra & Wellman, 2007). This can result in agents with quite sophisticated levels of cognition.

Other Kinds of Agents

We have already discussed breeds and various types of agents, but there are two other special kinds of agents that deserve at least a brief mention. The first type are meta-agents, agents made up of other agents; the second is proto-agents, placeholder agents that allow you to define interactions for your fully defined agents with other entities that have not been fully developed.

Meta-Agents   Many things that we would consider agents in reality are actually composed of other agents. In reality, all "agents" are composed of other agents; to cite the oft-told parable, "It's turtles all the way down."[5] In other words, there is always a lower level of detail that you can use to describe an agent in your model, at least until you reach the most basic level so far described by physics. For instance, if we have selected a human to be the agent, he or she is actually composed of many subagents, with these subagents in turn being different depending on how you view the human. You could view the subagents of a human as the systems of the body—e.g., the immune and the respiratory systems—or you could view the subagents of a human as psychological aspects like the intellect and emotion. Moreover, these subagents are not the most basic level; in our example, the systems of the body are made up of organs, tissues, and cells.

At each of these levels, we are describing the relationship between *meta-agents* (agents composed of other agents) and *subagents* (agents which compose other agents). Still, agents can also be both meta-agents and subagents at the same time. For instance, organs are composed of cells and are meta-agents. However, they also play a compositional role in the systems of the human body and are thus subagents. We can use meta-agents in our ABMs by defining the subagents that make up our agents and providing them with their own actions and properties.

From the perspective of another meta-agent, a meta-agent appears to be a single agent. If a person meets another person, they do not (usually) directly interface with the heart or the lungs (unless the meeting takes place at the surgical table). Instead, they interface with the person as a whole. The same is true in ABM. Suppose you have a meta-agent of a human that is composed of an intellect and an emotion. Everything that meta-agent "says" is the result of a dialogue between intellect and emotion. When another human meta-agent speaks to that meta-agent, the second meta-agent will only be aware of the utterance resulting from that dialogue, and not the individual factors that made it up.

When we think of modeling agents and their interactions, we have to determine what level of granularity we want to describe the agent behaviors. However, we always have the option of refining our model by converting agents into meta-agents that describe the agents that constitute other agents. Sometimes, it can be useful to represent the agents in our models not as autonomous individuals, but instead, as meta-agents composed of other agents. NetLogo doesn't include explicit language support for these meta-agents, though there are commands for locking together the movement of several agents (e.g., the TIE command) that may be useful in some circumstances. However, there is nothing to prevent you from designing models that have groups of agents representing single agents.

---

5. As the story goes, a visitor asks the wise man what keeps the earth from falling. The wise man says that the earth is held up on the back of a giant turtle. The visitor asks what is holding up the turtle, and the wise man replies, "Yet another turtle." The visitor smiles and asks, "What is holding up the first turtle?" The wise man responds, "It's turtles all the way down." The source of this quote is disputed, although William James seems the likeliest candidate.

Proto-Agents To truly be an agent within the agent-based modeling framework, an entity must have its own properties or actions. Sometimes, though, it can be desirable to create agents that, rather than having their own properties or behaviors, are instead placeholders for future agents. We call these agents *proto-agents*, and their primary purpose is to enable us to specify how other agents would interact with them if they were fleshed out into full agents. For instance, if you were creating a model of residential location decision making, you would have residents as agents; however, since where a resident lives is greatly influenced by places of employment and services (e.g., grocery stores and restaurants) you might also want to include these "service centers" as agents as well. The same level of detail necessary for the residents, who are the focal agents of concern, may not be necessary for the service centers. Instead, they might be rendered as placeholders to represent where residents might potentially find jobs and transact business. However, as you continue to refine the model, you might give the service centers additional decision-making abilities. For instance, they might have a more elaborate model of market demand and decide where to locate using their own properties and beliefs about the future growth of the world. Keeping these agents as proto-agents early on means that when you add in the more richly detailed versions to the model, you do not have to go back and revise your resident agents. Instead, you can use the interaction events that they had already been using to interface with the service center proto-agents. There are no special NetLogo commands to create proto-agents; rather, agents such as patches or turtles may serve the role of proto-agents depending on how they are treated in your model.

Both meta-agents and proto-agents provide a way to initially create a simpler model and late elaborate upon that model as we continue to refine it.

Environments

Another early and critical decision is how to design the *environment* of the agent-based model. The environment consists of the conditions and habitats surrounding the agents as they act and interact within the model. The environment can affect agent decisions, and, in turn, can be affected by agent decisions. For instance, in the Ants model from chapter 1, the ants leave pheromone in the environment that changes the environment, and in turn changes the behavior of the ants. There are many different kinds of environments that are common in ABMs. In this section, we will discuss a few of the most common types of environments.

Before we discuss the types of environments, it is important to mention that the environment itself can be implemented in a variety of ways. First, the environment can be composed of agents such that each individual piece of the environment can have a full set of properties and actions. In NetLogo, this is the default view of the environment—the environment is represented by the agentset of patches. This allows different parts of the environment to have different properties and act differently based on their local interactions. A second approach represents the environment as one large agent, with a global set of properties and actions. Yet another approach is to implement the environment outside of the ABM toolkit. For instance, it could be handled by a geographic information systems (GIS) toolkit, or it could be handled by a social network analysis (SNA) toolkit, and the ABM can interact with that environment. All of the "types" of environments we discuss in what follows are, in principle, independent of this implementation decision; still, some types may be easier to create using different implementations.

Spatial Environments

Spatial environments in agent-based models generally have two variants: discrete spaces and continuous spaces. In a mathematical representation, in continuous spaces between any pair of points, there exists another point, while in discrete spaces, though each point has a neighboring point, there do exist pairs of points without other points between them, so that each point is separated from every other point. However, when implemented in an ABM, all continuous spaces must be implemented as approximations, so that continuous spaces are represented as discrete spaces where the spaces between the points are very small. It should be noted that both discrete and continuous spaces can be either finite or infinite. In NetLogo, however, the standard implementation is a finite space, although it is possible to implement an infinite space (we explain how later in the chapter).

Discrete Spaces   The most common discrete spaces used in ABM are lattice graphs (also sometimes referred to as mesh graphs or grid graphs), which are environments where every location in the environment is connected to other locations in a regular grid. For instance, every location in a toroidal square lattice has a neighboring location up, down, to the left, and to the right. As mentioned, the most common representation of the environment in NetLogo is *patches*, which are located on a 2D lattice underlying the world of the ABM (see figure 5.9 for a colorful pattern of patches whose code is simply ASK PATCHES [SET PCOLOR PXCOR * PYCOR]). This uniform connectivity makes them different from network-based environments, which we will discuss in more detail later in this chapter.

The two most common types of lattices are square and hexagonal lattices, which we will discuss in turn later. There is one other type of regular polygon that tiles the plane (i.e., covers the plane with no "holes"), namely the triangle, but the triangle is usually not as useful for representing environments as squares and hexagons are. In addition, there are eight other (semiregular) tilings involving combinations of triangles, squares, hexagons, octagons, and dodecagons (Branko & Shephard, 1987). However, since these tilings

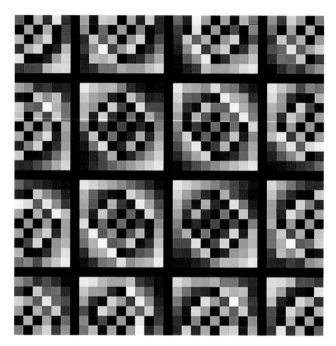

Figure 5.9
Patches displaying a range of colors.

have different cell shapes in different locations, they make the environment nonuniform; thus, they are not commonly employed in ABM, though nothing precludes their use.

Square Lattices   The square lattice is the most common type of ABM environment. A square lattice is one composed of many little squares, akin to the grid paper used in mathematics classrooms. As we discussed in chapter 2, there are two classical types of neighborhoods on a square lattice: the *von Neumann neighborhood*, consisting of four neighbors located in the cardinal directions (see figure 5.10a); and the *Moore neighborhood*, comprising the 8 adjacent cells (See figure 5.10b). A von Neumann neighborhood (named after John von Neumann, a pioneer of cellular automata theory among other things) of radius 1 is a lattice where each cell has four neighbors: up, down, left, and right. A Moore neighborhood (named after Edward F. Moore, another pioneer of cellular automata theory) of radius 1 is a lattice in which each cell has eight neighbors in the eight directions that touch either a side or a corner: up, down, left, right, up-left, up-right, down-left, and down-right. In general, a Moore neighborhood gives you a better approximation to movement in a plane, and since many ABMs model phenomenon where planar movement is common, it is often the preferred modeling choice for discrete motion.

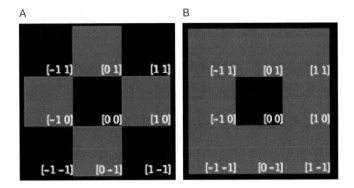

Figure 5.10
(a) Von Neumann Neighborhood. (b) Moore Neighborhood. The black cell in the center is the focal cell, and the red cells comprise its neighborhood.

These neighborhoods can be extended for neighborhoods with radii greater than 1; for example, a Moore neighborhood of radius 2 would have twenty-four neighbors, while a von Neumann neighborhood of radius 2 would have eight neighbors. An easy way to remember the difference between Moore and von Neumann neighborhoods is that a Moore neighborhood has "more" neighbors than a von Neumann neighborhood. We will discuss how neighborhoods affect interactions in the Interaction section later in this chapter.

Hex Lattices   A hex lattice has some advantages over square lattices. The center of a cell in a square grid is farther from the centers of some of the adjacent cells (the diagonally adjacent ones) than other such cells. However, in a hex lattice, the distance between the center of a cell and all adjacent cells is the same. Moreover, hexagons are the polygons with the most edges that tile the plane, and for some applications, this makes them the best polygons to use. Both of these differences (equidistance between centers and the number of edges) mean that hex lattices more closely approximate a continuous plane than square lattices. But because square lattices match more closely a Cartesian coordinate system, a square lattice is a simpler structure to work with; even when a hexagonal lattice would be superior, many ABMs and ABM toolkits nevertheless employ square lattices. However, with a little effort, any modern ABM environment can simulate a hexagonal lattice in a square lattice environment. For instance, you can see a hex lattice environment in the NetLogo Code examples, Hex Cells example, and Hex Turtles example (see figures 5.11 and 5.12). In the Hex Cells example, each patch in the world maintains a set of six neighbors, with the agents located on each patch having a hexagonal shape. In other words, the world is still rectangular, but we have defined a new set of neighbors for each patch. In the Hex Turtles example, the turtles have an arrow shape and start along headings that

Figure 5.11
Hex Cells example from the NetLogo models library.

are evenly divisible by 60 degrees; when they move they only move along these same 60-degree angles.

Continuous Spaces   In a continuous space, there is no notion of a cell or a discrete region within the space. Instead, agents within the space are located at points in the space. These points can be as small as the resolution of the number representation allows. In a continuous space, agents can move smoothly through the space, passing over any points in between their origin and destination, whereas in a discrete space, the agent moves directly from the center of one cell to another. Because computers are discrete machines, it is impossible to exactly represent a continuous space. We can, however, represent it at a level of resolution that is very fine. In other words, all ABMs that use continuous spaces are actually using a very detailed discrete space, while the resolution is usually high enough that to suffice for most purposes.

One of the interesting innovations of NetLogo absent in many other ABM toolkits is that the default space is a continuous space, with a discrete lattice laid on top of it. As a result, agents can move smoothly through the space, but they can also determine what

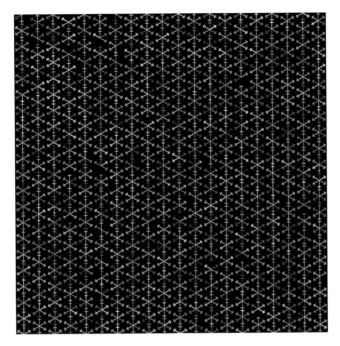

Figure 5.12
Hex Turtles example from the NetLogo models library.

cell they are in and interact with the lattice. To make this work, there has to be a mapping between the discrete space and the continuous space. In NetLogo, this is done by having the center of each patch be the integer coordinates of the patch, with each patch extending 0.5 units around this center. For instance a patch at –1, –5 has those coordinates at the center of the patch and includes every point from (–1.5, –5.5) to (–0.5, –5.5) to (–0.5, –4.5) to (–1.5, –4.5). However, this is not exactly true since the points along the edges can only belong to one patch: a patch at 0, –5, for example, includes the points along the edge from (–0.5, –5.5) to (–0.5, –4.5) including the points at the corners and the patch at –1, –4 includes the points along the edge from (–0.5, –4.5) to (–1.5, –4.5) including the points at the corner. In other words, a patch contains its bottom and left edges, but not its top and right edges.

NetLogo does not require that you specify whether you are using a continuous or discrete space ahead of time; model developers can write code that takes advantage of either spatial form. Many of the NetLogo sample models actually use both the discrete rectangular lattice and the continuous plane at the same time. For instance, the Traffic Basic model represents the cars as existing at points in the space but uses patch-ahead (i.e., the rectangular lattice) to determine if the car should speed up or slow down.

Box 5.5
Topologies

A topology is a class of environments with the same connectivity structure. For example, a sheet of paper represents the topology of a bounded plane. No matter how big that sheet of paper is, it still has fixed rectangular boundaries. A torus is the topology of a doughnut. Take a sheet of paper and roll it up. Now attach one open end to the other—you will get a doughnut-shaped (torus) topology. What makes topologies interesting is their connectivity properties and how these properties enable or block the movement of agents. When an agent on a bounded plane topology comes to the edge of the plane, there is nowhere else for it to go. By contrast, an agent on the torus topology encounters no edge to the world.

Boundary Conditions   One other factor that comes into play when working with spatial environments is how to deal with boundaries, an issue for Hex and Square lattices as much as for continuous spaces. If an agent reaches a border on the far left side of the world and wants to go farther left, what happens? There are three standard approaches to this question, referred to as *topologies* of the environment: (1) it reappears on the far right side of the lattice (toroidal topology); (2) it cannot go any farther left (bounded topology); or (3) it can keep going left forever (infinite plane topology).

A *toroidal* topology is one in which all of the edges are connected to another edge in a regular manner. In a rectangular lattice, the left side of the world is connected to the right side, while the top of the world is connected to the bottom. Thus, when agents move off the world in one direction, they reappear at the opposite side. This is sometimes called *wrapping*, because the agents wrap off one side of the world and onto another. In general, using a toroidal topology means that the modeler can ignore boundary conditions, which usually makes model development easier. If the world is nontoroidal, then modelers have to develop special rules to handle what to do when an agent encounters a boundary in the world. In a spatial model, this conflict is one of whether the agent should turn around simply take a step backward. Indeed, the most commonly used environment for an ABM is a square toroidal lattice.

A *bounded* topology is one in which agents are not allowed to move beyond the edges of the world. This topology is a more realistic representation of some environments. For example, if you are modeling agricultural practices, it is unrealistic for a farmer to be able to keep driving the tractor east and then end up back on the west side of the field. Using a torus environment may affect the amount of fuel required to plow the fields, so a bounded topology might be a better choice depending on the questions the model is trying to address. It is also possible to have some of the limits of the world be bounded while others are wrapping. For instance, in the Traffic Basic model, where the cars only drive from left to right, the top and bottom of the world are bounded (cars do not go up and down in this

Box 5.6
Exploring Environments and Topologies

Find a phenomenon that is better modeled on a hex grid than on a square grid and vice versa. Implement a model of the phenomenon in both kinds of grids and demonstrate your results. Find a phenomenon to model for which each of the three topologies (bounded, toroidal, and infinite) works best. Choose one of these three phenomena and implement it in all three topologies. Compare and contrast your experiences in the three different topologies.

model) while the left and right are wrapped (in effect, a cylindrical topology). This gives the world the appearance of an infinitely long piece of road. In NetLogo, you can specify whether each boundary set (north–south or east–west) is bounded or wrapping in the Model Settings dialogue.

Finally, an *infinite-plane* topology is one where there are no bounds. In other words, agents can keep moving and moving in any direction forever. In practice, this is done by starting with a smaller world such that whenever agents move beyond the edges of the world, the world is expanded. At times, infinite planes can be useful if the agents truly need to move in a much larger world. While some ABM toolkits provide built-in support for infinite plane topologies, NetLogo does not. However, it is possible to work around this limitation by giving each turtle a separate pair of x and y coordinates from the built-in ones. Then, when an agent moves off the side of the world, we can hide the turtle and keep updating this additional set of coordinates until the agent moves back onto the view (see the Random Walk 360 coding example for an implementation of this). In most cases, however, a toroidal or bounded topology will be the more appropriate (and simpler) choice to implement.

Network-Based Environments

In many real-world situations, especially in social contexts, interactions between agents are not defined by physical geography. For instance, rumors do not spread between individuals in a strictly geographical manner. If I call a friend of mine in Germany and tell her a rumor, it spreads to Germany without passing through all of the people between Germany and me. In many cases, we want to represent the way individuals communicate by using a network-based environment (See figures 5.13 and 5.14). Using a network-based environment, we can represent the fact that I called my friend in Germany by drawing a link between the agents that represent each of us in our model. A *link* is defined by the two ends it connects, which are frequently referred to as *nodes*. These terms are used in the rapidly growing field of *network science* (Barabási, 2002; Newman, 2010; Watts & Strogatz, 1998). Note that mathematical graph theory literature uses different terminology

A

B

Figure 5.13
(A) Bipartite network of cancers and protein complexes. (B) Network of archive documents shared by League of Nations personnel.

A

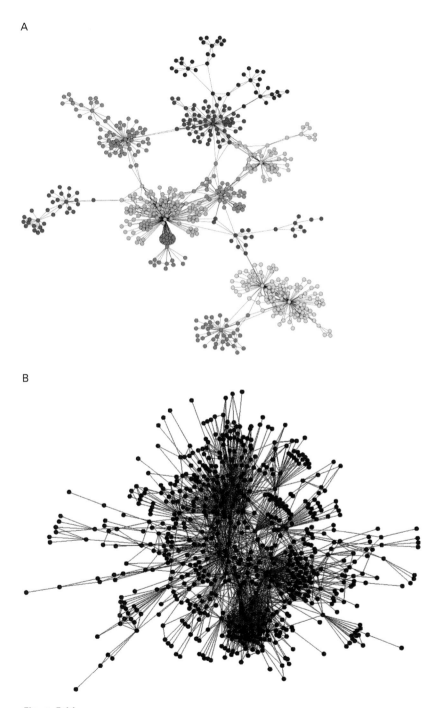

B

Figure 5.14
(A) Collaborations between researchers at McCormick School, Northwestern University. (B) Flights between cities in Asia and Middle East.

to refer to essentially these same objects, whereby a graph (network) consists of vertices (nodes) that are connected by edges (links). However, we will use the network/node/link vocabulary throughout this text.

In NetLogo, links are their own agent-type. Much like patches, links can either be passive conduits of information and descriptions of the environment or else full-blown agents with properties and actions all their own. The lattice environments described earlier can be thought of as special cases of network environments, with patches being nodes connected to their grid neighbors. In fact, lattice graphs can also be called *lattice networks*, with the property that each position in the network looks exactly like every other position in the network. However, ABM environments usually do not implement lattice environments as networks for both conceptual and efficiency reasons. Additionally, using patches as the default topology allows for either discrete or continuous representations of the space, whereas a network is always discrete.

Network-based environments have been found useful in studying a wide variety of phenomena, such as the spread of disease or rumors, the formation of social groups, the structure of organizations, or even the structure of proteins. There are several network topologies that are commonly used in ABM. Besides the regular networks described earlier, the three most common network topologies are *random*, *scale-free*, and *small-world*.

In *random networks*, each individual is randomly connected to other individuals. These networks are created by randomly adding links between agents in the system. For example, if you had a model of agents moving around a large room and connected every agent in the room to another agent based on which agent had the next largest last two digits of their social security number, you would probably create a random network. The mathematicians Erdös and Rényi (1959) pioneered the study of random networks and described algorithms for generating them. We show one simple methods for creating a random network. This code is also in the Random Network model in the chapter 5 subfolder of the IABM Textbook folder of the NetLogo models library:

```
to setup
    ca
    crt 100 [
        setxy random-xcor random-ycor
    ]
end

to wire1
    ask turtles [
        create-link-with one-of other turtles
    ]
end
```

In this code, we create a group of turtles and place them randomly on the screen. We then ask each turtle to create a link to another turtle chosen randomly. If we want the

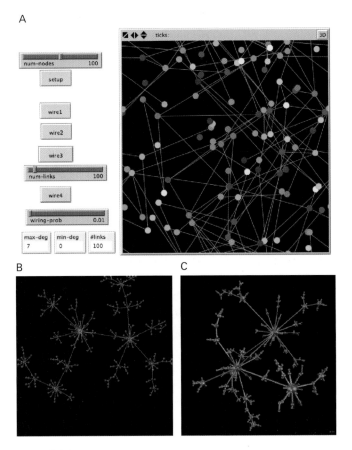

Figure 5.15
(A) Random Network model showing classic Erdös-Rényi random network. (B, C) Scale-Free Network from Preferential Attachment model. http://ccl.northwestern.edu/netlogo/models/PreferentialAttachment (Wilensky, 2001).

turtles to have more than one link we can ask each turtle to REPEAT this process several times. This code produces a network where each node has at least one link, meaning there are no isolates (i.e., nodes with no links). The Random network model shows several other ways to create random networks, including the classic Erdös-Rényi network. We will talk more about random networks in chapter 6.

Scale-free networks have the property that any subnetwork of the global network has the same properties as the global network. A common way to create this type of network is by adding new nodes and links to the system so that extant nodes with a large number of links are more likely to receive new connections (Barabási, 2002). This technique is sometimes called *preferential attachment*, since nodes with more connections are attached to preferentially. This method for network creation tends to produce networks with central nodes that have many radiating links; because of the resemblance to a bicycle wheel, this network structure is sometimes also called hub-and-spoke. Many real-world networks such as the Internet, electricity grids, and airline routes have similar properties to a scale-free network.

To create a scale-free network, we start by creating a couple of nodes and linking them. This code is also in the Preferential Attachment Simple model in the chapter 5 subfolder of the IABM Textbook folder of the NetLogo models library:

```
to setup
    ca
    set-default-shape turtles "circle"
    crt 2 [ fd 5 ]                              ;; create two turtles and space them out
    ask turtle 0 [ create-link-with turtle 1 ]  ;; create a link between them
end
```

This code clears the world and then changes the default shape of turtles to circles so that they look more like abstract nodes. After that, it creates two nodes and draws a link between them. Our GO procedure systematically adds nodes, one at a time, using the existing links to choose an endpoint. The code to add new nodes (up to the limit NUM-NODES) is:

```
to go
    if count turtles > num-nodes [stop]
    ;; choose a partner attached to a random link
    ;; this gives a node a chance to be a partner based on how many links it has
    let partner one-of [both-ends] of one-of links
    ;; create new node, link to partner
    crt 1 [ fd 5 create-link-with partner ]
tick
end
```

The crux of this code is determining a partner node that connects to the new node. One way to think of this code is that the partner node is determined by giving each node in the network a number of lottery tickets equal to the number of connections it has. Then a random ticket is drawn and whichever node has that lottery ticket is the partner node. This code is based on the Preferential Attachment model (see figure 5.15) in the Networks section of the NetLogo models library, which in turn is based on the Barabási-Albert network model (1999).

The final standard network topology is known as a *small-world network. Small-world* networks are made up of dense clusters of highly interconnected nodes joined by a few long distance links between them. Due to these long distance links, it does not take many links for information to travel between any two random nodes in the network. Small-world networks are sometimes created by starting with regular networks, like the 2D lattices described before, then randomly rewiring some of the connections to create large jumps between occasional agents (Watts & Strogatz, 1998). The example of a rumor spreading could be modeled using a small world, since much of it will happen in a local geography (i.e., friends in a nearby physical location), but there will be occasional long jumps (like a distant friend). For an example of how to create a small-world network, see the Small-World model in the Networks section of the NetLogo models library (Wilensky, 2005a).

There are many ways to characterize networks. Two commonly used ways are average path length and clustering coefficient. The *average path length* is the average of all the pairwise distances between nodes in a network. In other words, we measure the distance between every pair of nodes in the network and then average the results. Average path length characterizes how far the nodes are from each other in a network. The *clustering coefficient* of a network is the average fraction of a node's immediate neighbors who are also neighbors of the node's other neighbors. In other words, it is a measure of the fraction of my friends who are also friends with each other. In networks with a high average clustering coefficient, any two neighboring nodes tend to share many of their neighbors in common, while in networks with a low average clustering coefficient there is generally little overlap between groups of surrounding neighbors.

Random networks have low average path lengths and low clustering coefficients, indicating that that it does not take long to get from any particular node to any other node, since the nodes all have some connections to other nodes and there is no regularity to their connections. Completely regular networks, like the lattice-based environments, have a high average path length and a relatively high clustering coefficient. It takes a long time for information to travel around a regular network, but neighbors are very tightly connected. Small-world networks have a low average path length despite having a higher clustering coefficient. Neighbors tend to be tightly clustered, but since there are a few long-distance links, information can still flow quickly around the network. Scale-free networks also tend to have low average path lengths, since those nodes that have many neighbors serve as hubs for communication. We will present an example of creating and using network-based environments in chapter 6. NetLogo also includes a special extension, the network extension, for creating, analyzing, and working with networks. This extension enables full integration of network theory methods into ABM. We present uses of the network extension in chapter 8.

Special Environments

The two methods we have demonstrated for defining the environment, two-dimensional (2D) grid-based (i.e., lattice) and network-based, are both instances of "interaction topologies." Interaction topologies describe the paths along which agents can communicate and interact in a model. Besides the two interaction topologies we have looked at so far, there are several other standard topologies to consider. Two of the most interesting topologies involve the use of 3D worlds and Geographic Information Systems (GIS). 3D worlds allow agents to move in a third dimension as well as the two dimensions in traditional ABMs. GIS formats enable the importation of layers of real-world geographical data into ABMs. We will discuss each of these in turn.

3D Worlds

An unspeakable horror seized me. There was a darkness; then a dizzy, sickening sensation of sight that was not like seeing; I saw a Line that was no Line; Space that was not Space: I was myself, and not myself. When I could find voice, I shrieked loud in agony, "Either this is madness or it is Hell."
    "It is neither," calmly replied the voice of the Sphere, "it is Knowledge; it is Three Dimensions: open your eye once again and try to look steadily."
—Edwin A. Abbott, *Flatland: A Romance in Many Dimensions*

The traditional ABM uses a 2D rectangular lattice of square patches. However, many of the systems we are interested in studying operate in 3D space. In many cases, it is okay to simplify the model to 2D space, because the systems we are working with only move in two dimensions, e.g., most humans cannot fly or the extra dimension of movement does not serve an important role in the model's outcomes. Sometimes, however, it can be important to incorporate a third dimension into our models. In general, 3D environments enable model developers to explore complex systems which are irreducibly bound up with a third dimension as well as sometimes increasing the apparent physical realism to their models.

There is a version of NetLogo called NetLogo 3D (it is a separate application in the NetLogo folder) that allows modelers to explore ABMs in three dimensions. There are many implementations of classic ABMs that have been developed for this environment in the NetLogo 3D models library (*Wilensky, 2000*). For instance, there is a three-dimensional version of the Percolation model that we discussed in chapter 3 (see figure 5.16).

Some elements of ABM remain the same in 3D, but others change. For instance, we can still use the concept of a square lattice in 3D to describe the environment, but we need to extend it in one more dimension, to a cubic lattice. Working with 3D worlds is not much different from working with 2D worlds. Although, using a 3D world does require additional data and commands. For instance, agents now have a Z-coordinate, and new commands are needed to manipulate this new degree of freedom.

In 3D, the orientation of an agent can no longer be described by its heading alone, we must also use *pitch* and *roll* to describe the orientation of the agent. If you think about an agent as an airplane, then the *pitch* of the agent is how far from horizontal the nose of the airplane is pointing. For instance, if the nose of the airplane is pointing straight up then the pitch is 90 degrees (see figure 5.17). Using the airplane metaphor the *roll* of an agent is how far the wings are from horizontal. For instance, if the wings are pointing up and down then the roll of the agent is 90 degrees (see figure 5.18). In many 3D systems,

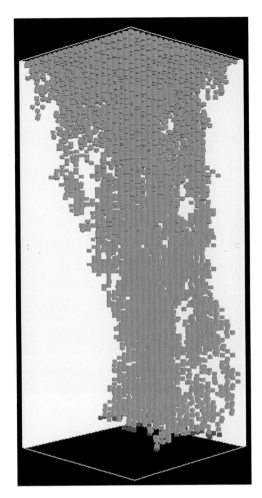

Figure 5.16
Percolation 3D. http://ccl.northwestern.edu/netlogo/models/Percolation3D (*Wilensky & Rand, 2006*).

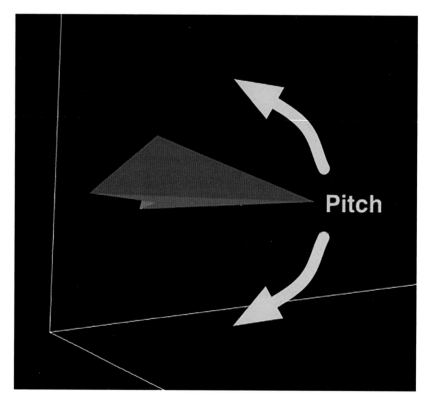

Figure 5.17
Pitch.

heading has a new name, which is *yaw*, but in NetLogo we still use HEADING regardless of whether you are in 2D or 3D NetLogo to keep things consistent.

To see the difference between writing 3D models and 2D models, let us examine the code in each model. The code for the PERCOLATE procedure in 2D Percolation looks like this:

```
to percolate
    ask current-row with [pcolor = red] [
        ;; oil percolates to the two patches southwest and southeast
        ask patches at-points [[-1 -1] [1 -1]]
            [ if (pcolor = brown) and (random-float 100 < porosity)
                [ set pcolor red ] ]
        set pcolor black
        set total-oil total-oil + 1
    ]
    ;; advance to the next row
    set current-row patch-set [patch-at 0 -1] of current-row
end
```

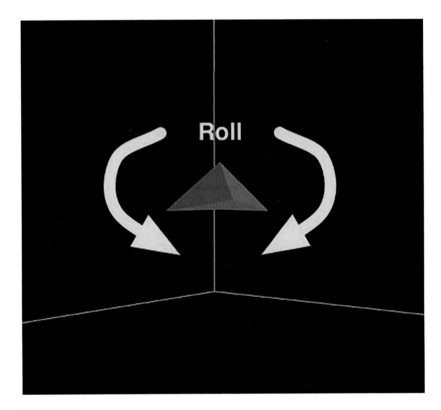

Figure 5.18
Roll.

Notice that in the 2D version, the code has each patch look at patches that are below, left, and right of the patch. This will change in the 3D version. In 3D Percolation (Wilensky & Rand, 2006), PERCOLATE looks like this:

```
to percolate
    ask current-row with [pcolor = red] [
        ;; oil percolates to the four patches one row down in the z-coordinate and
    ;; southwest, southeast, northeast, and northwest
        ask patches at-points [[-1 -1 -1] [1 -1 -1] [1 1 -1] [-1 1 -1]]
            [ if (pcolor = black) and (random-float 100 < porosity)
                [ set pcolor red ] ]
        set pcolor brown
        set total-oil total-oil + 1
    ]
    ;; advance to the next row
    set current-row patch-set [patch-at 0 0 -1] current-row
end
```

The only difference between the 3D percolate and its 2D counterpart is that instead of percolating a line of patches at a time, we percolate a square of patches. As a result, each patch must ask four patches below it (in a cross shape) to percolate, not just two as it does in the 2D version.

As in the preceding case, it can sometimes be very easy to translate a model from two dimensions into three dimensions. In many cases this adds a level of realism to the model. Since many phenomena that exhibit percolation, percolate in all three dimensions, like oil through rock, it is reasonable to use three dimensions to model percolation. However, in some situations a two-dimensional representation of the complex system may be an adequate representation (or even better than a 3D representation). In the end, the decision to include a third dimension or not is driven primarily by the question that the model developers are trying to answer. If a third dimension is necessary to properly address the question at hand, then it should be included. However, if a third dimension is not necessary then using a two-dimensional representation can expedite and facilitate model development. This question might not always be easy to answer. For instance, if a researcher is interested in examining land use and land change on a mountainside, it might at first be assumed that a 3D representation is necessary, since mountains change greatly in elevation and thus have a height as well as a width and length. But as long as the only aspect that is of concern is the surface coverage of the mountain, then there is no data of concern that is either above or below the current area of interest. We can instead model the change in elevation as a patch variable. In fact, this is exactly what is done in the Grand Canyon model in the Earth Science section of the models library.

In NetLogo the 3D view is a separate window, and provides controls to manipulate the point of view such as "orbit," "zoom," and "move," which allow you to better visualize the model (see figure 5.19).

GIS-Based   Geographic Information Systems (GIS) are environments that record large amounts of data that are related to physical locations in the world.[6] GISs are widely used by environmental scientists, urban planners, park managers, transportation engineers, and many others, and help to organize data and make decisions about any large area of land. Using GIS, we can index all the information about a particular subject or phenomenon by its location in the physical world. Moreover, GIS researchers have developed analysis tools that enable them to quickly examine the patterns of this data and its spatial distribution. As a result, GIS tools and techniques allow for a more in-depth exploration of the pattern of a complex system.

Agents moving on a GIS terrain may be constrained to interact on that terrain. Thus, GIS can serve as an interaction topology. However, GIS systems need not be solely

---

6. It is important to note that a GIS environment is, in fact, a spatial environment, and it can also contain within it both continuous and discrete spaces, but since the way GIS data is handled is very different from traditional mathematical spaces, we have decided to address it separately in this textbook.

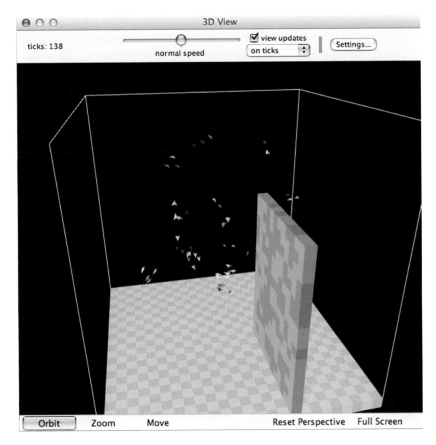

Figure 5.19
The 3D model, Flocking 3D Alternate, in which a flock of birds move around a wall. http://ccl.northwestern.edu/netlogo/models/Flocking3DAlternate (*Wilensky, 2005*).

employed for strictly geographical data such as elevation, land use, and surface cover. Whenever we have large amounts of data about a particular subject or phenomena, we can take advantage of the GIS to encode that data. For instance, we can embed the socioeconomic status of neighborhoods in a location related to that neighborhood.

Where does ABM fit in to this picture? GIS can provide an environment for an ABM to operate in. Since ABM encompasses a rich model of process of a complex system, it is a natural match for GIS, which has a rich model of pattern. By allowing ABM to examine and manipulate GIS data, we can build models that have a richer description of the complex system we are examining. GIS thus enables modelers to construct more realistic and elaborate models of complex phenomena.

To illustrate this, examine the Grand Canyon model in the NetLogo models library (see figure 5.20). This model shows how water drains in the Grand Canyon. We use a digital

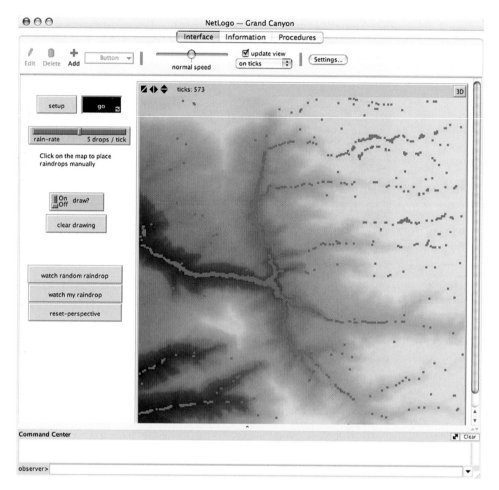

Figure 5.20
Grand Canyon model. http://ccl.northwestern.edu/netlogo/models/GrandCanyon (*Wilensky, 2006*).

elevation map of the Grand Canyon (created from a GIS topographical elevation dataset) to enable the user to visualize a simple model of a complex process (water drainage) in a real environment (the Grand Canyon).

How was the GIS data incorporated into this model? The first step was to examine the data in a GIS toolkit. This data was gathered from the National Elevation Dataset (http:// seamless.usgs.gov). It was then converted from the original ESRI grid file format to an ASCII grid file. ESRI is a large producer of GIS software, and many datasets are found in this format. You can use one of many ESRI products, e.g., ArcGIS, to examine ESRI data. After changing the file format, the data file was rescaled to lie in the range 0 to 999, while the headers were stripped out of the file, allowing the data to be more easily managed by NetLogo. The end result is a file stored as one large list with 90,601 entries. This list represents 301 rows, with each row containing 301 elevation values. The first row looks like this:

```
819 820 822 828 830 832 834 835 836 837 839 841 842 844 845 846 847 848 849 848 847
844 840 833 829 826 825 825 826 827 828 830 832 835 838 841 841 842 842 843 844 845
847 849 850 850 852 855 858 862 864 866 865 864 864 870 873 876 878 880 880 880 880
879 878 877 877 879 879 881 884 887 888 888 887 883 881 880 879 873 870 866 864 860
860 861 860 856 853 852 853 852 851 850 848 845 843 841 840 836 834 833 833 834 835
835 836 838 838 839 840 843 845 847 848 853 856 859 863 871 874 876 879 884 887 890
894 902 905 908 910 912 912 912 912 911 908 906 906 901 897 897 900 904 909 913 918
919 919 916 914 915 915 914 912 913 911 907 904 899 899 903 906 911 913 915 917 922
923 921 918 907 903 904 908 910 911 911 910 909 912 915 918 918 918 920 921 919 918
918 919 921 922 924 924 926 929 931 932 935 938 940 942 944 945 946 947 947 945 942
943 949 950 952 953 956 957 958 959 960 960 960 959 957 956 955 955 956 956 957 957
959 960 961 962 963 964 964 963 963 963 962 960 954 951 949 948 950 954 959 963 965
966 966 967 968 969 970 971 972 973 974 974 975 975 975 975 975 975 974 975 976 976
977 978 979 980 981 981 981 981 981 981 981 982 982 983 985 987 988 989 991 992 993
993 990 990 992 993 994 993
```

This data file was saved as "Grand Canyon data.txt." The NetLogo model was created with a world of 301 x 301 patches. The data file is read into the NetLogo model using the following code:[7]

```
file-open "Grand Canyon data.txt"
let patch-elevations file-read
file-close
set color-max max patch-elevations + 200
;; put a little padding on the upper bound so we don't get too much
                ;; white, and higher elevations have a little more variation.
let min-elevation min patch-elevations
                ;; adjust the color-min a little so patches don't end up black
set color-min min-elevation - ((color-max - min-elevation) / 10)
                ;; transfer the date from the file into the sorted patches
( foreach sort patches patch-elevations
  [ ask ?1 [ set elevation ?2 ] ] )
```

The first line opens the file. Then, a temporary variable, PATCH-ELEVATIONS, is created to store the data from the file as one big list, after which the file is closed. We then determine how to color the world by determining the minimum and maximum values of the elevations. Finally, we assign each patch of the world an elevation equal to the corresponding data point that was read in from the file. Later on in the code, this information is used to color the patches:

---

7. As a side note, this code is contained in the STARTUP procedure. STARTUP procedures are special NetLogo procedures that are run when the model is opened before any button is pressed.

Box 5.7
The Special Local Variable: ?

The Grand Canyon model code makes use of variables of the form ?1 and ?2. ?, ?1, ?2, and so on are special local variables in NetLogo that hold the current inputs to a reporter or command block for certain primitives. For example, in FOREACH, these variables are set to different values every time the FOREACH primitive goes through its loop, as shown below:

```
( foreach sort patches patch-elevations
        [ ask ?1 [ set elevation ?2 ] ] )
```

For each iteration, ?1 will be set to the next patch as sorted. The default patch sort sorts the patches such that the first item is in the upper left corner and then lists them left-to-right and top-to-bottom, with ?2 set to the next item in the list (PATCH-ELEVATIONS). Another example of these local variables is evidenced in the SORT-BY primitive, which takes a comparator reporter and a list and returns a sorted list. Consider two examples:

```
sort-by [?1 < ?2] [8 5 4 7 2 1]

sort-by [?1 < ?2] [8 5 4 7 2 1]
```

In both cases, ?1 is always the first item being compared; ?2, the second. The result of the first sort-by is [1 2 4 5 7 8], whereas the second sort-by reports [8 7 5 4 2 1].

```
ask patches
        [ set pcolor scale-color brown elevation color-min color-max ]
```

SCALE-COLOR tells an agent to choose an appropriate shade of a color on the basis of a numerical value. In this case, we asked the patches to set their color to some shade of brown, on the basis of their elevation. This means that patches with lower elevations will be colored darker shades of brown, while patches with higher elevations will be colored lighter shades of brown.

This demonstrates one way to include a minimal amount of GIS data in to an agent-based model that will work with almost any agent-based modeling toolkit. One can also modify this data and export the results back to a GIS (see exploration 4). We will also discuss more advanced ways to integrate GIS and ABM in chapter 8, including the NetLogo GIS extension that is a standard part of the NetLogo package. Using the NetLogo

GIS extension is the preferred method of importing large amounts of GIS data into a NetLogo model.

Interactions

Now that we have discussed both agents and the environments in which they exist, we will look at how agents and environments interact. There are five basic classes of interactions that exist in ABMs: *agent-self*, *environment-self*, *agent-agent*, *environment-environment*, and finally, *agent-environment*. We will discuss each in turn along with some examples of these common interactions.

Agent-Self Interactions   Agents do not always need to interact with other agents or the environment. In fact, a lot of agent interaction is done within the agent. For instance, most of the examples of advanced cognition that we discussed in the Agent section involve the agent interacting with itself. The agent considers its current state and decides what to do. One classic type of self-agent interaction that we used in chapter 4, have yet to discuss, is birth. *Birth* events are a typical event in ABMs where one agent creates another agent. Though we tend to discuss birth within the biological paradigm of physically giving birth, similar types of interactions exist in other domains, from social science (e.g., an organization can create another organization) to chemistry (e.g., the combination of two atoms can create a new molecule). Below is the birth routine that we used in chapter 4:

```
;; check to see if this agent has enough energy to reproduce
to reproduce
   if energy > 200 [
      set energy energy - 100  ;; reproduction costs energy to the parent
      hatch 1 [ set energy 100 ] ;; which is transferred to the offspring
   ]
end
```

1. As you can see, the agent considers its own state and, based on this state, decides whether or not to give birth to a new agent. It then manipulates its state, lowering its energy and creating the new agent. This is the typical way of having agents reproduce: they consider whether enough of a resource exists to "give birth" to an offspring and, if so, "hatch" one. Though our example above was one of a turtle creating another turtle, it is also possible to have a patch create a turtle (in NetLogo, this is accomplished with the command SPROUT). Notice that the environment (represented by patches) can create a new turtle, but not new patches for a new environmental area. This is because,

as the old saying goes, "The reason why land is valuable is because they're not making any more of it."

Of course, the opposite of birth is death, and we also had a death procedure in chapter 4. This is also a self-agent interaction in NetLogo. There is no "kill" command that directly causes another agent to die, but rather, another agent may ask a turtle to kill itself (die). (Note: there is also the CLEAR-TURTLES command, which will cause all turtles to die.) Following is the code that we used in chapter 4:

```
;; asks those agents with no energy to die
to check-if-dead
if energy < 0 [
      die
   ]
end
```

This is a fairly typical way of having agents die: If an agent does not have enough of a resource to go on living, they then remove themselves from the simulation.

In Traffic Basic, we have another kind of agent-self interaction where the agents decide what speed they should be traveling at:

```
ask turtles [
    let car-ahead one-of turtles-on patch-ahead 1
    ifelse car-ahead != nobody
        [ slow-down-car car-ahead ]
        ;; otherwise, speed up
        [ speed-up-car ]
;; don't slow down below speed minimum or speed up beyond speed limit
    if speed < speed-min [ set speed speed-min ]
    if speed > speed-limit [ set speed speed-limit ]
    fd speed ]
```

If we ignore the beginning section of this code (where the car senses the cars ahead) and the end of this code (where the car actually moves), all of the actions in between (where the car changes its speed) are agent-self interactions, since the car looks at its current speed and then changes that speed. This is another typical type of self-agent inter-action, where an agent considers the resources it has at its disposal and then decides how to spend them.

Environment-Self Interactions Environment-self interactions are when areas of the environment alter or change themselves. For instance, they could change their internal state variables as a result of calculations. In chapter 4, the classic example of an environment-self interaction is when the grass regrows:

```
;; regrow the grass
to regrow-grass
   ask patches [
      set grass-amount grass-amount + grass-regrowth-rate
      if grass > 10 [
         set grass 10
                        ]
recolor-grass
   ]
end
```

Each patch is asked to examine its own state and increment the amount of grass it has, but if it has too much grass then it is set back to the maximum value it can contain. Finally the patch colors itself based on the amount of grass it contains.

Agent-Agent Interactions   Interactions between two or more agents are usually the most important type of action within agent-based models. We saw a canonical example of agent-agent interactions in the Wolf Sheep Predation model when the wolves consume the sheep:

```
;; wolves eat sheep
to eat-sheep
   if any? sheep-here [ ;; if there are sheep here then eat one
      let target one-of sheep-here
      ask target [
         die
      ]
      ;; increase the energy by the parameter setting
      set energy energy + energy-gain-from-sheep
   ]
end
```

In this case, one agent is consuming another agent and taking its resources, whereby the wolf always eats the sheep. However, it is also possible to add competition or flight to this model, where the wolf gets a chance of eating the sheep and the sheep gets a chance to flee. Competition is another example of agent-agent interaction.

Traffic Basic features another typical kind of agent-agent interaction: the sensing of other agents by an agent. At the beginning of the GO loop

```
   ask turtles [
      let car-ahead one-of turtles-on patch-ahead 1
      ifelse car-ahead != nobody
         [ slow-down car-ahead]
   ...
```

We can see that the current car is sensing whether there are cars ahead of it. If there are, it then changes its speed to reflect that of the cars ahead of it. When developing or interacting with agent-based models, it can be tempting to anthropomorphize our agents. That is, we may assume that they will have the knowledge, properties, or behaviors that come naturally to the thing being modeled, but are not automatically present in the modeled agents. It is important to remind yourself that computational agents are very simple, in that the rules about how agents sense the world around them, and how to act in response to that information, must be spelled out completely. In addition to sensing other agents, agents can also sense the environment, a phenomenon we will discuss in a later section.

A final example of agent-agent interaction is communication. Agents can share information about their own state as well as that of the world around them. This type of interaction allows agents to gain information to which they might not have direct access. For instance, in the Traffic Basic model, the current car asks for a car ahead of it to communicate its speed. A more classic example of agent-agent communication is the Communication T-T Example model in the Code Examples section of the NetLogo models library. In this model, one turtle starts with a message and then communicates it to other turtles using this procedure:

```
;; the core procedure
to communicate ;; turtle procedure
    if any? other turtles-here with [message?]
        [ set message? true ]
end
```

The turtles communicate by choosing another local turtle with which to communicate. If the other turtle has a message, the current turtle copies that message. If the turtles are linked together over a network, we can then change the procedure so that the turtles communicate with others with which they are linked instead of just local turtles. This code is also in the Communication-T-T Network example model in the chapter 5 subfolder of the IABM Textbook folder in the NetLogo models library:

```
;; the core procedure
to communicate ;; turtle procedure
    if any? link-neighbors with [message?]
        [ set message? true ]
end
```

This allows turtle-turtle interaction over links. In this instance, the links serve more as part of the environment than as full agents. Communication is not the only type of interactions that can occur over links. Links can be used for many kinds of agent interactions.

Environment-Environment Interactions   Interactions between different parts of the environment are probably the least commonly used type of interaction in agent-based models. However, there are some common uses of environment-environment interactions: one of these is diffusion. In the Ants model discussed in chapter 1, the ants place a pheromone in the environment, which is then diffused throughout the world via an environment-environment interaction. This interaction is contained in the following piece of code in the main GO procedure:

```
diffuse chemical (diffusion-rate / 100)
ask patches
    [ set chemical chemical * (100 - evaporation-rate) / 100
;; slowly evaporate chemical
        recolor-patch ]
```

The first part of this code is the only environment-environment interaction—the DIFFUSE command automatically spreads the chemical from each patch to the patches that immediately surround it. The second part of this code is actually an example of an environment-self interaction. Each of the patches loses some of its chemical over time to evaporation, changing its color to reflect how the chemical has changed over that period.

Agent-Environment Interactions   Agent-environment interactions occur when the agent manipulates or examines part of the world in which it exists, or when the environment in some way alters or observes the agent. A common type of agent-environment interaction involves agents observing the environment. The Ants model demonstrates this kind of interaction when the ants examine the environment to look for food and sense pheromone:

```
to look-for-food ;; turtle procedure
    if food > 0
    [ set color orange + 1      ;; pick up food
        set food food - 1                ;; and reduce the food source
        rt 180                                     ;; and turn around
    stop ]
    ;; face in the direction where the chemical smell is strongest
    if (chemical >= 0.05) and (chemical < 2)
    [ uphill-chemical ]
end
```

In the Ants model, the patches contain food and chemical, so the first part of this code checks to see if there is any food in the current patch. If there is food, the ant then picks up the food and turns around back to the nest, and the procedure stops. Otherwise, the ant checks to see if there is chemical, wherein it follows the chemical in that direction.

Another common type of agent-environment interaction is agent movement. In some ways, movement is simply an agent-self interaction, since it only alters the current agent's state. But since a major property of any given area in the environment is the agents contained in it, movement is also a form of agent-environment interaction. Depending on the topology of the world, agent movement will have differing effects on the environment.

Consider the following two types of movement.

In the Ants model the ants move around by "wiggling":

```
to wiggle ;; turtle procedure
    rt random 40
    lt random 40
    if not can-move? 1 [ rt 180 ]
end
```

Note that in the last line of this procedure, the ant checks to see if it has reached the edge of the world. If it has, it turns back around and heads in the other direction.

You can also have environment interactions where an agent goes off one of the edges of the world but comes back on the other edge. In the Traffic Basic model, the topology "wraps" horizontally. As a result, the cars continuously move in a straight line (or, viewed as a torus, on a circular track).

We have reviewed here the five basic different types of interactions: agent-self, environment-self, agent-agent, environment-environment, and agent-environment. While there are many other different examples of these types of interactions, we have covered here some examples of their most common applications. More of these will be covered in the explorations at the end of this chapter.

Observer/User Interface

Now that we have talked about the agents, the environments, and the interactions that occur between agents and environmental attributes, we may discuss who controls the running of the model. The *observer* is a high-level agent that is responsible for ensuring that the model runs and proceeds according to the steps developed by the model author.[8] The observer issues commands to agents and the environment, telling them to manipulate their data or to take certain actions. Most of the control that model developers have with an ABM is mediated through the observer. However, the observer is a special agent. It does not have many properties, though it can access global properties like any agent or patch can. The only properties that one could consider to be specific to the *observer* are those relating to

---

8. In NetLogo, this agent is called the Observer; in other ABM toolkits, it goes by other names, such as *Modeler* or *Controller*.

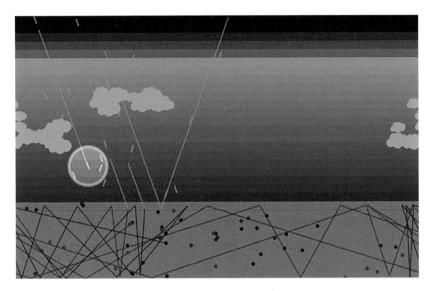

Figure 5.21
Climate Change model (with a sun ray turtle being watched, which is shown by the transparent "halo" around it). http://ccl.northwestern.edu/netlogo/models/ClimateChange (*Tinker & Wilensky, 2007*).

the perspective from which the modeled world is viewed. For instance, in NetLogo the view may be centered on a specific agent, or focusing a highlight on a certain agent, using the FOLLOW, WATCH, or RIDE commands (See figure 5.21).

The 2D NetLogo world can also be viewed from a 3D perspective by clicking the 3D button in the top right corner of the view control strip. In NetLogo 3D models, the observer's vantage point can also be manipulated (using the commands FACE, FACEXYZ, and SETXYZ, or with the 3D controls), and the world can be seen from a particular turtle's eye view, rather than the usual bird's-eye view. (Other than that, the observer's basic actions are asking agents to do things, and manipulating data and properties.)

In NetLogo there are observer buttons and agent buttons. Observer buttons tell the observer to do something. For instance, we can create a SETUP button and place the following code in it:

```
create-turtles100 [ setxy random-xcor random-ycor ]
```

Only the observer can run this code. We cannot ask a turtle to create turtles using the CREATE-TURTLES primitive (though we could use HATCH to achieve the same effect). If we then wanted the turtles to do something, we could create a turtle button (by selecting turtle in the drop-down box in the edit button dialog), with the following code:

A   B

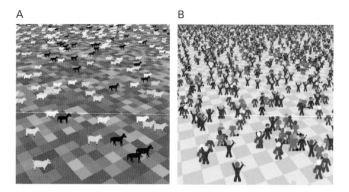

Figure 5.22
3D views of 2D models. (A) Wolf Sheep Predation model. (B) Rebellion model.

```
fd random 5 rt random 90
```

We can also create an observer button that does the same thing, but if we put the exact same code in we will get an error that only turtles can execute FD. So we have to tell the observer to ask the turtles to do something:

```
ask turtles [
fd random 5 rt random 90
]
```

Thus the observer plays the role of a general supervisor for the model. Usually when building models we interact with the model through the observer.

User Input and Model Output   We have already made use of many of the standard ways to interface with an ABM when we extended models in chapter 3 and when we built our first model in chapter 4, but it is worth recapping some of them herein. ABMs require a control interface or a parameter group that allows the user to setup different parameters and settings for the ABM. The most common control mechanism is a *button*, which executes one or more commands within the model; if it is a *forever button* it will continue to execute those commands until the user presses the button again. A second way that the user can request that actions be performed within the ABM is via the command center (along with the mini–command centers within agent monitors). The command center is a very useful feature of NetLogo, as it allows the user to interactively test out commands, and manipulate agents and the environment.

The other interface controls that are usually provided to the model user are data-driven as opposed to action-driven. Among data-driven interface controls, one can differentiate input controls and output controls. The input controls include sliders, switches, choosers, and input boxes. The output controls consist of monitors, plots, an output area, and notes. Though these names are specific to NetLogo similar controls exist in most ABM toolkits. In NetLogo's interface, buttons are colored blue-gray, input controls are green, and output controls are khaki-colored.

Sliders enable the model user to select a particular value from a range of numerical values. For instance, a slider could range from 0 to 50 (by increments of 0,1) or 1 to 1,000 by increments of 1. In the Code tab the value of a slider is accessed as if it were a global variable. *Switches* enable the user to turn various elements of a model off or on. In the Code tab, they are also accessed as global variables, but they are Boolean variables. *Choosers* enable a model user to select a choice from a predefined drop-down menu that the modeler has created. Again these are accessed as global variables in the Code tab, but they are variables that have strings as their values, these strings being the various choices in the chooser. Finally, *input boxes* are more free-form, allowing the user to input text that the model can use.

As for output controls, *monitors* display the value of a global variable or calculation updated several times a second. They have no history but show the user the current state of the system. *Plots* provide traditional 2D graphs enabling the user to observe the change of an output variable over time. *Output boxes* enable the modeler to create free-form text-based output to send to the user. Finally, *notes* enable the modeler to place text information on the Interface tab (for example, to give a model user directions on how to use the model). Unlike in monitors, the text in notes is unchanging (unless you manually edit them).

These methods among many other ways of creating output will be discussed in more depth in chapter 6 where we will discuss how to analyze ABMs. However, one last method should be mentioned before we move on. Besides these direct manipulation methods of interfacing with an ABM, there are also file-based methods. For instance, you can write code to read data in from a file. This allows the user to modify that file to change the input to the model. Similarly, besides the traditional output methods within NetLogo, the modeler can also output data to a file. This is often useful because it creates a historical trace of the model run that does not disappear even after NetLogo has been closed. Moreover, using tools or analysis packages like Excel and R, it is possible to aggregate this file data into summary statistics. This will also be discussed in more depth in chapter 6.

Visualization   Visualization is the part of model design concerned with how to present the data contained in the model in a visual way. Creating cognitively efficient and aesthetic visualizations can make it much easier for model authors and users to understand the model. Though there is a long history of work on how to present data in static images (Bertin, 1967; Tufte, 1983, 1996), there is much less work on how to represent data in real-time dynamic situations. However, attempts have been made to take current static guidelines and apply them to dynamic visualizations (Kornhauser, Rand & Wilensky, 2007). In general, there are three guidelines that should be kept in mind whenever designing the visualization of an ABM: simplify, explain, and emphasize.

Simplify the visualization   Make the visualization as simple as possible so that anything that does not present additional usable information (or that is irrelevant to the current point being explained) has been eliminated from the visualization. This prevents the model user from being distracted by unnecessary "graph clutter" (Tufte, 1983).

Explain the components   If there is an aspect of the visualization that is not immediately obvious then there should be some quick way to determine what that visualization is illustrating, such as a legend or description. Without clear and direct descriptions of what is going on the model user may misinterpret what the model author is attempting to portray. If a model is to be useful it is necessary that anyone viewing the model can easily understand what it is saying.

Emphasize the main point   Model visualizations are themselves simplifications of all the possible data that a model could present to the model user. Therefore, a model visualization should emphasize the main points and interactions that the model author wants to explore, and, in turn, to communicate to end users. By exaggerating certain aspects of the visualization they can draw attention to these key results.

Model visualization is often overlooked, but a good visualization can make a model much easier to understand, and can provide a visceral appeal to model users who are thus more likely to enjoy working with the model. So how is good visualization actually accomplished? A full description would be beyond the scope of this textbook but a good place to start is with shapes and colors. Every NetLogo agent has a shape and color, and by selecting appropriate shapes and colors we can highlight some agents while backgrounding others. For instance, to simplify visualization if agents in our model are truly homogenous, like the ants, then we might make all the agents the same color, as in the Ants model. To explain the visualization we might change their shape to indicate something about their properties. For instance, in the Ethnocentrism model based on Hammond and Axelrod's model (2003) agents employing the same strategies have the same shape, even if they are different colors. Finally, to emphasize a point, we can use color as well as other tools. For instance, in the Traffic Basic model we have one car that is both red and haloed, in order to highlight that car. If this car were blue and not haloed, it would be hard to pick out from the rest of the cars, and thus it would be hard to figure out what a typical car was doing. Investing effort and attention to detail will be rewarded when designing a model's user interface.

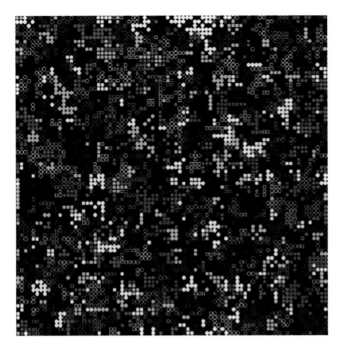

Figure 5.23
NetLogo Ethnocentrism model. This model uses the shape of agents to visualize agent strategy. http://ccl
.northwestern.edu/netlogo/models/ethnocentrism (*Wilensky, 2003*).

Batch vs. Interactive   When you open a blank NetLogo model, it starts with a command center that says "Observer." This blank window allows you to manipulate NetLogo in an interactive manner. If you open a model, you still have to press SETUP and GO to make the model work. Moreover, with most models, even when they are running, you can manipulate sliders and settings to see how these new parameters affect the performance of a model even during the middle of a run. This kind of spur-of-the-moment control is called *interactive running*, because the user can interact as the model is running. When designing an ABM, it is important to think about how a model user is going to interact with your model. For instance, can they manipulate all of the parameters of the model while it is running? Or do you want to only allow them to manipulate a subset of the parameters? In the latter case, it is useful to try and indicate that to the model user? For example, in NetLogo it is a convention to put any controls the user is going to initialize before the model runs (and leave unchanged during the model run) above the SETUP button. Controls that the user can manipulate while the model is running are placed below the SETUP button. Regardless of the solution used, modelers should be mindful of these considerations when developing their model.

In contrast to interactive running, another type of user running of a model is called *batch running*. With batch running, instead of controlling the model directly, the user writes a script to run the model many times, usually with different seeds for the pseudo-random number generator and with different parameter sets. This allows the user to conduct experiments on the model they are running and to collect results about multiple runs of the same model under different conditions. NetLogo provides two typical ways to conduct batch runs: (1) BehaviorSpace and (2) NetLogo's Controlling API. BehaviorSpace, which we will explore more in chapter 6, is an interactive tool that allows a model user to specify initial conditions and parameter sweeps for a model. BehaviorSpace can run either from the NetLogo user interface or in a *headless* mode without any graphics (e.g., from a command line interface). NetLogo's Controlling API is a method of interacting with NetLogo that involves writing Java code (or another JVM-compatible language) to control the NetLogo model. The Controlling API can either control the NetLogo GUI, or it can run headless as well. More details about headless running and NetLogo's Controlling API are beyond the scope of this book, but additional information can be found in the NetLogo documentation. However, when designing the user interface for your model, it is important to keep in mind that some users are going to want to be able to interact with your model via batch running. Usually this means that you should build your model so that the model clears the world every time it is run and does not rely on any past information.

Schedule

The *schedule* is a description of the order in which the model operates. Different ABM toolkits can have more or less explicit representations of the schedule. In NetLogo, there is no single identifiable object that can be identified as "the schedule." Rather, the schedule is the order of events that occur within the model, which depends on the sequence of buttons that the user pushes, and the code/procedures that those buttons run. We will first discuss the common SETUP/GO idiom which is employed in almost all agent-based models, and then move on to discuss some of the subtler issues concerning scheduling in ABMs.

SETUP and GO   First of all, there is usually an initialization procedure that creates the agents, initializes the environment, and readies the user interface. In NetLogo this procedure is usually called SETUP and it executes whenever a user presses the SETUP button on a NetLogo model. The SETUP routine usually starts by clearing away all the agents and data related to the pervious run of the model. Then it examines how the user has manipulated the various variables controlled by the user interface creating new agents and data to reflect the new run of the model. For instance, in Traffic Basic the SETUP procedure looks like this:

```
to setup
    clear-all
    ask patches [ setup-road ]
    setup-cars
    watch sample-car
end
```

As is typical of many ABMs, this procedure calls a bunch of other procedures. It starts by clearing the world (CA), and then asks the patches to SETUP-ROAD, which creates the environment for the model. Afterward, it creates the cars using SETUP-CARS, which checks the value of the NUMBER-OF-CARS slider and uses that to determine how many cars will be created. Back in the SETUP procedure, the WATCH call tells the observer to highlight one particular car.

The other main part of the schedule is what is often called the main loop, or in NetLogo, the GO procedure. The GO procedure describes what happens in one time unit (or tick) of the model. Usually that involves the agents being told what to do, the environment changing if necessary, and the user interface updating to reflect what has happened. In Traffic Basic the GO procedure looks like this:

```
to go
;; if there is a car right ahead of you, slow down to a speed below its speed
    ask turtles [
        let car-ahead one-of turtles-on patch-ahead 1
        ifelse car-ahead != nobody
            [   slow-down-car car-ahead]
            ;; otherwise, speed up
            [ speed-up-car ]
    ;; don't slow down below speed minimum or speed up beyond speed limit
        if speed < speed-min [ set speed speed-min ]
        if speed > speed-limit [ set speed speed-limit ]
        fd speed ]
    tick
end
```

In this procedure, the agents change their speeds and move, and then the tick counter is advanced, which allows all of the components of the model to know that a tick has passed. In this model, the environment remains constant, but it is possible for potholes and repairs to be made to the road, which would cause another call to be included in the GO procedure.

SETUP and GO provide a high level view at the schedule of a NetLogo model. However, to get a full description of the schedule, it would also be necessary to examine the procedures that are called within SETUP and GO.

Two issues must be considered when thinking about the schedule of an ABM. The first is whether the ABM uses synchronous updates (all agents updating at the same time) or asynchronous updates (some agents updating before others). Relatedly, one must determine whether the model operates sequentially (agents take turns acting), in parallel (agents operate at the same time) or in a simulated concurrency (somewhere between sequential and concurrent). We will examine these issues in turn.

Asynchronous vs. Synchronous Updates   If a model uses an *Asynchronous* update schedule, this means that when agents change their state, that state is immediately seen by other agents. In a *Synchronous* update schedule changes made to an agent are not seen by other agents until the next clock tick—that is, all agents update simultaneously. Both forms of updating are commonly used in agent-based modeling. Asynchronous updates can be more realistic, since asynchrony is more like the real world where agents all act and update independently of each other rather than waiting for each other. The Traffic Basic, Wolf Sheep Predation, Ants, Segregation, and Virus models all use asynchronous updating. However, synchronous updates can be easier to manage and debug and are therefore commonly used. In the NetLogo models library, Fire, Ethnocentrism, and the Cellular Automata models are examples of models that use synchronous updating. The form of updating can make quite a bit of difference to the behavior of the model. For instance, in a synchronous update, the order in which agents take actions does not matter, because they are only affected by the state of other agents at the end of the last tick, rather than the most current state of the agents. However, in asynchronous updating, it is important to know in what order and how agents take actions, which is what we will discuss in the next paragraph.

Sequential vs. Parallel Actions   Within the realm of asynchronous updating, agents can act either sequentially or in parallel. *Sequential* actions involve only one agent acting at a time while *Parallel* actions are those in which all agents act independently. In NetLogo (versions 4.0 and later), sequential action is the standard behavior for agents. In other words, when you ASK agents to do something, one agent completes the full set of actions that you have requested before passing on control to the next agent. In some ways, this is not a very realistic model of actions since in reality agents are constantly acting, thinking, and affecting other agents all at the same time and they do not take turns to wait for each other. Still, sequential actions are easier to design from a model implementer's viewpoint because it is more difficult to understand how parallel actions interact. Moreover, for the agents to act truly in parallel, you would need parallel hardware so that the actions of each agent would be carried out by a separate processor.

However, there is an intermediate solution. *Simulated concurrency* uses one processor to simulate many agents acting in parallel. Very few agent-based modeling toolkits support simulated concurrency, although NetLogo does have limited support for it. One way to take advantage of this is through the use of "turtle forever" buttons. With a turtle forever button, each agent acts completely independently of the others, and the observer is not involved at all, For example, examine the Termites model (*Wilensky, 1997c*) in the Biology section of the NetLogo models library. In this case, all of the turtles are executing this procedure:

```
to go   ;; turtle procedure
    search-for-chip
    find-new-pile
    put-down-chip
end
```

In this example, some termites can be on their second SEARCH-FOR-CHIP, even though some other termites have not finished the PUT-DOWN-CHIP command. While the difference is subtle, it can be important in some cases, providing a way to implement simulated parallel actions.

Wrapping It All Up

Now that we have reviewed all the components of an ABM, you should have a solid foundation for creating an agent-based model. In particular, there are three parts of any ABM that are essential to keep in mind as you are creating your model: the code, the documentation, and the interface. The *code*, which we have discussed and worked with for the last three chapters, tells the agents what to do and tells the model how to execute. The *documentation* describes the code, placing the model in the context of the real world. The *interface* is what allows users to control the model and thus manipulate its results.

In NetLogo, the code is placed in the Code tab (see figure 5.24). We have already discussed the code in some detail in the previous chapters so we will not discuss it much more here, except to highlight the importance of placing documentation in your code as well. In the code examples and models that we have developed, we have placed comments alongside the code (using the semicolon "comment" character). This is done to help anyone who reads your code to understand what is going on. In fact, it can even help you. Often modelers will reuse code or get asked questions about code, years after they have written it. If they have not documented their code well, it can take much longer to figure out what the code does, or why it was written as it was. In the end, documenting your code is a short-term cost for a long-term benefit, which usually outweighs the initial cost.

In NetLogo, the documentation is placed in the Info tab (see figure 5.25). This is in addition to the documentation that you have already placed in your code comments. This documentation should give an overall purpose and structure to your model. In

Figure 5.24
Code tab.

NetLogo, this documentation is typically broken down into eight sections (See the "Sections of the Info tab" text box), though model authors are free to add their own sections. Though this format of eight sections is specific to NetLogo, in general it makes sense to provide documentation that covers the same basic aspects of the model. A general overview to give the context of the model (WHAT IS IT?), a user's guide for how to take advantage of the model (HOW TO USE IT), interesting results (THINGS TO NOTICE and THINGS TO TRY), future improvements for the model (EXTENDING THE MODEL), special techniques employed in the model (NETLOGO FEATURES), and related work that inspired the model, as well as other places for information on the model (RELATED

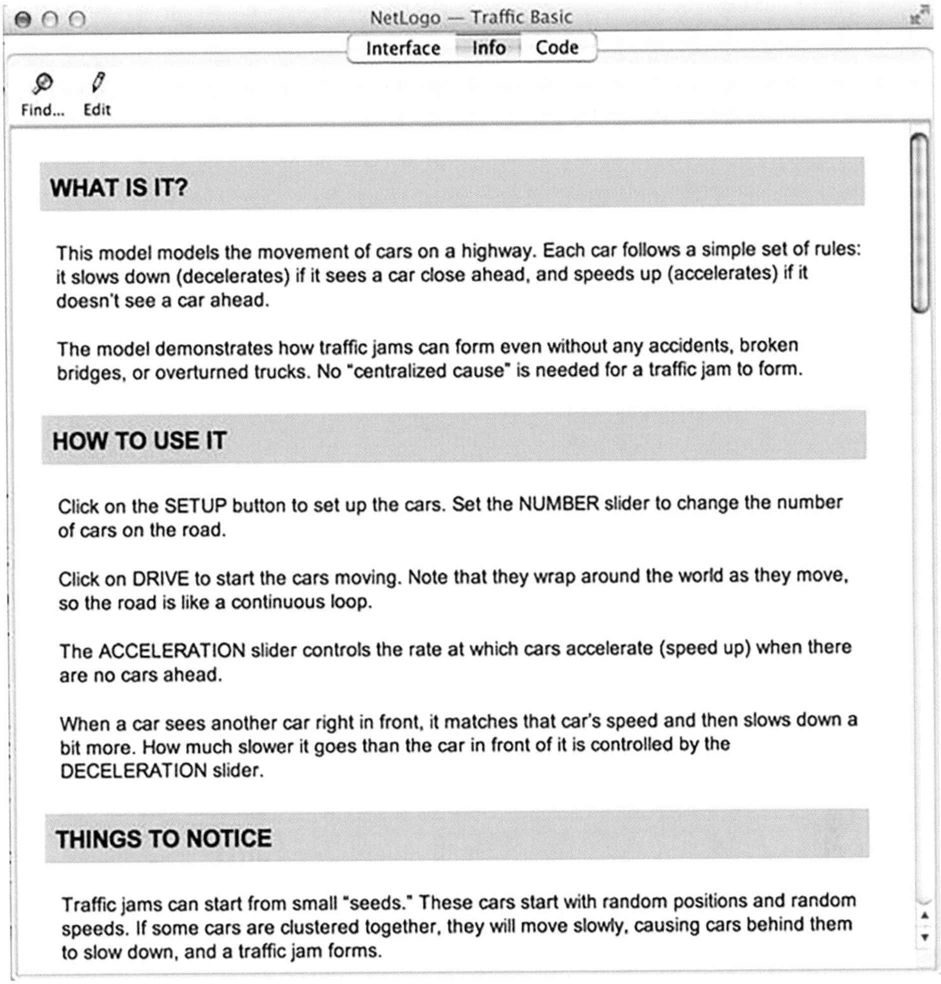

NetLogo — Traffic Basic

Interface   Info   Code

Find...   Edit

WHAT IS IT?

This model models the movement of cars on a highway. Each car follows a simple set of rules: it slows down (decelerates) if it sees a car close ahead, and speeds up (accelerates) if it doesn't see a car ahead.

The model demonstrates how traffic jams can form even without any accidents, broken bridges, or overturned trucks. No "centralized cause" is needed for a traffic jam to form.

HOW TO USE IT

Click on the SETUP button to set up the cars. Set the NUMBER slider to change the number of cars on the road.

Click on DRIVE to start the cars moving. Note that they wrap around the world as they move, so the road is like a continuous loop.

The ACCELERATION slider controls the rate at which cars accelerate (speed up) when there are no cars ahead.

When a car sees another car right in front, it matches that car's speed and then slows down a bit more. How much slower it goes than the car in front of it is controlled by the DECELERATION slider.

THINGS TO NOTICE

Traffic jams can start from small "seeds." These cars start with random positions and random speeds. If some cars are clustered together, they will move slowly, causing cars behind them to slow down, and a traffic jam forms.

Figure 5.25
Info tab.

Box 5.8
Sections of the Info tab

WHAT IS IT? Provides a general description of the phenomenon that is modeled.

HOW TO USE IT   Gives instructions on how to run the model and describes the interface elements of the model.

THINGS TO NOTICE   Describes interesting phenomena that the model exhibits.

THINGS TO TRY   Describes how the user can manipulate the model to produce new results.

EXTENDING THE MODEL   Gives suggestions and challenges on how to change the model to examine new features and phenomena. (This is similar to the future work section of a research paper.)

NETLOGO FEATURES   Discusses some particularly interesting features of NetLogo that are used in the model.

RELATED MODELS   Lists other agent-based models (often from the NetLogo models library) that are related to this model.

CREDITS AND REFERENCES   Tells the user who created the model and where the user can go to find more information about the model.

MODELS and CREDITS AND REFERENCES). There are several other formats for documenting a model. One popular format is the ODD format, developed by Grimm and colleagues (2006) that specifically aims to be a standard protocol for describing simulation models. Documentation completes the loop of tying the model to the real world phenomenon it is supposed to be describing. No model is complete without accompanying documentation.

The final part of the model that is necessary for it to be complete is the user interface. In NetLogo, the user interface is in the Interface tab (see figure 5.26). The UI enables the user to set the parameters for a particular model run and to watch the model unfold. Also, as we have discussed in previous sections, a good visualization choice can help the model user to gain insights into the model that they may not have gotten based purely upon numerical outputs. In fact, in many cases ABM modelers learn more about their model from watching runs than they do from the raw data that the model outputs at the end of a run.

The other components that we have described (i.e., agents, environments, interactions, interface/observer, and schedule) are central to code, documentation, and interfaces. They are formally controlled in the code, described in the documentation, and employed by the user interface. Together, these three parts are the necessary wrapping to deliver the full model.

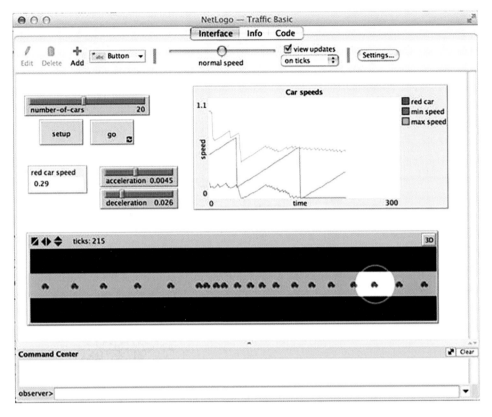

Figure 5.26
Interface tab.

Summary

We have described five classes of ABM components: agents, environments, interactions, observer/user interface, and schedule. These five classes of components of ABMs are described at a conceptual level. When creating your own models, you will find that you will need many instances of components, but they will all fall within these five general categories. Agents can have many different properties and behaviors, and there are many kinds of agents, but they are the basic component of an agent-based model, no agents, no ABM. The environment is where agents reside, and thus adequately describing the environment is important to an agent-based model. Interactions are how the dynamics of the model evolve, and therefore are critical to the operation of an agent-based model. The observer/interface is how the model is controlled and how data is extracted from the model.

Without the observer and interface, the model would not be usable. Finally, the schedule tells the model when to do what when, and there are important details about the schedule that must be considered when building a model.

These five components come together to form an agent-based model. They come together in the three parts of a model, the code, the documentation, and the user interface. The code is the formalistic description of the model, while the documentation ties the model to its real-world system, and the user interface enables the user to control the inputs, outputs, and operation of the model.

These components and parts are also a useful starting point for the design of an ABM. For example, suppose you want to expand on the traffic model to model a full urban transportation system. You might start by asking what the basic agents of the model are. Do you want to model trains, cars, buses, ferries, cyclists, and even pedestrians? After this, you might consider the environment. Trains tend to move on a network of rail systems, but pedestrians and cyclists are less geographically constrained. Your decisions about agents will affect your decisions about the environment and vice versa. After this you have to consider how agents and the environment interact. Can city hall create new transportation systems, or are you considering the current transport network to be exogenously fixed? Can some agents delay other agents? Do you just want to model commuters on their way to work or also agents on leisure trips? How does the observer and user interface interact with all of this? Will the movement of agents be visualized or will the system simply compute the mean time for a given commute? How does the schedule work? Who gets to decide where they are going? Can commuters change their minds based upon their previous workday? By thinking about these basic components, we can begin to frame the discussion that we will use to create our new model.

After completing this chapter, you have learned how to use simple agent-based models, extend an ABM, and build your own agent-based model, while familiarizing yourself with the components of an agent-based model. In the next chapter we will start to learn how to analyze a model so as to create useful results for answering the question that launched your model.

Explorations

1. Choose a model from the sample models in the models library. What are the agents in the model? What is the environment? What are the interactions? What responsibilities does the observer have? How is the schedule set up?
2. NetLogo turtle agents come with a default set of properties (heading, xcor, ycor, color, and others). Look at the complete list, which be found in the NetLogo documentation, then come up with a new property that you think might be a good addition to the default properties of agents. What are the arguments for including this property? What are the reasons that this property should not be included?

3. We have talked about geographic and network-based environments. Is there a model where you would want to use both geographic and network-based environments at the same time? Describe the model. Why would using both environment types simultaneously be needed for this model? Can the two environments interact with each other?

4. Modify the Grand Canyon model so that the water slowly erodes the elevation over time. Run the model several different times and export the resulting elevation maps back to a GIS package. Compare and contrast these different maps.

5. We have presented several basic interactions that agents often exhibit in agent-based models. Many times though the typical set of interactions that agents carry out is based upon the particular domain that you are trying to model. Thus, it is often useful to create a set of interactions for a particular domain. Can you describe a set of interactions that might be typical in a particular domain? For instance, what kinds of interactions might agents routinely carry out in economic models? Biological models? Engineering models?

6. Both the observer and the schedule require the model author to put together components of an agent-based model so that they will work together. How is the observer different from the schedule? Are these two components separate? Or can they be conceived of as one large component, with one part of the componentry controlling time and the other controlling the interaction topology?

7. *The human body as an ABM*   In the world of agent-based modeling, sometimes the term *meta-agent* is sometimes used to describe a group of agents that act together in such a way that they can be collectively thought of as an agent themselves. For instance, a company can be thought of as an agent when it is interfacing with other companies, even though that company is itself composed of individual agents (i.e., the company's employees). That company could in turn be part of a larger conglomerate of companies that act together as another meta-agent. Describe the human body in terms of meta-agents. What are the basic agents of the human body? What are its meta-agents?

8. *Preferential attachment*   Open the Preferential Attachment Simple model in the IABM chapter 5 folder. This model grows a network in which new nodes being added to the network are more likely to be connected to nodes that already have many links. These types of networks are common in real-world situations that are both engineered and emergent, like airline networks, the Internet, Hollywood actors in the same film, and the power grid. In many of these cases, if you are joining a network you would want to be more connected to a higher degree node. However, the model does not take a node's value into account at all. What if a node has an intrinsic value in addition to its connectedness? Modify this model to give the nodes an intrinsic value. Have new nodes attach to the network taking both degree and intrinsic value into account. Add a slider so that you can control this relationship. What are the results of your model what happens when the new nodes use only degree to make their decision? What happens when they only use intrinsic value to make their decision? What happens in between?

9. Modify the Preferential Attachment model so that as hubs get more and more attachment requests, they decrease their probability of accepting them. How does this change affect the resultant network?

10. *Giant component* Another model in the Networks section of the models library is the Giant Component model. This model starts with a group of nodes and then adds random links to them. The giant component is the largest connected subcomponent of this network. One question you might ask is, is there a point at which the giant component size grows quickly? How many links do you have to add for this to occur? Does this value change as you change the number of nodes? What if you want all of the nodes to be in the giant component? How many links do you have to add for this to occur? Run the model several times and examine how many ticks it takes to have all the nodes be part of the giant component. Is there any regularity to this amount of time?

11. In the Giant Component model, the probability of any two nodes getting connected to each other is the same. Can you think of ways to make some nodes more attractive to connect to than others? How would that affect the formation of the giant component?

12. Another model in the Networks section of the models library is the Small Worlds model (*Wilensky, 2005a*). That model is initialized with a set of nodes connected in a special circular network. Can you find another initial network to start with that can be easily modified to be small world?

13. Another model in the Networks section of the models library is the Virus on a Network model, which demonstrates the spread of a virus though a network of nodes each of which may be in one of three states: susceptible, infected, or resistant. Suppose the virus is spreading by emailing itself out to everyone in the computer's address book. Since being in someone's address book is not a symmetric relationship, change this model to use directed links instead of undirected links.

14. Try making a model similar to Virus on a network model but where the virus has the ability to mutate itself. Such self-modifying viruses are a considerable threat to computer security, since traditional methods of virus signature identification may not work against them. In your model, nodes that become immune may be reinfected if the virus has mutated to become significantly different from the variant that originally infected the node.

15. Another model in the Networks section of the models library is the Team Assembly model, which illustrates how the behavior of individuals in assembling small teams for short-term projects can give rise to a variety of large-scale network structures over time. Collaboration networks can alternatively be thought of as those networks consisting of individuals linked to projects. For example, one can represent a scientific journal with two types of nodes, scientists and publications. Ties between scientists and publications represent authorship. Thus, links between a publication multiple scientists specify coauthorship. More generally, a collaborative project may be represented by one type of node, and participants another type. Can you modify the model to assemble teams using bipartite network?

16. *Different topologies*   Build a model of a phenomenon where agents communicate with nearby agents in a Euclidean space. Then build another model of the same phenomenon in which agents communicate across a social network. When would you use each of these models? What advantages does each topology have? What disadvantages? Compare the results of the two models.

17. *Möbius strips*   We discussed many different topologies that can be used for agent interactions. One interesting topology is that of the Möbius strip. To create a Möbius strip you take a strip of paper, twist it and connect one end to the other end of the strip. The interesting thing about the Möbius strip is that while a normal sheet of paper has two sides, it only has one. You can prove this to yourself by tracing a line on the Möbius strip. Build an agent-based model with this topology. For instance, can you modify the Flocking model to have the birds fly on a Möbius strip? (Hint: One way to do this would to use a bounded topology in the top-bottom, and have a toroidal wrapping topology in the left-right.)

18. *Smarter agents*   Examine one of the Artificial Neural Net models from the Computer Science section of the models library. This model shows how you can use a simple machine learning technique to develop an algorithm that matches inputs to outputs. In this chapter, we discussed how machine-learning algorithms can be used to make agents smarter. Take the Neural Net code and embed it in another model to make the agents smarter. For instance, take the Wolf Sheep Predation model and have the wolves use neural nets to decide in what direction to move to most efficiently predate.

19. *Adaptive Traffic Basic*   In the section on adaptive agents, we gave you some of the basic pieces of code necessary to build an adaptive Traffic Basic model. Take this code and make it fully work. To do this you may need to rewrite the SETUP procedure and add some global declarations.

20. *Individual Adaptive Traffic Basic*   In the adaptive Traffic Basic model that we discussed and developed in the previous exploration, all of the turtles have the same acceleration rates. Modify this code so that each turtle has its own acceleration and adapts this acceleration based on its own experience.

21. *Info Tab*   We have discussed how important documentation is to a model. The Info Tab is a critical part of that documentation, since it describes what the model represents. In fact, some scientists argue that without proper documentation detailing the relationship between an implemented model (i.e., the code) and the real-world phenomenon, a model is not a model; it is simply a piece of software that computes some numbers. Substantiate this argument. What is a sufficient level of documentation that a model author must provide to complete a model? Provide an explanation for your decision.

22. *Interface Tab*   The Interface Tab enables a model user to interact with a model that you have designed. It is important that the Interface Tab provide both a clear visualization and an easy-to-use set of interactive tools to control the model. Describe three guidelines for designing an informative visualization. Describe three guidelines for designing an easy-to-use interface.

23. *Discrete event scheduler*   We have discussed several different issues to consider when designing the schedule for your agent-based model. There is one other approach to scheduling that we did not discuss in this chapter. Discrete Event Scheduling (DES) is when the agents and the environment of your model schedule events to take place at discrete times. For instance, examine the Mousetraps model in the Mathematics section of the models library. Right now, whenever a ball flies through the air it simply moves until it comes to a resting place and then attempts to trigger a mousetrap. Instead of this method, you could imagine implementing this model without any ball agents; instead, when a mousetrap is tripped, it schedules two other mousetraps to trip within a radius at a certain time in the future. This would be a discrete event scheduler. Reimplement this model using a DES.

24. The DES idea of discrete ticks being used to represent time is very useful. However, this may not be the most computationally efficient mechanism for all systems. Can you speculate about how to move away from a discrete scheduler toward something that would allow the model builder to specify when something was executed rather than how often it was executed? What would such a system look like? How would it differ from the standard tick based system? What are the costs and benefits of this new approach?

25. *Activation*   The order in which agents execute can greatly affect how a model runs. Open the Life model in the NetLogo models library under Computer Science > Cellular Automata. This model operates with all of the patches running in synchronous order, that is, each patch waits to update its state until all other patches have updated their state. Modify this model so that it operates in an asynchronous order. How do the two models compare? Describe the patterns that arise from each model. Is it possible to create the glider (discussed in chapter 2) in the asynchronous model?

26. *3D models*   It is often possible to create a 3D version of a 2D ABM. Sometimes the behavior of the model is similar, but other times it can have quite different results. Create a 3D version of the Segregation model in the Social Science section of the models library.

27. In the NetLogo 3D Flocking model, can you extend the model so that the birds can fly around obstacles in the middle of the world?

28. In the NetLogo 3D Termites model, can you extend the model to have the termites sort several colors of wood? Create some informative plots that are useful to measure the termites' progress.

29. In the section on goal-directed agents, we described how the goal-directed agents in Traffic Grid were not very smart because they would get caught in infinite loops of going back and forth between the same squares both of which are equally distant from their goal. As a result, they never reach their goal. Modify the algorithm so that the agents always reach their goal.

30. After modifying the Traffic Grid model as in the previous exploration, the traffic still might not flow that smoothly as cars are turning around while on the road. Modify the model so that when a car reaches its goal, it moves off the road into the house or work

and remains there for some time, STAY-TIME. Which values of STAY-TIME result in the most efficient traffic?

31. *Turtles vs. patches*   Both turtles and patches can be agents in a model. In fact many models could be implemented as either turtle-based models or patch-based models. Open the AIDS model in the Biology section of the models library. Currently this model is turtle-based. Reimplement this model without any turtles, using only patches. Open the Life model in the computer science of the models library, which is patch-based. Reimplement this model without using patches, but instead have turtles that are hatched and killed. Describe your experience in reimplementing these models. At what times is it more beneficial to use turtles as agents? At what times is it more beneficial to use patches as agents?

32. Open the Robby the Robot model in the Computer Science section of the NetLogo models library. Robby is a virtual robot that moves around a room and picks up cans. This model demonstrates the use of a genetic algorithm (GA) to evolve control strategies for Robby. The GA starts with randomly generated strategies and then uses evolution to improve them. Vary the settings on the POPULATION-SIZE and MUTATION-RATE sliders. How do these affect the best fitness in the population as well as the speed of evolution? Try different rules for selecting the parents of the next generation. What leads to the fastest evolution? Is there ever a trade-off between fast evolution at the beginning and how effective the winning strategies are at the end?

33. Many times in both nature and society, distributed elements can synchronize their behavior. This occurs with physical systems such as coupled oscillators, with biological systems such as synchronized firefly flashing and with human systems such as audiences clapping.

Open the Fireflies model from the Biology section of the NetLogo models library. It presents two strategies for fireflies to synchronize their flashes: "phase advance" and "phase delay."

(a) Change the strategy chooser between "delay" and "advance" while keeping the other settings steady (in particular, keep FLASHES-TO-RESTART at 2). Which strategy seems more effective? Why?

(b) Try adjusting FLASHES-TO-RESTART between 0, 1 and 2 using both phase delay and phase advance settings. Notice that each setting will give a characteristically different plot, and some of them do not allow for synchronization at all (for example, with the delay strategy, contrast FLASHES-TO-RESTART set to 1 as opposed to 2). Why does this control make such a difference in the outcome of the simulation?

(c) This model explores only two general strategies for attaining synchrony in such cycle-governed fireflies. Can you find any others? Can you improve the existing strategies?

(d) There are many other possible situations in which distributed agents must synchronize their behavior through the use of simple rules. What if, instead of perceiving only other discrete flashes, an insect could sense where another insect was in its cycle (perhaps by hearing an increasingly loud hum)? What kinds of strategies for synchronization might be useful in such a situation?

(e) If all fireflies had adjustable cycle-lengths (initially set to random intervals) would it then be possible to coordinate both their cycle-lengths and their flashing?

34. *List Manipulation* Write a reporter that takes two lists as input and reports a list of the pairwise sums.

35. Write a procedure that takes a list of turtles and a list of numbers and asks each turtle to move the corresponding number forward.

36. Write a reporter that takes a list as input and reports the list in reverse order.

6 Analyzing Agent-Based Models

My answer to him was, "… when people thought the Earth was flat, they were wrong. When people thought the Earth was spherical they were wrong. But if you think that thinking the Earth is spherical is just as wrong as thinking the Earth is flat, then your view is wronger than both of them put together."

—Isaac Asimov

Measure twice, cut once.

—Proverb

Types of Measurements

Heretofore, we have examined ABMs, modified them, built them from scratch, and analyzed their behavior. In this chapter, we will learn to employ ABM to produce new and interesting results about the domain that we are investigating. What kinds of results can ABMs produce? There are many different ways of examining and analyzing ABM data. Choosing just one of these techniques can be limiting; therefore, it is important to know the advantages and disadvantages of a variety of tools and techniques. It is often useful to consider your analysis methods *before* building the ABM, to enable you to design output that is conducive to your analysis.

Modeling the Spread of Disease

If someone catches a cold and is coughing up a storm, he might infect others. Those that he comes into contact with—his friends, co-workers, and even strangers—may catch the cold. If a cold virus infects someone, that person might spread that disease to five other people (six now infected) before they recover. In turn, those five other people might spread the cold to five more people each (thirty-one are now infected), and those twenty-five people might spread the cold to five additional people (a hundred and fifty-six people are now infected). In fact, the rate of infection initially rises exponentially.

However, since this infection count grows so quickly, any population will eventually reach the limit of the number of people who can be infected. For instance, imagine that the 156 people mentioned above all work for the same company of 200 individuals. It is impossible for the remaining 125 people to each infect five new people, and thus the number of infected people will tail off because there is no one left to infect. As we have described it so far, this simple model assumes that each person infects the same number of people, which is manifestly not the case in real contexts. As a person moves through their workspace, it might be the case that, they happen to not see many people in one day, whereas another individual might see many people. Also, our initial description assumes that if one person infects five people and another person infects five, there will not be any overlap. In reality, there is likely to be substantial overlap. Thus, the spread of disease in a workplace is not as straightforward as our initial description suggests. Suppose that we are interested in understanding the spread of disease, and we want to build an ABM of such a spread. How should we go about doing it?

First, we need some agents that keep track of whether they are infected with a cold or not. Additionally, these agents need a location in space and the ability to move. Finally, we need the ability to initialize the model by infecting a group of individuals. That is exactly how the NetLogo model we will be discussing in this chapter behaves (See figure 6.1). Individuals move around randomly on a landscape and infect other individuals whenever they come into contact with them.

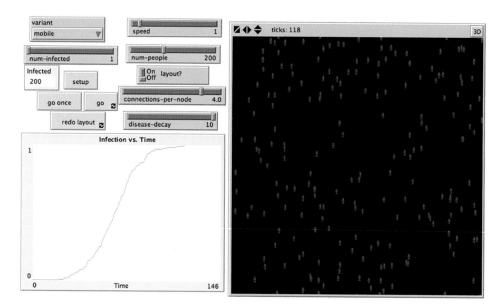

Figure 6.1
Spread of Disease model.

Table 6.1
Infection Data

Population	50	100	150	200
Time to 100% Infection	419	188	169	127

Though this model is simple, it exhibits interesting and complex behavior. For instance, what happens if we increase the number of people in the model? Does the disease spread quicker throughout the population, or does it take a longer time because there are more people? Let us run the model at population sizes of 50, 100, 150, and 200, and examine the results. We will keep the size of the world constant, so that, as we increase the number of individuals, we are also increasing the population density. Along the way we will write down at what time the entire population becomes infected (see table 6.1).

Based on these results, we conclude that as the population density increases, the time to full infection dramatically decreases. This makes sense upon further contemplation. In the beginning, when the first person becomes infected, if there are not many other people around, the person has no one to infect, and thus the infection rate increases slowly. However, if there are many people around then there will be plenty of infection opportunities. Moreover, at the end of the run, when there are only one or two uninfected agents, they will be more likely to run into someone with an infection if the population count is high. This is true despite the fact that the total number of people that need to be infected increases.

Box 6.1
Language Change

In the Spread of Disease model, we discuss how diseases can spread from one individual to another. However, there is no reason to restrict this model to just disease spread. Ideas can also spread from one individual to another. One classic example of this is language change. There are many different types of language change that can occur but one clear example is the introduction of new words into a language (Labov, 2001). To view the Spread of Disease model in this way, we assume that when any two individuals come into contact, they talk to each other. If one of the speakers uses a new word, then he or she provides the other speaker with the ability to use that word in future encounters. In this way, we can see how the introduction of a new word into a language spreads through a population in much the same way that an infection does (Enfield, 2003). One difference between the current Spread of Disease model and language change, is that usually in language change there is a resistance to change, and that also needs to be included in the model. In the Explorations for this section you can explore how to change the Spread of Disease model to make it a more robust model of language change. See also the Language Change model (*Troutman & Wilensky, 2007*) in the Social Sciences section of the NetLogo models library.

Table 6.2
Your Friend's Data

Population	50	100	150	200
Time to 100% Infection	305	263	118	126

Table 6.3
Raw Data

Population	Run 1	Run 2	Run 3	Run 4	Run 5	Run 6	Run 7	Run 8	Run 9	Run 10
50	419	365	305	318	323	337	432	380	430	359
100	188	263	256	205	206	205	201	181	202	231
150	169	118	163	146	143	167	137	121	140	140
200	127	126	113	111	133	129	109	101	105	133

Let us suppose that we show this data to a friend of ours and she does not believe it. She believes that the time to 100 percent infection should grow linearly with the population. She looks over the code and determines that it seems to match the description (a process called verification, which we will discuss in the next chapter). After that, she runs the model and collects the same data that we did (a form of replication which we also discuss in the next chapter). Her data is in table 6.2.

These results do not support our friend's prediction that the time to 100 percent infection will grow as the population increases, but, on the other hand, they are quite different from the results that were originally collected. In fact, the time to 100 percent infection for 150 and 200 increases in our friend's data, seemingly contradicting our original results. Moreover, if we run the model several more times you might again get different results. We need some methods for determining if there are trends in the data.[1]

The data is inconsistent because most ABM models employ randomness in their algorithms—i.e., the code makes use of a random number generator. How the agents move around on the landscape is not specifically determined, but instead is the result of several calls to the random number generator at each time step that determine the actions of any particular agent. Moreover, these random decisions occur at least once for each agent in the population for each time step. Clearly, then, one set of runs is not enough to characterize the behavior of this model. Suppose, then, that we collect additional data for a set of population densities for ten different model runs as in table 6.3. Though most of these runs look more like our original results than our friend's results, it might be difficult to see

---

1. In the particular case of this simple model, it is relatively straightforward to determine what the rate of increase in the model will be by using heuristic methods or by generating a closed-form solution. However, we will explore how to discover this rate directly from the data as that will often be the only method available.

clear trends, and to analyze the results overall. Thus, to describe these patterns of behavior it makes sense to turn to some statistics.

Statistical Analysis of ABM: Moving beyond Raw Data

Statistical results are the most common way of looking at any kind of scientific data whether it is computational models, physical experiments, sociological surveys, or other methods that generate data. The general methodology behind descriptive statistics is to provide numerical measures that summarize a large data set and describe the data set in such a way that it is not necessary to examine every single value. For instance, suppose we are interested in determining whether a coin is fair (i.e., it is as likely to turn up heads when flipped as it is to turn up tails) then we can conduct a series of experiments where we flip the coin and observe the results. One way to determine if the coin was fair would be to simply examine all of the observations: HHHHTTHTTT and, based upon our exami-nation, make a determination if the coin was fair or not. However, if we wanted to examine a thousand, or ten thousand, or even a million such observations, it would take too much time to examine all of them. A better way is to simply count the frequency with which heads occurs, i.e., the observed probability of success, and the standard deviation of this observed probability. It is much easier to look at means and standard deviations than it is to examine large series of data (e.g., for HHHHTTHTTT, the observed probability is 0.5, and the expected outcome for ten trials is to observe five heads with a standard deviation of 1.58).

To apply this technique to our Spread of Disease model in more depth, we can create summary statistics of the table 6.3 results, which we display in table 6.4.

From these summary results, we see that the mean time to 100 percent infection declines as the population density increases. Another interesting result is that as the population density goes up, the standard deviation goes down. This means that the data is less varied. In other words, more trials are closer to the mean than farther away from it. This happens because when there are few agents, there is a possibility that individuals might not run into each other to transmit the disease for quite a while, but when there is a high density of individuals, there is less probability of this occurring, which means that the time to 100 percent infection remains closer to the mean time.

Table 6.4
Summary Statistics

Population	Mean	Std. Dev.
50	366.8	47.39385802
100	213.8	27.40154091
150	144.4	17.65219533
200	118.7	12.12939497

These results seem to confirm our original hypothesis that as population density increases the mean time to infection declines. Within ABM, statistical analysis is a common method of confirming or rejecting hypotheses. When initially examining an ABM we may start by exploring the space of possibilities (the parameter space) observing the variations in the results, but over time we will start to create hypotheses about how the inputs to the ABM generate various outputs. Devising an experiment like the one above, and analyzing the results is how we begin to confirm or reject these hypotheses.

If you are conversant with basic statistical methods, it is straightforward to carry out further statistical analysis on this data and attempt to describe the rate at which the time decreases as the population density increases. We could also carry out a statistical test to prove that changes in population density lead to different times to achieving 100 percent infection. Statistical tests for analyzing ABMs will be touched upon briefly in the next chapter. A detailed discussion of statistical analysis is beyond the scope of this textbook, but for a more in-depth introduction to statistical analysis, see an introductory statistics text.

Because of the natural "compression" of data that occurs when conducting statistical analysis, this is a useful technique when examining ABMs. ABMs create large amounts of data (the Spread of Disease model is just a small example), and if we can summarize that data we can examine large amounts of output in an efficient manner.

Numerous easily available tools can facilitate the conduction of statistical analysis. For instance, Microsoft Excel, the open source R package, SAS, Mathematica, and Matlab, all have packages and sets of functions that assist in the analysis of large data sets. It is usually quite easy to take data from an ABM and import it into one of these packages. Most ABM toolkits allow you to export your data to a CSV (Comma Separated Value) file, and all of the preceding tools can import such data. You can then carry out any statistical analysis necessary in these toolkits. In addition, most ABM toolkits give you the basic ability to carry out simple statistical analysis within the package itself (e.g., in NetLogo there are MEAN and STANDARD-DEVIATION primitives). Thus, while the model is running, the ABM itself can generate summary statistics. Finally, some ABM toolkits provide the ability to connect to statistical packages while the model is running (e.g., in NetLogo you can use Mathematica Link (*Bakshy & Wilensky, 2007*) to control NetLogo from within Mathematica, which allows you to retrieve any results from your model within Mathematica. Similarly, you can use the NetLogo R extension to conduct analyses with the R statistical package).

The Necessity of Multiple Runs within ABM

As illustrated earlier, when you are trying to collect statistical results from an ABM you should run the model multiple times and collect different results at different points. Most ABM toolkits will provide you with a way to collect the data from these runs automatically (e.g., in NetLogo there is a tool called BehaviorSpace[2]) and it is important to know how to access these features. However, even when these features do not exist, ABM toolkits are often full-featured programming languages, allowing you to write your own tools for creating experiments to produce the data sets you want to analyze. In fact, in the analysis described before, that is what we did to generate the data. We simply wrote the following code:

```
repeat 10 [
    set num-people 50
    setup
    while [count turtles with [ not infected? ] > 0 ]
      [ go ]
    print ticks
]
```

By modifying the value of NUM-PEOPLE, we were able to generate the four sets of data presented in table 6.3. This technique can become tedious if you want to explore a large number of variables, or a large number of settings for one variable. Consequently, to aid in this process, most ABM toolkits have a *batch experiment tool*. These tools will automatically run the model multiple times with multiple different settings and collect the results in some easy to use format like the CSV files mentioned earlier. For instance, if we wanted to run the same experiment described before using NetLogo's BehaviorSpace, we would begin by starting BehaviorSpace and selecting a new experiment. The resulting dialog is illustrated in figure 6.2.

It is instructive to go through the steps of setting up a BehaviorSpace experiment. We start by giving a name to the experiment. Let us call this experiment "population density," which will correspond to the name of the output file that BehaviorSpace generates to hold the results of our experiment. We can then select the parameters and parameter ranges for BehaviorSpace to "sweep" so as to recreate the same experiment within BehaviorSpace. We can then set each parameter using the BehaviorSpace syntax. For instance, ["num-people" 50] sets NUM-PEOPLE to 50, or we can set NUM-PEOPLE to a range of values, and BehaviorSpace will automatically run the model for each value in the range. If we want to recreate the results above we need to vary NUM-PEOPLE by using ["num-people" [50 50 200]]. This tells BehaviorSpace to start at 50 and increment that number by 50 until it reaches 200. Additionally, we can modify two parameters at the same time. For instance, if we wanted to modify the number of people originally infected (NUM-INFECTED) at the same time as NUM-PEOPLE, we could specify ["num-infected" [1 1 5]]. This will

2. Wilensky & Shargel (2001).

3. The print primitive will print the data to the command center. It is often useful to write the data to a file using the file-open, file-print, and file-close primitives.

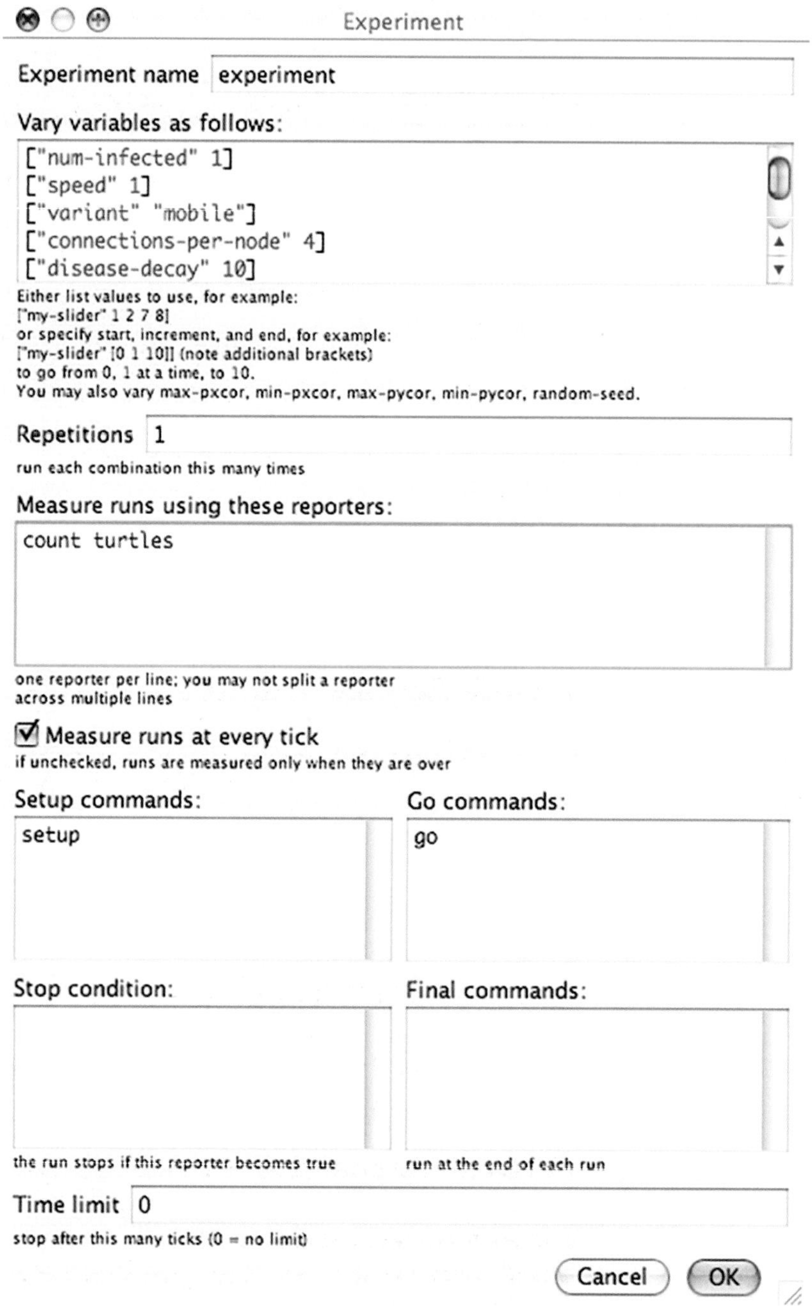

⊗ ○ ⊕   Experiment

Experiment name experiment

Vary variables as follows:

```
["num-infected" 1]
["speed" 1]
["variant" "mobile"]
["connections-per-node" 4]
["disease-decay" 10]
```

Either list values to use, for example:
["my-slider" 1 2 7 8]
or specify start, increment, and end, for example:
["my-slider" [0 1 10]] (note additional brackets)
to go from 0, 1 at a time, to 10.
You may also vary max-pxcor, min-pxcor, max-pycor, min-pycor, random-seed.

Repetitions 1

run each combination this many times

Measure runs using these reporters:

```
count turtles
```

one reporter per line; you may not split a reporter
across multiple lines

☑ Measure runs at every tick
if unchecked, runs are measured only when they are over

Setup commands: Go commands:

```
setup                              go
```

Stop condition: Final commands:

the run stops if this reporter becomes true   run at the end of each run

Time limit 0

stop after this many ticks (0 = no limit)

                                        Cancel   OK

Figure 6.2
BehaviorSpace, a batch experiment tool in NetLogo.

then run the various values of num-people and num-infected at the same time (i.e., (num-infected, num-people) = (1, 50), (2, 50), (3, 50), (4, 50), (5, 50), (1, 100), (2, 100), (3, 100), (4, 100), (5, 100), (1, 150), (2, 150), (3, 150), (4, 150), (5, 150), (1, 200), (2, 200), (3, 200), (4, 200), (5, 200)) or 20 different parameter settings). Next we can look at the number of times we want each set of parameters to repeat. In our experiment, we collected the results of 10 repetitions, so we set this to 10. After that we can specify the values that we are interested in, since we want to examine the time it takes until 100 percent infection occurs, and we can put the special reporter "ticks," which reports the current time, in this box. We can then turn off "Measure runs at every tick" and all we will collect is the final number of ticks. The SETUP and GO commands allow you to specify any additional NetLogo code that you need to make the model start and go. "Stop condition" allows you to specify special stop conditions for each run, and "final commands" allows you to insert any commands that you want executed between runs of the model. Finally, the time limit box allows you to set a limit to the number of ticks for which the model will run if no stop conditions are reached. After we make these changes, the BehaviorSpace dialog looks like figure 6.3.

After we click OK, we go back to the experiment selection dialogue. From here we can run the experiment and select whether we want it in table (row-oriented) or spreadsheet (column-oriented) format (or both or neither), and we specify where we want the file saved. If, after we run the experiment, we want to look at the results, we can start up a spreadsheet or another statistical package and load the CSV file. The results of our experiment are illustrated in table format in table 6.5. In addition to the actual data we are interested in (NUM-PEOPLE vs. TICKS), BehaviorSpace also displays all of the additional parameters, such as NUM-INFECTED and SPEED.[4] These results are similar to the results described earlier, but they do not correspond exactly, since different random number seeds were used.

In general in ABM, it is important to carry out multiple runs of your experiments so that you can determine if some result is truly a pattern or just a one-time occurrence. One common way is to start by manually running your model multiple times, but to get a better sense of the results it is usually much easier to use a batch experiment tool. We have illustrated the BehaviorSpace tool, which is the batch experiment tool for NetLogo but most ABM toolkits have a similar method of sweeping parameters and collecting multiple runs.

Using Graphs to Examine Results in ABM

As you look over the summary statistics in table 6.4 (or, even worse, the full data set in table 6.3), you may become aware of a deficiency in such information. The summary

---

4. In fact, one of the additional variables that BehaviorSpace automatically reports every time it prints out a row of this spreadsheet is the tick count, so our ticks reporter was actually superfluous.

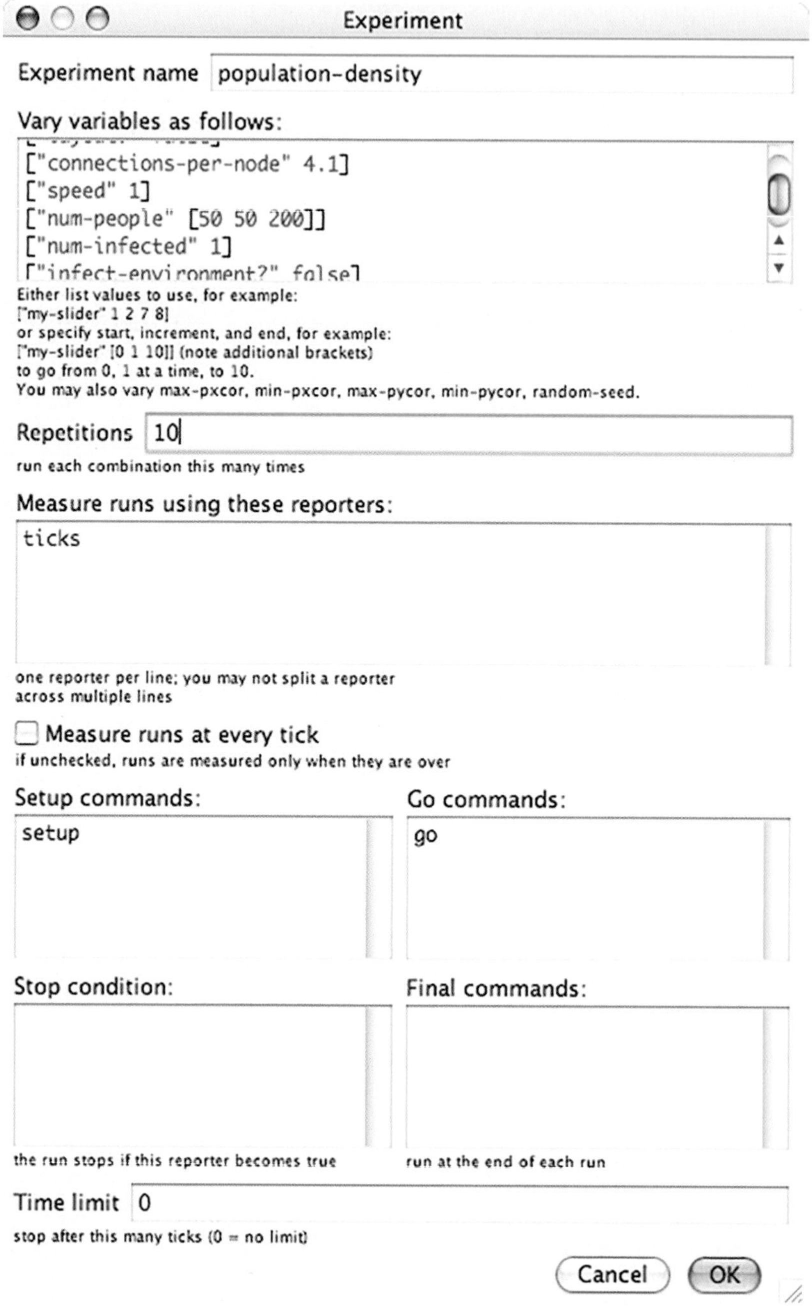

Experiment

Experiment name population-density

Vary variables as follows:

```
["connections-per-node" 4.1]
["speed" 1]
["num-people" [50 50 200]]
["num-infected" 1]
["infect-environment?" false]
```

Either list values to use, for example:
["my-slider" 1 2 7 8]
or specify start, increment, and end, for example:
["my-slider" [0 1 10]] (note additional brackets)
to go from 0, 1 at a time, to 10.
You may also vary max-pxcor, min-pxcor, max-pycor, min-pycor, random-seed.

Repetitions 10

run each combination this many times

Measure runs using these reporters:

```
ticks
```

one reporter per line; you may not split a reporter
across multiple lines

☐ Measure runs at every tick
if unchecked, runs are measured only when they are over

Setup commands:
```
setup
```

Go commands:
```
go
```

Stop condition:

Final commands:

the run stops if this reporter becomes true

run at the end of each run

Time limit 0

stop after this many ticks (0 = no limit)

Cancel   OK

Figure 6.3
Final settings for BehaviorSpace.

Table 6.5
BehaviorSpace Data Imported into a Spreadsheet

BehaviorSpace Table data

population-density

DATE

TIME

[run number]	network?	layout?	connections-per-node	speed	num-people	num-infected	infect-environment?	[tick]	ticks
1	FALSE	FALSE	4.1	1	50	1	FALSE	299	299
2	FALSE	FALSE	4.1	1	50	1	FALSE	432	432
3	FALSE	FALSE	4.1	1	50	1	FALSE	444	444
4	FALSE	FALSE	4.1	1	50	1	FALSE	400	400
5	FALSE	FALSE	4.1	1	50	1	FALSE	467	467
6	FALSE	FALSE	4.1	1	50	1	FALSE	397	397
7	FALSE	FALSE	4.1	1	50	1	FALSE	337	337
8	FALSE	FALSE	4.1	1	50	1	FALSE	280	280
9	FALSE	FALSE	4.1	1	50	1	FALSE	366	366
10	FALSE	FALSE	4.1	1	50	1	FALSE	257	257
11	FALSE	FALSE	4.1	1	100	1	FALSE	268	268
12	FALSE	FALSE	4.1	1	100	1	FALSE	165	165
13	FALSE	FALSE	4.1	1	100	1	FALSE	183	183
14	FALSE	FALSE	4.1	1	100	1	FALSE	200	200
15	FALSE	FALSE	4.1	1	100	1	FALSE	151	151
16	FALSE	FALSE	4.1	1	100	1	FALSE	206	206
17	FALSE	FALSE	4.1	1	100	1	FALSE	217	217
18	FALSE	FALSE	4.1	1	100	1	FALSE	234	234
19	FALSE	FALSE	4.1	1	100	1	FALSE	197	197
20	FALSE	FALSE	4.1	1	100	1	FALSE	209	209
21	FALSE	FALSE	4.1	1	150	1	FALSE	131	131
22	FALSE	FALSE	4.1	1	150	1	FALSE	127	127
23	FALSE	FALSE	4.1	1	150	1	FALSE	173	173
24	FALSE	FALSE	4.1	1	150	1	FALSE	179	179
25	FALSE	FALSE	4.1	1	150	1	FALSE	203	203
26	FALSE	FALSE	4.1	1	150	1	FALSE	124	124
27	FALSE	FALSE	4.1	1	150	1	FALSE	128	128
28	FALSE	FALSE	4.1	1	150	1	FALSE	190	190
29	FALSE	FALSE	4.1	1	150	1	FALSE	170	170
30	FALSE	FALSE	4.1	1	150	1	FALSE	141	141
31	FALSE	FALSE	4.1	1	200	1	FALSE	103	103
32	FALSE	FALSE	4.1	1	200	1	FALSE	124	124
33	FALSE	FALSE	4.1	1	200	1	FALSE	124	124
34	FALSE	FALSE	4.1	1	200	1	FALSE	138	138
35	FALSE	FALSE	4.1	1	200	1	FALSE	211	211
36	FALSE	FALSE	4.1	1	200	1	FALSE	137	137
37	FALSE	FALSE	4.1	1	200	1	FALSE	115	115
38	FALSE	FALSE	4.1	1	200	1	FALSE	110	110
39	FALSE	FALSE	4.1	1	200	1	FALSE	142	142
40	FALSE	FALSE	4.1	1	200	1	FALSE	130	130

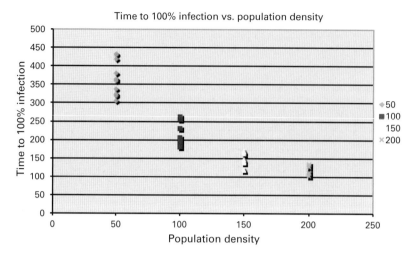

Figure 6.4
All raw data in a graph-based form.

statistics provide a check that you were correct when you thought that time to 100 percent infection decreased as population increases, but they do not tell the whole story. They do not provide you with a total description of the distribution of the data. Moreover, looking at the data itself is difficult, since it is hard to look at a series of numbers, as in table 6.3, and discern any meaningful pattern quickly. It would be nice to present the data in a way that you could quickly understand the full data set. Graphs, which embed the full set of data in a pictorial representation, facilitate understanding while still providing all the data available. For instance, we can take the data from table 6.3, and create a graph of the four population densities versus the time to 100 percent infection, as illustrated in figure 6.4. In NetLogo creating simple graphs is easy to do and will often suffice for simple data analysis. But with complex data sets, designing a useful and immediately informative graph can be challenging and is the subject of an extensive body of literature (Tufte, 1983; Bertin, 1983).

From figure 6.4, we can quickly see how the data is distributed and how the data changes with population density. This data seems to indicate that as population increases the differences between times to infection decreases. If we kept looking at higher and higher population values, it might be that the time to infection starts leveling off, i.e., regardless of whether there are 2,000 or 3,000 individuals, it still takes 100 time steps to fully infect the population. For instance, it appears that the times to 100 percent infection is not very different whether the population is 150 or 200.

However, this data might still be too complicated to understand. We can use the same technique to make the summary data easier to understand as is illustrated in figure 6.5.

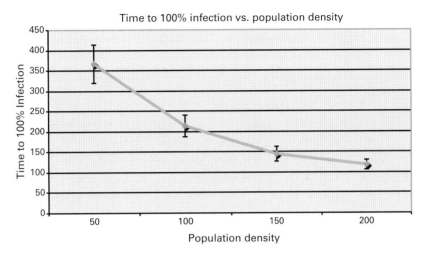

Figure 6.5
Summary data.

In this figure, the mean of each data series is plotted as well as error bars of one standard deviation. This new figure might not be easier to understand than figure 6.4, but if there were one hundred data points in figure 6.4 rather than ten data points, then a figure like figure 6.5 might be very helpful.

Graphs are not only useful to help clarify your data after a model run, but they are also useful during the running of a model. Many ABM toolkits include capabilities for continually updating graphs and charts during the running of a model and thus enable you to see the progress of the model temporally. This can be very useful for understanding the dynamics and temporal evolution of the model. For instance, in the Spread of Disease model there is a graph that illustrates the change in the fraction of infected agents as time proceeds (see figure 6.6). If you were to examine one run from table 6.3 for one value, then you would be looking at the final x-value on this graph, since table 6.3 records the x-value of this graph when the y-value hits 1.0.

This graph (figure 6.6) is an example of a *time series* since it is data collected over time. Time series analysis is very important in agent-based modeling because much of the data generated by ABMs is temporal in nature. One way to analyze a time series is to determine if there are particular phases that data goes through during the course of a run. For instance, in the preceding results there seem to be three very different phases of behavior. In the beginning, the number of infected agents grows very slowly. After around fifty time steps, the number of infected agents grows very quickly. Finally, after around one hundred time steps, the number of infected agents increases slowly. Usually, it is useful to compare these three phases of data to the behavior in the model. During the first phase, there are only a

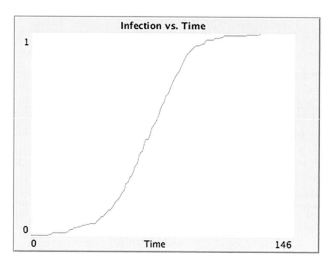

Figure 6.6
Fraction infected versus time for 200 agents.

few infected agents spreading the disease, and so the spread is very slow. During the second phase, the number of infected agents grows fast because there are a lot of infected agents and a lot of agents being infected. During the final phase, there simply are no longer that many agents who can be infected and so the number of infections slows considerably. This is one example of how we can use time series to help understand the behavior of a model.

Many times within ABM, it is useful to look not only at one particular run like in figure 6.6, but also at multiple runs overlaid on each other. This can help you see not only the general trend of the model, but the possible paths that the model usually takes. For instance, it might be possible that a model always winds up taking one of two paths: either the disease spreads throughout the population in the S-shaped curve above, or it spreads very slowly and then quickly spreads to all members of the population. Such a bifurcation in the path of the model would show up in a graph of overlaid characteristic runs. Looking at a set of characteristic runs allows you to observe the characteristic behavior of the system rather than just a particular run.

Analyzing Networks within ABM

As we mentioned in chapter 5, having agents walking around and interacting is useful if you want to examine physically proximate interactions, but many types of interactions do not occur in physical space, but rather across social networks. The Spread of Disease model we have explored relied on contact between moving agents to spread the infection. Diseases do indeed spread in part by people walking around and infecting other people, but

Box 6.2
Time Series Analysis

Time series analysis is a research area in and of itself. The basic question in this area is
how to characterize a data set that is temporal in nature. Many times the goal of time series
analysis is to predict what will be the next set of data points in the series. One way to do
this is to decode the past time series experience in to both short term and long term
components. By differentiating between these two, it is possible to predict the long-term
behavior of the time series. There are many subject areas for which times series analysis is
useful, such as ecology, evolution, political science, and sociology. Time-series analysis
also has applications to stock market analysis, where if it is possible to predict the
long-term behavior of a stock, it is possible to make money off of that stock. For more
information on time series analysis see (Box, Jenkins, & Reinsel 1994).

the spread of diseases relies heavily on the social network of individuals. In fact, some
diseases such as sexually transmitted diseases are not spread by casual contact at all but
only through certain kinds of social networks. The Spread of Disease model was designed
to explore that possibility as well. There is an interface element, the chooser, which allows
you to select different variants of this model. When the chooser is set to "network," instead
of agents moving around on the plane, they are connected via a network, and the disease
spreads over the network. The network that is created in this model is a particular type
of network, a random graph,[5] which we saw in the previous chapter (in this case an
Erdös-Rényi random graph [1959]).

In a network model, the location of the agents in physical space does not matter—what
matters is who is connected to whom. Herein we analyze the effect of varying an important
network property, the connections-per-node (i.e., average degree of the network). This
factor determines how many connections, on average, each individual has to other individuals in the network. Let us analyze this case.

We begin by setting the VARIANT chooser to "network," and the connections-per-node
to a reasonable number such as 4.0. Then we can run the model and see the results as
illustrated in figure 6.7.

We now need to create an experiment to explore how connections-per-node affects
disease spread. If you play around with the model, you will notice that often the disease
does not spread to all of the individuals. For instance, in figure 6.7, the disease has only
infected 197 of the 200 individuals. As you adjust the sliders back and forth, you will
realize that there seems to be a critical point near 1.0. If the connections-per-node is less
than 1.0, then the disease does not infect very many individuals, but if it is greater than

5. This is not as realistic a social network as other types of well known networks such as small world networks
or scale-free networks (Barabasi & Albert, 1999; Watts & Strogatz, 1998), but it is a good base case to analyze.

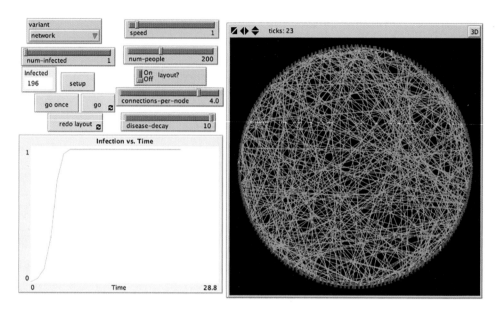

Figure 6.7
Network variant of the Spread of Disease model.

1.0, then it infects a much larger proportion of the population. Let us proceed to create an experiment to explore this.

There is no guarantee that the entire population will become infected, and consequently it is necessary to create a new termination criteria for the experiment. One way to do this would be to look at the number of agents that are infected at a particular time step, allowing the model to run for a while so that there is as much spread as possible. We can do this in BehaviorSpace by setting a time limit for our run. Here we set this time limit to 50. We create a BehaviorSpace experiment that varies the connections-per-node from 0.5 to 4.0 at 0.5 increments. Importing these results into a spreadsheet yields the data summarized in table 6.6.

From these results, the average number of individuals infected grows substantially as the connections-per-node exceeds 1.0. This is in fact a well-known property of random graphs, as the average degree (connections-per-node) exceeds 1.0, a giant component (a large connected subset of the nodes) forms in the network (Janson et al., 1993). If an infection occurs inside this giant component, then the disease will infect a large percentage of the population. This result corresponds exactly to a result in classical (non-network-based) epidemiology models. In these classical models, if the rate of infection over the rate of recovery of a disease exceeds 1.0 then an epidemic will occur in the population, if it is below 1.0 the disease will die out. You can think of the links in the network-based

Table 6.6
Number of Agents Infected after 50 Ticks

connections-per-node	mean # infected	std. dev.
0.5	1.8	1.229272594
1	15.1	21.75852323
1.5	68	59.11946474
2	145.3	50.64922946
2.5	181.1	3.348299734
3	189.3	3.093002856
3.5	174.5	61.03050239
4	196.4	2.170509413

model as infections that the individual will transmit during the time that the individual carries the disease. Given this way of thinking of links, the average degree and the ratio of the rate of infection to rate of recovery are equivalent. In other words if the average individual will at some point infect at least one individual then you will have an epidemic, i.e., all of the individuals in the model will become infected. Consequently, you are likely to have an epidemic if the connections-per-node parameter is greater than 1.0.

Average degree (connections-per-node) is just one property of a network. There are many more. For instance, the property of average path length is a measure of the average distance between any two nodes in the network. This property affects the spread of disease, since if a network has a high average path length, it will take a long time for the disease to reach everyone. However, if the network has a low average path length, the vast majority of people will be infected very quickly. Another widely used property is the clustering coefficient of a network. A clustering coefficient is a measure of how tightly clustered the network is—that is, a measure of how many of the nodes an agent is linked to are also linked to each other (or how many friends of your friends are also your friends). These measures are just two examples of a wide variety of metrics and analysis tools that have been created within the field of Social Network Analysis (SNA). SNA and ABM often work well together. ABM provides a rich model of the process of a phenomenon, while SNA provides a detailed model of the patterns of interaction. Together they allow you to model both the pattern and process that exist within these complex systems.

Each of these network properties can be analyzed as to their effect on the spread of disease. You would need to create reporters to measure these properties, but you could also export the network that you are examining and import it into a standard network analysis toolkit like UCINet or Pajek for further examination.[6]

---

6. Some of these reporting functions may be provided as primitives in the ABM toolkit. NetLogo does include many of these. NetLogo's network extension also provides a more comprehensive set of primitives.

Box 6.3
Diffusion of Innovation

We have discussed this model as a spread of disease, and we have also mentioned how it shares commonalities with models of language change. Another way to view this model is as a diffusion of innovation model. One agent becomes "infected" or adopts an innovation, like a new audio device, a new business process, or a new movie that the agent likes (Rogers, 2003). This agent then spreads this innovation by word of mouth to their friends and co-workers. The network-based version of the Spread-of-Disease model is particularly good for modeling diffusion of innovation since innovations usually spread across social networks and not necessarily across physical space (Valente, 1995). One commonly discussed topic in innovation diffusion is the role of influentials, i.e., are there some people in social networks who are better able to spread innovations than others (Watts, 1999). In the Explorations we will propose extending this model to more explicitly model the diffusion of innovation.

Box 6.4
Social Network Analysis

Social Network Analysis (SNA) is a burgeoning field of research. The basic premise of SNA is that, within social systems, the structure of interactions is at least as important as the type of interactions that occur. In other words, it's not just how *you* interact, but it's also *who* you interact with and *who* they interact with. One of the major findings of this area of research is that most people are connected through only a few intermediate connections. This is colloquially known as the Six Degrees hypothesis: that everyone in the world is only six connections away from everyone else. This hypothesis is based on a Stanley Milgram experiment where it was found that on average it took six letters for someone from Iowa to contact someone in New York City. Recently, this has been formalized as the idea of Small World networks in the book Six Degrees by Duncan Watts (2003), building upon work he carried out with Strogatz (1998). For a set of classical papers in Social Network Analysis, see Newman, Watts and Strogatz (2006) and for an introductory textbook, see Newman (2010).

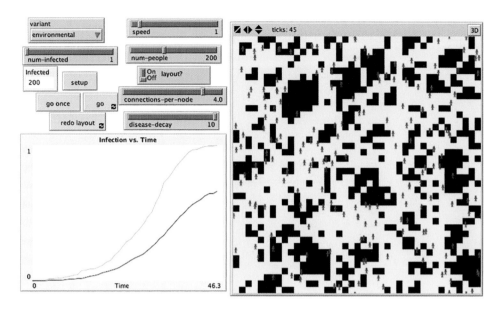

Figure 6.8
Environmental variant of the Spread of Disease model.

Environmental Data and ABM

After looking at the model for some time, we might realize that for the diseases we are interested in studying, such as the common cold, the mobile agent model makes more sense. However, the mobile agent model did not go far enough. Besides agent-to-agent transmission of cold germs, there can also be agent-to-environment and environment-to-agent transmission. For instance, if someone has a bad cold and wipes his nose with his hand, and then opens a door, someone else who comes through that door shortly after the person with the disease might catch the cold. Of course, germs do not live very long outside the body so these environmental infections might decrease after time; so we would want the model to reflect this.

In fact, the Spread of Disease model allows us to examine this scenario. There is an environmental interaction effect. This variant can be seen in figure 6.8. If you turn this variant on (by choosing "environmental" in the VARIANT chooser) then the patch below any infected agent will become yellow. For a limited amount of time (DISEASE-DECAY), this patch will infect any other agent who steps on it. Let's investigate how disease-decay affects the time to 100 percent infection. We carry out an investigation in a similar manner to the one described before. This experiment is very similar to the one described for the original variant, but instead of changing the NUM-PEOPLE, which we fix at 200, we change the rate of DISEASE-DECAY from 0 (which exactly represents the original variant) to 10 at single time step intervals. We create a BehaviorSpace experiment to carry this out and import the results into Excel summarizing our findings in table 6.7.

Table 6.7
Time to 100% Infection, Environmental Variant

disease-decay	Average	Std. Dev
0	126.4	12.2854928
1	71	4.988876516
2	62	7.363574011
3	51	4.242640687
4	51.2	2.780887149
5	49.4	2.716206505
6	49.9	2.643650675
7	46.5	2.758824226
8	48.5	3.341656276
9	47.4	3.062315754
10	47.3	2.213594362

We can see that as the environmental decay parameter increases (i.e., the disease remains in the environment for a longer period of time) the time to 100 percent infection decreases. In the original model or when DISEASE-DECAY is set to 0, the only thing that can infect agents is other agents, but when the DISEASE-DECAY is positive then patches and agents can infect other agents. As DISEASE-DECAY increases, the number of patches that can infect other agents increases as well, meaning there are simply more objects in the environment, which can cause the spread of the disease.

It might be possible that the effect of DISEASE-DECAY is not completely separate from the population density. After all, if there are not many individuals in the model then a long DISEASE-DECAY might have a negligible effect over having a small DISEASE-DECAY. This can also be investigated using BehaviorSpace. We set it up to vary both DISEASE-DECAY and NUM-PEOPLE at the same time and report the number of ticks until full infection. To make sure we do not get anomalies, we average the data over ten runs. This results in a large number of runs, since we are looking at four values for NUM-PEOPLE and eleven values for DISEASE-DECAY, resulting in 440 runs. We can display this data using a three-dimensional graph (e.g., figure 6.9). As we see from this chart, both NUM-PEOPLE and DISEASE-DECAY have an effect on the results. However, it is clear that it is only when both of these values are very small that the model is sensitive to their results. The sharp peak in the results of the values as we decrease each variable indicates this. If NUM-PEOPLE is small and so is DISEASE-DECAY we will see a dramatic change in the time to full infection if we alter either of these variables.

A powerful aspect of ABMs, is that in addition to showing us the dynamics of how a disease spreads, it also shows us the pattern of infection. The yellow patches indicate

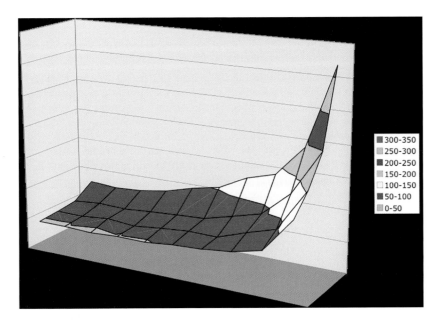

Figure 6.9
3D Chart of NUM-PEOPLE and DISEASE-DECAY versus time to 100 percent infection.

where the disease is still alive and how it might infect other agents. This could be useful if we are trying to control a disease. This disease model leaves long, stringy patterns of environmental infection, which is a product of how the individuals move through the landscape. Since these patterns of disease are not well clustered, then it does not make much sense to try and quarantine an area of the world to prevent the disease from spreading. Instead, we have to track down each individual in the world that is infected and attempt to cure them of the disease they have. Yet, if the disease spreads out from a single point, then if we were aware that there was an outbreak of a disease in an area it would make sense to create a ring of immunity around the disease through vaccination, for example, and slowly move toward the center of the ring, curing individuals along the way. This can be a successful method for smallpox control (Kretzschmar et al., 2004).

These qualitative stories of patterns in the environment are interesting, but there are also quantitative ways to attempt to capture the same results. For instance, we can take a map of yellow disease trails and measure what is called, in landscape metrics (McGarigal & Marks, 1995), the *edge density* of the yellow trails.[7] The edge density, as described in

7. Typically, landscape metrics are analyzed utilizing a computational tool like FRAGSTATS (McGarigal & Marks, 1995).

Box 6.5
Geographic Information Systems (GIS)

> The central idea of the field of Geographic Information Systems (GIS) is that most data in the world can be indexed via a spatial location. Moreover, by representing this data in spatial ways we can gain a better understanding of complex phenomena. GIS is used to analyze everything from the spread of disease as described in this chapter, to the environmental effects of suburban sprawl (Brown et al., 2008), to the flow of commuters in a transportation network. Since GIS has developed a powerful model of the spatial pattern of data, it is useful to combine GIS with ABM, which has a powerful model of the process of data transformation. Together, GIS and ABM can provide rich pictures of both the pattern and process of complex spatial systems. For an introduction to GIS, please see (Longley, Goodchild, Maguire, & Rhind, 2005).

chapter 5, is the ratio of the number of edges between two different states of the environment (in this case infected and noninfected patches) to the overall area. If the edge density is low, then similar patch states are highly clustered and have very few shared edges with different patch states; when studying the spread of disease, this would suggest that you should use a ring type of intervention. If the edge density is high, which is the case in the preceding environmental interaction model, then the different location types are interwoven; when studying the spread of disease, this would suggest the use of a targeted intervention.

Edge density is just one of many types of landscape metrics that have been created. Geographic Information Systems (GIS) is an entire field devoted to the study of patterns in the environment. GIS provides a rich description of the pattern within an environment when those patterns are geographically related. This is similar to the model of pattern that SNA provides within network-related environments. GIS combines well with ABM because together they enable the creation of elaborate models of both pattern and process.

We could implement some of the measures such as edge density within our ABM, and some ABM toolkits provide tools to make this easier. However, it might be better to simply export the data from your ABM to a GIS tool like ArcView Grass or MyWorld (Edelson, 2004), which have been developed specifically for understanding geographic patterns. This can be done in a number of ways from passing text files, to a tightly coupled application-programming interface (API) (Brown et al., 2005). We saw an example of a loosely coupled ABM model in chapter 5, the Grand Canyon model (*Wilensky, 2006*). This model reads in a digital elevation map that was created in a standard GIS software package, and it uses the elevation map to predict how rain flows across the terrain of the Grand Canyon.

Summarizing Analysis of ABMs

Measuring and analyzing ABMs presents different challenges from the analysis of equation-based models and even from other types of computational models. This is because of the large number of inputs and outputs that are normally associated with ABMs. Because ABMs enable the model user to control so many aspects of the agents, there are often a large number of inputs that must be specified. For instance, in a model of commuter patterns in an urban area, each agent or commuter may have characteristics such as age, wealth, environmental group membership, children, and ethnicity, not to mention nondemographic parameters such as personal preferences for waiting times and aesthetic qualities. On the output side since we are modeling the micro-level behavior of the system, it is possible not only to generate aggregate patterns of data, but also individual patterns. For example, in the commuter model mentioned earlier, we could observe the average commuting time over all individuals, but we could also break that down by any other characteristic. We can examine data along orthogonal dimensions as well. For example, we could examine the commuting time for anyone who takes a particular highway to work.

The large number of possible inputs and outputs gives researchers the ability to precisely control and measure their models. However, trying to control for them all can cause combinatorial explosion. If the commuting model has one thousand agents (commuters) that each have five characteristics (e.g., wealth, eco-friendly, children, age, work location) each of which can take just two values (e.g., high/low, yes/no, yes/no, old/young, north/south), then there are 2^{10} or 1,024 possible different types of individuals and $1,024^{1000}$ possible populations of individuals. This is one of the core reasons behind the ABM Design principle we presented in chapter 4—when building an agent-based model, start as simple as possible, and add complexity only as it is necessary to improve the model. The example we just gave is actually a relatively small parameter space since most agent characteristics will be real-valued not binary, and most models will have not only agent parameters but also environmental and global parameters. Despite its relatively small size, this number is much too large to exhaustively examine, especially when we are interested in a set of results for each run and not just one number. For example, in the commuter model imagine that there are five measures we are interested in, the average commuting time for all individuals and the commuting times for five subclasses of the individual types described before (e.g., wealthy individuals, individuals heading north). Essentially our model becomes a mapping from $1,024^{1000}$ possible inputs to five real-valued outputs. However, even this conceptualization is limiting, because often when examining an ABM we are interested not only in the final value of a particular output but also the dynamic patterns of the model, like the time series we examined. Thus, we are not really interested in just five outputs, but the dynamics of five outputs over many time steps. If in the commuter model we assume we are observing the results for a year of working days, then we are talking about $5 \cdot 20 \cdot 12 = 1,200$ real-valued outputs.

Thus, though the vast number of ABM inputs gives a model author a very precise level of control and the vast number of outputs gives the author a lot of detail, it also presents some challenges. First, the vast number of inputs means that there are that many more parameters of the model to validate. Each parameter must be examined carefully and either tested against real-world data or explored well enough to show that within a reasonable set of choices the model is robust to changes. Second, the vast number of outputs makes it easy for a model author to become lost in all the data that the model generates. Moreover, it makes it difficult to extract clear patterns of behavior. Often model authors will need to look at many different relationships between the input and output data before they are able to find a salient pattern of behavior that is compelling.

The four distinct formats of ABM data that we have talked about in this chapter are: (1) statistical, (2) graphical, (3) network-based, and (4) spatial. Statistical results are standard model output: means, standard deviations, medians, and other methods of analyzing the values of a variable. Graphical results are an outgrowth of statistical results; they transform statistical results into graphs that can be more easily examined by the observer. Network-based results, like cluster analysis and path length examinations, are another particular way of analyzing data that is often useful in ABMs. Finally, spatial results address the analysis of patterns of variables in a one-, two-, or higher dimensional space, and they frequently address questions regarding the pattern of data in the space.

However, these four formats of data output can also be used as data input. As we have seen, this is very clear in the case of network and spatial data. In the network variant of the Spread of Disease model we initialized the model using network properties (e.g., the number of connections per node). We then ran the model and used the output of the network data in combination with the model measures, such as time to 100 percent infection, to describe the model. In the spatial case, we initially start with a world in which there is no infection except in one location, but it would be a simple extrapolation to "seed" the world with multiple pockets of environmental infection. We can also use statistical and graphical data as input to the model. For instance, when we set the parameter of DISEASE-DECAY to 4, we are really setting the parameter to a mean of 4 with a standard deviation of 0. We could add another parameter to control the standard deviation as well, and then whenever a new agent becomes infected they might have a slightly slower or faster DISEASE-DECAY because it would be generated using the "random-normal" primitive instead of being set to exactly 4. This could indicate whether that individual practices hygiene habits or participates in infectious behavior. Finally, we can also use graphical data as model input. Graphs can embody equations, and we might place equations within agents to govern their behavior. For instance, rather than having the DISEASE-DECAY be constant based on the agent, we could make it a variable based on the time since they have been infected (e.g., DISEASE-DECAY = $e^{\text{TIME-SINCE-INFECTION}}$), indicating that the longer an individual has been infected, the more infectious he becomes. By using all of these results and inputs together, we can obtain a better understanding of how any model works, and by understanding the model we gain a deeper understanding of the phenomenon we are modeling.

Explorations

1. In all of the Spread of Disease models that we discussed, a contact results in an infection, but in reality diseases do not often spread based on one contact. Instead, there is usually a probability of a contact resulting in a spread. How would you modify the model and its variants described earlier to account for the probability of disease spread?

2. In the experiments discussed in this chapter, we discussed how density of individuals affects the Spread of Disease; however, there is also the speed with which individuals move throughout a landscape. One might hypothesize that if individuals move faster, that is the same as there being more individuals. What arguments exist for and against this hypothesis? How can you construct an experiment to test this hypothesis?

3. In the environmental model variant, the disease impact left behind by an individual dissipates at a constant rate (10 time steps). One could instead imagine that the disease diffuses through the local environment and as the concentration falls below some critical level, it becomes impossible for the disease to still be infectious. How would you model the phenomenon instead of the current constant rate of dissipation?

4. The social network variant, the mobile/spatial variant, and the environmental variant described earlier were all separate variants. However, in many cases of the spread of real diseases, all of these factors interplay. How would you modify the models described so that they took into account social networks, random meetings, and environmental effects?

5. Throughout this chapter, we have modeled the spread of disease. Researchers have hypothesized that innovations spread in similar ways to disease. How would you modify our model to model the diffusion of innovation instead of disease? What about the spread of rumors or urban legends? Carry out one of these modifications and analyze the results.

6. This class of disease-spread models is also related to percolation that we discussed before. Compare and contrast the Spread of Disease model and the Fire model that we discussed in chapter 3. How can you modify the Spread of Disease model so that it represents a forest fire instead of the spread of an infection?

7. The focus of this chapter has been on measuring the results of ABM. Why is measuring a result different in ABM as compared to classical science? What advantages and disadvantages does the multitude of results and inputs have for ABM as compared to classical experiments?

8. *Dynamic networks* In the Spread of Disease model, when we switched from a spatial relationship between agents to a network-based relationship, we also switched our output measure. In the spatial case we were measuring the time to full infection given the population size, but since in the case of a network we may not have full infection, we had to

switch to measuring the number infected after a certain time period for a given average degree. How can we compare these two numbers? Why is the degree of a node in the static case not the same as the number of individuals contacted every time step in spatial case? Design a measure that describes a dynamic degree. Use this measure to compare the results of the two models. Does the Network model or the Spatial model result in faster infection? Why?

9. *Testing parameter spaces* The Fur model in the Biology section of the models library can generate a lot of different patterns. For instance, you can create both horizontal and vertical stripes by manipulating the four parameters that control the repulsion and attraction radii. Find all the sets of parameters that will create at least one strip that of the nondominant color that goes all the way around the world. Keep in mind that this model is nondeterministic. Hint: It might be easier to first create a new measure then create a BehaviorSpace experiment to explore this space.

10. *Spread runs* Sometimes it can be useful to examine a group of runs at once. Run the Spread-of-Disease model one hundred times and plot the number of infected versus time on the same graph. What does this Spread Run graph tell you that a single instance does not? What does this graph tell you that graphing the mean of the number infected does not?

11. *Batch runs* We have discussed how you can run a model multiple times from BehaviorSpace, but you can also run a model multiple times without ever opening up the NetLogo application. Read in the NetLogo documentation about the Controlling API about "headless" running. Run the simple Spread of Disease model this way multiple times and collect the results in a single graph showing time versus number infected. What are the advantages to running your simulation in this manner?

12. *Language change* Rewrite the Spread of Disease model as a Language Change model. Think of the infection as a new way of pronouncing a word. Whether or not an individual adopts the new pronunciation depends on how many of the people he or she interacts with use the same pronunciation. This is in contrast to an infection model where there is a probabilistic chance of infection based on every contact. How does this new infection method affect the results?

13. *Birth and death* Some diseases are fatal. Add birth and death to the Spread of Disease model, but make the death of an individual dependent on how long he or she has had the disease. Is it possible to adjust these birth and death rates such that the disease persists but does not kill off all of its hosts?

14. *Recovery* The model that we have created is what is called an SI (Susceptible and Infected) model. Modify this model to create an SIR (Susceptible, Infected, and Recovered) model. Add a third state to the agents where after individuals become infected they have a chance of becoming recovered. Recovered agents are immune to the disease and cannot become re-infected. Describe the results of the new model.

15. *Different distributions* In the results of the Spread of Disease model that we have presented herein, we have described the statistical distributions of the results using a mean and a standard deviation. This is fine if the results are normally distributed, that is, they all fall around a central mean, with most of them being closer to that mean and fewer of them being far from the mean. However, some results are better described as two groupings of data instead of just one, and thus the results can be more naturally divided into subgroups. What parameters would you use to describe these types of results? When looking at data, how would you know to split them into multiple groups? Describe a general-purpose method that will enable you to take a raw set of data and determine the number of means that it takes to adequately describe the data.

16. *Different thresholds of infection* In the current model every individual has the same threshold of infection. In fact, this threshold is a constant and cannot be changed by a parameter. In the current model, as soon as an individual is in contact with an infected individual, he becomes infected himself. Change this so that different individuals have different thresholds of infection. There are at least two different ways to do this. One way would be to have each individual have a probability of becoming infected every time he comes in contact with an infected individual. Another possibility is to have individuals have to contact at least *x* infected individuals before they become infected themselves. Implement both of these methods. Is there any difference in the results? Describe why this difference is or is not meaningful.

17. *Time series analysis* We discussed how time series analysis can be used to examine data that is time-dependent. The typical way this is done is by describing a relationship between time and some input parameters. For instance, fraction-infected(t) = population/$(1 + e^{-at})$ creates a graph that looks somewhat like the increase in the fraction-infected over time, but this function must be tuned to more closely approximate the results of our model. Create a function that represents the change in fraction-infected over time as a function of the population, for the original "mobile" Spread of Disease model. Describe your function. Highlight which areas of the graph it more closely matches and which areas it does not.

18. *Clustering coefficient and average path length* We discussed how the clustering coefficient and average path length of a network model can help us to analyze a network. Create reporters for both of these in the network variant of the Spread of Disease model. Examine the relationship between these values and the mean number infected after fifty ticks.

19. *Mean patch size and edge ratio* Similar to the previous exploration, the mean patch size and edge ratio of geographical systems can contribute to an understanding of the system. Implement these reporters in the environmental variant of the Spread of Disease model. Do these measures change as you vary the disease-decay time? If so, describe how they change. If they do not change, describe why they do not change.

20. *Exponential decay of disease* At the end of the chapter, we talked about how you can give agents rules that are equations. Implement an exponential decay of disease model in the patches. How does this change compare with the original environmental variant of the Spread of Disease model?

21. *Other types of measurements* Throughout this chapter, we measured the number of individuals infected and the time to 100 percent infection. Create another measure that may be of interest to someone studying the spread of disease. Why did you choose this measure? Explain why it would be useful to someone interested in this subject.

7 Verification, Validation, and Replication

Essentially, all models are wrong, but some are useful.

—George Box

The word model sounds more scientific than the word fable or tale, but I think we are talking about the same thing.

—Ariel Rubinstein

There are two ways of constructing a software design: One way is to make it so simple that there are obviously no deficiencies, and the other way is to make it so complicated that there are no obvious deficiencies. The first method is far more difficult. It demands the same skill, devotion, insight, and even inspiration as the discovery of the simple physical laws which underlie the complex phenomena of nature.

—Tony Hoare

In the previous seven chapters, we have made a case for the importance and utility of ABM, learned to extend existing ABM and build new ones, taken a wide view of the components that go into an ABM environment, and learned how to collect and analyze results from an ABM. In this chapter, we will learn to assess the correctness and usefulness of an ABM. How can we know if our implemented ABM corresponds to our conceptual model? How can we assess the match between our ABM and the real world?

Correctness of a Model

If a model is to be useful for answering real-world questions, it is important that the model provides outputs that address the relevant issues and that the outputs are accurate: The model must provide outputs that are useful to the model user. Model accuracy can be evaluated through three different modeling processes: validation, verification, and replication. *Model validation* is the process of determining whether the implemented model corresponds to, and explains, some phenomenon in the real world. *Model verification* is the process of determining whether an implemented model corresponds to the target conceptual model. This process is equivalent to making sure that the model has been correctly implemented. Last, *model replication* is the implementation by one researcher or group of researchers of a conceptual model previously implemented by someone else.

By ensuring that an implemented model corresponds to a conceptual model (verification) whose outputs are reflected in the real world (validation), confidence grows in the correctness and explanatory power of both the conceptual and implemented models. Furthermore, as other scientists and model builders replicate the work of the original scientist, the scientific community as a whole comes to accept the model as correct. Verification, validation, and replication collectively underpin the correctness, and thus utility, of a model.

However, demonstrating that one particular set of results from a model corresponds to the real world is not sufficient. As discussed in previous chapters, due to the stochastic nature of ABMs, multiple runs are often needed to confirm that a model is accurate. Therefore, the methodologies of verification, validation, and replication often rely upon statistical methods. We start our discussion by looking more closely at verification.

Verification

As an agent-based model grows larger, it becomes more difficult to simply look at its code to determine whether it is actually carrying out its intended function. The process of verification addresses this issue, having as its goal the elimination of "bugs" from the code. However, this is not as simple as it may sound, and if the model designer(s) and implementer are different people, the debugging process can become much more complex.

A general guideline for enabling model verification involves building the model simply to begin with, expanding the complexity of the model only as necessary. Thus, adhering to the core ABM design principle described in chapter 4 renders an important side benefit: If a model is simple to begin with, it is easier to verify than a complex model. Likewise, if the additional parts added to the model are also incremental in nature—building toward your question of interest rather than trying to develop all of the elaboration of the model at once—those components will also be easier to verify (and by extension, the model of which they are a part). Even so, it should be noted that even if all of the components of a model are verified, the model itself may not be, since additional complications can arise from the interactions between model components.

Throughout this section, we examine the issue of verification in the context of a simple ABM of voting behavior, using the following fictitious narrative to guide our discussion:

Imagine that we are approached by a group of political scientists who want to develop a simple model of voting behavior.[1] They explain that they think that people's social interactions largely determine voting in elections. Based on their observations of polls and

---

1. Since we have spent the last few chapters learning how to write ABM code, in this example, we will take the role of an ABM implementer. However, the processes of verification, validation, and replication are important if you are the model author or the model implementer.

election results, they think that people have some initial way that they want to vote, and when they are initially polled, they express those feelings. However, in the interval between when they are polled and when they actually cast their vote, they talk to their neighbors and colleagues and discuss the way they plan to vote; this may change the way they decide to vote. In fact, this may happen several times during the period leading up to an election. The political scientists ask us to build an ABM of this phenomenon.

Communication

Often, the model implementer and the model author are the same person, but this is not always the case. Sometimes a team of people builds a model, wherein one or more people describe the conceptual model while other team members actually implement the model. This frequently happens when the domain expert does not have the technical skills to create the model on their own. In these situations, verification becomes especially critical, as no one individual has a full knowledge of all parts of the modeling process. When models are built in this fashion, communication is critical to ensure that the implemented model correctly reflects the domain expert's conceptual model. The best way to verify models constructed in these types of teams is for the domain expert (or experts) to gain familiarity with the model tools and, likewise, the implementers to learn about the model's subject matter. While one cannot expect the two parties to become experts in each other's domains, building this common ground is essential to make sure ideas are effectively communicated and the model correctly reflects the intentions of the modelers.

For example, in our voting model, it would be useful if the political scientists knew the difference between Moore and von Neumann neighborhoods, what a small-world network looked like, and the affordances of a hexagonal versus a rectangular grid. This knowledge would enable them to make informed decisions about how their conceptual model should be implemented. In addition, it would help if the implementer had a basic idea of how voting mechanisms are conceptualized within the discipline of political science, since it might help them realize possible simplifications for the model or even potential conceptual pitfalls in the model as it is being implemented. For example, is it reasonable to assume that there are only two parties? Is it reasonable to assume that each person's group of friends does not change over the time period modeled in the simulation?

When it comes to communication of the conceptual model, there is often room for human error and misunderstanding. In an ideal situation, the model author and the implementer is the same person, which averts the sort of communication errors that can result from different vocabularies and different assumptions. However, the time required for domain experts to learn computer programming, or conversely, the time required for computer programmers to learn a particular domain, can be substantial. This was particularly true in past decades, when it was often unfeasible to become both an expert model implementer and model author. However, new, low-threshold ABM languages, such as NetLogo, have an explicit goal of decreasing the amount of time necessary to learn how to write ABMs, thus narrowing (or eliminating) the gap between the author and the implementer.

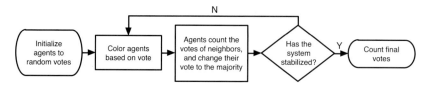

Figure 7.1
Flowchart of Voting model.

Describing Conceptual Models

As we begin to implement the voting model, we might realize that there are some mechanisms and agent properties that we did not understand completely when we talked with
the political scientists. To alleviate this problem, we decide to write a document describing
how we plan to implement the model so that we can verify that we and the political scientists have the same conceptual model in mind. This document will serve as a more formal
description of the conceptual model.

One way to describe conceptual models in more formal terms is to use a *flowchart*. A
flowchart is a pictorial description of the model that depicts the flow of decisions that
occur during the operation of a piece of software code. For the conceptual model described
above, we could use a flowchart like the one in figure 7.1.

Flowcharts use *rounded squares* to indicate the start and stop states of the system,
squares to indicate processes, and *diamonds* to indicate decision points in the code. These
symbols provide a clear way of understanding how control flows through the software.

We can also take the flowchart diagram and rewrite it in *pseudo-code*. The goal of
pseudo-code is to serve as a midway point between natural language and formal programming language. Pseudo-code can be read by anyone, regardless of his or her programming
knowledge, while, at the same time, containing algorithmic structure that makes it easier
to implement directly into real code. For instance, in describing the voting model, we could
use pseudo-code like this:

```
Voters have votes = {0, 1}

For each voter:
    Set vote either 0 or 1, chosen with equal probability
Loop until election
    For each voter
        If majority of neighbors' votes = 1 and vote = 0 then set vote 1
        Else If majority of neighbors' votes = 0 and vote = 1 then set vote 0
        If vote = 1: set color blue
        Else: color = green
    Display count of voters with vote = 1
    Display count of voters with vote = 0
End loop
```

In addition to flow charts and pseudo-code, several other methods for describing conceptual models deserve mention. For instance, Booch, Rumbaugh, and Jacobson devised the Unified Modeling Language (UML). UML is designed so that different readers have different entry points to the conceptual model description—for example, different entry points for model users vs. model creators (2005). UML uses a combination of graphical views and natural language text to describe models. There have also been recent attempts to integrate ABM-specific concepts into UML (Bauer, Muller, & Odell, 2000). Another method involves choosing a language that is similar enough to pseudo-code that it can be clearly understood by a nonexpert. Using a low-threshold language such as NetLogo helps facilitate the verification process because its code syntax corresponds closely with natural language.

Verification Testing

After designing the conceptual model with our political science colleagues, we can start coding. We follow the ABM core design principle and start simple, incrementally verifying the alignment between our conceptual model and the code. For instance, we can write the setup procedure, as here:

```
patches-own
[
    vote  ;; my vote (0 or 1)
    total ;; sum of votes around me
]

to setup
    clear-all
    ask patches [
        if (random 2 = 0) ;; half a chance of this
        [ set vote 1 ]
      ]
    ask patches [
      if (random 2 = 0) ;; half a chance of this
        [ set vote 0 ]
    ]
    ask patches [
      recolor-patch
    ]
end

to recolor-patch ;; patch procedure
    ifelse vote = 0
      [ set pcolor green ]
      [ set pcolor blue ]
end
```

We can then write a small test that examines whether the code created the correct number of green and blue voters.[2] In the voting model's initial state, the number of voters with vote 0 should be roughly equal to the number of voters with vote 1. We can easily verify this by setting up our model a number of times, comparing tallies of each vote. If the difference across these many setups is more than roughly 10 percent, for instance, our code might have a bug.[3] If the difference is less than 10 percent of the total number, we can feel relatively confident that the populations are generated as we intended. This code would look like this:

```
to check-setup
    let diff abs ( count patches with [ vote = 0 ] - count patches
with [ vote = 1 ] )
    if diff > .1 * count patches [
        print "Warning: Difference in initial voters is greater than 10⁴%."
    ]
end
```

We can insert a call to CHECK-SETUP at the bottom of the SETUP procedure. This test will then be run every time the model runs SETUP and, if there is a problem, will alert whoever is running the model that there is a voting imbalance.

Using this SETUP procedure, the warning appears almost every time we run the model, which tells us that the code is not achieving what we intended. Additionally, it is visually apparent that this code creates many more patches that are green (vote = 0) than blue (vote = 1). Because all errors are not visually apparent, writing verification tests is important. (Readers are encouraged to examine the setup code above and determine its flaw.) After discovering the error, we can rewrite the setup procedure with the following (simpler) code, which achieves the correct balance of initial voters.

```
to setup
    clear-all
    ask patches [
        set vote random 2      ;; 0 or 1, with equal probability
    ]
    ask patches [
        recolor-patch
    ]
    check-setup
end
```

2. It is often good practice to write the tests even before writing the code. That way, the test is both specifying your intention for the code and providing a way to verify the code.

3. Rather than use 10 percent of the population as a rule of thumb, we could use statistical tests and report if the difference between the two populations is greater than three standard deviations, for instance, but for our case this simpler test will work just as well.

4. It is sometimes useful to use the "user-message" primitive here instead of print, which requires the user to type OK, acknowledging having read the message.

This verification technique is a form of unit testing. *Unit testing* (related to Component testing) is an approach that involves writing small tests that check whether individual units are working correctly in the code (Rand & Rust, 2011). By writing unit tests as we develop our code, we can make sure that future changes to our code do not disrupt previous code. Since this unit test will run every time we run this model, it ensures that we can modify the code without fear that our changes will undetectably disrupt the previous code. Of course, this is just one unit test, and there are many more that could be written.

The preceding is an example of "in-model" unit testing, sometimes called "online" unit testing because it happens while the model is running. It is also possible to write a separate set of unit tests that are not part of the implemented model, but instead are written to run the model with particular inputs and test whether the outputs correspond to the expected results. This approach is sometimes called "offline" unit testing. (A more detailed account of unit testing is beyond the scope of this textbook, but for more information on software testing, refer to Patton, 2005.) After we are confident that the SETUP code is verified, we begin a similar process for the GO procedure. We translate the pseudo-code into NetLogo code as follows:

```
to go
    ask patches [
        set total (sum [vote] of neighbors)
    ]
    ;; this is equivalent to count neighbors with [vote = 1]
    ;; use two ask patches blocks so all patches compute "total"
    ;; before any patches change their votes
    ask patches [
        ifelse vote = 0 and total >= 4 [
            set vote 1
        ]
            [if vote = 1 and total <= 4 ] [
                [set vote 0
            ]
            recolor-patch
    ]
    tick
    end
```

In this code, we first ask the patches to compute the total number of neighbors with vote = 1. If the patch is voting 0 and has a total greater than or equal to 4, then it switches to voting 1. Similarly, if the patch is voting 1 and has a total less than or equal to 4, it switches its vote to 0. After verifying both SETUP and GO procedures, we can begin to investigate the model results.

Beyond Verification

Despite the best efforts to verify that the implemented agent-based model corresponds to the conceptual model, it will sometimes produce results that do not seem to correspond

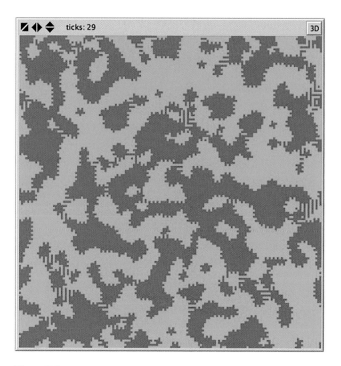

Figure 7.2
Voting model, first version.

to what the implementers and authors hypothesized. Over time, it may become clear that there is no "bug" in the model, but rather, that the emergent and surprising results of the model are unintended consequences of individual-level decisions that the modeler has encoded.

For example, after coding the preceding model, we present the results to our political science colleagues (figure 7.2). The results of the model confuses the political scientists, because they expected the model to coalesce with voters forming static blocks with smooth edges, rather than the jagged edges that appear in the figure. In fact, this model never reaches equilibrium; it continually cycles through a set of states.

After further examination, it becomes clear that what is causing the model to cycle and have jagged edges is tie votes. As we coded it, the model has the voters change their vote if the vote count of their neighbors is tied. Thus, voters on the edge of the concentrated blocks keep cycling back and forth between the two votes. We can change the model so that voters do not change their vote if their neighbors' votes are tied. After we make this change, the blocks coalesce with smooth edges (figure 7.3). However, as the political

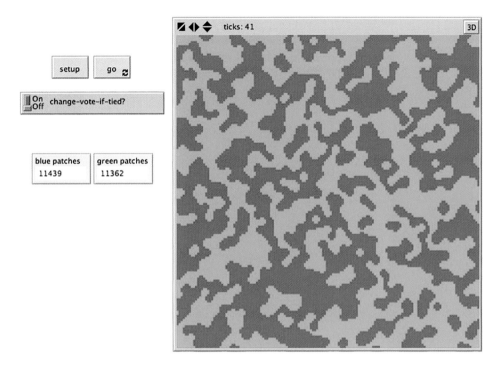

Figure 7.3
Voting model, ties stay with same vote.

scientists have become interested in how an apparently small change creates a large difference in the result, they decide to make this an element of the model that they can control by adding a switch, called CHANGE-VOTE-IF-TIED?

Having this option as a controllable element enables us to explore new voting behavior. For instance, what would happen if voters decide to side with the minority party in their neighborhood? That is, imagine a community where, when a member's neighbors are closely divided between two candidates, the member decides to vote for the underdog (whoever the majority of his/her neighbors are *not* voting for), as the member might be able to ensure the underdog's victory. Note that this hypothetical perversity of agents may not reflect real-world voting practices. However, this is a question of model *validation* (which we will discuss later), rather than *verification*. Below is the code for the go procedure with the two added options:

```
to go
  ask patches
    [ set total (sum [vote] of neighbors) ]
    ;; use two ask patches blocks so all patches compute "total"
    ;; before any patches change their votes
  ask patches
    [ if total > 5 [ set vote 1 ]
      if total < 3 [ set vote 0 ]
      if total = 4
        [ if change-vote-if-tied?
          [ set vote (1 - vote) ] ] ;; switch vote
      if total = 5
        [ ifelse award-close-calls-to-loser?
          [ set vote 0 ]
          [ set vote 1 ] ]
      if total = 3
        [ ifelse award-close-calls-to-loser?
          [ set vote 1 ]
          [ set vote 0 ] ]
      recolor-patch ]
  tick
end
```

The opportunity to explore intriguing hypothetical situations is one of the strengths of agent-based modeling. When the "vote for the underdog" option is turned on, which is controlled by our AWARD-CLOSE-CALLS-TO-LOSER? switch, another emergent pattern results (figure 7.4). In this case, blocks of blues and greens coalesce while irregular boundaries between the zones gradually drift and distort as time passes.

If we decide to turn on both the "CHANGE-VOTE-IF-TIED?" option and the "AWARD-CLOSE-CALLS-TO-LOSER?" option, we get a different outcome. This final option (figure 7.5) results in a seemingly random pattern of colors, without any large solid blocks of either color.

This example illustrates that, when examining model results, it can be hard to decipher whether the outcome of a model is a result of bugs in the code, a miscommunication between the model author and implementer, or a "correct" but unanticipated result of the agent rules. Thus, it is vital that the model implementer and model author discuss both model rules and results as frequently and regularly as possible, and not simply when finalizing the model. Skipping over this communication process may result in the model implementer creating a model with agent behavior that the model author did not intend. However, by maintaining these communications, the model author may discover that small variants in their conceptual model result in dramatically different outcomes. Even if the same person is model author and implementer, it is helpful to review the model rules and results iteratively and discuss them with people who are familiar with the modeled phenomena.

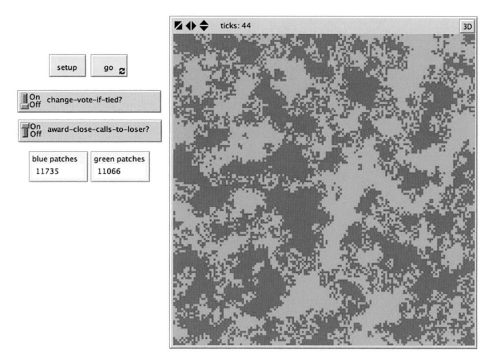

Figure 7.4
Close calls go to loser, Voting model.

Sensitivity Analysis and Robustness

After we have finished building a model and found some interesting results, it is important to explore these results to determine how sensitive our model is to the particular set of initial conditions that we are using. Sometimes, this just means varying a group of the parameters that we already have within our model, but other times, this entails adding new parameters to the model. This process, called *sensitivity analysis*, creates an understanding of how sensitive (or robust) the model is to various conditions.

One type of sensitivity analysis involves altering input values of the model. For instance, one of the political scientists is concerned about the initial conditions of the model, thinking that the current behavior of the model may depend on initially having a balanced number of voters for each party (color). She wonders whether tipping the initial balance in one direction or the other would result in one color dominating the landscape. To test out this hypothesis, we create a parameter (a slider in the model's interface) that controls the percentage of green agents in the initial state of the model. Using BehaviorSpace (as discussed in chapter 6), we then run a set of experiments where we vary this percentage from 25 percent to 75 percent at 5 percent increments. In setting the stop condition for this experiment, we must keep in mind that it is possible to have never-ending, oscillating

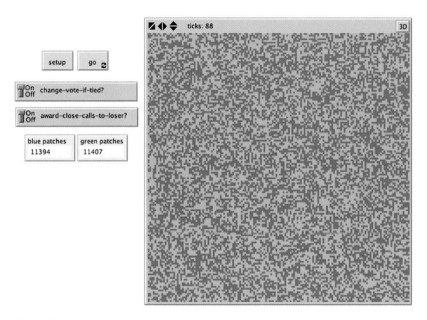

Figure 7.5
Outcome of Voting model with both "CHANGE-VOTE-IF-TIED?" and "AWARD-CLOSE-CALLS-TO-LOSER?"

patterns. For this reason, we decide to set two different stop conditions: (1) the model will stop if no voter switched votes in the last time step, and (2) the model will stop after one hundred time steps have executed, since that seems to be enough time to arrive at a final state of the model. This investigation will mean that we have to reevaluate our component test (check-setup created during the initial verification process, since now, we are deliberately altering the initial distribution. Therefore, we can alter this code so that it takes into account the new parameter:[5]

```
to check-setup
    let expected-green (count patches * initial-green-pct / 100)
    let diff-green (count patches with [ vote = 0 ] ) - expected-green
    if diff-green > (.1 * expected-green) [
      print "Initial number of green voters is more than expected."
    ]
    if diff-green < (- .1 * expected-green) [
      print "Initial number of green voters is less than expected."
    ]
end
```

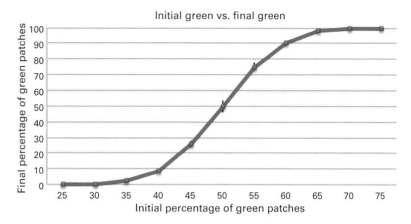

Figure 7.6
Initial Green Patches vs. Final Green Patches, Voting model.

We can examine the relationship between initial voter distribution and final vote count by executing ten runs for each initial percentage. The simplest measure of the dominance of each political party is to count the percentage of final voters that are either green or blue. After running our BehaviorSpace experiment, we can plot the results of the final percentage against the input percentage, obtaining the graph in figure 7.6.

These results show that, as we move away from an initial distribution of half blue voters and half green voters, there is a nonlinear effect on the final distribution of voters. The model is sensitive to these parameters, and thus, a slight change in the number of initial voters for a party results in a larger number of final voters for that same party. However, the definition of "sensitivity" depends on what model results you are considering. For example, sensitivity in the quantitative results does not necessarily mean there will be sensitivity in the qualitative results. If your primary model result is the qualitative finding that solid islands of voters of both colors form, leaving segregation, then this qualitative result remains true even if you perturb the initial distribution of voters by 10 percent in either direction. When perturbed, the islands of one color or the other may be much smaller, but there will still be solid blocks. Hence, for this qualitative measure, you could conclude that this model is insensitive to small changes in the initial voter balance.

Sensitivity analysis is an examination of the impact of varying model parameters on model results. To determine how sensitive a model is, we examine the effect that different initial conditions and agent mechanisms have on the model results. Additionally, we can examine the environment in which the model operates. For instance, in the voting model, we are using a two-dimensional torus grid, but these results might dramatically change if the voters were located on a hex grid, network, or some other topology.

There has also been past research on methodologies for automating the process of sensitivity analysis. NetLogo's BehaviorSpace facilitates the process of sensitivity analysis

Box 7.1
Statistical Analysis

Verification, validation, and replication all require at least some knowledge of statistics so that the aggregate results of model outcomes, in the form of numerical data, can be compared. In many cases, it is insufficient to simply examine means and standard deviations in order to understand the results of your model. Often, you will want to compare two results of your model to show that they are sufficiently different from each other. The two basic statistical tests that allow you to compare and contrast distributions are the Student's *t*-test and the Kolmogorov-Smirnov test. The Student's *t*-test assumes that the underlying distribution is normal, and describes the probability that two samples are drawn from the same distribution. The Kolmogorov-Smirnov test makes no assumptions about the underlying distributions. Instead, it compares all of the data to determine the likelihood that the two data sets could be drawn from the same distribution. Descriptive statistics and statistical tests are summaries of results, rather than results in and of themselves. Often, it is useful to actually run the model and observe what behaviors are creating the results. One intermediate method between watching the model run and looking at summary statistics is to examine spread runs. A *spread run* is when, instead of taking all of the data for a particular set of parameters (a *treatment*) and averaging the data, you instead plot all of the data separately. This allows you to see the true underlying distribution, as opposed to some summary of the underlying data based on the assumption that the data is distributed in any particular way.

by making it easier to sweep a large set of parameters and examine the results. Miller (1998) developed a methodology called Active Nonlinear Testing (ANT), which takes a set of parameters, a model, and a criterion as its inputs. The criterion is the aspect of the model that we would like to test, such as the amount of green voters at the end of the run. ANT then uses an optimization technique, such as genetic algorithms, to find a set of parameters that maximize this criterion. It presents the user with a set of parameters that best "break" the model according to some criteria. Stonedahl and Wilensky (*2010b, 2010c*) have developed techniques and a tool, called BehaviorSearch,[6] for automating parameter exploration and analysis by searching for target model behaviors. BehaviorSearch can be very useful when the parameter space is too large to search exhaustively.

Verification Benefits and Issues
There are many benefits to performing verification analysis, which include developing an understanding for the cause of unexpected outcomes and exploring the impact of small changes in rules. The basic level of verification is for the model implementer to compare

6. BehaviorSearch does not do gridded search to sweep the entire parameter space. Instead, it uses genetic algorithms to try and hone in on the parameters that produce the specific behavior you are looking for. BehaviorSearch is free and open-source. See behaviorsearch.org.

the conceptual description of the model to the implemented code to determine whether the implemented model corresponds to the conceptual model. The more rigorous the model verification process, the more likely it is that the resultant implemented model will correspond to the conceptual model. If the two models correspond exactly, then the model authors understand the model's low-level rules. This means that they understand how the model generates its results. Still, understanding the low-level components of the model does not guarantee an understanding all of the interactions of these components or of why the model generates the aggregate results that it does. Verification is important because it helps ensure that the author (or authors) understand the mechanisms that underlie the phenomenon being explored. Without going through this process, the authors cannot be confident in the conclusions drawn from the model.

Verification can be difficult to achieve because it is challenging to determine whether a surprising result is the product of a bug in the code, a miscommunication between the model author and implementer, or an unexpected outcome of low-level rule. Furthermore, it can still be difficult to isolate and eliminate a bug, or fix the miscommunication. Even if we are sure that the result is an unexpected, yet accurate, consequence, it can be difficult to discover what caused the results to be different from what we expected.

The process of understanding how a model operates can also help us to understand the "why" question. For instance, in the preceding model, as the political scientists examine the model, they begin to understand the reason the second model coalesces into blocks. Thinking through the rules of the model from the agent's point of view, it becomes clear that once a block of individuals forms it will remain constant, while if the majority of an agent's neighbors are voting one way and none of them are changing, then the agent will continue to vote the same way. Therefore, once all the agents have reached a majority consensus of their neighbors, they will stay that way forever. It is only when we give agents the ability to switch colors based on the counts around them, as in the other two rules, that we see perpetual change in the results.

The verification process is not binary. A model is not either verified or unverified, but rather exists along a continuum of verification. It is always possible to write more component tests or to carry out more sensitivity analyses. Thus, it depends on the model author and implementer (and later a model replicator) to decide when verification proves the correspondence between the conceptual model and the implemented model.

Validation

Validation is the process of ensuring that there is a correspondence between the implemented model and reality. Validation, by its nature, is complex, multilevel, and relative. Models are simplifications of reality; it is impossible for a model to exhibit all of the same characteristics and patterns that exist in reality. When creating a model we want to incorporate the aspects of reality that are pertinent to our questions. Thus, when undertaking the validation process, it is important to keep the conceptual model questions in mind and validate aspects of the model that relate to these questions.

There are two different axes along which to consider validation issues (Rand & Rust, 2011). The first axis is the level at which the validation process is occurring. *Microvalidation* is making sure the behaviors and mechanisms encoded into the agents in the model match up with their real world analogs. *Macrovalidation* is the process of ensuring that the aggregate, emergent properties of the model correspond to aggregate properties in the real world. The second axis of validation is the level of detail of the validation process. *Face validation* is the process of showing that the mechanisms and properties of the model look like mechanisms and properties of the real world. *Empirical validation* makes sure that the model generates data that can be demonstrated to correspond to similar patterns of data in the real world.

To help illustrate the process of validating an ABM, we will use the Flocking model from the Biology section of the NetLogo models library. This model attempts to recreate patterns of birds flocking as they exist in nature (see figure 7.7). The flocking model is

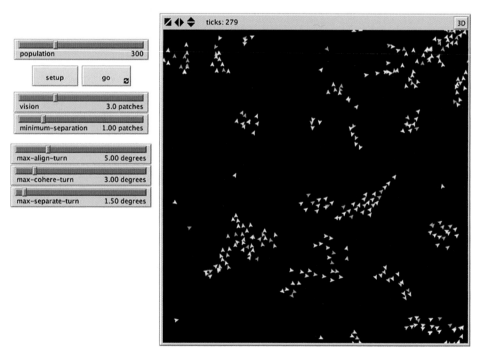

Figure 7.7
NetLogo Flocking model. http://ccl.northwestern.edu/netlogo/models/Flocking (Wilensky, 1998a).

a classic agent-based model based on the original Boids models by Reynolds (1987). The model demonstrates that bird flocks can arise without being led in any way by special leader birds. Rather, each bird is following exactly the same set of rules, from which flocks emerge. Each bird follows three rules: "alignment," "separation," and "cohesion." "Alignment" means a bird turns so that it is moving in the same direction as nearby birds. "Separation" means a bird turns to avoid hitting another bird. "Cohesion" means a bird moves toward other nearby birds. The "separation" rule overrides the other two, meaning that if two birds are approaching each other, they will always separate. In this case, the other two rules are deactivated until the minimum separation is achieved. The three rules affect only the bird's heading. Each bird always moves forward at the same constant speed. The rules are remarkably robust and can be adapted to swarming of insects, schooling of fish, and patterns of flocking such as the "V" flocking of geese (Stonedahl & Wilensky, 2010a).

Let us briefly describe the implementation of these three rules. The alignment rule is coded as follows:

```
to align    ;; turtle procedure
    turn-towards average-flockmate-heading max-align-turn
end
```

This code tells the bird to turn toward the average heading of its flockmates, but not more than the slider MAX-ALIGN-TURN, which specifies the maximum angle a bird can turn for the purposes of aligning with its flockmates. This code requires two helper procedures: one to find a bird's flockmates and another to find their average heading. The first is straightforward:

```
to find-flockmates ;; turtle procedure
    set flockmates other turtles in-radius vision
end
```

This code sets a bird's flockmates to be all the birds that it can see, as specified by the VISION slider. The second is a bit trickier, as averaging headings is not straightforward. If you try to average the flockmates' headings by summing them and dividing by the number of flockmates, it won't work. For example, if the bird has two flockmates, one with a heading of 1 and the other with a heading of 359, the straightforward averaging would get us an average heading of 180, whereas the average we want is 0. We solve this problem with a little trigonometry, as follows:

```
to-report average-flockmate-heading    ;; turtle procedure
    ;; We can't just average the heading variables here.
    ;; For example, the average of 1 and 359 should be 0,
    ;; not 180. So we have to use trigonometry.
    let x-component sum [dx] of flockmates
    let y-component sum [dy] of flockmates
    ifelse x-component = 0 and y-component = 0
      [ report heading ]
      [ report atan x-component y-component ]
end
```

We now turn to the separation rule:

```
to separate    ;; turtle procedure
    turn-away ([heading] of nearest-neighbor) max-separate-turn
end
```

This role simply asks the bird to find the bird closest to it and turn away from that bird, but not more than allowed by the slider MAX-SEPARATE-TURN.

Last, we turn to the coherence rule:

```
to cohere    ;; turtle procedure
    turn-towards average-heading-towards-flockmates max-cohere-turn
end
```

This code asks the bird to calculate the heading to each flockmate, average those headings, and turn toward that average heading, but not more than allowed by the slider MAX-COHERE-TURN. This again involves a helper procedure with some trigonometric wizardry as follows:

```
to-report average-heading-towards-flockmates   ;; turtle procedure
    ;; "towards myself" gives us the heading from the other bird
    ;; to me, but we want the heading from me to the other bird,
    ;; so we add 180
    let x-component mean [sin (towards myself + 180)] of flockmates
    let y-component mean [cos (towards myself + 180)] of flockmates
    ifelse x-component = 0 and y-component = 0
      [ report heading ]
      [ report atan x-component y-component ]
end
```

Now that we have understood the code for each of three rules for birds' behavior, we can turn back to validation. A question one might ask of this model is: How do we know that the model is representative of the behavior of real birds? We think our model looks like real birds flocking, but how can we be sure? These are validation questions.

Macrovalidation vs. Microvalidation

When determining whether a model is a valid representation of a phenomenon, we start by comparing the actions and data that exist at the lowest level of the model. ABMs are particularly amenable to this approach. Since ABMs are built from agents, we can directly compare the agents that exist in our model with those that exist in the real world.

For instance, in the flocking model, we can ask whether the agents have properties similar to real birds. We can examine all of the relevant properties of the birds, such as location in the world, heading, flockmates, and nearest neighbor, using NetLogo's inspector (as seen in figure 7.8). Like the agents, real birds also have locations and headings and, based on their vision, are aware of the birds around them. However, real birds have many more properties as well. They can be young or old, hungry or well fed, sick or healthy. None of these are captured in our model. Similarly, real birds also move in three dimensions, but our bird agents only move in two. Does this make our model invalid? Not necessarily. It is always important to keep in mind that a model is only valid or invalid relative to the questions it is being used to answer. We examine each of these possible validity threats to assess if they are relevant to our question.

Since our question is whether the agent-birds flock like real birds, it seems reasonable to start with the provisional assumption that their location, heading, and range of vision are sufficient to describe their behavior in this regard. Thus, our model is face valid in regard to these properties. Whether or not two dimensions are sufficient is difficult to determine in advance. Given that the notion of a flock seems to carry over to two dimensions, and given how we can imagine a flock would look, we can provisionally assume that it is fine to model the birds in only two dimensions. Alternatively, if we suspect another property may be necessary, we can add it to the model to see if it makes any significant difference to the model results. If it does not, we have evidence that it is not an important property to include. For example, we could build the flocking model in three dimensions and examine the resultant flocks to see if they are relevantly different from the 2D flocks.

The other major avenue of validation is to investigate the relationship between the global properties of the model and the flocking patterns of real birds, a process called macrovalidation. Because ABM's are implemented by describing micro-level agents and interactions, it is especially important that the macro or emergent properties correspond to the real world. By showing that our model corresponds to the macro-level phenomenon we are modeling, we further validate that our model is descriptive of real world systems. You can conclude different things from the two types of validation. Macrovalidation tells you if you have captured the important parts of the system, whereas microvalidation tells you if you've captured the important parts of the agent's individual behavior.

In the flocking model, we need to consider whether the flocks in the model correspond to those that we see in reality. Running the model, we can observe that the bird-agents do

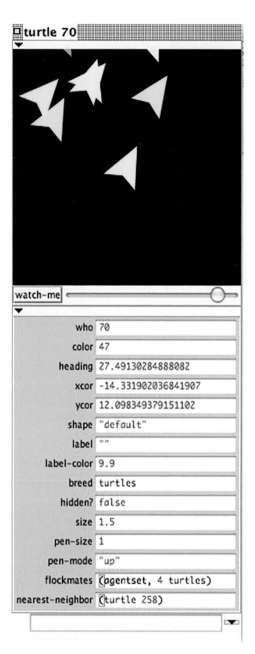

Figure 7.8
Properties of Birds in the Flocking model.

A   B

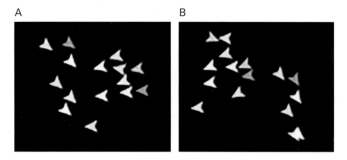

Figure 7.9
Two mini-flocks (A) before and (B) after a collision.

group together like real flocks. They also seem to interact with each other in other ways that we would expect. For instance, if one flock runs into another in the model, it is not consumed by the first flock, but instead, passes through it, maybe losing a few birds to the new flock (see figure 7.9) much like what occurs in real flocks. We could also calculate the average flock size in our model to see if it corresponds to the average flock size in the real world. Still, although we can macrovalidate this model in many different ways, at first glance, this model corresponds to many of our basic ideas of how birds flock.

We have described microvalidation vs. macrovalidation as a binary choice, but in reality, it is better to think of these as a part of a validation spectrum. Indeed, it is possible to show many levels of validation in-between. In the flocking model, we could begin by showing that individual birds behave as expected. After this, we could ask if flockmates react to each other as expected. Finally, we could determine the validity of the behavior of the flocks as a whole.

In many traditional modeling forms, like equation-based modeling, only macrovalidation is carried out. The aggregate results of the model are compared to the aggregate results of the real phenomenon. Equation-based models typically model at the aggregate level only; often, there is little to no correspondence between micro-level elements of the model and micro-level objects in the real-world phenomenon. Because ABM produces data at all levels of aggregation, ABM not only allows microvalidation to be carried out, but also, validation at almost any level in between.

Face Validation vs. Empirical Validation

Validation involves making sure that the implemented model mechanisms and objects bear resemblance to reality in those aspects that are important to your questions of interest. However, there will rarely be just one correct interpretation of your questions of interest leading to a single, correct ABM. Rather, there may be, and often are, many equally good reality-to-model mappings. In order to use a model to make claims about the world, there has to be a defensible connection between the two.

Face validation helps ensure that someone who looks at the model "on face" (i.e., without detailed analysis) can easily be convinced that the model contains elements and components that correspond to agents and mechanisms that exist in the real world. In the flocking model, on the surface, the birds appear to behave like real birds: They generally move in a straight line, have the ability to change directions, and make decisions based on local information. Most importantly, there are no behaviors that seem unreasonable for a bird to enact. For instance, the Flocking model does not require the birds to conduct complex calculations in order to determine which way they should be moving. Face validity can exist at both the micro- and macro-levels. Determining whether the birds in the model correspond to real birds is face microvalidity, while determining if the emergent flocks correspond to the appearance of real flocks is face macrovalidity. All together, these indicators confirm that the Flocking model has face validity.

Empirical validation sets a higher bar: Data produced by the model must correspond to empirical data derived from the real-world phenomenon. This is a comparison based not on how things look, but rather, on the measures and numerical data generated both by the model and the actual phenomenon. Empirical validation involves running statistical tests on the comparable data sets to determine how similar these data sets are. One challenge in doing this is that inputs and outputs in "the real world" are often poorly defined or nebulous. Empirical validation combines the epistemological challenges of the real world with those of models. Since the real world is not a computational machine with precise inputs and outputs, it can be hard to isolate and measure parameters from a real-world phenomenon. In many cases, there are natural correspondences that can be measured. For instance, in the Flocking model, we can compare the birds' known properties and behaviors as input parameters while the output parameters consist of measures of the flocks that form.

It is possible to show that the Flocking model generates many numerical similarities to real flocks. The angular momentum, size, and velocity of the flocks are all comparable to real flocks and, depending on the model's parameters and initial conditions, the model can produce results similar to real flocks. Finding the parameters and initial conditions that cause the model to match up with real-world data is a process called calibration. *Calibration* involves using empirical data to adjust the parameters and mechanisms of a model so that it can be used to examine a particular situation. Empirical validation can be carried out on the micro- and macro-levels. The comparison described here is a case of empirical macrovalidation. An empirical microvalidation might entail comparing how quickly birds in the model can turn compared to real birds or how fast the model's birds move compared to real ones.

Pattern-oriented modeling (Grimm et al., 2005) presents a particular use of empirical validation. By matching patterns of empirical data at multiple levels, the model author is able to create a more valid model. Many times, when building any kind of model, authors will show that their model creates a pattern similar to reality at only one level of detail,

Box 7.2
The Artificial Anasazi Model

The Artificial Anasazi model (Axtell et al., 2002; Dean et al., 2000; see figure 7.10) is an agent-based model that is particularly renowned for the level of empirical validation it has undergone. The Kayenta Anasazi (now called Kayenta Ancestral Pueblo) was a group of people living in the Long House Valley in the Black Mesa region of modern-day Arizona. The people lived in this area as early as 1800 BCE, but disappeared very suddenly around 1300 CE. There is an extensive archeological record from about 200 CE until their disappearance. The Artificial Anasazi project was an attempt to discover why this group suddenly vanished from Black Mesa. To do this, they created an agent-based model of the Ancestral Pueblo inhabitants of the area. Validation of the Artificial Anasazi model was carried out by comparing the results of the model to the historical data. These comparisons were favorable, and it is now believed that the Artificial Anasazi model explains the disappearance of the real people as a combination of environmental and social causes.
A NetLogo version of the Artificial Anasazi model (*Stonedahl & Wilensky, 2010b*) can be found in the Social Sciences section of the NetLogo models library.

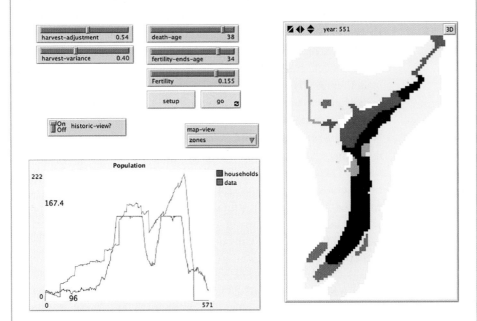

Figure 7.10
NetLogo version of the Artificial Anasazi model. In the population plot, the red line plots the simulated population and the blue line the real population data.

such as the macro-level. For instance, it could be shown that the flocking model creates realistic distributions of birds across the entire space. With pattern-oriented modeling, the more (i.e., different) levels of patterns that are validated, the more likely the model will provide a good explanation of the phenomenon. At an extreme, this must be true. If patterns of behavior were matched at every single level and for every single type of behavior, then the model would be a perfect replica of reality. Thus, it seems reasonable that the greater the number of patterns of behavior that your model is able to replicate, the more likely it is that your model is valid.

Together, these four types of validation (micro-face, macro-face, micro-empirical, and macro-empirical) characterize the majority of validation efforts carried out. However, it is important not to get too caught up in validation. A model, being a simplification of reality, will never perfectly correspond to the real world. The goal of model building is to answer a question and explain a result, but not to simulate all of the aspects of a phenomenon—or, to paraphrase Resnick, "to stimulate, not to simulate" (1994b).

Stochasticity, Invariant and Variant Results, and Path Dependence   Agent-based models are usually stochastic in nature, rarely producing the same result twice even given the same initial parameters. This can present a problem when attempting to validate a model. In many cases, reality will only present itself with a few instances of a phenomenon we would like to model; thus, we have few data points for our set of initial conditions. Running the model repeatedly may produce thousands of different results, even when only one result (or a subset of them) may exactly match the results of the real system. Given this fact, how do we determine if our model is valid?

This is where a final level of statistical testing comes in. We can assume that our model is creating a distribution of results, just as the real world is also creating a distribution of results. Therefore, we can use standard statistical tools such as the t-test and the Kolmogorov-Smirnov test to determine if our model is producing a distribution consistent with that produced in the real world. In this way, we do not conduct validation by comparing the exact results of the real world to the exact results of our model. Instead, we assume that there will be some noise affecting the production of both sets of results.

It is often the case that an ABM produces so many different end results of data that it becomes very difficult to compare it to the real phenomena. Usually, the output from these runs can be classified into two different types: *invariant results* and *variant results* (Brown et al., 2005). Invariant results are those that occur no matter how many times we run the model. Variant results, by contrast, are those that change depending upon how the model evolves. For instance, if we had a model of city growth, it might show that the western section of the city will always be developed. However, in 50 percent of the model runs, the northern section may develop and the southern section does not, while in the other half of runs, the southern section may develop and the northern section does not. By partitioning the space of model results into variant and invariant areas, we can cut down on the amount of data we need to compare while simultaneously examining how well the model passes validation tests in these two different areas.

Many times, when there are variant results that are quite pronounced, it is caused by a path dependent process in the model. A path dependent process is one where the history of the process greatly affects its final state. For instance, in the city growth model introduced earlier, it may be that the western section of the city is always undervalued at the beginning of the model. As a result, people choose to move to this section first, because it is cheaper to live there. However, this is not a path dependent process, since it always happens as a result of the initial state of the model. However, if the northern and southern sections of the city were to have an equal chance of being developed, then once a significant concentration of individuals settle in one section or other of the city, a positive feedback loop forms, whereby the more people who settle, the more desirable it becomes. This would be a prime example of a path-dependent process. Another classic example of path dependence involves the process of erosion (see the Erosion model in the Earth Science section of the NetLogo models library). Starting with a perfectly rounded mound of dirt, if rain falls randomly on it, the runoff channels could form anywhere. However, even after shallow channels have formed, they will continually deepen, and it is unlikely that a new deep channel will form in a new area that hasn't been eroded yet.

Path dependence is interesting in that it often identifies leverage points in systems. For instance, if there were an area of ecological sensitivity south of the city we just discussed and the agent-based model showed the south and north were equally likely to be developed, it would make sense for urban planners to offer incentives to develop north of the city in the early stages of city growth. On the other hand, if the model had shown that the southern region was going to be developed regardless, then such an incentive program might be useless. In this way, models can often tell you a lot about how to manipulate the world while not telling you how the world will change without manipulation.

Validation Benefits and Questions

Why is it important to validate? A valid model can be useful for extracting general principles about the world. By validating a model, you show that the model actually works in a similar fashion to the real world. Changing the mechanisms and parameters of the model can often help predict what might occur in the real world. This is particularly useful when you cannot directly carry out the same experiments in the real world. For example, while it can be very difficult (or even impossible) to change the basic operating mechanisms of the financial system, this can easily be explored in an ABM.

To the extent that a model has been validated, insights from the model are transferable to real-world systems. Only by validating our models can we hope to show that they actually do make statements that are useful outside of the model.

As we saw with respect to verification, a model is not either valid or invalid: validation is not a dichotomy. Instead, a model can be said to be more or less valid based upon how closely it has been compared to the real process it is modeling. One should always be mindful of the purpose of the model, since validation only makes sense within the context of the question being investigated. A model is never inherently valid; rather, its validity comes from the context of what it is being used for. It is up to the model authors to assess how well it answers their questions and up to the model consumers and the scientific community to determine how well it fits their purposes.

As we have hinted at, there are deep philosophical questions with respect to the concept of validation. Validation assumes that something in the model corresponds to something in reality. However, how do we compare simulations against reality? Some philosophers of science have argued that the instruments and devices used to measure reality are themselves models of the world around us (Taylor, 1996); therefore, comparing them to another model raises questions of infinite regress. For our purposes, we can assume that, when building a model, the user intends to explain something that they have observed about the world and is willing to use those observations as the basis for his or her validation attempts.

Replication

One of the foundational components of the scientific method is the idea of replication (Latour & Woolgar, 1979). From this vantage point, in order for an experiment to be considered acceptable by the scientific community, the scientists who originally performed the experiment must publish the details of how the experiment was conducted. This description of can help subsequent teams of scientists carry out the experiment themselves to ascertain whether their results are similar enough to confirm the original results. This process confirms the fact that the experiment was not dependent on any local conditions, while the written description of the experiment is satisfactory enough to record the knowledge gained in the permanent record.

Replication is an important part of the scientific process and is just as important within the realm of computational models as it is within the realm of physical experiments. Replicating a physical experiment helps prove that the original results are not due to mistakes or oversights in execution by testing and comparing both the experimental setup and ensuing results. Replicating a computational model serves this same purpose. Additionally, replicating a computational model increases our confidence in the model verification since a new implementation of the conceptual model has yielded the same results as the original. Replication can also aid in model validation as it requires the model replicators to try to understand the modeling choices that were made and how the original modelers saw the match between the conceptual model and the real world. Wilensky and Rand (2007)[7] give a detailed account of replicating an agent-based model using Axelrod and Hammond's

---

7. Parts of the rest of this section are adapted from Wilensky and Rand (2007).

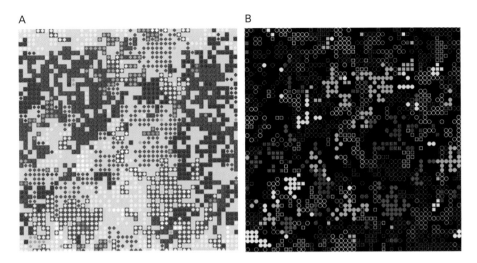

Figure 7.11
(A) Screenshot of the original Axelrod-Hammond Ethnocentrism model. (B) The replicated Ethnocentrism model.

Ethnocentrism model (2002, 2006; see figure 7.11). In this model, agents compete for limited space via Prisoners' Dilemma type interactions. Agents have one of four possible ethnicities and each agent has a strategy that includes whether it cooperates or defects with agents of its own ethnicity and with other ethnicities. "Ethnocentric" agents treat agents within their group more beneficially than those outside their group. The model includes a mechanism for inheritance (genetic or cultural) of strategies. The model suggests that "ethnocentric" behavior can evolve under a wide variety of conditions, even when there are no native "ethnocentrics" and no way for agents to know beforehand if another agent will cooperate with them.

In the process of attempting the replication, differences were discovered between the Wilensky-Rand model and the Axelrod-Hammond model; the replicated model had to be modified to produce the original results. The replication effort ultimately succeeded but the process that was required to determine that the replication was successful was complicated and involved unforeseen problems. Wilensky and Rand described the considerations that must be carefully examined, and extracted some principles for both model replicators and model authors. We will review those herein.

Replication of Computational Models: Dimensions and Standards
Replication is the implementation by one scientist or group of scientists of a conceptual model (*replicated model*) described and already implemented (*original model*) by a scientist or group of scientists at a previous time. The implementation of the replicated model must differ in some way from the original model and must also be executable (rather than

another formal conceptual model). Since replication refers to the creation of a new implementation of a conceptual model based on the previous results of an implementation, the terms *original model* and *replicated model* always refer to implemented models.

An original model and an associated replicated model can differ across at least six dimensions: (1) time, (2) hardware, (3) languages, (4) toolkits, (5) algorithms, and (6) authors. This list is ordered based upon how likely the replication effort is to produce different results from the original model. More than one of these dimensions are usually varied in the course of a single model replication.

Time A model can be replicated by the same individual on the same hardware and in the same toolkit and language environment but rewritten at a different time. This change in dimension is the least likely to produce significantly different results but, if it did, would indicate that the published specification is inadequate, since even the original researcher could not re-create the model from the original conceptual model. This is the only dimension of replication that will always be varied.

Hardware The model could be replicated by the same individual but on different hardware. At a minimum, by a change in hardware we mean that the implemented model was run on a different machine. Hardware changes may also be obtained by replicating the model on a different hardware platform. Regardless, given the prevalence of hardware independent languages, neither of these changes should provide significantly different results. If, however, the results are different, investigations (often technical) are warranted and could, for example, point to the model being susceptible to small changes in the order of behavior execution.

Languages The model could be replicated in a different computer language. By a *computer language*, we mean the programming language that was used to encode the instructions in the implemented model. Java, Fortran, Objective-C, and NetLogo are all examples of different languages. Often, the syntax and semantics of a language (e.g., procedural versus functional languages) have a significant effect on how the researcher translates the conceptual model into an actual implementation. Thus, replication in a new language can highlight differences between the conceptual model and the implementation. Even apparently minor details in language and algorithmic specifications, like the details of floating point arithmetic or differences between implementations of protocols, can cause differences in replicated models (Izquierdo & Polhill, 2006; Polhill & Izquierdo, 2005; Polhill, Izquierdo & Gotts, 2005, 2006). For a model to be widely accepted as part of scientific knowledge, it should be robust to such changes.

Toolkits The model could be replicated in a different modeling toolkit based in the same computer language. A toolkit, in this sense, is a software library or set of libraries written in a particular language for the purpose of aiding the development of a model. For instance, Repast (Collier, Howe & North, 2003), Ascape (Parker 2000), and MASON (Luke et al., 2004) are distinctly different toolkits for building ABMs, though they are all written in Java. NetLogo is an interesting example because, while the NetLogo software itself is written in a combination of Java and Scala, modelers use another language (also referred to as NetLogo) to develop models. Therefore, we classify NetLogo as both a toolkit and a language. With many different modeling toolkits available for use, the results of replicating a model in a different toolkit can often illuminate issues not only with the conceptual model, but also, with the toolkits themselves.

Algorithms The model could be replicated using different algorithms. For example, there are many ways to implement search algorithms (e.g., breadth-first, depth-first), or to update a large number of objects (e.g., in order of object creation, in a random order chosen at the beginning of the run, in a random order every time). In fact, a replicated model may simply carry out the steps of a model in an order different from that of the original model. All of these differences can potentially create disparities in the results. On the other hand, it is also possible that the algorithmic description differs, but that the results do not. This could happen because two individuals describe the same algorithm differently, or that the algorithmic differences do not affect the results.

Authors Individuals apart from the original researcher can replicate the model. This is a strong test of a model's replicability. If another researcher can take a formal description of the model and recreate it to produce the same results, we have reasonable evidence that the model is accurately described and the results are robust to changes in the dimensions of replication that have been altered.

A *successful replication* is one in which the replicators are able to establish that the replicated model creates outputs sufficiently similar to the outputs of the original. This does not necessarily mean that the two models have to generate the exact same results. Many times it is more important that similar changes generate similar effects, but determining the standard for success is left up to the researcher conducting the replication. The criterion by which the replication's success is judged is called the *replication standard* (*RS*). Different replication standards exist for the level of similarity between model outputs. Axtell et al. (1996) examined this question of standards. They developed three categories of replication standards for a replication experiment. The first category of replication standards, "numerical identity," is difficult to establish, as it entails showing that the original and replicated models produce the exact same numerical results. One way of minimizing the risk of failure of numerical identity is by using specified random seeds.[8] The second category of replication standards is "distributional equivalence." Here, the goal is to show that the two implemented models are sufficiently similar to each other according to statistical measures. To meet this criterion, RS researchers often try to show statistical indistinguishability, that is, that given the current data, there is no proof that the models are not distributionally equivalent (Axtell et al., 1996; Edmonds and Hales, 2003).[9] The final

---

8. Even when the code controls for all random seeds, research has shown that running the same program on the same machine with the same parameters does not guarantee "numerical identity" (Belding, 2000).

9. It should be noted that it might be impossible to conclusively prove that two models are distributionally equivalent due to the problem of induction and the stochastic nature of these models.

category of replication standards is "relational alignment." Relational alignment exists if the results of the two implemented models show qualitatively similar relationships between input and output variables. For example, if you increase input variable x in both models, the output variable y should respond in the same way in both the first model and the second model.

After deciding on the category of RS for a replication effort, it is important to define the details of the particular RS you intend on following more concretely since there are many more specific replication standards that could be defined. ABMs usually produce large amounts of data, much of which is usually irrelevant to the actual modeling goal. Only data that are central to the conceptual model should be measured and tested during replication. For example, replication of outputs like x and y coordinates for every agent over time, or the generation of particular random numbers, can be ignored during the replication process if they are not integral to the phenomenon being modeled. Usually, one must choose appropriate functions on a subset of the output variables to be the measures for replication.

After the particular measures have been chosen, it is also necessary to choose how often the results will be compared. One specific RS is to simply match a particular set of outputs at the end of the run. Another more detailed RS would be to match a set of values at various intermediate points throughout the run. Alternatively, one could attempt to match all the outputs throughout the run to demonstrate equivalence in the evolution of the outputs over time. This last RS is perhaps most in the ABM spirit in that it is concerned less with equilibrium and more with dynamics over time. As Epstein asserts in his seminal 1999 paper, "If you didn't grow it, you didn't explain its emergence." In other words, to fully understand a phenomenon, it is important to model the *process* that creates it rather than simply fitting a curve to some of the numbers that characterize it.

Note that the measures themselves must also be reproduced in the replicated model. In order to prevent an infinite regress of replications, model replicators often proceed with the assumption that a determination of the successful replication of the measures can be achieved by comparing the replicated measures to their conceptual description (i.e., "verification" of the measures).

Benefits of Replication

A successful replication of a physical experiment advances scientific knowledge because it demonstrates that the experiment's design and results can be repeatedly generated to show that the original results were not exceptional or statistical abnormalities. As a "side benefit" of a replication, the knowledge and data resulting from that experiment is available to the model replicator as a tool to advance their own research agenda and further explore the phenomenon beyond the original publication. Replication of a computational model has these benefits as well.

Additionally, the process of replicating a computational model can contribute to the scientific community in other ways. As we will describe, replicating computational models specifically contributes to the processes of model verification, model validation, and the development of a shared understanding of modeling. By *shared understanding*, we mean the creation of a set of terms, idioms, and best practices that can be utilized by model authors to communicate about their models.

Replication supports the model verification process because if two distinct implementations of a conceptual model are capable of producing the same results, confidence that the implemented model accurately captures the conceptual model grows. During the model replication process, if differences between the original model and the replicated model are discovered, the replicated model may need to be fixed; conversely, concerns may be raised over the correctness of the original implementation.

Replication supports model validation because validation is a process that determines a correspondence between the outputs from an implemented model and real-world measures. If the replicated model produces different outputs than the original model, this raises questions as to which outputs correspond more to real world data. If the replicated model's outputs are closer to the real-world data, by contrast, this lends greater support to the validity of the replicated model as compared to the original. More important, model replication raises questions about the details of the original modeling decisions and how they correspond to the real world. These questions help clarify whether there is sufficient correspondence between the original model and the real world. Replication forces the model replicator to examine the face validity of the original model by reevaluating the original mapping between the real world and the conceptual model, as the replicator must reimplement these same concepts. Most model replicators do not simply blindly follow directions, but rather, are themselves researchers with a vested interest in understanding the model and its ability to explain the phenomenon that they are investigating. In this way, they become engaged in the validation process through the act of replication.

The replication process helps us develop a language for describing the modeling process. Creating a culture of replication fosters a shared understanding of the modeling process in the ABM community. In much the same way that statisticians share an understanding of what is meant by "mean" and "standard deviation" and when to apply various statistical tests, over time, replication of ABM experiments will help us define such terms as "time-step," "shuffled list" and "vision cone," helping us classify ABM rules to better match up with patterns of data.

Recommendations for Model Replicators

There are several issues that should be considered when undertaking a replication. Foremost, it is important to think about the replication standard—what criteria will be used to determine whether replication has been achieved. Typically, a scientist working on a physical experiment will not attempt to exactly reproduce numerical results produced by another scientist. Instead, the RS is to reproduce to the level of precision necessary to establish the hypothesized regularity. As such, the RS itself changes depending upon the question being asked. As discussed earlier, Axtell et al. (1996) listed three general categories of replication standards: "numerical identity," "distributional equivalence," and "relational alignment." These are examples of how different experiments can achieve different levels of replication. Specifying the RS in advance facilitates the replication effort.

A second issue is that model replicators need to consider how detailed the description of the conceptual model is in the original paper and whether to communicate with the authors and/or implementers of the original model. Due to page limits and the desire to limit technical detail in a paper, research papers are usually quite concise—every word may have meaning for model replicators and it may sometimes be necessary to contact the original implementers of the model.[10] Many times they will be able to quickly clear up misunderstandings or fill in missing details about the original model. Sometimes, the researchers who developed the conceptual model may not have implemented the model, having delegated that job to a programmer. In that case, it may be important to talk with both the author and implementer, as there is an increased chance that, unbeknownst to the author, the original implementation made unintended assumptions with respect to the conceptual model (i.e., an error that would have been found if the original model had undergone a complete verification process).

On the other hand, it is beneficial to delay contacting the original authors until after a first attempt to recreate the original model has been made, since part of the goal of reproducing scientific results is to make sure that the published papers detail the process well enough to preserve the results. By first constructing the replicated model from the original paper, the model replicator provides a valuable service by noting which parts of the conceptual model are not sufficiently described in the original paper. These differences have an impact on the verification of the model because they may indicate that the conceptual model is not detailed enough to be verifiable based on the published research alone. It is also possible that the differences between the published conceptual model and an implementation can be scientifically interesting, resulting in new discoveries. These discoveries could affect the validation of the original model because it may be shown, for example, that the replicated version of the model produces outputs that better correspond to measures of the real world.

As part of this process, it may be necessary to become familiar with the toolkit in which the original model was written. Taking the time to learn the toolkit can result in a better understanding of how the original model operates. All ABM toolkits have metaphors or

---

10. This is a strategy that may have limited applicability. However, because ABM is still relatively young, the majority of original model implementers are still alive and accessible.

central constructs that they use to structure their primitives and inform the practice of constructing ABMs. Becoming familiar and working with these concepts will often help the replicator understand the subtler workings of the original model they are attempting to reproduce. A different approach that we discussed earlier is to deliberately implement a strategy that is distinct from the paradigm of the original model. By replicating a model in a new language or toolkit differences between the conceptual and implemented models may be easier to observe.

To facilitate the model replication process, it is often necessary to obtain the source code of the original model. This will enable the model replicator to examine the source in detail and even do line-by-line comparisons with the replicated model. This strategy is effective for illuminating discrepancies in the two model implementations that are not obvious from the text descriptions. In addition, the published results of the original model often do not completely explore the parameter space of results that the original model can produce. By obtaining a copy of the original model, it is possible to explore unpublished parts of the parameter space and determine if the two model implementations produce similar results. Exploring beyond the published space may significantly alter the conception of what the model results can teach us about the real world. Such was the case in at least two replication attempts that have been previously attempted (Fogel, Chellapilla & Angeline, 1999; Edmonds & Hales, 2003). In both instances, the validation of the original model was called into question by the replication of that model. This replication process illuminated differences in the results that were not expected from the description of the conceptual model and were not obtained from the original model.[11] As a result, the replicators published a view of the world that was slightly different from the original conceptual view of the world.

Though exposure to the source code and the original model is important, if it is done too early in the replication process, it may result in "groupthink." In groupthink, the replicator unconsciously adopts some of the practices of the original model developer without maintaining the independence necessary to replicate the original model; essentially, he or she "copies" the original model (Janis, 1982). These considerations represent important trade-offs and merit careful consideration of the level and timing of communication between the original model authors and the model replicators.

Table 7.1 presents a list of items that replicators should include in publications of replication. Alongside these items, some possible ways to specify these items are described. These issues and possible answers are not meant to be a complete list but to be the start of a conversation about such norms in the ABM community.

---

11. Sometimes these differences can be quite small and still cause huge differences in the replication. The authors of this textbook discovered quite different results in a social science model when they used floating-point division (which was implied by the conceptual model) versus integer division, which the original implemented model used. This difference in division techniques drastically altered the model results.

Table 7.1
Details to be included in published replications. For each category, sample options to choose from are listed.

Categories of Replication Standards:

Numerical Identity, Distributional Equivalence, Relational Alignment

Focal Measures:

Identify particular measures used to meet goal

Level of Communication:

None, Brief email contact, Rich discussion and personal meetings

Familiarity with Language/Toolkit of Original Model:

None, Surface understanding, Have built other models in this language/toolkit

Examination of Source Code:

None, Referred to for particular questions, Studied in-depth

Exposure to Original Implemented Model:

None, Reran original experiments, Ran experiments other than original ones

Exploration of Parameter Space:

Examined results from original paper, Examined other areas of the parameter space

Recommendations for Model Authors

Model authors can also make a model replicator's job easier by considering a few issues when building new ABMs. First of all, the section of a research paper where the conceptual model is described needs to be well specified. Details of the specification may not appear to be important to the model developer but are important if a model replication is to be successful. It is important to carefully consider the level of detail articulation of the conceptual model. For example, is it sufficient to describe the model using text alone? Or to expand into a pseudo-code description of the model? Or to publish the full source code of the model? Even the complete source code for the model may not suffice. For discovering differences between some replications, replicators may require source code of the modeling toolkit in which the model was authored. That could in turn necessitate a description of the machine the model was run on, and so on, and so on. Publishing the complete source code of the original model facilitates the replication process, but it may also have costs. In practice, scientists make some assessment of the balance between the advancement of scientific knowledge and their own professional advancement. Once the complete source for a model is made public, it gives competing researchers quick and easy access to the author's research methods, which may entail the professional cost of enabling another scientist to leap ahead of the original model developer. Determining a standard of model publication is necessary for ABM to move ahead as a methodology. It is our strong recommendation that model authors make their source code publicly available, or at the very least, make publicly available "pseudo-code" of how the model was implemented.[12] This allows the scientific process to proceed most reliably. In recent years, there has been an increasing trend to publish source code on websites that accompany the published article. In the long run, we expect the field to converge on a common standard form or language for model publication.

Another issue is to what extent the model developer presents a sensitivity analysis of the results generated by their model. In some cases it may be clear that there are small modifications to the original implementation of the model that drastically affect the results. It is exactly these sensitive differences that model authors need to publish. Even if they do not as yet have explanations for the sensitivity, it is important to point these out as directions for future research. It is also important to consider how the details of the model correspond to the process that the model is attempting to recreate. If the original model makes a different simplification choice than the replicated model and either choice appears to be irrelevant in the real world, then the results should match.

As noted earlier, the model author may not be the original implementer. Such a division of labor can be efficient, but it has significant costs. In essence, translating a conceptual model that someone else designed into an implemented model is quite similar to the process of replication. Knowing how hard it is to do a faithful replication, there is a danger that when the model author and implementer are different, the implementation will not be veridical (i.e., if/when the model undergoes the verification process, it will turn out to be an incorrect implementation of the conceptual model). This will in turn make further replication attempts even harder to do. Our recommended resolution of this trade-off is to suggest that model authors implement their own models using "low-threshold" (Papert, 1980; Tisue & Wilensky, 2004) languages and toolkits. "Low-threshold" languages and toolkits are designed to be simple enough that model authors need not be experienced programmers, yet can faithfully implement their models. These design affordances reduce the costs and inefficiencies of having a single person be both the model designer and implementer and enable model authors to gain the benefit of more likely verity. An additional benefit of this approach is that the author can experiment more freely with alternative implementations and thus uncover and resolve threats to model validity. In cases where authors, implementers and domain experts are not the same person, and perhaps are not even collocated, collaboration tools such as the NetLogo modeling commons (Lerner, Levy & Wilensky, 2010) facilitate collaboration between team members.[13] In table 7.2, we present these issues as a list of items that model authors should consider when making results available.

In order to truly facilitate the model replication process, it is advisable for model authors to examine their conceptual models through the lens of a potential model

---

12. Grimm et al. (2005) have recently explored this issue with respect to ecological modeling.

13. http://modelingcommons.org.

Table 7.2
Details to be included in published models. For each category, sample options to choose from are listed.

Level of Detail of Conceptual Model:

Textual description, Pseudo-code

Specification of Details of the Model:

Order of events, Random vs. nonrandom activation

Model Authorship/Implementation:

Who designed the model, who implemented the model, and how to contact them

Availability of Model:

Results, beyond those in the paper, available, Binary, or Source Code available

Sensitivity Analysis:

None, Key parameters or All parameters varied, Design of experiment analysis

replicator. It is only by going through the replication process that a researcher can understand how to adequately describe their conceptual model for other researchers. If model authors consider whether their conceptual model descriptions are detailed enough that a model replicator could replicate the model from those descriptions, published models would undoubtedly be more replicable. Moreover, by establishing a norm for model authors to also engage in replication of models, we will accumulate a body of cases of model replications, and the field will gain a better understanding of best practices for model replication.

Summary

Now that we have explored the three broad topics of verification, validation, and replication, what do these concepts tell us about the accuracy and correctness of a model? Through verification, we have explored how to make sure that our implemented model corresponds to our conceptual model. This improves the correctness of our model because it tells us that the implementation is based on the concepts and ideas that we had in mind when constructing the model. Validation is the process of making sure that our model actually tells us something about the real world. A model that has been shown to be valid, to some degree, is more correct in that it provides more information about the real world. Finally, replication is a tool by which we can make sure that the results from a model run were not anomalous. By replicating a model, we show that its results are repeatable, and thus we can be more certain in the knowledge that the model provides us. In addition, replication helps us improve the verification and validation of a model. Through the use of these three techniques, we can increase our confidence that our model tells us something interesting about the complex system that we are examining.

Explorations

1. We have described a unit test for the Voting model that ensures that the initial conditions are correct. Can you describe a unit test that ensures the voting mechanism is functioning correctly for an individual agent? Implement this test in the Voting model in the Social Science of the NetLogo models library.

2. Choose a model from the Sample Models section of the NetLogo models library. Describe how you would test the validity of the model in four different ways: (1) face microvalidity, (2) face macrovalidity, (3) empirical microvalidity, and (4) empirical macrovalidity. Apply each test and describe the results.

3. Find a (relatively simple) model written in another ABM language/toolkit like Repast, Swarm, or MASON. Replicate this model in NetLogo. What replication standard would you use? How would you judge that you had completed a successful replication? What issues did you encounter while attempting this replication?

4. Validation can be difficult. Some philosophers of science argue that it is impossible to compare computational models with the real world. Even when you agree on which measures to match, there is no proof that these measures are actually referring to the same underlying phenomenon. In fact, they cannot be since one is empirical and one is computational. Present an argument against this view, and justify why models are valid ways of gathering knowledge about the world.

5. *Simplifying models* The Voting model discussed in this chapter is related to the Ising model found in the chemistry and physics of the models library. In the Ising model, there is an exponential formula that calculates the probability of flipping from one state to another. Design a different rule that is simpler, more discrete, and results in similar behavior. Create a replication standard for comparing these two models. Show whether or not your new model meets this replication standard.

6. *Docking models* Model docking is a process that shows that two models that were written separately confirm the same general result. Typically, the process involves changing the parameters of the models until they can produce the same answer to the question of interest. For example, both the Altruism model (in the Biology section) and the Ethnocentrism model (Social Science section) in the NetLogo models library examine how people decide to cooperate. Can you dock the findings of these models? Find a set of parameters for both models such that selfish people (ethnocentrics, defectors) always win. By contrast, find a set of parameters for both models where the altruists always win. What does it mean for both models to have the same results? Can you define this in terms of the model outputs? Can you describe the relationship between the two sets of model parameters that produce the same results in the two models? What can you learn from this relationship about the two models?

7. *Distributing agents* Imagine you read a scientific paper in which the authors describe their model initialization as "agents randomly distributed in the world." Consider two ways

to implement that description. The first method involves writing a model in which a group of agents is created at the center of the world and then all move outward a random amount. The second requires you to create a group of agents and use SETXY to place them randomly in the world. Examine the scattering of agents that results from each of these techniques. Are they equivalent? Can you create a unit test that distinguishes between them? How would you refine the authors' original description if you found out they used one of these methods?

8. *Measuring agents* As described in the Validation section, we can compare measures of agent-based models to real-world descriptions. Suppose we have three measures of real-world bird flocks that we want to compare to data from the Flocking model. Implement measures of average angular velocity (how quickly each bird changes its heading), average flock size, and percentage of singleton birds. Can you think of another interesting measure? Graph these results over time.

9. *Adding networks to models* The voting model is currently based on local neighborhoods. Imagine that political scientists come back to you because they realize that many times, people talk not only to their local neighbors, but also to people at a distance. Modify this model to connect each agent in the world to another random agent as well as their neighbors. Neighbor relationships can be represented in several different ways. One way stores a group of neighbors (agentsets); another way is to use links. If you use links, you will need to represent voters as agents on patches, rather than patches themselves, because NetLogo only allows creating links between turtles (not between patches). How does the behavior of the model change as a result of these networks?

10. *Replicating additional results* In Axelrod and Hammond's original Ethnocentrism model, one change that prevented ethnocentrism from evolving was changing the way reproduction occurs. If children are not born near their parents, then ethnocentrism is much less likely to evolve. Implement nonlocal reproduction in the Ethnocentrism model to show how ethnocentrism is less likely to evolve.

11. Change the Voting model so it can start with a nonrandom green-and-blue pattern. For example, one could make half of the world blue and half green. How does this affect the model results?

12. In the Voting model, can you think of other possible voting rules? Modify the model to use these rules and compare the results to the original model.

13. Can you enhance the Voting model to incorporate multiple colors and multiple votes? One might interpret shades of color to represent the degree of a patch's opinion about an issue: strongly against, against, neutral, etc. Each patch could have more than two choices and weighted votes: blue patches' vote could count twice, etc.

14. In the Flocking model (in the Biology section of the NetLogo models library), currently the birds can "see" all around them. What happens if birds can only see in front of them? The "in-cone" primitive can be used for this.

15. Can you get the birds in the Flocking model to fly around obstacles in the middle of the world?

16. Introduce a predator bird into the Flocking model. How will this affect flocking?

17. Adapt the Flocking model so it models the schooling of fish.

18. Add more ethnicities to the Ethnocentrism model (in the Social Science section of the NetLogo models library). Does the behavior change?

19. Modify the Ethnocentrism model so that some patches are "richer" than others, that is, agents on them have a higher chance of reproducing. Distribute this advantage across the world in different ways such as randomly, in blobs, or in quarters. How does this affect the behavior of the model?

20. Modify the Ethnocentrism model so that patches can be tagged with a color. Distribute the colors across the world in different ways: blobs, randomly, in discrete quarters. Agents use the patch color under other agents to determine whether to cooperate with them or not. How does this affect the behavior of the model?

8 Advanced Topics and Applications

Any sufficiently advanced technology is indistinguishable from magic.

—Arthur C. Clarke

We have now examined most of the basic topics related to agent-based modeling. We have addressed the following questions about the field of ABM: What is an ABM? Why, how, and when should you use ABM? How do you build ABMs, and how do you conduct (and analyze) experiments with ABM? We have covered the basics of what you need to know in order to start working with ABM.

In this final chapter, we will discuss some advanced topics in ABM that you may go on to pursue. We will also survey select applications in which ABM has been productively used.

Many readers will not need to read through this chapter from start to finish, but might want to use it more as a reference, or browse the subheadings and read the topics most relevant to you.

Advanced Topics in ABM

Having laid the groundwork for basic knowledge of ABM, the modeling process, and complex systems, we want now to discuss many related topics that we simply do not have time or space to address in detail in this textbook. In the following pages, we will briefly survey some of the major topics we did not address and provide references where you can learn more about them. We will discuss a range of topics, including some advanced methods of designing ABMs, calibrating ABMs, communicating with ABMs that involve other types of agents (e.g., humans and robots); combining ABM with other modeling techniques; and using advanced data sources and data analysis tools in combination with ABM.

We will start with some advanced methods for designing ABMs. In this text, we stressed the ABM design principle of starting simple and building toward your question. This basic principle is very useful and it can be employed in combination with other design guidelines. First, we will discuss Full Spectrum Design, which is the process of building models so that they can exhibit both simple and elaborated, realistic mechanisms at the same time. Second, we will discuss Iterative Design, which involves the rapid development of models so that domain experts can regularly review them.

We can also use more advanced methods to help us come up with the rules for our ABM. For example, we might extract rules from empirical data sets. By employing machine-learning methods (such as decision trees), we can use already existing data to automatically create simple rules for the agents in our model to follow. We can also create new data sets through the use of participatory simulations, a method that involves humans interacting with agents in a model. We can then observe the human actions, encoding their responses as new rules within the ABM.

So far, we have primarily discussed the use of ABMs for research, but they may also be used in other ways. For instance, ABMs can be used as communicative devices to express a claim about the world and illustrate that claim to other individuals. In this way, ABMs can be used to persuade people that a particular statement about the world is true. Another very powerful use of ABMs is in education. ABM lends itself to many educational uses—from introductory activities, such as demonstrating a complex systems principle or visualizing the mechanisms underlying a scientific phenomenon, to more advanced uses, such as students modifying or creating models on their own to explore a content area.

Virtual agents do not need to be the only kind of agents involved in an ABM. Human agents can be used, as we just mentioned when discussing participatory simulations. Human agents can interact with simulations, pushing them in certain directions. Agent-based models can also be connected to physical robot agents. The ABM can receive input from the robots just as it would a virtual agent and is capable of sending outputs such as turning motors on or off.

By combining ABM with other modeling methods, we can sometimes create hybrid or multilevel models. For example, we can use another modeling method such as system dynamics modeling to describe the hydrodynamics of a particular pond while using ABM on top of that to describe fish behavior. Similarly, we could use ABM to describe agents in a stock market and how they interact while using machine-learning models to describe how agents change their strategies over time.

We have already demonstrated in chapter 6 how combining GIS and SNA data with ABM can be especially useful. This is a particular instance of a broader challenge: that of combining ABM with advanced data sources and data analysis packages.

We will now discuss each of these topics in more detail. In some cases, we will be addressing advanced topics that have already been well examined and researched within the field of ABM; in other cases, the methods we will be discussing are only in early stages of development.

Model Design Guidelines

The Basic Design principle of ABM that we introduced in chapter 4 is to start simply and then elaborate in the direction of the question you want to answer. This design principle is, of course, quite broadly applicable, but there are also additional design principles that can be useful in guiding model construction. In this section, we will discuss two additional design principles that can be useful for creating ABMs: Full Spectrum Modeling and Iterative Modeling.

Full Spectrum Modeling   Many agent-based models, like Schelling's (1971) original segregation model that we discussed in chapter 3, are very simple. In spite of their simplicity, these simple models often illustrate very general principles about the world that can best be understood through a "caricature" of the real world, which is exactly what these models provide. For instance, in the case of Schelling's model, the simplified version of the world illustrates quite well that even minor racial biases can cause segregated neighborhoods to emerge. Though simple models lack all the mechanisms that exist in the real world, they can provide us with tools for understanding complex phenomena.

Elaborated, realistic (ER) models, on the other hand, contain a variety of different mechanisms, use empirical data, and can be shown to match real-world outcomes. One could imagine a more elaborated version of Schelling's model that read in real data from Chicago neighborhoods to examine what people's preferences were, using cognitive modeling to determine how they would choose where to live. Within the context of a complex system, realistic models can be used to explore particular situations and particular problems. This increased amount of specificity leads some critics to charge that ER models are impossible to understand and that they apply only to the particular details around which they are built (Grimm et al., 2006). But sometimes that is exactly the desired outcome, a *particular* prediction. For instance, a realistic model of residential housing choice might be able to predict land development patterns in neighborhoods of Chicago for years to come.

Researchers have discussed this tension between ER models and simple models both explicitly and implicitly (Axelrod, 1997; Carley, 2002). For instance, some researchers argue that simple models provide for better transparency and a deeper level of understanding. Other researchers, however, argue for an increased emphasis on elaborated and realistic models, since they are more consistent with the scientific method and more easily falsifiable. However, this forced choice between simple models and realistic models is not required. Grimm et al. (2006), for instance, argue with their pattern-oriented modeling (POM) approach that the optimal level of modeling complexity resides somewhere in the middle. This approach allows a single model to reproduce multiple levels of observed patterns. While being able to create patterns at multiple levels of hierarchy is important, there is no need to restrict the process to building one model at the "sweet spot" of complexity. One solution is to build several models at different levels of complexity, thus exploring both general principles and specific applications at the same time. This approach is called *full spectrum modeling* (Rand & Wilensky, 2007). As the name implies, it involves modeling phenomena at multiple levels of detail—that is, modeling not just at the level of "simple" and/or "elaborated and real" but also at the levels in between. Sometimes this can take the form of a series of models, in which one starts with simple models and becomes progressively realistic, or else starts with realistic models and becomes progressively simplified. A full spectrum approach allows for a deeper and fuller understanding of the given phenomenon than any single-level approach.

Full spectrum modeling combines the benefits of simple and ER modeling and provides some additional benefits. Full spectrum modeling does not require that there be a single simple model or a single ER model. Instead, there can be many different simple models, ER models, and models at the levels of elaboration and realism in between. By building models at multiple different levels of elaboration and realism, it is possible to extract general principles from the phenomenon being analyzed and embed those general principles in simple models. In addition, researchers can calibrate ER models to real-world data to show how those models create accurate descriptions of the world around them.

Researchers gain additional benefits from pursuing models at multiple levels of elaboration and realism at the same time. Simple models enable us to explore small numbers of mechanisms in-depth and show that those mechanisms can have profound effects on our results. These simple models can be used to determine what mechanisms should be in the ER models and help to validate that these mechanisms are important to the system being studied. Likewise, by examining ER models, scientists can highlight mechanisms that they want to explore in more depth and create simple exploratory models that emphasize only certain aspects of the ER models. Thus, full spectrum modeling may involve building sequences of models either by starting with caricature-like simple models and elaborating on them, or by simplifying more elaborate realistic models.

This approach to creating model sequences suggests a principle for the design of agent-based models to be used in combination with the ABM design principle laid out in chapter 4. To facilitate full spectrum modeling, it is important, whenever possible, to allow different mechanisms to be turned on and off. This can be done with one large model and many switches or with a progressive sequence of models. This fine-grained control over mechanisms allows the model (or model sequence) to be made more or less elaborate/realistic as the need arises. The general principle of this approach to model design is to make it easier to add mechanisms and empirical data to simple models, as well as to remove mechanisms and look at simplified or idealized situations in ER models.

There are no clear-cut methods for determining when it is best to use a full spectrum approach. Creating a large number of models will likely require more time than focusing all of your efforts on building a single model. Will the benefit discussed here make this time worthwhile? When is it better to build a palette of full spectrum models, versus building a single elaborated model? What about only building multiple simple models? These are judgment calls that you will have to make. Formally investigating these trade-offs is an active area of research within the methodology of ABM.

Iterative Modeling   The Iterative Modeling methodology rests on the idea that frequent feedback between the conceptual model design process and the model implementation process can be very fruitful both for model building and data collection/theory generation processes. As we discussed in chapter 6, often the same individual or team conducts these two processes. However, it is also common that one team generates the conceptual model while another team implements it. Both of these ABM development scenarios can benefit from an iterative modeling process but, for clarity, we separate the conceptual model authors from the implementers in the following text.

ABMs are often developed on the basis of individual-level data sets or from theories about how individuals behave. In such cases, ABM implementers typically sit down with domain knowledge experts to discuss the various components that are part of the complex system under investigation. After this information-gathering phase, the authors design the conceptual model, while the ABM implementers are tasked with creating the code for this conceptual model. In traditional modeling practice, the model implementation is independent of the model design process is subsequent to the completion of the design. In contrast, iterative modeling methodology posits that it is useful to get feedback throughout the model design and model implementation processes. Following this design approach, the model is incrementally built in small stages; this allows the model designer to see the model at various stages of completeness and make changes to the model as needed. When the model designer and model implementer are separate individuals or teams, iterative modeling can play a helpful role in catching miscommunications. It might seem that this benefit is less important when one individual is both model author and implementer. In fact, it is easy when implementing a design to forget assumptions you made in the conceptual model, and iterative modeling enables you to revisit and refine those assumptions regularly.

An ideal iterative modeling process proceeds as follows: After a meeting in which an initial conceptual model is designed, the implementers implement the model and show it to the model designers as quickly as possible with the most basic mechanisms working. At this point, the model designers provide the implementers with feedback as to how to improve the model and new mechanisms to add in to the model. These requested changes may have already been clear to the designers/authors at the outset, but were imperfectly communicated to the implementers. Alternatively, the need for explicit specification that arises from the implementation process may cause the designers to realize that components of their model were underspecified. The model implementers may recognize this underspecification as they detect ambiguity in how to transform a rule of the conceptual model into code. Sometimes, the authors can address these underspecifications directly; other times, they may provoke new data gathering processes to identify an answer to the model implementers' questions.

To review, the iterative modeling cycle involves (1) designing the model based on initial data/theories, (2) implementing the model with basic mechanisms, (3) revising the data/theories based on realization of underspecification or results of model runs, (4) revising the implementation based on the data/theories, and (5) repeating steps 1–4. In other words, modeling is not only driven by theory generation and data collection, but it can also drive theory generation and data collection. By elucidating areas where theory and data cannot be directly translated into computational formats, ABM facilitates the empirical and theoretical aspects of research as well. Because ABMs require both low-level descriptions of objects to generate the models and high-level descriptions of systems in order to validate the models, they are particularly well suited to the task of uncovering underspecified areas of research.

One of the benefits of Iterative Modeling is that, by encouraging frequent communication between the model author and model implementer, it can facilitate the identification of verification problems early on in the lifecycle of the model. By developing model versions quickly, differences between "expected" outcomes and actual outcomes become obvious at an earlier stage in the process. Since fewer changes will have been made than if the model was not examined until all the mechanisms were in, it can become easier to identify what components of the model are causing the differences in expected outcomes. As we discussed in chapter 7, these differences may be the result of (1) bugs, (2) miscommunications/misunderstanding, or (3) unexpected emergent results. Iterative modeling will help to more quickly identify the cause, and allow for earlier appropriate action.

Rule Extraction

As we discussed in chapter 4, while models are abstractions and do not correspond one-to-one with reality, they nonetheless must match up with reality in some useful way. Therefore, we must sometimes adjust the model's parameters so as to fit a particular situation (we discussed this process in chapter 7). However, sometimes calibration goes beyond just fitting particular parameters to input data. It requires adjusting the rules of behavior of the agents. In fact, it is often the case that the rules of behavior can be directly extracted from the data. In this section, we will discuss two ways of extracting rules for ABMs. The first method involves the examination of large data sets to extract simple decision rules. The second method is also a data-mining process but, instead of examining previously collected data, involves placing human agents in interaction with a model in order to extract simple rules of behavior.

Extraction of Rules from Empirical Data   Many large data sets have already been collected about social, natural, and physical phenomena. These data often describe what has happened in the past, but they do not usually provide us an explanation of why things happened the way they did, or what might have happened had things been different. If we could somehow transform these past descriptions of events into rules of behavior, we could use them to produce agent-based models that could be more explanatory than these data sets are by themselves.

The field of *machine learning*, which we discussed in chapter 5, has developed a variety of techniques that can be useful in this situation. One way to think of agents is that they take output actions as a result of input observations. Machine learning has developed methods to classify inputs into outputs and abstract general rules that describe these relationships. Using these techniques, we can take large data sets and use machine-learning techniques, such as decision trees (Quinlan, 1986), to describe general relationships between independent input variables in the data and dependent output variables. A decision tree determines when a particular input variable will provide the maximum amount of discriminatory information among the output variables, creating a branch point based on this information. They are called decision trees for their variety of decision nodes, which form branchlike structures with leaves at the end as outputs and thus resemble upside-down trees (see figure 8.1).

For example, imagine that we have a data set that describes the demographics of families in Chicago that attend public schools. In Chicago, a school choice policy allows families to choose where to send their children to school (Maroulis et al., 2010). Suppose our data set includes the choice of school system that each family made in the past ten years. We might use decision tree induction to create decision trees from

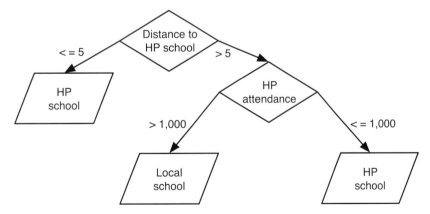

Figure 8.1
School Decision Tree.

this data set that model the choices families have made. For instance, suppose a section of this tree is responsible for deciding if a family will send their child to a (possibly distant) high-performing (HP) school or a local neighborhood school. Their decision might then look like figure 8.1 since, if the high-performing school is close by, they might go to it regardless, but if its crowded and far away, they might decide to leave their child in the local school.

The first branch in figure 8.1 asks whether the distance to the closest HP school is less than or equal to five miles. If yes, they then choose to go to the HP school. Otherwise, the decision branches on whether the attendance of the HP school is less than or equal to one thousand. If yes, the family will decide to attend the HP school; if no, they will attend the local school. This is just one possible example tree. Machine-learning algorithms for decision-tree induction will automatically create trees that are consistent with the data set while also being reasonably parsimonious. Decision trees enable you to easily visualize the results of a large amount of empirical information. They also allow you to trace data in the system one of two ways: You can start at the top of the tree and work your way down, or, if you are interested in how individuals come to be in certain states, you can start at a final decision state at the bottom of the tree and work your way up.

Decision trees highlight decision points or critical points in the data where individuals can easily be split into categories. Decision trees can serve as an intermediate form between conceptual models and code, and they can be easily turned into code. These qualities make them well suited for explicating a conceptual model and ensuring agreement among collaborators. Other machine-learning methods that can extract rules or behavior from data include training artificial neural networks, support vector machines, and Bayesian frameworks, among others. (For an overview of various machine-learning methods, see Flach, 2012; Mitchell, 1997.)

After we have extracted a decision tree from a set of empirical data, we can then create an ABM rule for each agent that represents this tree. For instance, the tree coded in NetLogo would look like this:

```
to-report decide-on-school
    ifelse (distance HP-school <= 5) [
        report "HP-school"]
        [ifelse (attendance <= 100) [
            report "HP-school"
          ]
          [report "local-school"
          ]
    ]
end
```

Box 8.1
Data Mining

Data mining is the use of automated computational techniques to extract patterns of information from large amounts of empirical data. Data mining enables knowledge discovery and prediction. Knowledge discovery is the process of analyzing large data sets to find useful patterns. For example, a company may record where shoppers at their stores are from. By data-mining this information, they may be able to choose an optimal location to build a new store. Prediction is the use of empirical data sets to forecast future trends; the company in our previous example might seek to forecast sales around the holidays next year based on data from the previous ten years of sales. An in-depth account of data mining methods is beyond the scope of this textbook; instead, see Tan, Steinbach, and Kumar (2005) for a technical introduction and Ayres (2007) for a general audience introduction.

At first glance, this does not tell you any more about the modeled decision process than the decision tree itself. But if we embed this code in an agent-based model, we can see how the dynamics of the decision-making process. Running this mode, we learn that attendance at the schools will fluctuate over time, with the decisions made early in the model run affecting the choices made later on. In short, examining the behavior of an ABM that is based on the decision tree will tend to prove more insightful into the dynamics of the decision-making process than merely examining the initial decision tree.

It can often be very difficult to create or hypothesize a set of rules that govern an ABM decision. Data mining that uses machine-learning techniques holds the promise of automatically creating decision rules from large data sets. This may help jumpstart the ABM process. For example, in the school choice example, our data might be presented in tables. One table might list each individual, the school he or she chose to attend, and the distance to the school. Another table would list each school, its status as high- or low-performing, and its enrollment. By mining these tables, we could come up with two important parts of our tree: the branching points and the values for branching. If our data set indicates that people are making their school choices using similar criteria, then we could extract one decision tree (the average tree) from the data set, using it as the rule for our agents. If a clustering algorithm shows us that there are numerous different rules in play, we could divide our population into different "breeds," populate our model with the numbers of each breed indicated by the data, and give each breed its own separate decision rule. Developing a more thorough understanding of how to do this and the dangers of automatically extracting rules of behavior are subjects of current research in the field of ABM.

Participatory Simulations and Extraction of Rules from Participatory Simulations   Participatory simulation (Colella, 2000; Wilensky & Stroup, 1999a, 2000, 2002) is a type of social simulation where individuals, from subject matter experts to the general public, directly participate in a complex systems model. Participatory simulations have important uses both in education and in research. One early use of participatory simulation was as an educational tool. NetLogo contains a participatory simulation module called HubNet (Wilensky & Stroup, 1999c), which has been widely used in classrooms to teach students the relationship between their individual decisions and global outcomes.

A classic model widely used in classrooms is the Disease HubNet activity (see figure 8.2). In the Disease HubNet model, each student controls an individual agent moving around on a landscape.[1] One of these individuals becomes infected (symbolized by red circles attached to the agents), and the disease spreads through the population by contact. The students observe the relationship between the spread and the graph of the number of people infected over time, learning about the characteristic "shapes" of disease spread. They experiment with different rules and conditions for spread and analyze the resulting infection curves.

Participatory simulations have been shown to be very engaging and effective in educational contexts (Colella, 2000; Klopfer, Yoon & Perry, 2005; Wagh & Wilensky, 2013; Wilensky & Stroup, 2000; 2014). Participatory simulations can also be useful for research in such areas as cognitive psychology, social psychology, sociology, political science, economics, and other fields that study human interaction. By presenting individuals with various simulated scenarios, researchers can begin to understand how those individuals respond under experimentally controlled conditions (see, e.g., Frey & Goldstone, 2013). Researchers can then analyze participants' actions to create rules of behavior that can be embedded in the agent-based model. This is similar to the data mining technique described earlier: By logging the inputs presented to the participant in how they made their decision, it is possible to extract decision trees and rules that describe the participants' general behavior.

For instance, in the Disease model described in the preceding box, it is possible to observe that many individuals would move away from other infected individuals to the extent that they could (given the boundaries of the world). This rule of behavior could be encoded into the model if you wanted to systematically explore how it affects the spread of the disease. The Disease model can also have "androids," computer-controlled agents that move around in the view. Normally, they move around randomly or stay in one place. However, a rule could easily be added to avoid infected individuals. This procedure, based on the androids-wander procedure, might look like this:

---

1. http://ccl.northwestern.edu/netlogo/models/HubNetDisease (Wilensky & Stroup, 1999b).

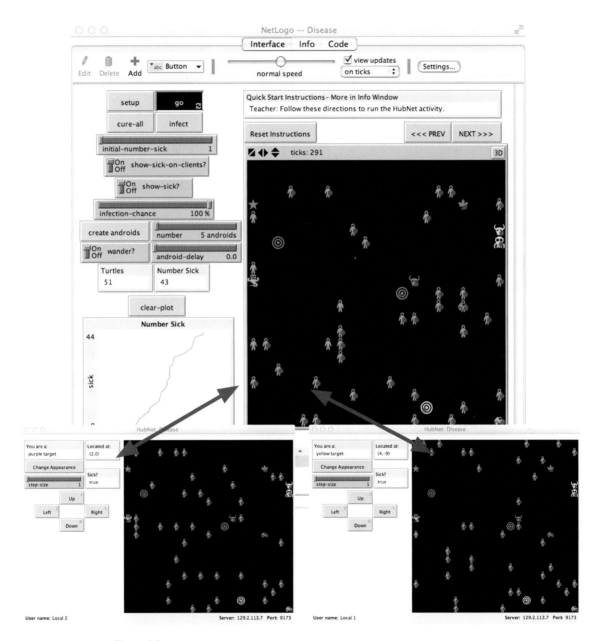

Figure 8.2
HubNet Disease Activity (*Wilensky & Stroup, 1999b*). The NetLogo model on the left is the HubNet server, and there are two clients on the right.

Box 8.2
HubNet Exploration

You can begin to explore HubNet models locally by opening a HubNet model from the
NetLogo models library and launching a few local clients (interfaces) on your personal
computer. However, to explore a HubNet model more fully, you will need several
computers and a few volunteers. For instance, open the Disease model under the HubNet
Activities in the NetLogo models library. This model is similar to the Spread-of-Infection
model we talked about in chapter 6. After opening the model, that model acts as the
"server" in a client-server architecture. Ask the participants to open their HubNet client
(which is another application distributed with NetLogo, in the NetLogo folder) and connect
to the server model. Ask the volunteers to move their avatar and try out different strategies
of movement, evasion, and capture. For example, suggest they try to avoid infected
individuals or, alternatively suggest they try to move toward infected individuals. How do
these different strategies affect the results of the spread of infection in this model?

```
to androids-avoid
   ask androids
   [
      ;; choose a target which is a neighboring patch free of infected turtles
      let target one-of neighbors4 with [ not any? turtles-here with [infected?] ]
      ;; if there is such a patch, head in that direction
      ifelse ( target != nobody ) [
         face target
      ]
      [
         ;; if there is no such patch, face a random cardinal direction
         face one-of neighbors4
      ]
      fd 1
   ]
end
```

This procedure looks to see if there is any nearby location without infected agents (either
human or computer-controlled); if there is, it then chooses randomly among the noninfected places and heads in that direction. This is a primitive form of avoidance, which can
be refined through calibration to the data gathered in the participatory simulation (see
Berland & Rand, 2009 for a discussion of this possibility).

   As a tool for research, participatory simulations have a number of advantages. Researchers can collect data on human behavior in a large number of alternative scenarios, a feat
that would be difficult to accomplish in the real world for a host of pragmatic reasons.
Moreover, participatory simulation enables recording and playback of the behavior as well
as the capacity to rewind, wherein behavior can be rewound to an earlier point, examined
at that point and continued from there to lead to possibly different outcomes. This allows

researchers to explore a larger space of alternatives to find points of leverage. In addition, as they refine the model, they can present the refined simulation back to the participants, allowing them to interact with the revised agents and further elaborate upon the model. This combination of participatory simulation and ABM often reveals new insights into how individuals process information (Abrahamson & Wilensky, 2004; Berland & Wilensky, 2006; Wilensky & Stroup, 2000).

Participatory simulations can be used both to help calibrate an ABM and to test its validity. If an ABM exhibits a particularly surprising or unusual pattern of behavior for a given set of inputs, a researcher can create a situation similar to those inputs for humans to participate in. If the results of the simulation correspond with the results of the ABM, this increases our confidence in the validity of the ABM. Determining how to find equivalences between ABM and participatory simulations is an open research question.

ABM gives us the ability to model as many different types of actors as necessary and evaluate a heterogeneous set of scenarios and policies that interact in nonlinear ways. Participatory simulation, by comparison, gives us the ability to refine our model and examine how real individuals respond to this complex world. Participatory simulation and ABM can be used together to gain insight into how individuals decide when and how much to take actions while likewise examining their response to a variety of inputs.

There are many challenges shared by both of the aforementioned calibration techniques (machine learning from empirical data sets and extraction of rules from participatory simulation). For instance, what do you do when you have conflicting data? What if participants in the simulation decide to take two different actions, even though they are given the same inputs? What if your data set provides no clear rules of behavior because people seem to decide what to do based on data that is only available to them? Is it possible to extract these rules in a parsimonious way without your agents becoming overburdened with computational complexity? These are all open questions in ABM research.

Before we leave the topic of participatory simulations, we present an example of how to build one with HubNet.

Creating a HubNet Model   In HubNet models, there is a single, central computer that acts as the host for the Participatory Simulation and runs the NetLogo model. Often this computer is connected to a projector so that the display of the host can be viewed and discussed in common. The participants connect as "clients" to the host computer, using the HubNet Client application. In this example we will describe how to build and test a simple HubNet model. Several other, more elaborate examples can be found in the models library.

As you create your HubNet model, you may have an initial idea of the interface you would like the clients to see. You can design this interface from within NetLogo, using the HubNet Client Editor (under the Tools menu; see figure 8.3). For our example, try adding two interface items: a View and a Button called "forward." (Optionally, you can

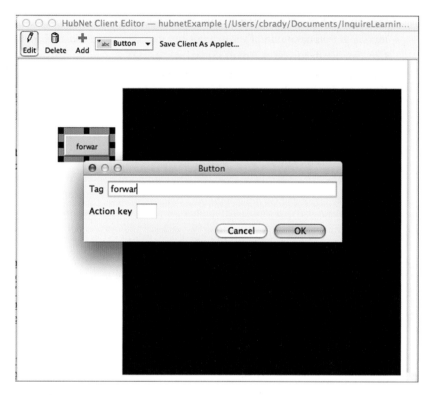

Figure 8.3
The HubNet Client Editor.

specify a "quick key" for the button, so that the client users can activate it through key presses.)

Now we need to see how to communicate with clients. The first thing to do is to create a SETUP procedure in your NetLogo model:

```
to setup
    clear-all
    hubnet-reset
end
```

The HUBNET-RESET command initializes the HubNet network, dropping communications with any clients that are attached. (The first time it is called, it also displays a dialog box that allows you to give the Host session a name that the clients will see. This is the name that participants will use to identify this activity.)

The HubNet Control Center opens when you start up the network using the HUBNET-RESET command, and offers the option to create a "local client"—a client that runs on the same computer as the host. This is a handy tool for testing or demonstrating a HubNet model. If you open one of these local clients, you should see a window appear that looks like the interface you designed. However, the View element will probably show up as a gray rectangle, because by default clients do not see the full view. To display the View from the Host model on the client, you need to select the option "Mirror 2D View on Clients" in the HubNet Control Center (see figure 8.4).

Once you have selected that option, you should be able to see any changes in the view on the screen of the local clients (see figure 8.5). For example, if you go to the host's command center and type the command:

```
ask patches [ set pcolor one-of base-colors ]
```

You will see that the view on the local client is the same as that of the host. This is our first communication from the host to the client (see figure 8.6).

Now let's see how clients can communicate to the host. The LISTEN-CLIENTS procedure shown below provides logic to handle client communications. We will discuss several key concepts that will help to illuminate this code.

```
to listen-clients
    while [ hubnet-message-waiting? ] [
        hubnet-fetch-message
        ifelse hubnet-enter-message? [
            print (word "Client with id: " hubnet-message-source " entered")
        ]
        [
            ifelse hubnet-exit-message? [
                print (word "Client with id: " hubnet-message-source " exited")
            ]
            [
                print (word "Message from: " hubnet-message-source ":")
                print (word " message tag: " hubnet-message-tag )
                print (word " message body: " hubnet-message )
            ]
        ]
    ]
end
```

The first of the concepts that helps illustrate this code is the idea of a message queue. Whenever the user of a connected client interacts with the interface, a message is sent to the host. These messages accumulate in a queue, and they remain there until processed.

The reporter, HUBNET-MESSAGE-WAITING? in the first line of the listen-clients procedure, is a Boolean reporter that indicates whether there are any messages in queue. If there are messages in the queue, the command in the next line, HUBNET-FETCH-MESSAGE takes the first message in the queue and makes it available for processing.

A

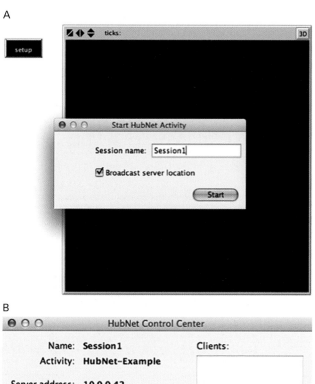

B

Figure 8.4
Starting a HubNet session.

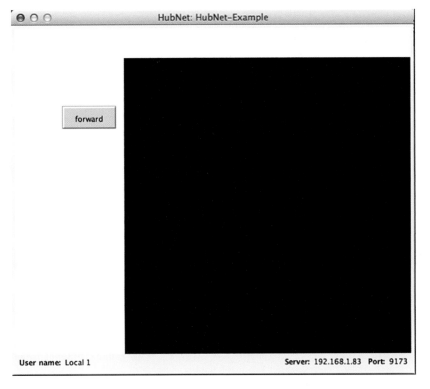

Figure 8.5
A local HubNet client.

Whenever this is called, the first message of the queue is removed from the queue and the contents of the message are made accessible through three reporters:

- HUBNET-MESSAGE-SOURCE, which reports the network id of the client
- HUBNET-MESSAGE-TAG, which reports a string indicating the interface element on the client that emitted the message, and
- HUBNET-MESSAGE, which contains the body of the message (or the value "false" if the message has no body).

The same HubNet message stays in focus until the command HUBNET-FETCH-MESSAGE is called again. Thus, if you need to refer to the in-focus message multiple times, you can do so simply by repeatedly calling these reporters.

Once you have entered the LISTEN-CLIENTS procedure, you can create a forever button to run it. Then, when you interact with the client interface in your local client, you can see the results in the Command Center on the host. Notice that when you press the "forward" button, you receive a message with the tag "forward" and an empty body

Figure 8.6
The HubNet host communicating to the HubNet client.

(FALSE). And when you click in the View, you receive two messages: a first message with tag "View" when you press the mouse button down, and a second message with tag "Mouse Up" when you release the mouse. In both cases, these messages have bodies that are two-element lists, indicating the patch coordinates of the mouse action.

With these message-handling functions, your NetLogo model can receive notice of all client user interactions and respond accordingly. In addition to this "upstream" client-to-host data flow, there are three additional basic concepts to understand about HubNet:

1. The mapping of clients to turtles, common to many HubNet Participatory Simulations.
2. The methods for programmatically sending information from the Host to the clients.
3. The methods for customizing the view that clients see, so that it can be different from the host display.

In many participatory simulations, each client is associated with an individual turtle. This is typically achieved through logic that is activated in response to the HUBNET-ENTER-MESSAGE and HUBNET-EXIT-MESSAGE commands. In the LISTEN-CLIENTS code, you could respond to a client entering by creating a turtle and assigning the value HUB-NET-MESSAGE-SOURCE to a turtles-own variable: "USER-ID," for example. Then, you could respond to a HUBNET-EXIT-MESSAGE with code such as:

```
ask turtleswith [ user-id = hubnet-message-source ] [ die ]
```

This line would identify the turtle associated with the client that is leaving the simulation, and ask it to die.

Once we have a turtle in the Host world associated with the client, then we can interpret client interactions as instructions to control the associated turtle. For example, we could interpret the forward button as an instruction to the turtle to move forward, and a click in the View as an instruction to turn toward the point clicked. The code to achieve this would go in the block of code above where we have just printed the in-focus message values. Instead of those lines, we could write:

```
ask turtles with [ user-id = hubnet-message-source ]
[
    if hubnet-message-tag = "forward" [ forward 1 ]
    if hubnet-message-tag = "View" [
        facexy (item 0 hubnet-message) (item 1 hubnet-message)
    ]
]
```

The second important idea is how to send information back to clients. In our example, suppose we wished to send the clients an indication of their current patch coordinates. We could do so by adding a *monitor* interface element to the HubNet Client Interface. Try this, and call the monitor "location." (Note: you must run HUBNET-RESET for the changes you make to the Client interface to get sent to new clients. You can do this by running your SETUP procedure.) Now, the only times that the turtle's location needs to be updated are (1) when it is created, and (2) when the client user presses the "forward" button.

Using ABM for Communication, Persuasion, and Education

We have been proceeding throughout this textbook as if a scientist or researcher is using an agent-based model to gain insight into the way the world works. However, ABM can be very useful in contexts other than scientific research. It can be used to communicate ideas to people who might not be able to understand those same ideas when conveyed in other forms. It can also be used to persuade or to convince individuals of a result that might run counter to their intuitions or prior beliefs. As we discussed in chapter 0, ABM can be profoundly useful in the educational process of restructurating "difficult material" to make it more accessible to much larger (and younger) audiences. This greater accessibility can have dramatic consequences for learning (Wilensky & Papert, 2010). Here we discuss each of these additional uses of ABM.

Communication The study of complex systems can require knowledge from many different subject areas and perspectives. When individuals come in to a group setting with different backgrounds and conceptualizations about the way the world works, it can be difficult for them to communicate. For instance, say a group of individuals is interested in understanding how population growth will affect a city and its services over the next fifty years. Some of these individuals may be academics interested in this topic for purely research reasons; some of these individuals may be private citizens concerned with how the city will change as a result of population trends; and other individuals may be urban planners and city officials who are trying to figure out where they need to spend money to best anticipate the future needs of the city. All of these individuals, or stakeholders, have different backgrounds, desires, and understandings of the problem at hand, which poses a challenge to finding a shared language and understanding.

ABM provides one solution to this problem. If all the individuals involved work together to develop an agent-based model, then the model becomes a touchstone of communication. It becomes, in the words of Seymour Papert, "an object to think with"—a shared focal object that they can discuss and analyze. Moreover, using a language like NetLogo, which is similar to natural language and thus can be more easily "read," makes it simpler for the stakeholders to examine how the model is implemented and what assumptions it makes. With minimal training, they can learn to tweak the assumptions themselves. This provides for a whole new method of communication, as the stakeholders involved can use the model to codify their knowledge of the situation and subsequently use the elements of the model to explain their vision and analysis. Although a nice graphical user interface (GUI) is not required to create an ABM, it is very useful for communication. It allows stakeholders to see agents "moving" around the world and making decisions, and enables them to quickly grasp the crux of the model.

Persuasion A common form of communication is persuasion. For example, the stakeholders involved in the city model described earlier may not just be interested in communicating their ideas to the other individuals involved, they may instead want to persuade the other stakeholders to accept a particular point of view.

For instance, let us assume that a model of population growth and its effect on the city has been created, which the stakeholders have named CitySim. Now, imagine that one of the urban planners for the city wants to implement a zoning ordinance that would place a minimum lot size on any new residential development. They hope that by requiring each household to take up a minimum amount of space on the landscape, they will prevent large subdivision-based tract development, thus limiting overall population growth within the city. One of the researchers claims that this may be true, but that the zoning policy will ultimately force the same population density to other outlying areas, creating longer commute times for individuals working in the city. This will, in turn, increase the cost of road maintenance and infrastructure support for the city, so that the zoning policy may have unexpected consequences.

In a traditional debate, this discussion would take place without any shared objects and, consequently, may render it hard for the academic researcher and the urban planner to reach a mutual understanding of each other's assumptions and inferences. However, given that they both have access to the model CitySim, they can both (either by themselves or through a developer) implement their particular assumptions and understanding of how individuals will respond to local conditions, run the model to see what effect their respective policies would have, and use the results of the model to persuade each other of the validity of their assumptions and beliefs.

This is a good example of using ABM for what Holland called a "policy flight simulator" (1996). An ABM may not necessarily be predictive of real-world results, but it can be predictive in the same sense as a flight simulator. A flight simulator enables a would-be pilot to understand the possible ramifications of his/her actions, and to try out different ways of flying. There is no guarantee that if a pilot takes the exact same actions while flying a plane that she or he did while in the flight simulator, the results will be the same. Similarly, the model of city growth enables the stakeholders to see possible outcomes of their policies, but there is no guarantee that these policies would turn out the same way in the real world. Nonetheless, in both cases, we gain a deeper understanding of the possible ramifications of our actions through interacting with the model.

Education   ABM also provides a new way of approaching education. ABM has already been used to educate K-12 and undergraduate students in a wide range of subjects such as chemistry (Levy & Wilensky, 2009; Stieff & Wilensky, 2003), materials science (Blikstein & Wilensky, 2006, 2009), psychology (Smith & Conrey, 2007), biology (Grimm et al., 2006 Wilensky & Reisman, 2006), geoscience (Brown et al., 2005), electromagnetism (Sengupta & Wilensky, 2008, 2009), statistical mechanics (Wilensky, 2003), economics (Epstein & Axtell, 1996; LeBaron & Tesfatsion, 2008), anthropology (Dean et al., 2000), sociology (Macy & Willer, 2002), marketing (Rand & Rust, 2011), medicine (An & Wilensky, 2009), and evolution (Centola et al., 2000; Wilensky & Novak, 2010). Because educational use is a central goal in the design of NetLogo, there are several curricular packages included as part of the NetLogo models library that enable individuals to explore these subjects in-depth. By allowing students to take the point of view of individual atoms, electrons, species, traders, or organizations and experiment with how interactions of these individuals aggregate into systemwide patterns, students are able to learn more complex subjects at a much earlier age.

One of the significant events in ABM educational research was the realization by Wilensky and Resnick (1999) that ABM had particular "learnability" properties that made it much easier for most people to learn. This work, carried on by several researchers over the past two decades, has generated strong evidence that it is easier for students (across all age groups) to work up from the rules governing a single agent in understanding a system composed of many such agents than it is to start with an aggregate description of the system (such as an equation) and break it down into the behavior of its constituent parts (Abrahamson & Wilensky, 2004; Blikstein & Wilensky, 2006; Klopfer, 2003; Levy & Wilensky, 2009; Resnick, 1994b; Wilensky, 1999b, 2003; Wilensky & Resnick, 1999). For instance, to study the behavior of a chemical reaction, a student using agent-based modeling would start by observing and articulating the behavior of individual molecules—that is, the chemical reaction as construed from the emergence of myriad interactions between these molecular "agents." Once the student-modeler understands the agents' local, "micro" rules, she or he can set them into motion and watch the overall patterns that emerge. Behaviors of individual atoms, molecules, or animals are more intuitive and easier to understand than the corresponding macrobehaviors of chemical reactions, flocks of birds, or whole populations. Microbehaviors, in general, are simpler to understand than the macrobehaviors they generate, and microbehaviors can be simulated to produce macrobehavior that can then be observed. In this way, ABM enables learners to deeply understand and work with scientific phenomena without using advanced mathematical machinery or possessing great mathematical sophistication. Such mathematical sophistication has served as a gatekeeper barring large numbers of students from access to these ideas; as such, ABM can greatly democratize access to these ideas.

Human, Embedded, and Virtual Agents through Mediation

So far, our discussion of ABM has been primarily about the use of virtual, computational agents. We briefly discussed the use of human agents in ABM earlier, but only in the context of observing human agents to understand how to create virtual agents from them. There is yet a third type of agent, sometimes known as a robotic agent, a physical agent, or an embedded agent—this is, an agent that is embedded in the physical world, gets data from that world, and can act in that world. From a certain point of view, human, embedded, and virtual agents can be treated equivalently. Each type of agent has properties (i.e., descriptions of itself and knowledge about the world) and methods (i.e., actions that it can take to achieve goals). Moreover, in all three cases, the agent—whether human, embedded, or virtual—examines the world around it and its own internal state to decide what action it should take on the basis of these inputs.

Each of these three systems presents its own challenges. For instance, with human agents, the logic that connects the input to the output may not be well known as it is internal to the human agent and people can act in unexpected ways. This makes it hard to uncover the agent rules. Still, confusion about the relationship between inputs and outputs is not limited to the human case. Robots can have noisy (inconsistent) sensors that affect their perception of the world around them. For example, a robot may have a bump detector to tell when it runs into something, but if that bump detector gets stuck for a few seconds, it may cause the robot to perceive incorrect information about its environment. Moreover, a robot's effectors or manipulators may not always be working perfectly. For instance, even if a robot has computed an exact route through a room, its wheels may not turn precisely the amount needed due to unevenness in the flooring or in the turning of the motor. As we have described earlier in this book, there are many challenges to designing virtual agents correctly. Nonetheless, there are many reasons why you might want to combine these systems into one integrated platform.

Robotic and virtual agents working within a shared model can be very fruitful. Robotic agents can use virtual ones to plan out routes and simulate their movements ahead of time, which can be useful in cases where physical movement is risky or costly, such as the development of planetary rovers. However, the integration of virtual systems with robotic systems can also present researchers with many difficulties. How does one model the noisiness and inefficiency of the physical world within a virtual system so that virtual and robotic agents can remain in step with each other? How should virtual agents interpret data from a robotic agent?

Human agents differ from virtual agents in many of the same dimensions as the robotic agents we just discussed. Human also have "noisy sensors" and "fallible actuators." Moreover, from a virtual agent's standpoint, human agents present many problems. They can adapt to their surroundings in new and surprising ways—making them less predictable—and can be deliberately obstinate or malicious—attempting to confuse and take advantage of virtual agents. Notwithstanding, the integration of human and virtual agents within a shared model has a lot of potential. For instance, as we discussed earlier, a model developer can have humans play the role of agents, subsequently capturing and embedding their decisions into virtual agents and enabling a richer and more elaborate examination of the behaviors employed by humans. (For more information on work on virtual and human agents using the HubNet platform, see Abrahamson & Wilensky, 2004; Berland & Wilensky, 2006; Wilensky & Stroup, 2002). Alternatively, human agents could work together with virtual agents to accomplish some mutual goal. For example, in a simulation of a business environment, humans could place emphasis on trading different stocks while allowing the virtual agents to take care of the low-level planning. However, all of this requires the development of new protocols. For example, how does one automatically capture human decisions and embed them in agent-based rules? How can human agents express new beliefs, desires, and intentions to a virtual agent?

Of course, there has been substantial research in the past into human-computer interaction (Shneiderman & Plaisant, 2004; Card, Newell & Moran 1983; Dix et al., 2004) and robotic control. However, very little of this research has been within the context of agent-based modeling, and almost none of it has been in the context of humans, robots, and virtual agents inhabiting a shared model. Even in the preceding discussion, we have been discussing these relationships between human and virtual agents, and robotic and virtual agents, as separate entities, but all three types of agents can be combined together in interesting ways. Researchers are beginning to explore the combination of all of these agents within one integrated platform (Blikstein, Rand & Wilensky, 2007; Rand, Blikstein & Wilensky, 2008). One such unified conceptual framework is the HEV-M framework,

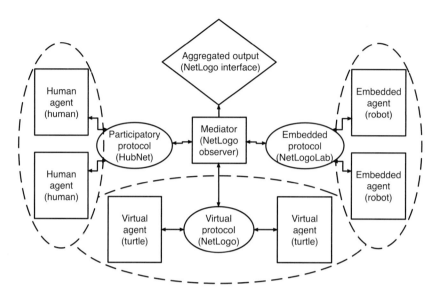

Figure 8.7
HEV-M Framework.

which stands for Human, Embedded and Virtual agents in Mediation. The HEV-M frame-work describes how to integrate human agents, embedded sensory-enabled robotic agents, and autonomous virtual agents, all of which communicate via a central mediator (see figure 8.7). The three different agent groups may have different goals, and even different tasks, but the mediator takes messages from any of the three groups of agents, transforms the messages, and relays the information to the other groups.

Let us explore how this framework might be useful through the use of three hypothetical examples: Widget Factory, Planetary Rover, and Demon Soccer. In Widget Factory, humans and virtual agents control simple machines that create parts of widgets. This environment shows how minor errors in the creation of the parts can dramatically alter the resultant outcome. In Planetary Rover, humans cooperate with virtual agents to control a robotic agent. The virtual agents utilize sensory data about their environment to make independent decisions. This environment can enable the exploration of collaborative human-robot protocols. In Demon Soccer, human agents interact with virtual agents to control a robotic soccer ball that has four wheels to control its movement. The human agents, who play on opposing teams, attempt to steer the soccer ball in to their opponent's goal. The four wheels are controlled by four different agents, two different humans, and two different hostile agents that either malignantly or randomly alter their speed and direction. This environment enables the exploration of mediation between hostile agents.

This HEV-M framework for agent integration is more than a hypothetical framework: it has been explored using NetLogo (see figure 8.7). In this prototype, NetLogo provides the infrastructure to control the virtual agents as well as the mediator, which is embodied by the NetLogo observer. The control of the robotic agents is handled by the GoGo extension (Blikstein & Wilensky, 2007), while the input of the human agents is handled by HubNet (Wilensky & Stroup, 2000). This system has been demonstrated through an example of human and virtual agents working together to guide a robotic agent through a maze (see figures 8.8, 8.9).

NetLogoLab: Connecting ABMs with the Physical World   The NetLogoLab environment provides the means to make a two-way connection between NetLogo and the physical world.[2] On one hand, a NetLogo model can take input from various kinds of sensors; on the other hand, you can connect hardware outputs such as buzzers, LEDs, motors, or servos to your model so that these devices will respond to features of the model as it runs. In general, this link between NetLogo ABMs and the physical world is mediated by a hardware device that can translate commands from NetLogo into signals to read sensors or control outputs. A variety of different kinds of devices can provide this interface to sensors and motors.

One such device is the GoGo Board.[3] Since the GoGo *extension* is bundled with NetLogo, you can interact with GoGo boards without installing any additional software. If you have access to a GoGo Board (see figure 8.10), connect it to your computer and open the GoGo Monitor model that is located in the Code Examples section of the NetLogo models library. Notice that the GoGo Board has dedicated ports for eight inputs (labeled 1–8) and for four outputs (labeled A–D). The GoGo extension provides NetLogo language primitives for communicating directly with these ports. To see how it works, if you have a GoGo board, connect a few sensors (such as a light sensor, a switch, or a pressure sensor) to the GoGo Board and connect the board to the computer, and examine how changing the sensor inputs affects the monitors and plots in the NetLogo interface. Open the monitors to see how the GoGo extension allows access to the current readings on the dedicated sensor ports. For instance, the reporter:

```
gogo:sensor 8
```

reports the raw resistance value that the GoGo Board detects on the port labeled 8. Translating this value into a meaningful reading depends on the characteristics of the sensor. For example, if a light sensor is attached to the board, you may want to know the

2. http://ccl.northwestern.edu/netlogolab (*Blikstein & Wilensky, 2005*).
3. See http://www.gogoboard.org (*Sipitakiat et al., 2004*).

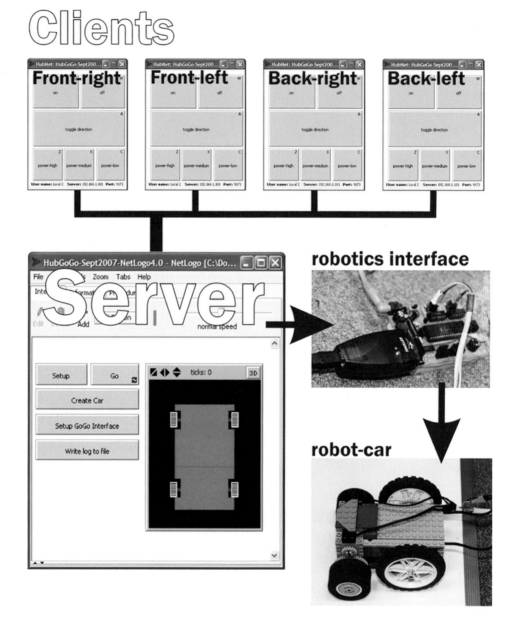

Figure 8.8
Diagram of the HEV-M system, with its three components: the client computers, the robot car, and the server.

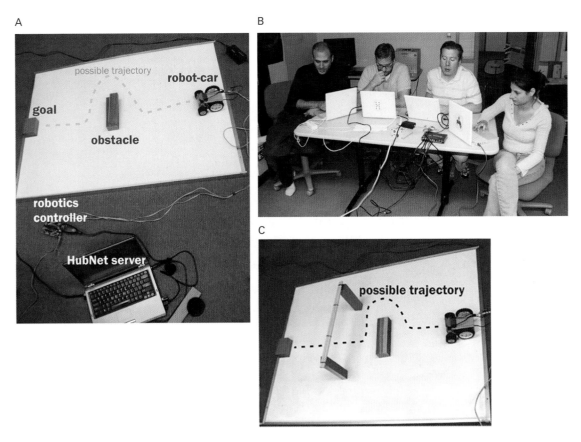

Figure 8.9
Clockwise from the left: Some participants using an implementation of the HEV-M Framework (Blikstein, Rand, & Wilensky, 2007).

translation of these resistance readings into lumens. You can determine a conversion formula by referring to the sensor's datasheet, and/or by matching the readings of your sensor with readings from another light sensor that has already been calibrated. The GoGo Board comes with a range of devices that act as sensors in this way and provide resistance that varies with: light intensity, pressure, temperature, magnetic field, rain (detecting the presence of water droplets), and soil humidity. In addition, switches can be considered as *binary* sensors of this kind, since they provide either "infinite" resistance (when the switch is open) or zero resistance (when the switch is closed).

To experiment with outputs, connect motors or LEDs to the output ports on the GoGo Board and control them using the interface in the GoGo Monitor model. Here again, the GoGo extension provides primitives for direct control of the output ports. For example, inspect the code for the button labeled "a-on" and you will see:

Figure 8.10
GoGo Board. Notice the output ports along the top and the input ports along the bottom of the board.

```
gogo:talk-to-output-ports [ "a" ]
gogo:output-port-on
```

The first line here sets the communications mode for the board; the second tells all addressed ports to supply power to attached output devices. The input for the first command can take a list of port names. Thus the commands

```
gogo:talk-to-output-ports [ "a" "c" ]
gogo:output-port-on
```

would turn on motors attached to *both* ports A and C at the same time.
   The command

```
gogo:set-output-port-power <number>
```

enables you to provide a variable power level to the output device, where <number> is a value between 0 and 7. Thus, the commands

```
gogo:talk-to-output-ports [ "d" ]
gogo:set-output-port-power 5
gogo:output-port-on
wait 10
gogo:output-port-off
```

would turn the output device connected to port D on at power-level 5, leave it running for ten seconds, and then turn it off.

Taken together, the NetLogo primitives for interacting through sensor inputs and motor outputs are the basic components you would need to enable NetLogo to control an embedded agent/robot using the GoGo Board.

Another popular interface device, the Arduino, can also be connected to NetLogo. As with the GoGo board, the Arduino extension (*Brady, 2013*) also comes bundled with NetLogo, allowing you to get started with ABMs and Arduinos easily as well.

The Arduino (see figure 8.11) offers a more flexible and configurable physical interface than the GoGo, in the sense that its ports (or "pins") are identified as *digital* or *analog*, but any of them may be configured for input *or* output. As we will see, this openness has some important advantages, but it also means that the Arduino requires a custom program, or "sketch," to run on the board for every new situation. Fortunately, the language in which these sketches are written, Wiring, is quite straightforward.

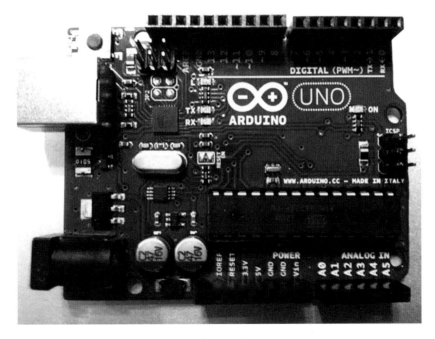

Figure 8.11
The Arduino.

To give a sense for the process of connecting the Arduino with a NetLogo ABM, we will go step by step through a very simple example. In it, we will use only the Arduino's onboard LED, located next to pin 13 (and connected to that pin). Our example will simply allow NetLogo to turn that LED on or off.

To write your Arduino sketch, you will need to use the Arduino IDE (Integrated Development Environment). This is a small download available from the Arduino site (http://www.arduino.cc). That site also has excellent "getting started" documentation.

The code for our Arduino sketch is shown below:

```
int ledPin = 13;

void setup()
{
    // start listening to the serial port at 9600 bps,
    // the baud rate expected by NetLogo's Arduino extension
    Serial.begin(9600);

    //set up the LED pin to act as an output
    pinMode(ledPin, OUTPUT);
}

void loop()
{
    // if we get a valid byte, turn the led on or off,
    // depending on the value
    if (Serial.available() > 0) {
        // actually read the incoming byte…
        int inByte = Serial.read();
        if (inByte == 0) {
            digitalWrite(ledPin, LOW);
        } else {
            digitalWrite(ledPin, HIGH);
        }
    }
    delay(100);
}
```

You will notice that there are two main procedures, called "setup()" and "loop()," along with one statement ("int ledPin = 13";), which is outside of any procedure. Setup and Loop are similar to the conventional "setup" and "go" procedures in many NetLogo models. When the Arduino receives power, it will first process the sketch, executing the variable assignment "int ledPin = 13"; It will then run setup() once. Finally, it will run loop() repeatedly, as fast as its processor allows and until it loses power or its Reset button is pressed.

To understand the sketch, let's go through it line by line. The line, "int ledPin = 13"; defines a global integer variable, ledPin, and assigns it the value 13. Then, in setup(), two things happen: First, the built-in Serial library is invoked and started. This opens a channel of communication between the computer and the Arduino over the USB cable. Next, the ledPin is put in output mode, since we are going to set that pin's state to turn the attached onboard LED on and off.

After setup() completes, the loop() procedure begins to run. Each time loop() is executed, we begin by checking to see if there are any bytes in the Serial communications buffer. (In fact, the available() function returns the *number* of bytes that are available for reading.) If no signal has come in from the computer, this value will be zero, and execution will pass to the delay() command at the bottom of the loop() procedure. So the code in the if-block executes only when a message arrives from the computer.

Within the if-block, the line "int inByte = Serial.read()"; actually reads the (first) available byte from the computer into a local integer variable inByte. Next, if that integer is a 0, we turn the LED off (by setting the digital pin to the constant value LOW). Otherwise, we turn the LED on (by setting the pin to the value HIGH).

Finally, after the if-block, we wait for 100 milliseconds (0.1 second) before running loop() again and checking for communications. (This delay statement is optional.)

Once you send this sketch to your Arduino board, it will be ready to receive signals from NetLogo automatically, whenever it gets plugged in.

On the NetLogo side, you can make a model that simply turns the LED on and off as follows:

In the Code tab, type the line:

```
extensions [ arduino ]
```

This will load the Arduino extension. Now we're ready to connect to the board and send messages to the code running in our sketch.

We'll make just three buttons on the Interface tab to do this test. First, to start communicating with the Arduino we need to establish a connection on a specific USB port. So, we'll make a button to ask the user to identify which USB port the Arduino is attached to. Make a button called "Open" with the following code:

```
let ports arduino:ports
ifelse (length ports > 0) [
    arduino:open user-one-of "Select a Port:" ports
]
[
    user-message "No available ports: Check your connections."
]
```

Here, the first line uses the Arduino extension to search for USB ports that might have an Arduino board attached. In many cases, the extension can narrow the options down to one;

in others, the user may have to choose the correct USB port from several options. In the next statement, if there are any candidate ports, NetLogo opens a user select dialog for the user to choose one. The command "arduino:open" attempts to establish communications with the device attached to the port that the user selects.

If everything is set up correctly and all the appropriate cables are plugged in, pressing this button puts us in a position to communicate with the board. Meanwhile, because the Arduino is plugged into the USB port, we know that the it is receiving power, so it must be executing its loop() procedure repeatedly and waiting for us to send it a byte.

The second button we create should turn the LED on. Make a button called "On" that has the following line of code:

```
arduino:write-byte 1
```

Finally, we need an "Off" button to turn the LED off. The code here should be:

```
arduino:write-byte 0
```

Test the buttons to make sure you can turn your LED on and off. If they are, then your Arduino connection is working appropriately.

Arduino boards do not all come in kits with a fixed set of sensors and motors. However, you can get inputs and outputs for your Arduino in many places. Moreover, the Arduino user community is extremely large and active, so if you find a sensor that you are interested in, chances are that either the manufacturer or someone from the community has created a sketch to interface with it.

For example, several manufacturers make low-cost ultrasonic distance sensor that are useful for many projects, and for most of these, sample sketches are available online. These devices work by sending a high-pitched signal and receiving the echo that returns from the first object in the signal's path. The logic to operate such a sensor requires a send/receive pattern and a high-precision chronometer.

Here is the heart of the loop() method in the example code available from the Arduino website itself:

```
pinMode(pingPin, OUTPUT);
digitalWrite(pingPin, LOW);
delayMicroseconds(2);
digitalWrite(pingPin, HIGH);
delayMicroseconds(5);
digitalWrite(pingPin, LOW);
pinMode(pingPin, INPUT);
duration = pulseIn(pingPin, HIGH);
```

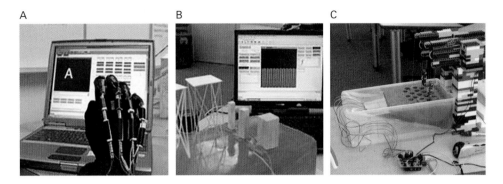

Figure 8.12
Bifocal models using GoGo Board with (A) an American Sign Language recognition glove, (B) models of earthquakes waves, and (C) Tsunami wave patterns.

Note that the pin wired to the signal line on the distance sensor (referenced by the pingPin variable) is switched rapidly between OUTPUT mode (to trigger the sensor) and INPUT mode (to retrieve the reading). Also, high time accuracy is necessary both to trigger the sensor (sending a 5-microsecond HIGH reading) and then to interpret the reading (the pulseIn() command returns a duration in microseconds). This example of the distance sensor shows the value that can be gained from Arduino's configurable hardware and the need to write custom sketches to manage each configuration of inputs and outputs.

Using GoGo or Arduino boards, it is possible to conduct many different activities that combine ABM and physical data. One such activity is bifocal modeling (Blikstein & Wilensky, 2007), in which NetLogo receives real-time data from the physical world and the modeler is challenged to build (or calibrate) a model that matches the real data, thus offering a potential explanation for the observed phenomenon (see figures 8.12, 8.13).

Hybrid Computational Methods
ABM is one powerful tool in the complex systems toolkit, but there are many other tools that have also been developed to model situations all around us. There are situations where ABM would be even more powerful if we could combine it with some of these other tools. In this section, we will discuss combining ABM with two specific tools: system dynamics modeling and machine learning.

System Dynamics Modeling and ABM   System Dynamics Modeling (SDM) (Sterman, 2000) is a useful tool for modeling how the aggregate properties of complex systems change over time. It is very good at dealing with systems that have nonlinearities and feedbacks. It represents numeric states of the world through the use of *stocks* and changes in these states through the use of *flows*. This ontology makes SDM very useful for

A

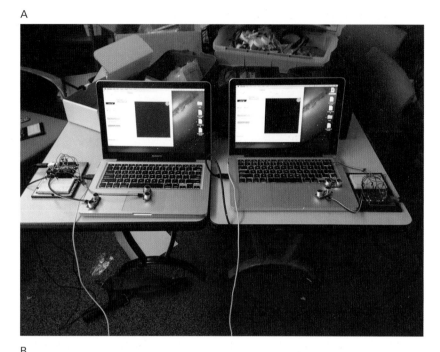

B

Bifocal electric current model

Figure 8.13
(A) Each NetLogo model is connected to two distance sensors through an Arduino. For each model, the distance sensors control the x-step and y-step sizes of each turtle. (B) An ultrasonic (distance) sensor connected to an Arduino board reports the distance of any object placed within a range (~90 inches) and thus detects the marbles rolling down the inclined plane.

describing phenomena that have continuous variables and continuous changes, such as the atmosphere, economic systems, and resource production.

As part of the NetLogo software package, there is a simple and easy-to-use System Dynamics Modeler included.[4] This tool, which provides functionality similar to many common system dynamics modeling toolkits such as STELLA (Richmond, Peterson & Vescuso, 1989), allows users to define the stocks and flows of their model graphically by pointing and clicking. While the SDM can be used by itself, similar to other SDM toolkits (for a quick example, see the Exponential and Logistic Growth models in the System Dynamics section of the NetLogo models library), its true power lies in its integration with the full NetLogo ABM environment, which allows for the model author to build models which use ABM and SDM either in parallel or in a more integrated manner.

One common way to use SDMs in an ABM environment is to simultaneously build both an ABM and an SDM model of a complex system and compare run results. One example of this is the Wolf-Sheep Predation Docked model (*Wilensky, 2005b*) in the System Dynamics section of the NetLogo models library (see figure 8.14). By allowing for the easy comparison of results between the two methods, this approach builds an understanding of when and how these two modeling techniques differ. In the Wolf Sheep Predation Docked model, the System Dynamic Modeler presents a representation of the Lotkba-Volterra equations (discussed in chapter 4), while the agent-based model similar to the one that we built in chapter 4 in the ABM side of NetLogo. These two models can either be started up separately with different parameters or initialized with the same parameters and run in lockstep, facilitating an examination and comparison of both models.

Besides using SDM and ABM in parallel, a model author can use SDM to model part of the system they are interested in examining and ABM to model another part of the system. If some portions of the complex system are more naturally understood using SDM, then it can be used to model those parts of the world, and vice versa for ABM. For an example of a hybrid model, look at the Tabonuco-Yagrumo Hybrid model in the System Dynamics section of the models library (see figure 8.15), which was inspired by the Journey to El Yunque project (http://www.elyunque.net/).[5] (There is also a simple Tabonuco-Yagrumo model that just uses the SDM.)[6] Tabonuco and Yagrumo are two varieties of trees that grow in the Caribbean islands and compete for resources. They both grow at different rates and have different resistances to the hurricanes that occur on a regular basis. In the hybrid model, the growth rates of individual trees, as well as the strength and frequency of hurricanes, are controlled by the SDM, but the ABM controls the location of the trees that are destroyed (by the hurricanes) and the new trees that

4. http://ccl.northwestern.edu/netlogo/docs/systemdynamics.html (*Wilensky & Maroulis, 2005*).
5. http://ccl.northwestern.edu/netlogo/models/TabonucoYagrumoHybrid (*Wilensky, 2006b*).
6. http://ccl.northwestern.edu/netlogo/models/TabonucoYagrumo (*Wilensky, 2006a*).

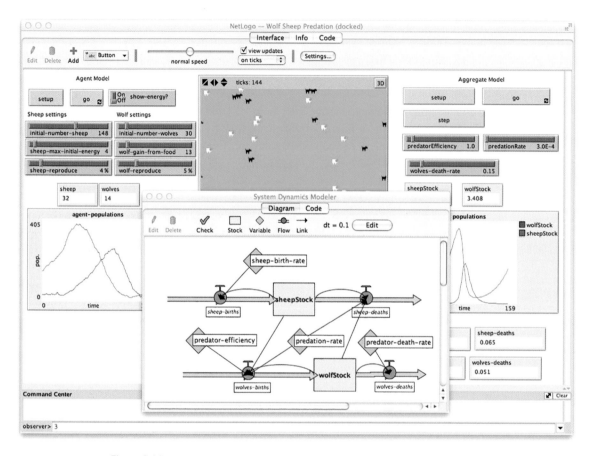

Figure 8.14
Wolf Sheep Predation Docked model. http://ccl.northwestern.edu/netlogo/models/WolfSheepPredation(docked)
(Wilensky, 2005).

are grown. This setup takes advantage of the respective power of both systems, since trees grow in a continuous (nondiscrete) fashion, while hurricanes, though individual events, tend to occur regularly. Thus, these two events should be modeled using the SDM, while the particular locations of new trees and those trees that are destroyed are much more discrete events, better suited to ABM. By choosing the correct modeling technique for the appropriate part of a complex system of interest, we can build more elaborate, interesting models of the world around us.

Machine Learning and ABM   We already discussed some of the reasons why you might integrate ABM and Machine Learning (ML) in chapter 5 when we talked about using adaptive agents in ABM. However, we never really discussed how these two systems

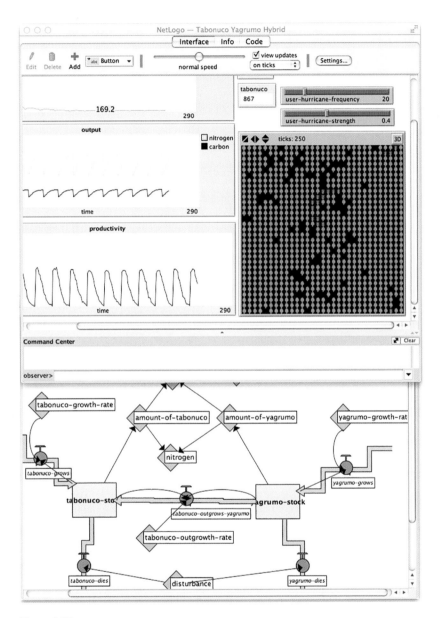

Figure 8.15
Tabonuco-Yagrumo Hybrid model.

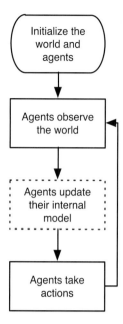

Figure 8.16
The ABM cycle.

could be integrated. At a high level, ABM and ML both utilize fairly simple algorithmic structures to control their flow of operation by (a) initializing the system, (b) observing what is happening, (c) refining the system, (d) taking actions, and (e) repeating as needed. To give this high level description more context, let us examine three cycles: the *ABM cycle*, the *ML cycle*, and finally, the *integrated cycle* (Rand, 2006). The ABM cycle can be broken down into three steps: (1) the world and a population of agents are initialized, (2) each agent observes its world, and (3) each agent takes an action based on the current observations, with the model repeating by going back to (2). This cycle becomes an *adaptive* agent-based model if we incorporate a fourth step between (2) and (3), where each agent updates their internal model of the world and decides what action to perform based on that internal model. The adaptive ABM cycle is illustrated in figure 8.16.

   The second distinct cycle, shown in figure 8.17, is the machine-learning cycle as exemplified by an agent updating in an online environment. The machine-learning cycle can also be broken down into four steps: (1) create an initial internal model, (2) observe the world and take note of rewards received, (3) update the internal model, (4) take an action based on the internal model and the current observations, and (5) go back to (2) and repeat.

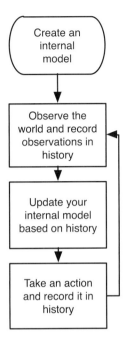

Figure 8.17
The machine-learning cycle.

As you can see, the two cycles are quite similar to each other, which facilitates the integration of the two frameworks. However, this integration process can be practically accomplished in a number of different ways. Here, we have chosen to explore the use of the ML cycle as a model refinement engine for the ABM. Thus, the integrated cycle focuses on the ABM and interrupts its standard flow in step three by sending data to the ML cycle to handle the model refinement. This is illustrated in figure 8.18.

One of the most interesting possibilities for the integration of these two techniques is the use of evolutionary computation with ABM. Evolutionary computation (EC) and ABM both involve populations of agents. EC is a learning technique by which a population of agents (commonly called individuals) adapts according to the selection pressures exerted by an environment (Ashlock, 2006). A typical use case for EC starts with a design problem, such as designing a bumper for a car. An EC algorithm will then generate a group of random solutions (individuals) to the problem. Based on a fitness function specified by the designer, the EC algorithm will give a fitness value to each individual in the population. The individuals with higher fitness are probabilistically more likely to be selected for reproduction. These individuals are then mutated, recombined, and copied into the next generation; the process is then repeated. Thus, EC can be viewed as a

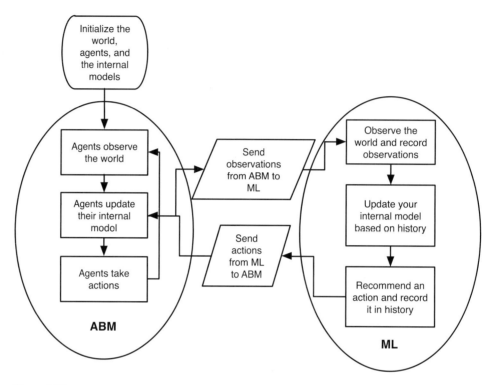

Figure 8.18
The integrated (ABM and ML) cycle.

process by which a virtual population changes in reaction to a selection pressure. ABM, on the other hand, seeks to understand how to coordinate the actions of a population of (possibly selfish) autonomous agents that share an environment insofar as some outcome is achieved.

In certain respects EC and ABM can be analogous. ABM addresses the bottom-up issue of how collective behavior emerges from individual actions, much like how low-level individual behaviors in EC create an overall population structure. Similarly, EC addresses the issue of how selective pressure drives the evolution of individual behavior. Thus, the methods used in EC and ABM can be viewed as natural counterparts, and it is not unusual to make use of the knowledge gained within one area while examining the other. Indeed, techniques from EC have often been embedded in ABM, and vice versa. For example, we can use EC to optimize the parameter settings for a particular ABM (e.g., Stonedahl, Rand & Wilensky, 2010), or we can also use EC techniques inside individual agents in an ABM to allow those agents to adapt to their environment. As a result, studying these two sets of methodologies in tandem is useful and has the potential to contribute to both fields.

Some Advanced Computational Methods in NetLogo

While this textbook is not meant as a NetLogo instructional manual, there are a few advanced computational methods in NetLogo that are useful in ABM and merit discussion here. Some of these methods are also supported by other languages and toolkits, while others relate to the particular nature of NetLogo as an outgrowth of Logo and Lisp. Specifically, these methods and associated NetLogo primitives enable you to run a piece of code on a number of different objects (MAP, REDUCE, and FILTER), create new code that was not specifically written beforehand to run during the execution of the model (RUN and RUNRESULT), or to pass code around in the same manner as values (TASK).

Higher-Order Operators: MAP/REDUCE/FILTER   The MAP, REDUCE, and FILTER primitives are often referred to as higher order operators. MAP takes a reporter and a list and applies that reporter to all of the elements of the list, outputting the resulting list. In other words, it "maps" the values of the list to a new set of values via the reporter. MAP is often useful in ABM when you have long lists of properties of agents that you want to change in some uniform way. For instance, if you are working with a model of income distribution, you may want to convert from dollars to thousands of dollars in order to make a display easier to read. To carry this out, you could use this code:

```
observer> show map [round (? / 1000) ] [34678 125000 75890 25000 35123]
observer: [35 125 76 25 35]
```

In this code, we also use the special ? variable (first introduced in chapter 5), which takes the values of each of the items in the list as we iterate over the list. MAP also works on multiple lists. For instance, if we wanted to take the income list we were working with earlier and divide by the cost of living in each area where the agent was working (which is stored in a second list) along with scaling it down by a factor of 1,000, we could use the following code:

```
observer> show (map [round ((?1 / ?2) / 1000)] [34678 125000 75890 25000 35123]
[1.0 1.2 1.4 0.9 1.0])
observer: [35 104 54 28]
```

In this code, we have to put parentheses around MAP and its inputs so that NetLogo can handle the multiple lists. We also use ?1 to refer to the current item in the first list and ?2 to refer to the current item in the second list. The code takes each income in the first list and divides by a cost-of-living index in the second list. It then divides that result by 1,000 and rounds to the nearest integer.

FILTER is much like MAP in that it applies a reporter to a list. Filter reports a list containing only those items of list for which the task reports true—in other words, the items satisfying the given condition.

```
observer> show filter is-number? [1 "5" 8]
observer: [1 9]

observer> show filter [? < 5] [1 5 4]
observer: [1 4]
```

REDUCE is useful for combining the items of a list together in some way. It is similar to MAP in that it applies a reporter to each element of a list, but instead of calculating each element of the list independently, it uses the result of each calculation as one of the inputs for the next. REDUCE progresses through the list from left to right cumulatively running the provided reporter. The final output is a single value. In this way, it reduces the list it is given down into a single value based on the reporter it was given.

Similar to MAP, REDUCE is useful because we often wind up working with long lists of agent values in ABM. For instance, we can take the output values we got from our above call to MAP and then use REDUCE to generate the average wealth of the population in thousands:

```
observer> show (reduce [?1 + ?2] [35 104 54 28 35]) / 5
observer: 51.2
```

REDUCE applies the [?1 + ?2] task to 35 and 104 which returns 139. This output from the first call becomes the first argument for the next calculation, so the second execution of the [?1 + ?2] reporters takes in 139 and 54 and returns 193. This patterns repeats as it progresses through the list, so the next calculation is 193 + 28, then finally calculating 221 + 35 to ultimately return 256. The last step is to divide the result by five (the number of incomes we are examining), which gives us the average income of the group.

Because the REDUCE function requires exactly two inputs, NetLogo also allows you to use shortcuts for tasks, so that the above code can be shortened to:

```
observer> show (reduce + [35 104 54 28 35]) / 5
observer: 51.2
```

This is not a particularly powerful use of REDUCE, as we could also have done this by using the SUM function:

```
observer> show sum [35 104 54 28 35] / 5
observer: 51.2
```

A better example of the unique power of REDUCE involves finding the number of occurrences of an item in a list. For instance, say we wanted to discover the number of people who made roughly $35,000. We could use the following code:

```
observer> show reduce [ifelse-value (?2 = 35) [?1 + 1] [?1]] [0 35 104 54 28 35]
observer: 2
```

As we have seen, the REDUCE operator applies a reporter to a list. The reporter in this case is [ifelse-value (?2 = 35) [?1 + 1] [?1]]. IFELSE-VALUE is a primitive that evaluates the first argument, which must be a Boolean reporter, in this case (?2 = 35). If it is true, then it reports the second argument, in this case, (?1 + 1); otherwise, it reports the third argument, (?1). The list we want to examine is [35 104 54 28 35]. In order to use REDUCE with this task on the list, we have to prepend a 0 to the list. This first element 0 is a counter that represents the number of occurrences of 35 counted so far. As this code processes each element in the list, it examines if the new element (?2) is 35. If it is, it adds 1 to the first element (the counter) and moves on to the next element in the list. If it is not 35, it then keeps the previous counter and uses it in the next comparison. So, for the first comparison, ?1 would be 0 and ?2 would be 35. That means the Boolean (?2 = 35) is true, so the reporter reports [?1 + 1], which is 1. In the next comparison, ?1 would be 1 and ?2 would be 104, so the Boolean is false and the reporter reports [?1], which is 1. This pattern continues until the last element of the list, which is 35, and add one more to the counter, with the final value of the REDUCE being 2. As REDUCE progresses through the list, the counter is preserved by always being the valued captured in the ?1 variable.

RUN/RUNRESULT   The RUN primitive takes a string of commands as input (such as " fd 10 rt 90") and runs the commands. RUNRESULT takes a reporter in the form of a string as input (such as "heading") and reports the result of running the reporter. Both RUN and RUNRESULT can also take TASKS, which we will describe next. The strings that are input to RUN and RUNRESULT can be created during the runtime of the model, and thus do not need to be compiled ahead of time. This is a very powerful formulation, because it means that the agents in the model can actually create the code that they themselves will be running during the model execution. For instance, imagine you are building a group of robotic agents, each of which is trying to run a maze. You could develop a set of commands, such as "MOVE-NORTH, MOVE-WEST, MOVE-SOUTH, MOVE-EAST," and then have the agents actually create new lists over time to evolve better strategies for solving the maze. One way of starting to code this idea might look like this:

```
turtles-own [ strategy ]
globals [ commands ]

to setup
    ca
    set commands ["BK 1" "LT 90" "RT 90" "FD 1"]
    crt 100 [
        pen-down
        set heading 0
        set strategy n-values 5 [ one-of commands ]
    ]
end

to go
    ask turtles [
        foreach strategy [ run ?1 ]
    ]
end
```

In this code, each turtle is given a list of five commands from the commands list. When it comes time to execute the code, this list is iterated over and each command is run. The exact commands given to each turtle are not decided until runtime, and for the most part, each turtle will have a unique set of commands.

RUNRESULT is similar to RUN, except that it takes a reporter and reports its result. For instance, if we wanted something similar to what we had above but also wanted the turtles to be able to choose headings based on their locations and other factors, we can use RUNRESULT:

```
turtles-own [ strategy ]

to setup
    clear-all
    let operators [" + " " - " " * " ]
    let inputs ["heading" "xcor" 1 2 10]

    crt 20 [
        pen-down
        set strategy ""
        repeat 5 [ set strategy (word strategy one-of inputs one-of operators) ]
        set strategy word strategy one-of inputs
    ]
    reset-ticks
end

to go
    ask turtles [
        set heading runresult strategy
        fd 1
    ]
    tick
end
```

The heart of this code is the part of SETUP that creates the strategy. This strategy is a string that is composed of series of inputs (HEADING, XCOR, 1, 2, and 10) followed by operators (+, –, *). The string starts with an input followed by an operator and ends with an input; in between, it has four pairs of inputs and operators. For example, a strategy could be the string "heading · 10 + 1 –2 –xcor · 2." Division is not included as an operator in order to avoid division by zero, which would cause the program to break.[7] In the GO procedure, each turtle's strategy is run, with RUNRESULT used to generate the heading for the turtle on the basis of its strategy. Finally, the turtle takes a step in the direction of this new heading. For example, if a turtle's strategy was the string "1 – 1 + 2 + 2 + heading · 2," then RUNRESULT would operate on that string performing the operations in it. That is, first, it would subtract 1 from 1, getting zero; second, it would add 2 twice to get 4; last, it would obtain the turtle's heading, multiply it by 2, and add that to the total. So, if the turtle's heading was 10, then it would add 14 to our total, getting 24, such that the GO procedure would result in that turtle setting its heading to 24 and moving forward 1.

A Simple Machine-Learning Example: Using Evolutionary Algorithms   This model that we have just created is useful for illustrating the machine-learning framework discussed in the previous section. In the RUNRESULT example model, the agents move randomly using the strategy that they had selected. However, what if we wanted them to move with a purpose, that is, to achieve some sort of goal? We could then use machine learning to automatically learn a strategy that would help achieve this goal.

In the framework we described in the previous section on machine learning, the internal model of the agents is the strategy highlighted in the RUNRESULT example, but the actual model of the interaction with the world is not clear. What do we want the agents to achieve in this world? Let us start with a simple task. Imagine that we want the agents to move to the upper right corner of the world in less than twenty ticks. We will start with some turtles with random strategies and see if they can learn strategies that are effective at accomplishing this task.

The first thing we will want to do is write a quick function to determine the "fitness" of a "solution" —that is, of a turtle's position after twenty ticks. A fitness function, or evaluation procedure, as it is sometimes called, is a method that can be used to determine how well a turtle did with respect to accomplishing its goal. In this example, our fitness function could be as simple as the straight-line distance from the turtle to the target patch after twenty ticks. First, we set up a global variable, goal, and initialize it to the upper-rightmost patch (PATCH MAX-PXCOR MAX-PYCOR). After this, we can write a fitness function procedure:

7. See the CAREFULLY primitive as a way of dealing with runtime errors.

```
        ;; turtle procedure
        ;; evaluate the fitness of a turtle as its distance from the upper-rightmost patch
        ;; this actually measures reverse fitness as the farther the turtle is from the
        ;; goal, the less it is fit.
to-report fitness
    report distance goal
end
```

The fitness reporter above is actually a reverse-fitness reporter—as the fitness reporter increases, the turtle is farther away from the goal, and thus less fit, meaning the lower the value returned from the reporter, the closer the agent is to achieving its goal.[8] Now we have a model as well as a fitness function. The next step is to build a machine-learning algorithm. This algorithm will take a population of solutions and improve the solutions until some criterion is met in terms of the performance of the system. In this case, we are going to use a variant on an evolutionary algorithm (Holland, 1994) that mimics natural evolutionary processes to improve the solutions. To do this, we are going to evaluate how well each turtle does at solving the problem. Then we are going to ask the 75 percent of the turtles that are the poorest performers to "die" and replace them with mutated versions of the best 25 percent. To introduce these "generations" of turtle strategies to our model, our GO procedure needs to change substantially.

```
to go
    clear-drawing    ;; clear the trails of the killed turtles
    ask turtles [
        reset-positions ;; send all the turtles back to the center of the world
    ]
    ask turtles [
;; each turtle runs its strategy and moves forward 25 times
        repeat 25 [
            set heading runresult strategy
            fd 1
            ;; set the turtle's label to show its fitness
            set label precision fitness self 2 ;; visualize the fitness of each turtle
        ]
    ]
    ;; replace 75% of the turtles
    let number-to-replace round 0.75 * count turtles
;; replace the turtles with maximum fitness which is really minimum fitness
    ask max-n-of number-to-replace turtles [ fitness] [
        die
    ]
;; need "let" so that best-turtles is not the special turtles agentset
;; and would expand
    let best-turtles turtle-set turtles
    repeat number-to-replace [
```

---

8. We could easily invert the fitness by multiplying by −1.

```
;; ask one of the turtles to hatch a new turtle with a mutated strategy
      ask one-of best-turtles [
          hatch 1 [
              set strategy mutate strategy
              set color one-of base-colors
          ]
      ]
    ]
    tick
end

;; turtle procedure, set position to origin with random heading
to reset-positions
    home
    set heading random 360
    pen-down  ;; put the pen down to draw the turtle's movement
end
```

This code can be made to work, but it is has a problem: in order to mutate the strategy, the mutate procedure must parse the strategy string, which requires some complex coding. To make the mutate code simpler, it is useful to encode the strategy as a list of strings, rather than as one single string:

```
to setup
    clear-all
    set operators ["+ " "- " "* " ] ;; set up the usable operators
    set inputs ["heading " "xcor " "1 " "2 " "10 "] ;; set up the usable inputs

    ;; create the first generation of turtles and have them put their pens down
    ;; so we can see them when they draw
    crt 20 [
        set strategy random-strategy
    ]

    ;; set the goal to the upper right corner
    set goal patch max-pxcor max-pycor
    reset-ticks
end

;; create a new strategy for how to set the heading for each turtle
to-report random-strategy
    let strat []
    ;; each strategy consists of 5 inputs and 4 operators alternating
    repeat 5 [ set strat (sentence strat one-of inputs one-of operators ) ]
    set strat sentence strat one-of inputs
    report strat
end
```

In this formulation, a strategy is not a single string, but rather, a list of strings such as ["10 " "+ " "xcor " "*" "1 " "*" "2 " "*" "2 " "+ " "10 "]. Note that the strings have a trailing space so that, when combined, they will form a well-formed expression. Though the format of the strategy is now quite different—the GO procedure only needs one line of modification—we use REDUCE to turn our new format string into an old format string to run. So, the GO procedure stays the same except that we replace

```
set heading runresult strategy
```

with

```
set heading runresult reduce word strategy
```

And the code for mutate is very simple:

```
;; mutate a strategy by replacing one of its inputs or one of its operators
to-report mutate [strat]
    ifelse random 2 = 0
    [set strat replace-item ( 2 * random 6) strat one-of inputs]
    [set strat replace-item (1 + 2 * random 5) strat one-of operators]
    report strat
end
```

The full version of this model is available in the IABM Textbook folder of the NetLogo models library under "Simple Machine Learning." This code accomplishes several things. First, it makes sure that the world has no drawings on it, moving the turtles to their initial positions at the center of the world. Then, it has each turtle run its own strategy twenty-five times, recording the fitness of its solution. After these observations have been recorded, the system updates its internal model by killing 75 percent of the lowest-performing turtles and replacing them with mutated versions of the best turtles. The mutation procedure takes a part of the agent's strategy, whether an input or an operator, and replaces it with a new part. The resultant new population can be considered the recommendation to the agent-based model of the best current solutions. The ABM is then run again, with the process repeating itself. (See figure 8.19.)

This model is a simplified version of a model invented and discussed by Melanie Mitchell in her book *Complexity: A Guided Tour* (2009) called "Robby the Robot." A version of Robby is in the Computer Science section of the NetLogo models library (*Mitchell, Tisue, & Wilensky, 2012*). If you are interested in the intersection of machine learning, agent-based modeling, and complex systems, then Robby is a good model to examine.

TASKS TASKS are NetLogo data structures that enable you to store code for later use. In other programming languages, tasks are known as first-class functions, closures, or

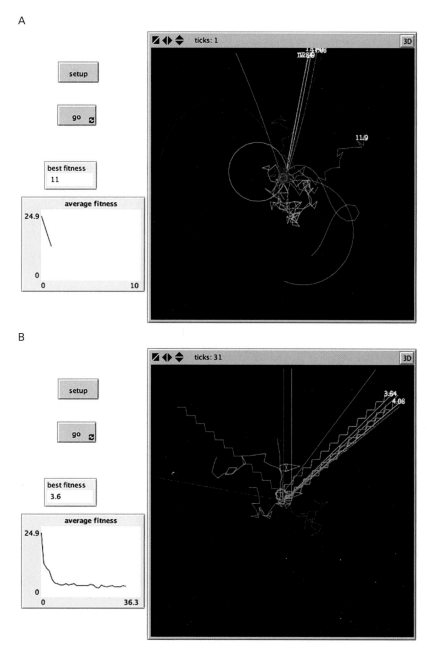

Figure 8.19
(A, B) Left: Results of first generation of solutions in Simple Machine Learning model. Right: Results after thirty generations of solutions in Simple Machine Learning model.

lambdas. Languages are said to have first-class functions if they treat functions in the same way that they treat other parts of the computer language, such as integers, characters, and strings. First-class functions can be passed to other functions and used as inputs to procedures. First-class functions are necessary for the functional programming style, wherein the use of higher-order procedures is standard.

The nice thing about tasks is that, though they are executable code, they are also values, which means that they can be passed around to other pieces of code. As we have seen, you can create code as strings and execute it on the fly with RUN or RUNRESULT. A great way to use tasks is to develop code that can take a number of different inputs—some of which are fixed values, and others, actually programmatically determined during runtime. For instance, in the Sandpile model in the IABM Textbook folder, the SETUP code is as follows:

```
to setup [initial-task]
    clear-all
    ask patches [
;; n is set to the result of running the initial-task (which is an input to the
;; setup procedure)
        set n runresult initial-task
        recolor
    ]
    set total sum [n] of patches
    reset-ticks
end
```

This code does the standard setup functions, such as clearing the world and resetting the tick counter, but, more importantly, sets a patch variable, *n*, on the basis of how this SETUP procedure was called. There are two procedures that invoke this SETUP procedure:

```
to setup-uniform [initial-value]
    setup task [initial-value]
end

 to setup-random
;; this creates a nameless procedure that when executed runs "random 4"
    setup task [random 4]
end
```

These two procedures allow the coder to use one version of the setup code to create two different setups. For instance, SETUP-UNIFORM 2 will create a world in which N for every patch is 2, while SETUP-RANDOM will set N to a number drawn from a random uniform distribution from 0 to 3. TASKS can be used (as is the case here) to modularize code and make it easier to read and verify. An additional benefit of this approach is that it will be much more efficient than passing in strings because TASKs are created as preassembled pieces of code. When RUN or RUNRESULT are given tasks as inputs, they can run *hundreds* of times faster than when they are given strings as inputs.

Extensions to ABM

NetLogo and many other ABM toolkits allow you to combine ABM with preexisting models, tools, and data sets. In this section, we will briefly discuss how this is done in NetLogo, although other ABM toolkits follow a similar model.

NetLogo provides two facilities to allow for this communication. The first is the NetLogo Extension API, which gives users the ability to write Java objects that can be accessed within NetLogo. The second is the NetLogo Controlling API, which enables users to control NetLogo from other applications using Java calls. These two APIs are the key to integrating NetLogo with other software packages. External data sources, formats, and tools are continuously being refined. An important feature of an agent-based modeling language and toolkit is extensibility, so that as these changes occur, they can be incorporated and integrated into the ABM toolkit.

As NetLogo has developed, extensions have been created to integrate NetLogo with a host of other capabilities. The extensions API provides a low-threshold way of accessing these powerful additional capabilities from within NetLogo. To keep the NetLogo language manageable, we chose not to integrate all of these extra capabilities into the core language, but instead made them available as optional extensions the modeler can choose to include if they are needed. A number of these extensions are bundled in with the NetLogo release, including extensions for dealing with arrays and matrices, for creating and analyzing networks, for accessing Geographic Information Systems data, for dealing with video and sound data, and for interfacing with physical devices and with the web. Many others are available for download from the NetLogo site, https://github.com/NetLogo/NetLogo/wiki/Extensions, including integration with advanced analysis tools (such as Mathematica), the operating system, advanced data storage, improved color capabilities, and interface to the popular Arduino hardware, among others. These extensions greatly enhance the capabilities of NetLogo. NetLogo extensions are open source and most are available on GitHub (https://github.com/NetLogo/), so users can add new capabilities to an extension.

Extensions can be added to a model by using the EXTENSIONS command in the very beginning of the NetLogo Code tab. Once the extension has been read in, the primitives contained in the extension can then be accessed by prefixing the primitive with the name of the extension. For instance, researchers have developed a GIS extension (Russell & Wilensky, 2008) that specifically facilitates the integration of GIS data into NetLogo both from standard GIS files, like GridASCII and Shapefiles, but also directly from specific GIS software, such as MyWorld (Edelson, 2004). This extension to NetLogo enables ABM developers to quickly access a large amount of publicly available GIS data. At the beginning of any NetLogo model that uses the GIS extension, you will find the following code:

```
extensions [ gis ]
```

Later in the code, you will set commands, such as GIS:SET-WORLD-ENVELOPE, by prefixing the command with the name of the extension, indicating to NetLogo that this command is part of the extension. We will explore the NetLogo GIS extension in more depth later in this chapter.

Integration of Advanced Data Sources and Output

There is a wealth of data and data sets available about groups of individuals. A common challenge facing modelers is how to make use of such data in their agent-based models. There have been many software packages that have already been created for advanced data analysis, and the examination of ABM could be facilitated if there was an easy way to export data from an ABM to these advanced packages. In this section, we will talk about connecting ABM to other input and output sources. We will discuss four types of connections in detail, though many more exist. These four types are Geographic Information Systems (GIS), Social Network Analysis (SNA) toolkits, physical sensor data, and advanced mathematical toolkits like Mathematica and MatLab.

Geographic Information Systems (GIS) Toolkits   In chapter 5, we described how GIS data can be imported into ABM toolkits using GridASCII data in the Grand Canyon model example. This enables model authors to make use of data from the physical world to initialize their model, thus grounding the model in a realistic environment. In chapter 6, in the Spread of Disease model, we went on to describe how sometimes, it can be useful to export data from an ABM toolkit back to a GIS package, such as ArcView, MyWorld, or OpenMap, so that many of the standard landscape metrics, such as mean patch size and edge ratio, can easily be calculated, with the results being used within the ABM.

However, so far, we have discussed only how this integration can be done via the passage of text files. A more sophisticated integration would allow for the ABM and GIS system to communicate at the same time while they are both running, passing information back and forth seamlessly. However, accomplishing this integration can be a difficult task, as ABM and GIS have different languages and use different data storage formats. Where ABM deals with agents, patches, properties, and methods, GIS deals with cells, layers, and transformations. Thus, the first step to integrating these two systems is to come up with a common language through which they can communicate about shared data (Brown et al., 2005).

NetLogo provides one way to do this using the GIS extension, which is included in the default NetLogo installation. The GIS extension gives NetLogo the capability of easily working with either vector or raster GIS data in NetLogo. Two code examples in the NetLogo models library that show how to do this, with the basic idea being that you first define a transformation of the coordinate space from the GIS data to the NetLogo world and then load the data. Once this has been done, you can then carry out basic GIS queries on the data. For instance, you can ask if one object contains another object, or if one object intersects another object. You can even manipulate the data in various ways, and then write it back out to a file for import in to a GIS analysis system.

To explore this in more detail, let us take a look at the GIS Ticket Sales example model in NetLogo. This example is from a marketing application and was partially inspired by a dissertation proposal and working papers on online ticket sales (Tseng, 2009). The general intent of this model is to simulate how individuals decide to buy tickets to a live event.

Most of the work of this model is contained in the setup example, a common feature of many GIS models. Establishing the correct coordinate system and reading in the data is important to get right in order to set up the relationship between the model world and the data contained in the GIS files. For instance, most of the GIS data is read in by the following procedure:

```
to setup-maps
    ;; load all of our datasets
    set nyc-roads-dataset gis:load-dataset "data/roads.shp"
    set nyc-tracts-dataset gis:load-dataset "data/tracts.shp"
    ;; set the world envelope to the union of all of our dataset's envelopes
    gis:set-world-envelope (gis:envelope-union-of (gis:envelope-of nyc-roads-dataset)
(gis:envelope-of nyc-tracts-dataset))
    set roads-displayed? false

    ;; display the roads
    display-roads

    ;; display the tract borders
    display-tracts

    ;; locate whether a patch intersects a tract, if it does assign it that tract
    foreach gis:feature-list-of nyc-tracts-dataset [
      ask patches gis:intersecting ? [
        set tract-id gis:property-value ? "STFID"
      ]
    ]

    ;; load the census data in to the patches
    load-patch-data
end
```

The first two commands use the command GIS:LOAD-DATASET to load the files for the roads and the census tracts for the model. These files are shapefiles, a GIS format that allows for the specification of points, lines, and polygons. Both of these files were obtained from the US Census Tiger website which provides a large amount of GIS data for free.[9] The command is also prefixed by "GIS," which, as mentioned, is NetLogo's way of denoting that the command is derived from an extension as opposed to being from the core NetLogo architecture.

The first step in using GIS data in an ABM involves relating the spatial boundaries of the GIS data to those of the model. Once this has been done, we can develop a mapping from the world of the model to the "real" GIS world, and vice versa. We do this by setting the world envelope (the largest space that contains all of the data which, in this case is defined to be the NetLogo world boundaries) via GIS:SET-WORLD-ENVELOPE to be the union (via GIS:UNION-OF) of the envelopes (via GIS:ENVELOPE-OF) of the underlying data files. In practice, this means that a model world's boundaries are set up such that they contain the full data contained in the GIS files. Of course, the underlying GIS data in this case (the data for Manhattan) is irregularly shaped, while the model world is a rectangle. As a result, NetLogo finds the minimal rectangle that will encapsulate the underlying irregular shape, which ultimately becomes the WORLD-ENVELOPE.

We then actually draw the lines contained in these shapefiles on the drawing layer using two other procedures, DISPLAY-ROADS and DISPLAY-TRACTS. DISPLAY-TRACTS shows how this is done:

```
to display-tracts

    ;; draw the census tracts in blue
    gis:set-drawing-color blue
    gis:draw nyc-tracts-dataset 1
end
```

GIS:SET-DRAWING-COLOR sets the pen used to draw the data in the drawing layer, while GIS:DRAW uses the data that has been read in and draws it at a thickness of one pixel.

If we go back to the SETUP-MAPS procedure, we can see that we loop through each feature in the census tracts data set—essentially, each and every census tract. We then ask patches that intersect with that tract to set their local variable TRACT-ID to the tract-id (under the heading STFID) of the tract.

The last call is to load the actual census data for the tracts. This data is located in a separate file, and is a flat text file, not GIS data. This file is scanned for each TRACT-ID,

---

9. http://www.census.gov/geo/www/tiger.

Figure 8.20
The results of one run of the Ticket Sales model.

Box 8.3
GIS Exploration

As we explored in chapter 6, one great example of how to use GIS data in an agent-based model is illustrated by the Grand Canyon model (Earth Science section) in the NetLogo models library. This model loads a digital elevation map (DEM) of the Grand Canyon and proceeds to explore where rain that falls on the Grand Canyon will drain toward—in particular, how it will collect in areas of low elevation. However, you could easily use this same data in another model. For instance, load the same elevation data into the Flocking model, and have the boids in the Flocking model move differently depending on their elevation.

while the number of households present in that tract is used to seed the model with the correct number of households.

After the GIS data has been imported, the model works just like any other NetLogo model. Each of the consumers decides at each time step whether or not to buy a ticket to the live event. Consumers' decisions are affected by the parameters of the model, such as their uncertainty of attending the event or how far they are from the event venue. However, in terms of the model, these decisions' outcomes do not utilize the GIS extension. (See figure 8.20 for a picture of the model at the end of the run.) In general, this dual method of using GIS data to initialize the model and the ABM power of NetLogo to execute the model is fairly typical among ABM-GIS integration, even as more sophisticated techniques can provide even more powerful explorations (Brown et al., 2005).[10]

If you want to explore additional uses of GIS data in NetLogo, there are a number of excellent resources including a book by Westerveldt and Cohen (2012) and example models created by Owen Densmore, Stephen Guerin, and their colleagues at the Redfish Group who have used NetLogo and GIS data to examine a number of interesting topics from Venetian boat traffic to Santa Fe traffic patterns to wildfire dynamics. For more information about their work, see www.redfish.com. (See figure 8.21.)

Social Network Analysis (SNA) Toolkits and the NetLogo Networks Extension   In chapters 5 and 6, we discussed the use of social networks in ABM. There are many large publicly available data sets of social networks available for use. The first step toward taking advantage of these large data sets in our own models is to import them. The Network Import Example in the Code Examples in the NetLogo models library provides an example of how to do this. The heart of this code example consists of the following lines:

10. http://ccl.northwestern.edu/netlogo/models/GrandCanyon (Wilensky, 2006c).

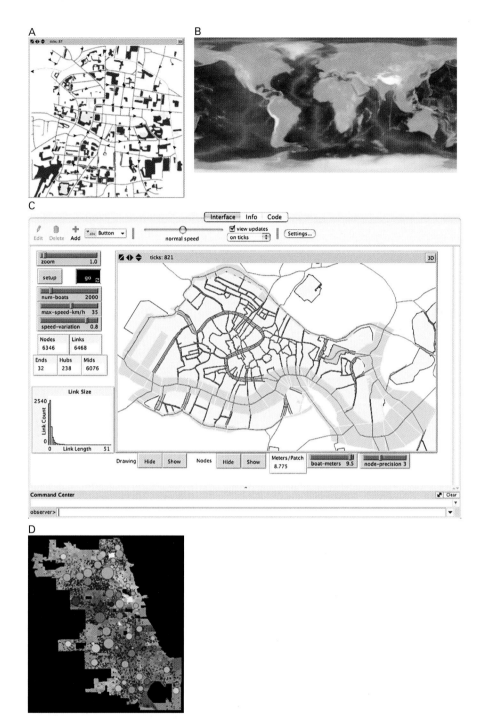

Figure 8.21
Examples of models using GIS data. (A) The Cruising model models cars driving in Santa Fe (*Densmore et al., 2004*). (B) The Climate Change Game model (Berland & Wilensky, 2006). (C) Venice model models boat traffic (*Densmore & Guerin, 2007*). (D) Chicago Public Schools model (Maroulis, Bakshy & Wilensky, 2007).

```
to import-links
    ;; This opens the file, so we can use it.
    file-open "links.txt11"
    ;; Read in all the data in the file
    while [not file-at-end?]
    [
        ;; this reads a single line into a three-item list
        let items read-from-string (word "[" file-read-line "]")
        ask get-node (item 0 items)
        [
            create-link-to get-node (item 1 items)
                [ set label item 2 items ]
        ]
    ]
    file-close
end
```

This code assumes that you have already created the nodes that will be linked together. In the code example, this is done in the IMPORT-ATTRIBUTES procedure. This code then starts by opening a file, and reading through that file line by line. Each line has three columns. The first column indicates the originating node of the link, the second column indicates the destination node, and the third column indicates the strength of the node. As each line is read, a link is created between the originating and destination nodes, and a label is set for each link equal to the weight. (See figure 8.22 for a picture of this model.) Here is the attribute file that we import:

1. 1.2 red
2. 1.0 blue
3. 1.5 yellow
4. 2 green
5. 1.8 orange
6. 1.4 red
7. 2 blue
8. 1.5 yellow
9. 1 green
10. 1.2 orange

This model could be expanded by adding new links, deleting old links, or changing the strength of existing links. As these properties change, and as the number of nodes becomes larger, it might be useful to analyze the results of this model in a SNA package like Pajek or UCINet. This can be done by exporting the network in a reverse pattern of the code above which reads it in. This data can then be analyzed in one of these SNA toolkits.

---

11. If you had your data in a GraphML file (a common network file format) rather than in a plain text file, you could use the network extension to import it with a single command: *nw:load-graphml*. See exploration 26 at the end of this chapter for more detail on how to do that.

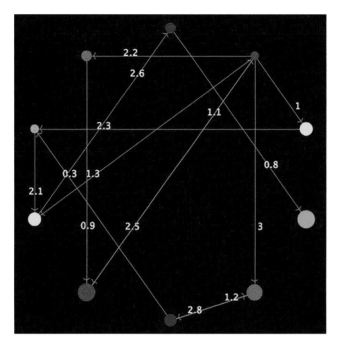

Figure 8.22
Network Import example (from the code examples in the NetLogo models library).

Another solution besides using NetLogo code to import, export, and analyze networks is to use the *Networks extension* toolkit, which is distributed as a built-in extension. The Networks extension (aka the "nw" extension) is a powerful package for doing network modeling in NetLogo and is the recommended method for doing so. The Networks extension works very similarly to the GIS extension and, like it, is included in the default NetLogo installation. Like other NetLogo extensions, it is open source and available on GitHub (https://github.com/NetLogo/NW-Extension). The Networks extension supplements NetLogo's core network primitives with various tools for performing more sophisticated network analyses. It gives you the ability to find shortest paths between turtles, to calculate various centrality measures, to find clusters and cliques in your networks, to generate random networks, and to read and write network data in the standard GraphML format.

Let us look at a sample model called Simple Viral Marketing (located in the IABM Textbook folder in the models library). Similar to the Ticket Sales model described in the GIS section, Simple Viral Marketing is based on a model from a paper (Stonedahl, Rand & Wilensky, 2010). The premise behind Simple Viral Marketing is that a brand manager wants to figure out who they should target in a social network with a promotion in order to maximize the spread of a product through a network.

In the SETUP of Simple Viral Marketing, there are two sections of code that use the network extension. First, there is CREATE-NETWORK. CREATE-NETWORK looks at what type of network the user wants to create and then creates a version of it. The two choices are RANDOM and PREFERENTIAL-ATTACHMENT. Random networks are networks where there is a random chance of a link between any two nodes (Erdös & Rényi, 1951); preferential attachment networks, by contrast, are networks where a few nodes have lots of connections and many nodes have very few connections (Barabási & Albert, 1999). Random networks are useful as a base case, but preferential attachment networks are often thought to more closely resemble real-world social networks. In the actual code, the CREATE-NETWORK procedure determines which network should be created and then calls the appropriate subprocedure. For random networks, it looks like this:

```
to create-random-network
    nw:generate-random turtles links 500 0.004 [
        set shape "circle"
        set color blue
        set size 2
        set adopted? false
    ]
end
```

The first thing this code does is use the network extension to create a random network using turtles (500 in all) and links, with a probability of an edge between any two nodes being 0.004. Since the number of possible edges is 500 · 499/2 (124,750) and the probability of an edge is 0.004, this means that, on average, there will be 499 edges, or just less than one edge per node.[12] This means that some nodes will not necessarily be connected to other nodes. As part of the network generation, a block of text appears that specifies actions for those turtles to take. In this case, the SHAPE is set to circle, the COLOR to blue, the SIZE to two, and ADOPTED? to false. ADOPTED? will be used to track whether this specific turtle has adopted the product/idea or not. Once some networks are created, we need to tell the network extension which nodes and links it should pay attention to when doing its calculations. The set of nodes and links that the network extension pays attention to is known as the *context*. In this case, we have only one kind of node and one kind of link, so we could have ended the procedure CREATE-RANDOM-NETWORK with the statement NW:SET-CONTEXT TURTLES LINKS. This bit of code essentially tells NetLogo what network you plan to work with in the near future (until you change the context). Since network calculations are expensive, this allows NetLogo to precache some of the calculations for future use. However, the context defaults to turtles and links, so there is no need to set the context in this case.

12. In general, the number of possible directed edges in any graph of size N is $N \cdot (N-1)$, since each node of N nodes can be connected to at most $N-1$ other nodes. However, when dealing with undirected edges, there can only be one edge between each pair of nodes, not two, and so we divide the result by two.

```
to create-preferential-attachment
    nw:generate-preferential-attachment turtles links 500 [
        set size 2
        set shape "circle"
        set color blue
        set adopted? false
    ]
end
```

CREATE-PREFERENTIAL-ATTACHMENT works in a similar manner to CREATE-RANDOM-NETWORK, except that a preferential attachment network is generated using a method based on Barabási and Albert (1999). As we saw in chapter 5, for preferential attachment networks, the probability of an edge existing is determined by a probabilistic generative method and is thus unspecified at the start. The code simply specifies the number of turtles (500) to create. The network will then be generated by iteratively adding nodes to the network, such that a new node is added with one edge to a node drawn probabilistically from all other nodes based on the number of neighbors it already has. This gives a scale-free or power-law distribution to the number of links in the network. After this, the properties of the nodes are set again. (See figure 8.23 for an example of such a resultant preferential attachment network.)

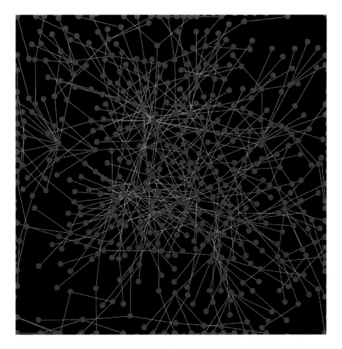

Figure 8.23
A preferential attachment network created by the network extension.

Box 8.4
Context in the Network Extension

The first thing that one needs to understand in order to work with the network extension is how to tell the extension which network to work with. Consider the following example situation:

```
breed [ teachers teacher ] breed [ students student ] undirected-link-breed
[ friendships friendship ] directed-link-breed [ classes class ]
```

Here, you have students and teachers. Students can have classes with teachers, but not the other way around. Anyone can be friends with anyone.

Now we might want to consider this whole thing as one big network. If that is the case, there is no need to set a context: by default, the NW extension primitives consider all turtles and all links to be part of the current network.

We could also, however, be only interested in a subset of the network. Maybe we want to consider only friendship relations. Furthermore, maybe we want to consider only the friendships between teachers. After all, having a very high centrality in a network of teacher friendships is very different from having a high centrality in a network of student friendships.

To specify such networks, we need to tell the extension both which turtles and which links we are interested in. Only the turtles from the specified set of turtles will be included in the network, and only the links from the specified set of links that are between turtles of the specified set will be included. For example, if you set the context to teachers and friendships, even the lonely teachers with no friends will be included in the network, but friendship links between teachers and students will not be included. The way to tell the extension about this is with the nw:set-context primitive, which you must call prior to doing any operations on a network. For instance:

• NW:SET-CONTEXT TURTLES LINKS will give you everything: teaches and students, friendships and classes, as one big network.

• NW:SET-CONTEXT TURTLES FRIENDSHIPS will give you a network where all the teachers and students are nodes and the links are friendships between any of them, but no class links

• NW:SET-CONTEXT TEACHERS FRIENDSHIPS will give you a network of all the teachers and the only links are friendships links between teachers

• NW:SET-CONTEXT TEACHERS LINKS will give you a network with all the teachers as nodes, and any links between them, whether these links are friendships or classes (it is possible for teachers to take classes with other teachers).

• NW:SET-CONTEXT STUDENTS CLASSES will give you a network of all the students, and links would be classes between students, but since in this example students cannot take classes from other students there will not be any links.

Box 8.4
(continued)

> Note that when using it with special agentsets (turtles, links, breeds or link-breeds), NW:SET-CONTEXT is dynamic: you call it once to tell the extension which turtles and links you want to work with, and the changes to your agents (births and deaths, namely) are automatically reflected in your network. You need to call NW:SET-CONTEXT again only if you want to redefine which agentsets you want in your network.
>
> NW: SET-CONTEXT works slightly differently for constructed agentsets; only deaths change the network context, while births or changes to the agentset criterion will not get updated automatically. For further information on this distinction, refer to the Special agentsets vs. Normal agentsets section of the documentation for the networks extension and the section on special agentsets in the NetLogo programming guide.

Another place where the Networks extension shows up in this code is in the SEED procedure. This procedure controls how nodes are selected to seed with the product:

```
to seed
    if seeding-method = "random" [
        ask n-of budget turtles [set adopted? true update-color]
    ]
    if seeding-method = "betweenness" [
        ask max-n-of budget turtles [nw:betweenness-centrality] [set adopted?
true update-color]
    ]
end
```

In this case, there are two choices: either RANDOM, which selects a random set of nodes to seed; or BETWEENNESS which seeds nodes based on their betweenness centrality. Betweenness centrality is a network measure of the number of shortest paths between any two nodes in the network this node is on (see e.g., Newman, 2005, which produces a measure of how important this node is to the overall diffusion of information through this network). SEED takes the BUDGET specified in the interface and seeds that many nodes either randomly or based on the betweenness centrality of the node. It does this by setting ADOPTED? to true and changing the color of the node to reflect this adoption.

While the rest of the code does not use the network extension at all, it does use some of the built-in network functionality of NetLogo as can be seen in the main decision procedure of the model, DECIDE-TO-ADOPT:

```
to decide-to-adopt
    ifelse random-float 1.0 < .01 [
        set adopted? true
    ]
    [
        if any? link-neighbors [
            if random-float 1.0 < 0.5 *
            count link-neighbors with [ adopted? ] / count link-neighbors [
                set adopted? true
            ]
        ]
    ]
end
```

This code checks to see if a random number is less than 0.01, and if it is, the agent adopts the product/idea regardless of its social situation. If it is not then, the code checks to see if the agent has any neighbors, and if so, it adopts so long as it is a random number less than 0.5 times the fraction of the neighbors who have adopted. This model is based on the classic Bass model (1959) that is widespread in the marketing literature. As you can see, it can be much easier to create models with the network extension than by hand. (See the finished model in figure 8.24.)

All in all, the ability to use social network data and analysis tools natively within an agent-based modeling platform is a powerful combination. As we have started to examine more and more complex systems, it has become clear that standard assumptions such as panmictic mixing (everyone interacting with everyone else) and even checkerboard-based environment, though very useful for gaining some elementary intuitions about phenomena, result in spurious and incorrect results at times. Using realistically synthesized (or even empirically derived) social networks enables a much richer and more robust modeling platform.

Physical Sensor Data   Scientists often need to validate computer models with empirical data. Traditionally, the computer modeling and the measurement processes are accomplished on different technological platforms. Collected experimental data is saved to a file, to be manually transferred to a software package for analysis. However, this process could be expedited by building a software link between the modeling toolkit and the data acquisition software. This would let users accomplish data acquisition on the fly by communicating with instruments (oscilloscopes, function generators, and probes) or other data sources (Internet feeds, external applications) directly from within an ABM toolkit. This connection would enable seamless communication with instruments via drivers and other commonly used communication protocols. With this link, the agent-based model could either generate data and send it out to an instrument or receive data for analysis and visualization. Users could then use a single, integrated environment for hardware interfacing and data analysis, bringing live, measured data into their model as

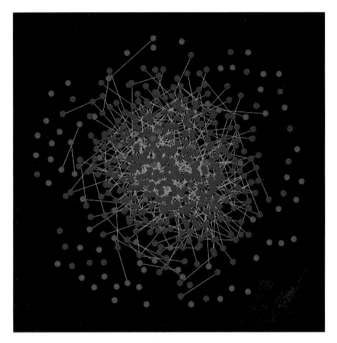

Figure 8.24
The Simple Viral Marketing model near the end of a run with a random network.

well as controlling external lab equipment. As discussed earlier, the NetLogoLab tool facilitates this process.

This sensory data often takes the form of images. Image analysis is one of the most common data-collection techniques in chemistry, biology, and medicine. Image analysis and ABM have great potential for research, since the "pixels" or "segments" in an image can easily be converted into agents in a computer model and assigned computational rules to perform predictive simulation. Having the ability within ABMs to connect with digital imaging equipment and automatically capture, filter, and process images and movies, as well as compare side-by-side images from real samples and the output of computer models, would be very powerful (see figure 8.25).

Advanced Mathematical Analysis Mathematica™ and MatLab™ are two of the most popular commercial mathematical and scientific analysis tools widely available. Mathematica is particularly powerful for symbolic algebraic manipulation and extensive graphing capabilities. MatLab is extremely popular in engineering schools owing to its vast collection of toolboxes, powerful matrix manipulation capabilities, and hundreds of built-in functions for control system design, signal and image processing, and test and

A

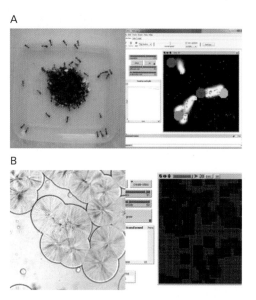

B

Figure 8.25
(A) Visualization of a solidifying salt, and its corresponding computer model. (B) Visualization of the video of an ant colony, and a corresponding computer model.

measurement, statistics, and data analysis. It also includes an extensive collection of drivers for communicating with external measurement devices. The integration of MatLab with ABM promises to be very fruitful.

There is an extension of NetLogo, called the Mathematica Link that enables model users to control and run models from within Mathematica.[13] Mathematica includes many features that ABM developers can find useful: advanced import capabilities, statistical functions, data visualization, and document creation. By linking NetLogo and Mathematica, model authors can build their models in an ABM toolkit but, at the same time, examine their results in the (more visually rich) analytic environment of Mathematica.

The results of this combination can be visually powerful (see figure 8.26). In this model, GIS data were used as the starting point of an agent-based model of patterns of school choice in a US city. This sophisticated visualization was made possible with Mathematica's graphing and analysis features (Bakshy & Wilensky, 2007b).

Advanced Visualization   Agent-based models are very useful for visually conveying the modeled phenomenon clearly and quickly. A good choice of visualization for your model can make a significant difference for the purposes of communication or persuasion. An

13. http://ccl.northwestern.edu/netlogo/mathematica.html (*Bakshy & Wilensky, 2007a*).

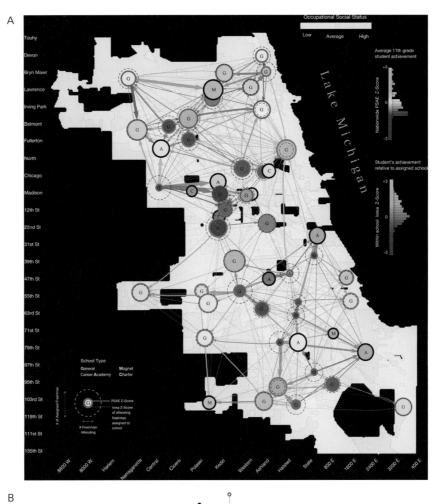

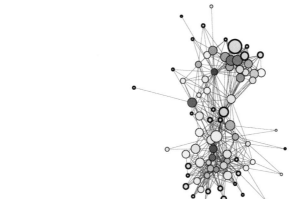

Figure 8.26
Visualization of complex, data-dense agent-based model made possible with Mathematica™ and the NetLogo-Mathematica Link (see Bakshy & Wilensky, 2007).

effective visualization of an ABM identifies the important model elements and helps the user to understand the model's behaviors. However, designing an effective visualization can be challenging for model authors, most of whom do not have visual design training. Establishing principles for designing cognitively efficient, aesthetic and communicative visualizations can guide researchers in their graphic design process of agent-based models. (See Kornhauser, Wilensky & Rand, 2009 for such guidance.) In addition to designing effective visualizations for model runs, you may have reason to produce a visually polished picture of your model for publication or presentation in a formal context. For this purpose, you can use the POV Ray extension, a NetLogo ray tracing extension that provides an interface with the popular open-source POV-Ray ray tracing rendering engine.[14] This allows you to create stunning high-resolution images from NetLogo 3D and the 3D view in NetLogo 2D (see figure 8.27). The authors and NetLogo community encourage advanced users of NetLogo to create even more extensions to NetLogo and make them publicly available to the ABM community through the NetLogo extensions website (https://github .com/NetLogo/NetLogo/wiki/Extensions).

Speed

Sometimes, especially with advanced models and models of empirical phenomena, models can have millions of agents and dozens of parameters. For example, in making a detailed model of emigration patterns in China, one might have millions of people agents, many thousands of land parcel agents, and many environmental and social parameters. In such cases, a run of the model may take a significant amount of time. When a single run of the model takes a long time, there are many possibilities for speeding up the model. A first step would be to turn off view updates (or increase the frame rate in the view) so that the model can run without sending graphical updates to the view. In addition, if you have access to a fast computer or compute server, most high-powered compute servers use an operating system compatible with NetLogo. As the core NetLogo engine is single threaded, you cannot run a single model run on multiple processors (cores). But, as we shall discuss, it is possible to run a BehaviorSpace experiment in parallel on multiple processors.

   Another way to increase the speed of your model would be to check if it is possible to reduce the number of agents. Sometimes you can move "up a level" in your moving agents, so that instead of atoms as agents, you can use molecules, or instead of individual people, you can use firms as agents. Similarly, you can reduce the granularity of the patch grid. Reducing the number of agents will yield proportionate speed savings. Another important way to increase the speed of your model would be to check your model thoroughly for unnecessary computation, especially in the main GO loop. As we have discussed in examples throughout the book, a common mistake is to compute something repeatedly in the GO loop that could be computed once before the loop began. Sometimes the ease of

14. https://github.com/fstonedahl/RayTracing-Extension (*Stonedahl, 2012*).

expression in NetLogo can mask the complexity of the operation. For example, it is easy to express ONE-OF TURTLES IN-RADIUS 100, but this is computationally expensive, because it must determine the distance to all turtles, and then choose one of them randomly. There is often a less expensive way to choose a turtle that meets your criterion. Similarly, primitives such as WITH and MAX-N-OF can be expensive as they evaluate reporters for every member of an agentset. As discussed earlier in this chapter, using the RUN primitive on varying strings can be very slow and is better done with TASKs. It is impossible to detail here all the ways one can speed up NetLogo code. For help with a specific model you want to speed up, email the users lists. Both "netlogo-users" and "stack overflow" have many NetLogo experts who are usually very responsive to questions. If performance of a single run is of great importance, and if you have the model in its final form, it may be worthwhile to rewrite the model in a lower level language, such as Java or C. Because these languages do not have the overhead of a language specifically designed for ABM, they can be tuned to run any specific model considerably faster.

A more common speed issue is not about the speed of a single run, but rather with the need for thousands of runs. If you want to do an experiment that varies five parameters, each with ten different values, you would need 5^{10}, or about a million runs. BehaviorSpace can run on multiple processors, which makes it straightforward to run an experiment on a large shared-memory machine, computing many runs at a time and thus finishing the experiment much more quickly. It is also possible to run NetLogo on a large cluster of computers enabling a great savings in runtime of an experiment, but that takes some additional scripts and job scheduling. For more information or running on clusters, see the documentation at ccl.northwestern.edu.

Sometimes an experiment is too large to run even on a large multiprocessor machine or cluster. In such cases, it may not be possible to search the parameter space exhaustively. However, if there is a particular target model behavior or measure that you are searching to find, then you may be able to find it by performing a heuristic search on the parameter space, selectively and more intelligently sampling the space to search for your target. As mentioned in the previous chapter, BehaviorSearch is a software tool to help with automating the exploration of agent-based models by using genetic algorithms and other heuristic techniques to search the parameter-space (Stonedahl, Rand & Wilensky, 2010). BehaviorSearch provides a low-threshold way to search for combinations of model parameter settings that will result in a specified target behavior. To use it, you must design a quantitative measure for the behavior you're interested in, choose which parameters to vary and select a search method.

Applications of ABM

Throughout this textbook, we have worked with and described applications of ABM to a wide variety of topics and domains. Our examples have spanned the gamut from animal

Figure 8.27
Ray traced images using the NetLogo ray tracing extension. (A) DLA 3D. http://ccl.northwestern.edu/netlogo/models/DLA3D (*Wilensky, 2006*). (B) Hydrogen Diffusion. http://ccl.northwestern.edu/netlogo/models/hydrogendiffusion3D (*Kim et al., 2010*). (C) Flocking Alternate 3D. http://ccl.northwestern.edu/netlogo/models/Flocking3DAlternate (*Wilensky, 2005*). (D) Mousetraps 3D. http://ccl.northwestern.edu/netlogo/models/Mousetraps3D (*Wilensky, 2002*). (E) Sandpile 3D. http://ccl.northwestern.edu/netlogo/models/Sandpile3D (*Wilensky, 2006*). (F) Percolation 3D. http://ccl.northwestern.edu/netlogo/models/Percolation3D (*Wilensky, 2006*). (G) Fire model with a 3D perspective. (H) Honeycomb model. http://ccl.northwestern.edu/netlogo/models/Honeycomb (*Wilensky, 2003b*). (I) A Twitter network visualization.

behavior to political science, from oil percolation to human segregation and communication. Many of these examples were pedagogical and were simplified to make a particular point. Still, they can serve as seeds for deeper and more comprehensive investigations.

Natural Sciences We have discussed how agent-based modeling has been used to help students learn about chemistry, from the ideal gas model to the difference between acids and bases (Connected Chemistry; Levy & Wilensky, 2009; Stieff & Wilensky, 2003). It has also been used in physics to describe properties of electromagnetic systems, such as series versus parallel circuits, or what defines current (NIELS; Sengupta & Wilensky, 2009). Some physics-based models have also been applied to non-physics-related inquiries. For instance, agent-based models of percolation were shown to compare favorably with forest fires (Fire model; Niazi et al., 2010), which has allowed researchers to better quantify the risk of large-scale forest fires. The recent introduction of GIS data into ABM has allowed for a more detailed application of some of these models.

Biology Biology is also a natural science, but because we have discussed many applications in this area, it deserves to be highlighted separately. This is in part because biology was one of the research fields to first embrace agent-based modeling when it was then called individual-based modeling. The predator-prey model that we have discussed at various points throughout this book is a primary example of the use of ABM in biology. There are many other biological applications as well, such as the Ants model discussed in chapter 1, which in turn has led to a large group of social animal models. This naturally follows from ABM's ability to model groups of individuals who interact in a shared space. Indeed, building on this strength, Holland's (1994) Echo models, among others, showed that ABM does not have to be limited to examining one predator and one prey; rather, it is also possible to examine the interaction of multiple species, considering their interaction with each other as well as the environment. Holland's Echo models went even further to develop a system where evolution was not an exogenous constraint placed by the researcher on the system, but rather, a process that arose naturally from life and death in the model.

Medicine Medicine may be considered as a form of applied biology, and thus, given the range of applications of ABM to biology, it should not be surprising that there are many applications within medicine as well. For instance, modeling of disease spread both within an individual (Tumor) and between individuals (AIDS, Spread-of-Infection, HubNet Disease) are common and successful uses of agent-based modeling. The introduction of social networks into epidemiological modeling has shown that many standard models of disease spread are improved when patterns of contact that reflect real human networks are considered (Morris, 1993).

Economics Humans do not just interact through exchanging viruses (thankfully), but also, via economic exchanges. The modeling of economic systems was one of the earliest uses of agent-based modeling. From examinations of systems as complex as the stock market (SFI Artificial Stock Market; Arthur et al., 1997) to those as simple as whether or not to go to a bar (El Farol Bar problem), ABM has given us new insights into economic systems. By highlighting such opportunities, regulatory agencies hope to prevent companies from manipulating the market by creating artificial demand and therefore higher prices. For instance, the Artificial Stock Market was used to explore and develop a new theory of asset pricing, while the El Farol Bar problem showed that even boundedly rational and inductively reasoning agents could achieve an economic equilibrium. Recently, ABM has been used to model the deregulation of electrical grids (Sun & Tesfatsion, 2007). ABMs of electrical grids may provide insight into locations in the electrical grid that could be used to keep companies from manipulating the market by creating artificial demand and therefore higher prices.

Organizations and Politics Organizational systems and political systems also play a key role in modern life, and ABM has been profitably employed in understanding these systems as well. Cohen's Garbage Can model (Cohen, March & Olsen, 1972) allowed organizational scientists to specify some of their conceptual models in a concrete way, which encouraged further refinements and improvement of these models. Schelling created one of the very first ABMs to show that even small preferences can have a dramatic effect on housing segregation, while Axelrod (1984) used ABM to examine the evolution of cooperation and, recently, the persistence of ethnocentrism. Democratic institutions require and rely on the ability of individuals to make decisions, and ABM provides a means of examining the emergent outcomes of individuals' decisions. The Voting model may not be reflective of any real political event, but it does illustrate how simple changes in rules can dramatically affect outcomes. Recently, there has been a trend to combine ABM with social network analysis (SNA) to create dynamic and rich models of human interaction across real social networks. This combination enables the creation of even more robust models of organizational systems. As we saw previously in this chapter, ABM done alongside social network analysis has been effectively used to explore the effects of educational policy on student performance.

Anthropology ABM has also been used to help understand how human systems work together systemically throughout a culture. For instance, an ABM of water irrigation in Balinese rice fields was used to show how farmers could solve the complex problem of distributing water using simple local rules (Lansing & Kremer, 1993). As we saw in chapter 7, the Artificial Anasazi model was used to explore theories of why the Anasazi population collapsed. By modeling each individual family, a higher resolution of description was possible than models that examined all families as a single big population.

Engineering ABM is used to examine not only social and natural systems but also engineered systems. The application of ABM to engineering typically takes one of two forms. The goal can be to simulate a system that has already been designed by humans (e.g., Traffic Basic, urban pattern formation) or, alternatively, to design a new system by configuring the interactions of low-level elements (e.g., using MaterialSim to design a new product). Sometimes, the model will straddle this divide. For example, ABM has been used to model computer networks. Once a successful model has been constructed, new optimization algorithms can be designed. The model can first be validated against empirical results, after which new mechanisms can be explored to see how throughput, bandwidth, and robustness of the network could possibly be improved. Interestingly enough, some of the new mechanisms and techniques that have been explored for computer networks were inspired by a model similar to the Ants model we discussed in chapter 1 (Dorigo & Stützle, 2004).

Math and Computer Science Many models in agent-based modeling explore fundamental properties of mathematical and computational systems. For example, cellular automata can be considered a subset of agent-based modeling that examines how agents in a fixed lattice change by interacting with their neighbors over time. Conway's Game of Life made it clear that these simple models can still exhibit powerfully rich behavior. Both Conway's model and Reynold's Boids model blur the distinction between computer and biological applications. Conway's model demonstrates how you can create complex replicating systems with very limited computational resources, while Reynolds's Boids shows how emergent behavior, such as flocking, in social animals like birds can be achieved through distributed control and absent of a leader or centralized controller.

Throughout these examples, we have discussed how ABM can be used predictively through careful calibration with real-world data. From electrical power grids (Li & Tesfatsion, 2009) to Balinese rice terraces (Lansing, 2006), the application of ABM to real-world problems has covered a wide range, and the potential applications are limitless. The advent of powerful computation has enabled us to move beyond simple approximations to complex systems, embracing nature and society in all their complexity—both beautiful and befuddling—to tease open the secrets of how they work. As we discussed in chapter 0, ABM is a new representational infrastructure that is enabling restructurations of disciplines and practices in much the same way as did the transition from Roman to Hindu-Arabic numerals. And, as in that restructuration, this not only enables great progress in science, it also democratizes access. We hope this book is part of that process, enabling a wide range of students to become fluent with agent-based representations and to make sense of a previously inaccessible complexity.

Revisiting the Trade-offs of ABM

It may be useful at this point to revisit the trade-offs and limitations of ABM that we discussed in the very first chapter. We have discussed many uses and advantages of ABM, but it is important to think about when ABM really generates the most reward for a particular unit of effort by the researcher.

As you have started to build your first agent-based models, it has probably become obvious that ABM can be computationally intensive. Often it is possible to write models that simply do not scale and when you attempt to increase the number of agents by orders of magnitude the system simply grinds to a halt as it attempts to calculate all of the interactions and actions of all of the agents. Of course, there are almost always ways to make a model more computationally efficient, but in many cases this involves giving up the power of ABM. For instance, you can create a representative agent that takes the place of 10,000 or even a million other agents, but then you lose the ability to track and observe every possible agent, and the model becomes more similar to a homogenous equation-based model. As we discussed in chapter 5 and earlier in this chapter, making decisions about granularity and resolution can be quite difficult. However, if this decision is made strategically it can be quite effective at scaling agent-based models up to a very large number of agents.

Strategic decisions about what level to model the agent at can also be seen as a limitation of agent-based modeling. Unlike other modeling frameworks which have fewer "free parameters" it is often the case that agent-based models need many more parameters and design choices. As we considered in chapter 4, there are a number of different aspects of designing an agent-based model that must be considered when building a model. However, this is not truly a limitation. Having a checklist of items that a model designer needs to consider when building a model forces modelers to consider many assumptions that go unquestioned and are simply hidden in other modeling frameworks. Moreover, most models can be built to be easily expanded, as was described earlier in this chapter, when we discussed the concept of full spectrum modeling.

Finally, it is important to remember that ABM requires knowledge about the lowest-level individuals/agents in the model, as opposed to simply data about the aggregate-level. As we discussed in chapter 4, the modeler needs to have some knowledge of agent properties and agent actions when designing an agent-based model, or at least have a theory about those agent properties and behaviors. With a theory, the model can be constructed and the results tested to see if they generate aggregate patterns of behavior that are reflective of real-world patterns, but without information about agent properties and behaviors, it is difficult to construct an agent-based model, since the rules of an agent-based model are constructed at the individual level.

The Future of ABM

In chapter 0, we discussed how ABM gives us the power to restructure the way we understand the world around us. By utilizing a complex systems perspective, we can understand the world in new and different ways.

The scientist and science fiction writer Isaac Asimov, in his *Foundation* series, talked about a scientist by the name of Hari Seldon. Seldon created a new science called psychohistory, which used statistics and mathematical descriptions of large groups of individuals to predict where the course of history would lead. He used this knowledge to foretell the destruction of a galactic empire and, based on his predictions, discovered leverage points where the future could be altered, allowing him to create a better future.

While agent-based modeling confers great modeling power, it will not soon give us the forecasting powers of a Hari Seldon. However, ABM does give us the ability to examine the world and features of it from a new perspective and has the potential for highlighting places in these systems where we can intervene to alter their shape and trajectory. The future course of ABM is not yet known. As we have seen, it has contributed new methods and insights to scientists, practitioners, theorists, and students, and it is likely to continue to do so. ABM can be a powerful and valuable tool for anyone interested in the complex natural, engineered, and social worlds around them. ABM gives us the ability and the insight to view the world through a completely new lens, a lens that is becoming increasingly important in a world where complexity surrounds and entangles every decision that we need to make. ABM is one of the few methods that enables us to pierce through this web and discern the simple rules that underlie most complex phenomena.

Explorations

1. What are the benefits of a simpler model? What are the benefits of a more realistic model? Under what conditions does it make sense to focus strictly on one form of modeling over the other?

2. Examine the Grand Canyon model in the Earth Science section of the models library. Create another model that illustrates the same principles but does not use a realistic data map.

3. Examine the Erosion model in the Earth Science section of the models library. Add a digital elevation map to the model so that it is more realistic. (See the Grand Canyon model for an example of adding a digital elevation map.)

4. Build a model based on the school choice decision tree discussed in the section on rule extraction. What other elements might you add to this model to make it more realistic?

5. Examine the Disease HubNet model in the HubNet Activities section of the NetLogo models library. How would you change this model to allow individuals to investigate how to best cure disease instead of simply watching the spread of it? (Hint: look at the Disease Doctors model, but make the actions of the doctors controllable by participants.)

6. Build a simple model of water dynamics using the systems dynamics modeler. Assume a flow-rate in and a flow-rate out. Compare how changing the flow rates affect the level of the water.

7. Open the Tabonuco-Yagrumo Hybrid model in the System Dynamics section of the NetLogo models library. Currently, the growth of new trees is random. Modify the code so it is spatially correlated. Also, modify the hurricane code so that trees that are removed are spatially correlated. Add a human agent that removes trees in a plot. How do all these changes affect the stability of the system?

8. Design a simple predator-prey model using the Systems Dynamics Modeler. Create a NetLogo agent-based model that produces the same population levels over time.

9. It is common in a NetLogo model to change the behavior of the model based on the value of a chooser. For example, in the Daisyworld model in the Biology section of the models library, the behavior of the PAINT-DAISIES button is defined by the PAINT-DAISIES-AS chooser. In the code this behavior is accomplished using conditional logic. The same result can also be achieved using the RUN feature. Try reimplementing the paint logic in this model using RUN. Is the RUN version an improvement over the conditional logic version? If so, why?

10. Look at the RUN and RUNRESULT examples. How are they different from each other? Is one clearly a better solution? The RUNRESULT version only modifies the heading of the turtle, while RUN modifies the basic commands. Can you combine RUN and RUNRESULT into one model so that you can use different commands (similar to the RUN example) and complex mathematical expressions for the inputs to those commands (similar to the RUNRESULT example)?

11. Add additional commands to the RUN example. For instance, have the turtles put their pen down or pull their pen up.

12. Add additional operators and values to the RUNRESULT example. For instance, create a division operator that works in all cases. Change the number of operators and values that the RUNRESULT code uses.

13. When would you use TASK? Can you describe what kind of circumstances might arise while coding a model that would inspire the use of TASK? Many of the models in the models library could be redone using TASKs. Select one and modify it to use TASKs.

14. Modify the Machine Learning model used in this chapter to use tasks instead of strings.

15. Often, the logarithm of a list of numbers is very useful for analyzing and visualizing data. However, if any of the numbers are 0, simply applying LN to every number will cause an error. Use MAP and FILTER to get a list of the natural logarithms of all positive numbers in a list.

16. Use REDUCE to create a reporter that gets the link neighbors of a turtle's link neighbors. In other words, the reporter should take in a turtle as an argument, and return an agentset containing all the turtles that can be reached from that turtle by traveling along exactly two links.

17. Use REDUCE to write a FLATTEN reporter that turns a list of lists into a single list containing the items from each list. For example, FLATTEN [[1 2] [3 4] [4 3] [2 1]] = [1 2 3 4 4 3 2 1].

18. (a) Use MAP to group turtles into agentsets according to color. That is, the output should be a list of agentsets, where all the agents in a given agentset have the same color. (b) Generalize your solution by making a reporter that will group turtles in this manner based off the result of a reporter task.

19. Write a reporter that uses REDUCE to report the largest agentset from a list of agentsets.

20. Write a reporter that uses MAP and REDUCE to get the largest of the pair of numbers with the largest ratio from two lists of numbers. That is, if the first list is [1 2 3 4] and the second list is [2 7 5 10], the reporter would report [3 5].

21. The geometric mean is very useful when dealing with percent growth. For example, if your population grows by 20 percent in the first tick, 50 percent in the next tick, and 30 percent in the third tick, you must take the geometric mean of 1.20, 1.50, and 1.30 to determine the average percent increase. The geometric mean of a list of n numbers is the nth root of the product of those numbers.

   (a) Use REDUCE, *, and ^ to define a GEOMETRIC-MEAN reporter.

   (b) One potential problem with the simple definition of geometric mean is that any 0s in the input list will cause the output to be 0. Often, we'd rather just ignore 0s. Using FILTER, modify your procedure in (a) to ignore 0s.

22. While it is often useful to employ REDUCE to combine elements together to produce an element of the same type, sometimes we want the result to be of a completely different type. For example, if we want to count the number of times a string appears in a list of strings, our list consists of strings but our result must be a number. A simple solution to this is to use FPUT to put the initial value of the result on the front of the list (what the value of the result should be if the list were empty). Use this technique to create an OCCURRENCES reporter. The reporter should take in a list and a value and return the number of times that the value occurs in the list.

23. Open the Flocking model in the Biology section of the NetLogo models library. Import data from a real mountain range into the world that the birds are flocking over. Modify the flocking model so that the birds avoid areas of high elevation.

24. Create a text file of the friendship connections in your class (as we did in the network import example). Import the network into NetLogo. Use the network to examine how a disease, such as a cold, might spread through your class.

25. Using the friendship network that you created in exploration 24, use NetLogo's network extension to calculate some properties of various members of your classmates. Who is the most central person? Who has the most friends? Who has the tightest clique (i.e., highest clustering coefficient)?

26. Many websites provide interfaces and APIs where you can access data sets. For example, netvizz provides an interface for obtaining your Facebook network. Using the network extension, we can load and analyze the network in NetLogo.

   If you have a Facebook account, go to https://apps.facebook.com/netvizz/ and follow the instructions for downloading your network (select the personal network option).

   After you have clicked "Start," netvizz will generate your network and give you some file types to choose from. Be sure to select GDF.

When you open the file you have downloaded, you will see an entry for each of the attributes that you have selected. Those will have names like "label," "name," "sex," "locale," etc. For these attributes to be filled when you load your graph in NetLogo, you need to declare them as turtle variables: "turtles-own [name sex]" and so on through the full list of attributes.

Once you have done that, loading your network is just one command: nw:load-graphml "/path/to/your/network.graphml." This will create a turtle for each of your friends and the links between them. Now is time to play with your friends! Can you visualize your network better by using layout-spring? Color your friends by "hometown_location." Are friends from the same hometown more likely to be connected? Can you figure out which of your friends are most central by using centrality measures available in the network extension? (See https://github.com/NetLogo/NW-Extension/blob/master/README.md for documentation.)

27. In the network you downloaded in exploration 26, try giving a "disease" to one of your friends and have the disease spread to their link neighbors with some probability. How long does it take for the disease to spread through the network? Does it spread faster if you first infect friends that are highly central?

28. Suppose you want to spread the news of having landed a new job, but you can't be bothered telling every single one of your friends. Instead, you're hoping that if you tell a few of your friends, word will spread. Knowing your friends, and knowing who your friends know, who would you tell first? What if you could tell three people? Why those three? Using the network you imported in exploration 26, write a model that spreads word across the network. Try, at first, to have the word spread like in the Virus on a Network model. You can also make the social contagion mechanics more complex: How could word spread besides between links with an equal, random chance? Are all people equally likely to spread the news? Maybe you know something about your friends that would impact your design—for instance, if you know some people that regularly update their Facebook status, versus others who are rarely on? How does frequency of use interact with network centrality? Is it better to tell someone central who uses Facebook rarely, or someone who uses Facebook all the time but knows only a few people in your network?

29. A clique is a subset of a network in which every node has a direct link to every other node. A maximal clique is a clique that is not itself contained in a bigger clique. Using the MAXIMAL-CLIQUES command, find how many maximal cliques are in your social network. What is the largest maximal clique? The smallest?

30. The networks extension also includes commands that let you find paths between nodes in a graph. Starting with a random person in your network, find the person who is the furthest from them (it takes the most hops to get to). How many nodes need to be visited to get to them? Can you figure out what the largest shortest path is in your network?

31. The network extension also comes with a set of network generators that allow you to easily create networks that have specific characteristics. Using the generators and the

centrality measures provided by the networks extension, figure out which of the available generators produces the graph with the lowest average closeness centrality? Which default graph has the highest average betweenness centrality? Is it the type of network you expected?

32. The network generators are convenient for quickly creating common networks, but it is a good exercise to create them manually to better understand their characteristics, the algorithms that produce them, and the similarities and differences across common network layouts. Try manually creating the networks that you can produce with the generators. Start with the simpler configurations like Ring and Star before attempting the preferential attachment or small world configurations.

33. Using the MAP primitive, take the two lists of strings ["FD" "RT" "LT"] and ["HEADING" "10" "XCOR"] and output lists of strings that you can then use REDUCE on to create a parsable code string.

34. Consider the list of lists [[1 2 5] [7 2] [3 10 1]]. Using higher-order operators, write a reporter procedure that reports the sum of the maximum values of each sublist.

35. Using higher-order operators, write a reporter procedure that takes a list of strings as input and reports the list of strings that do not start with a vowel or end with a consonant.

36. In chapter 2, we looked at the Heroes and Cowards model and mentioned that it was related to Dewdney's Party Planner game. In Dewdney's game, some people go to a party. Each person has a preferred distance that they'd like to be apart from every other party guest (that distance is zero for him/herself). Create a model that sets up a party with n guests with distance preferences. Each guest's unhappiness at the party can be calculated as the absolute value of the differences between its actual distance from a guest and the desired distance. Find an algorithm that minimizes the total unhappiness at the party.

37. Many of the models in the NetLogo models library lend themselves well to being augmented with physical computing devices like the GoGo Board or Arduino. For example, try adding an audio sensor as an input to the flocking models so that loud sounds cause the birds to scatter. Or, in the Climate Change model (in the Earth Science section), try replacing the add/remove cloud button with a humidity sensor that automatically adds and removes clouds from the model based on the current humidity reading.

38. Look through the NetLogo models library and try to find a model that can be augmented with an interface device such as a GoGo Board or Arduino, Modify the model to be able to take input from the real world.

39. NetLogo also has a sound extension that makes it possible to have a model produce audio. Paired with a GoGo Board or Arduino, it enables you to create custom instruments. Try combining a few inputs (like buttons and sensors) to build a one-of-a-kind computer instrument.

40. In this chapter we introduced the idea of bifocal modeling where the same phenomenon is represented in NetLogo code and also through feeding physical sensor data into a

virtual representation. Can you build a bifocal model to verify one of the models in the NetLogo models library? For example, can you recreate the phenomena shown in the Heat Diffusion model using a heat source and heat sensor?

41. The video extension (https://github.com/NetLogo/Gst-Video-Extension) allows you read video files as well as use live footage from the computer's webcam. This extension can be used for computer vision models. One simple way of doing feature detection is by tracking colorful objects. Make a model in which a turtle tracks the greenest object that your webcam can see. The first step in this process is to send the video data to the patches so that you can interact with the color information directly. Then, you must identify the greenest spot.

42. Building on the techniques from the previous exercise, modify the flocking model so that the turtles flock toward the greenest spot that your webcam can see, while still flocking together. Once you've done so, try slowly moving a small green object in front of your camera to influence the turtles.

Appendix: The Computational Roots of Agent-Based Modeling

The world can be resolved into digital bits, with each bit made of smaller bits.

—Ed Fredkin

It's ridiculous to live 100 years and only be able to remember 30 million bytes. You know, less than a compact disc. The human condition is really becoming more obsolete every minute.

—Marvin Minsky

Many different fields have contributed ideas and methods to ABM. In this appendix, we will focus on the key antecedents of ABM technologies from computer science and associated computational fields.

Besides the computational fields, we note that there have also been strong contributions from biology, physics, engineering, and social science. In biology, these contributions came largely from ecology and the independent development of Individual-Based Modeling alongside ABM (DeAngelis & Gross, 1992). Individual-based modeling foregrounds the role of individual animal or plant behavior in an ecosystem, as opposed to working with population-level variables (DeAngelis & Mooij, 2005). Moreover, like ABM, IBM models are often placed within particular landscapes or environments, and IBM modelers focus on how landscapes can greatly affect the results of a model (Grimm & Railsback, 2005). Much of IBM methodology has become incorporated into ABM work.

In physics, the Ising models were used to describe magnetics and showed that very simple models could produce phase transition. These models were also precursors of cellular automata. As described in chapter 3, physicist Per Bak created the classic Sandpile model, which Bak used to illustrate the concept of self-organizing criticality (SOC). He went on to apply physics-based methods to complex phenomena across many content domains (such as the Fire model in chapter 3 and various stock market models) and showed the relationship of power laws to SOC.

In engineering, process engineering and cybernetics, among other areas of research, contributed to ABM's development. In process engineering, the goal is to design an optimal output given low-level behaviors, which can be thought of as a similar framework to ABM, but with a different goal. As such, some of the tools and methods of process engineering are also useful in the context of ABM. The field of cybernetics branched off from process and control engineering, focusing on general properties of feedback in systems. This led to notions of system phase shifts, that is, areas of parameter-space where small changes can have disproportionate consequences (Wiener, 1961). In a similar vein, as engineering models became more complex, they needed to deal with stochasticity, which led to the techniques of Monte Carlo simulation (Metropolis & Ulam, 1949), wherein models are run repeatedly in order to understand its range of outputs or search for an optimal output.

As with process and cybernetic engineers, social scientists came to the realization that social organizations' complexities were not sufficiently captured by available modeling tools. As a result, social scientists started using algorithmic and computational models to describe social phenomena. These models could be reasoned about and falsifiable predictions could be made from them, thus allowing the models to be tested. This provided social scientists with a method of comparing empirical data to predicted data akin to that of natural scientists (Lave & March, 1975). Nash's (1950) game theory models were some of the earliest attempts to capture human behavior in mathematical equations. Most of these initial social science models used aggregate data averaged across individuals. For instance, the famous Club of Rome model made very simple assumptions about how world population would increase and how resources would be consumed (Meadows, 1972). These efforts gave rise over time to Systems Dynamic Modeling (SDM; Forrester, 1961), which proposed creating models using stocks (the quantities of goods, entities, or objects in particular locations) and flows (the rates of increase or decrease in these stocks). SDM modelers made important contributions to complex systems, but because the elements in System Dynamics models were mass quantities, a logical step was to shift down a level, modeling the individuals that make up the mass quantity. Thus, for modelers interested in SDM, agent-based modeling was a natural progression that enabled a deeper examination of the behavior of heterogeneous individuals. In fact, partly because of this need for social science to understand individual behavior in an increasingly rich framework, some of the earliest agent-based models arose in the social sciences. Schelling's model of segregation (discussed in chapter 3) is considered by many to be one of the first agent-based models ever devised, even though it was carried out manually using a checkerboard and coins (Schelling, 1971). Schelling's book *Micromotives and Macrobehavior* (1978) demonstrated how individual level actions could give rise to surprising social patterns. His Segregation model showed that housing segregation would occur even if no individual wants it, as long as people have a preference not be in an extreme minority in their neighborhood.

In the last decade, we have witnessed tremendous growth in the field of network theory and the incorporation of support for networks as a core element of agent-based modeling. This work was pioneered by the mathematician Euler in the 1800s in solving the problem of the seven bridges of Konigsberg (see Newman, 2010). In the 1950s and early '60s, mathematicians Erdös and Rényi characterized random networks (1960), which was then followed by the Barabasi-Albert model on preferential attachment networks (1999). Work by psychologists such as Stanley Milgram suggested that the average path length in human networks is short (six degrees of separation) (1967), an idea later formalized in the Watts and Strogatz small-worlds network models (1998). These types of networks and their associated methods of analysis have become staples of agent-based modeling.

A comprehensive history of ABM's roots in other fields and said fields' role in the origins of ABM is beyond the scope of this appendix. Here, however, we will explore some key discoveries that shaped the development of ABM. We present here six vignettes that describe several of the main antecedents to ABM technologies.

The Vignettes

Cellular Automata and Agent-Based Modeling

John von Neumann contributed greatly to a large number of scientific fields, including quantum mechanics, economic game theory, and computer science. The Hungarian-born mathematician was said to have been "the last of the great mathematicians," who possessed the "most scintillating intellect of this century." In the late 1940s, von Neumann, having invented the modern architecture of the computer, became interested in trying to create artificial machines that could reproduce autonomously. He speculated that humankind would eventually need to mine other celestial objects, and that the most effective way of performing large-scale mining operations (such as mining an entire moon or asteroid belt) would be the use of self-replicating machines, taking advantage of their exponential growth.

Influenced by his work on the first computer (ENIAC; von Neumann et al., 1987), he imagined this artificial reproducing machine as having a long set of instructions on a tape. This tape would hold not only a description of the entire machine, but also, a description of the tape that described this machine. Von Neumann sought to determine how to encapsulate an entire machine (plus the instructions to build that same machine) within a single program tape. Collaborating with his colleague Stanislaw Ulam, the two began to think of a computation machine hovering over a lake of parts, which would pick up parts from the lake and put them together to construct another machine that was an exact duplicate of the original (Von Neumann & Burks, 1966). This machine would be very simple in its operation—it would look at the pieces below it, consider its own state, and, on the basis of a rule table, alter its own state. Building on this thought experiment, von Neumann eventually created a simplified procedural version of the big lake, which he called a cellular automaton (CA).

Utilizing CAs, von Neumann was eventually able to design a hypothetical reproducing machine using twenty-nine different states (using pencil and graph paper!) that he called a Universal Constructor (Burks, 1970). Although a physical machine had not yet been built, the Universal Constructor was proof of the concept that a self-reproducing machine *could* be built. In addition, it introduced the notion of universality. The machine was called a universal constructor, as the description of the machine on the tape could be modified and extended in an arbitrary fashion; as long as it still contained the proper constructor instructions, it would continue to operate. Effectively, this meant that von Neumann had not only constructed a machine capable of self-replication, but also, one that could undergo evolution, since the instructions could be modified and added on to at the start of each succeeding generation to provide more and more capabilities.

Von Neumann's original universal constructor was unwieldy in that it required a CA where each lattice location had twenty-nine different states; such a large rule space was difficult to comprehend. However, in 1970, John Conway created a much simpler cellular automaton, which he called the "Game of Life" (discussed in detail in chapter 2). Due to the lack of sufficient computational power, Conway utilized a Go board to conduct his experiments and not a computer. "Life" became popular when Martin Gardner published the game in his popular *Scientific American* column (Gardner, 1970). As we saw in chapter 2, the CA that Conway came up with was very simple. Conway's Game of Life had three rules: (1) If a cell had exactly three neighbors (out of its eight immediate neighbors), it would go from being dead to being alive (birth); (2) If it had two or three neighbors and was alive, it would stay alive (no change); (3) If it had any other combination of neighbors, it would go to the dead state (loneliness or overcrowding).

When Conway seeded the game with a random set of live and dead cells, the system would create beautiful and intricate patterns of interesting objects. Many of them can be seen in chapter 2. Remarkably, although Conway's Life rule required only two dimensions, two states (dead or alive), and nine inputs (the cell and its eight neighbors), Conway and others proved that his "Life" rule (Berlekamp et al., 1982) contained the material necessary for self-reproduction—that is, the system could create a computational entity that could also create additional computational entities. However, the power of the Game of Life did not end there. In 2009, Adam Goucher built a universal computer/constructor within Conway's Game of Life that demonstrated that the rules of the Game of Life were sufficient to compute all possible problems (Hutton, 2010).

Around the same time of some of Conway's earliest work, and after von Neumann's death in 1957, Arthur W. Burks, one of von Neumann's collaborators, carried on examining CA as part of the Logic of Computers group at the University of Michigan. He eventually edited a collection of most of the original papers on CA in a book entitled *Theory of Self-Reproducing Automata* (von Neumann and Burks, 1966). Burks was also the graduate advisor of John H. Holland, who is discussed in a subsequent vignette. Burks's work preserved the study of CAs until Stephen Wolfram revived it in the early 1980s (Wolfram, 1983).

Wolfram made several notable contributions to the field of CAs. For instance, he undertook an extensive survey of all of the one-dimensional CA rules for cells with a neighborhood of just their left and right neighbors (radius = 1). Even this simple class of CAs exhibits surprisingly complex behavior. Wolfram divided them into four classes: uniform final state, cyclical final state, random final state, and complex final state. Wolfram showed that many patterns found in nature can be generated by CAs. Wolfram and Ed Fredkin of MIT stirred much controversy when they made the claim that the entire universe can be modeled using CAs or, even more striking, the possibility that the universe *itself* was a CA (Wolfram, 2002; Fredkin, 1990).

The historical relationship between CAs and ABM is somewhat messy. Many authors have written that CAs led directly to the development of ABM. In fact, CAs can be viewed as simple ABMs where all the agents are stationary: in contrast to CAs, more general ABMs can also include explicitly moving agents. Their ability to have mobile agents enables researchers to more naturally represent and model moving objects. As a result of this similarity, it might be assumed that ABMs were a natural scientific development from CAs. However, there is little evidence that the developers of the first ABMs; for example, Schelling and colleagues started with a CA from which an ABM was then developed. Most of these researchers were aware of CA work, but, to judge by interviews with several of them, it appears that they developed the notion of agent-based modeling independent of the ongoing work in CA theory.

In many ways, CAs (and Conway's Game of Life in particular) exhibit many of the properties of modern agent-based models. Each cell can be viewed as an agent with a simple description of state. The actions it takes to change its state on the basis of its neighboring inputs are akin to the actions that agents take in response to local interactions. Von Neumann's CAs were among the first attempts to create computational models of a biological system. In addition, the discrete time scale of the CA is very similar to the ABM's notion of a scheduler and "ticks." Moreover, the notions of self-reproduction, universality, and evolutionary processes are all concepts that live on as mechanisms within ABM. Conway's Life model also exhibited many behaviors that are often seen in ABMs. The final output of the model is hard to predict on the basis of the initial inputs, and there are emergent patterns that can only be described at a level higher than the micro-level (e.g., blinkers and gliders). Last, Wolfram's work on classifying CA rules into classes of behavior was an early example of complexity science's attempts to understand our world by taking large numbers of disparate phenomena and classifying them into groups that help us understand similarities between systems that, at first glance, seem completely unrelated.

Genetic Algorithms, John Holland, and Complex Adaptive Systems

In computer science, algorithms have traditionally been designed as engineered artifacts. The inspiration for these algorithms came from engineering applications such as assembly lines, bridge construction, and even sewer systems. In the late 1960s, a young electrical engineer by the name of John Holland stumbled upon the work of Donald Hebb. In Hebb's book *Organization of Behavior* (1949), the psychologist had written up his ideas for how neurons can be thought of as simple algorithms. Frank Rosenblatt (1962) was influenced by these ideas to build a computational model of human neurons, which he called a perceptron. Rosenblatt used this model to solve conventional computer science problems in ways he claimed were similar to the way that the human mind solves problems. This technique would eventually result in the modern field of neural networks. In this nascent field, Holland had a powerful insight: He realized that a perceptron was essentially a model of how a neuron adapts to inputs and outputs. Thus, the perceptron was not just a static model of the mind, but also, one of mental *adaptation* to the world. Holland started to wonder if it was possible to make this adaptation model more universal. Specifically, he began to think about evolutionary adaptation and how a computer might model evolution.

Foreshadowing a general principle of complex systems, Holland attempted to generalize his theoretical model in one domain, extract its computational core, and apply it more widely to other domains. Adaptation appeared (at least at some level) to exist in, for example, both neurons in the brain and species adapting to climate changes. By extracting the essence of adaptation into a universal principle, Holland shed new light on both of these examples while connecting them to many other adaptive systems, heralding a signal insight of a Complex Systems perspective.

In 1975, John Holland published his monograph *Adaptation in Natural and Artificial Systems.* This work was the culmination of his early years spent researching adaptation and resulted in the idea of the genetic algorithm (GA). In essence, GAs create a population of solutions to a problem, evaluate how effective the solutions are at solving a problem, and then combine and mutate the best solutions to create a new population. This new population can then be evaluated and the process, repeated. The GA was a unique development in computer science in that it postulated the use of biological models to solve computational problems by evolving populations of solutions to search problems. Holland described using GAs for "game-playing" among other concepts. His thoughts on computers and game playing were greatly influenced by Samuel's work on machine learning and checkers (Samuel, 1959). Holland thought that computers could solve even more complex problems if the game-playing program could not only change its *actions* but also its *strategies* over time. He imagined evolving computational strategies to use when playing games. These ideas led naturally to reifying adaptive agents that can change and adapt to their surroundings.

Holland started his study of adaptive agents much as he had previously studied evolutionary systems; he began with real world data and then developed computer models of those systems, investigating systems where adaptive agents already existed. Holland had become involved early on (circa 1985) with the Santa Fe Institute (SFI), a research institute devoted to studying complex systems. At a meeting at the Santa Fe Institute in September

1987, Holland presented his ideas of how the whole economy could be viewed as a complex adaptive system made up of adaptive agents (Holland, 1995). Holland's ideas were extensions of his views on evolutionary computation since he viewed the economic world as another ecology where individuals adapted and evolved over time. At this meeting, Holland met Brian Arthur, who was influenced enough by Holland's work to develop one of the first models in economics that did not rely on individuals having infinite amounts of knowledge and infinite computational power. Instead, agents employed Herbert Simon's concept of *bounded rationality*, where agents are limited in their computational power (Simon, 1982). This model, called the El Farol Bar problem (Arthur, 1994), was one of the first ABMs that showed that a very simple model could shed light on a complex theoretical discipline like economics. During this time, many Santa Fe Institute researchers, such as Holland, Arthur, Anderson, Arrow, and Pines, became interested in modeling the economy as a complex evolving system. This research effort would result in one of the first classical agent-based models, the Santa Fe Artificial Stock Market (Arthur et al., 1997).

In August 1986, a group of researchers including Holland, Kenneth Arrow, and W. Brian Arthur, were brought together at SFI by CEO of Citicorp, John Reed, because of a mutual frustration with the ability of traditional modeling methods to capture the complexity of the world. In many ways, this meeting and the financial backing of Citicorp, enabled the SFI to become one of the largest contributors to both the field of complex systems and that of agent-based modeling. SFI also developed one of the first agent-based modeling toolkits designed for researchers, Swarm (Minar et al., 1996). Swarm and similar toolkits have allowed the use of agent-based modeling to grow more rapidly, greatly simplifying the process of creating ABMs by providing the researcher with prebuilt libraries with many of the standard tools necessary to build ABM simulations.

Holland was also influenced early on by a group of his peers at the University of Michigan: Burks, Axelrod, Cohen, and Hamilton. All of these researchers (who together called themselves the BACH group) were to become influential in the field of complex systems, and some even dabbled in agent-based modeling. Axelrod created the tournament of prisoner's dilemma strategies (Axelrod, 1984) that showed that simple strategies (such as the well known Tit-for-Tat strategy) could do well in social games as long as the agents employing the strategies interacted with other agents multiple times. Cohen developed the Garbage Can Model of Organizations (Cohen et al., 1972), which described organizations as "organized anarchy" in which decisions are made by interactions between four independent streams: problems, solutions, participants and choice opportunities. Around this same time period, Holland began investigating a generalization of the genetic algorithm, the classifier system. Based on the principle of a default hierarchy, the classifier system would evolve rules, or "classifiers" that would translate inputs into outputs to satisfy a goal. The classifier system contained a population of simple rules that worked together to model complex phenomena. This is similar to the way that the ABM contains a population of simple agents that work together to model a complex phenomenon. Moreover, the classifier system was a first attempt at creating truly adaptive agents, since it contained an algorithm for agents to build up arbitrarily complex strategies.

In the following years, Holland worked with two graduate students, Melanie Mitchell and Stephanie Forrest. Together, they began exploring the use of the genetic algorithm in various scenarios related to artificial life (Mitchell & Forrest, 1994). Mitchell demonstrated (1998) that genetic algorithms could find better solutions to classic cellular automata problems. She went on to do core research and write an introductory textbook on complex systems (2009) that described the relationship between complexity and computation, evolution and artificial intelligence. Around the same time, the ECHO series of models was developed (Holland, 1993), which were a first attempt at building agent-based models where the agents had no explicit goals. Instead, the agents made use of resources in the environment and used them to stay alive. The agents were forced to find ways to gain more resources through trade, conflict, or harvesting, and to find ways to defend themselves. However, none of this was explicitly coded into the model; instead, the system was only coded so that agents without enough resources died, a principle known as an *implicit fitness function*. Even though ECHO was never implemented by Holland, it described many of the basic mechanisms in use in ABMs today. If you want to check out an implementation of ECHO, there is a version in the Biology section of the NetLogo models library.

ECHO influenced early work in the modeling of artificial life and is still used as a high-level description of the evolutionary process. Many of Holland's ideas about the ECHO models were summarized in Holland's 1995 Ulam Lecture series at the Santa Fe Institute, which was published as *Hidden Order* (1995). *Hidden Order* is one of the first books to outline the basic principles of ABM and cast them as a foundational to complex adaptive systems. These ideas are extended and revised in Holland's 1998 book, *Emergence*.

Forrest would continue to expand upon these ideas and create artificial immune systems (AIS; Hofmeyr & Forrest, 2000). AIS create populations of agents within a computer whose sole task is to determine whether activity within the computer is normal; if it is not, the agents must then isolate and stop the activity. This process is very similar to how the human body immune system works, and AIS are as such ABMs of the human immune system placed in a computer environment.

Echoes of Holland's work can be seen throughout ABM not just through his influence on individual modelers and their fieldwork, but also in the many first principles that he developed. His notion that many different types of adaptation, from neural to evolutionary to economic, have a common structure has greatly influenced agent-based modeling. Moreover, Holland's interest in parallel computation from population-based search techniques to the classifier system to neural modeling remains central in agent-based modeling today.

Seymour Papert, Logo, and the Turtle

In the late 1960s, Seymour Papert was appointed codirector of MIT's Artificial Intelligence Laboratory along with his colleague Marvin Minsky. Papert had arrived at MIT after finishing his doctorate in mathematics at Cambridge and spent several years studying children's mathematical thinking with Piaget at the Jean Piaget Institute in Geneva, Switzerland.

Shortly after his arrival to MIT, he began collaboration with scientists at Bolt Beranek and Newman, which had a research laboratory in Cambridge. Together, Papert, Feurzeig, Bobrow, and Solomon (See Feurzeig et al, 1969) created a programming language, Logo, designed to be used by children. Logo inherited much of its form and syntax from the language Lisp, which was prominently used in Artificial Intelligence work.[1] Papert believed that giving children access to programming would enable them to become computational thinkers and give them access to powerful ideas such as debugging and recursion (Papert, 1980). He called this educational approach Constructionism. After working with Logo for a year, Papert invented the "turtle," an object that was controlled by the Logo language. Some early turtles were mechanical (Walter, 1950) and tethered to the computer, but soon the turtle became virtual. Turtles had properties such as location on the screen, a "heading" (direction) they were facing, and a pen they carried. Each turtle obeyed some core Logo commands, such as "move-forward," "turn-left," etc. By issuing commands to the turtle, children were able to draw classic geometric figures as well as repeating and recursive figures that were quite intricate but were easily programmed in the computational medium.

Logo was thereafter introduced into schools, with millions of children worldwide participating in Constructionist Logo activities (Harel & Papert, 1990; Papert, 1987). Much of the success of Logo was attributed to the turtle. Papert described the turtle as a "body-syntonic" object (1980): A user could project oneself into the turtle and, in order to figure out what commands it should be given, users could imagine what they would do with their bodies to achieve the desired effect. So, to draw a square, the user would move forward, turn right, move forward the same amount, and so on. In thousands of Logo classrooms, children would "play turtle" and learn both about geometric figures and how to program in this way.

The Logo turtle may have been the *first computational agent* in the sense that we think of agents in agent-based models today. Like NetLogo agents, the Logo turtle has a location and direction, and its power is based on users being able to project themselves into it, that is to imagine being a turtle. NetLogo took much of its syntax from Logo and expanded the idea of a single turtle to thousands of turtles. NetLogo turtles typically "draw" with their bodies rather than with pens, and it is the configuration of their bodies that create a NetLogo visualization (Wilensky, 2001). NetLogo also borrowed the slogan "low threshold, high ceiling" from Logo, meaning that it should be simple enough for novices to be able to work with it right away and yet powerful enough for experts to conduct their

---

1. *Lisp* stands for *List* Processing.

research with it (Tisue & Wilensky, 2004). Moreover, NetLogo built upon the Logo syntax to make reading it as close to English as possible.

The influence of Papert and Logo can be seen not only in NetLogo, but also in the way that many agent-based modeling platforms conceptualize agents as entities with their own properties and actions. Most of the early agent-based modeling platforms, such as Swarm (Minar et al., 1996) and Repast (*Collier, 2001*), took as given the need to visualize agents on a 2D screen, in the same way that the Logo turtle was projected onto a 2D screen.

Object-Oriented Programming and the Actor Model

The original conception of "function" within a programming language was a simple procedure that would take a single number and output a single number or, at best, take as input a matrix of numbers and output a matrix of numbers. It was not until the invention of the Lisp language by John McCarthy in 1958 at MIT that this notion of function was expanded. McCarthy (1960) built upon Alonzo Church's lambda calculus (1932) to create a programming language where functions could take as input other functions and pass back as output a new function. This new development treated functions as first class objects within the Lisp programming language and rebranded numerical and matrix data as restricted forms of the full functional input and output that Lisp allows. This vastly expanded the computational power of functions since now they could not only respond to numerical and variable inputs, but also to functional inputs.

Although Lisp was a powerful programming language, it still maintained that functions and data were separate. This is a reasonable strategy when the functions are very simple, like addition and subtraction, and when the data is very simple, like integers and floating point numbers. However, as software engineering techniques advanced, it became clear that more complicated functional and data management power was necessary. For example, how does one describe an "addition" operator that works on a universal set of objects ranging from integers to address records to full databases? To solve this problem, several researchers came up with the idea of tying functions to the data that they manipulated. Ole-Johan Dahl and Kristen Nygaard in Norway realized while designing simulations of maritime ships that the easiest way to describe a ship, including all the attributes and behaviors it could have, was to place the ship in a class of similar ships (Holmevik, 1994). In order to facilitate this process, Dahl and Nygaard created the Simula programming language, the first programming language to combine data and functions together in a single object or "class." However, the term "object-oriented programming" was not used until the development of Smalltalk by Alan Kay and colleagues (Kay, 1993). Simula and Smalltalk were the first languages to allow the encapsulation of objects, a way to bind multiple functional units and data elements into one cohesive whole.

Object-oriented programming led to a new way of thinking about modeling as well. If we can encapsulate objects and methods together, then we can create classes that represent different objects in our universe. For instance, in the model of the ants discussed in chapter

1, we can create a class that represents the ant object. It can represent both what the ant can do in the world (move, eat, drop pheromone, etc.) and what the ant knows (where it is headed, whether it has found food, etc.). Not until the creation of object-oriented languages could many of the properties of agent-based models be easily instantiated in computational constructs.

Though Smalltalk and Simula were elegant and very expressive in their ability to send messages from one object to another, Carl Hewitt, a researcher at MIT, thought they were too complex. Hewitt wanted to create a computational model where the central computational construct was message passing and, moreover, wanted to emphasize concurrent computation over serial computation. He thus developed the Actor model, which was placed on formal footing by Bishop and Steiger (Hewitt et al., 1973). He was greatly influenced along this development by Papert and the little person model of computation (Hewitt & Baker, 1977), as well as Kay's work on object-oriented programming (1993), but Hewitt espoused a simplified design philosophy wherein the computational objects would be known as "actors."

Actors have a very limited set of things they can do, but despite this are able to perform complex computations. Actors can send and receive messages, create other actors, and have behaviors, which allow them to manipulate messages. Each actor has a mailing address, and actors can only send messages to other actors whose mailing address they already have. The only way for an actor to know another actor's mailing address is by having it sent to them in a message. Thus, all interactions are local; there is no global state of knowledge of all mailing addresses. In addition, since actors can learn new mailing addresses as well as forget old ones, the topology of interactions in the world of actors is dynamic, as opposed to one based on physical distance or some other static attribute of the world. Moreover, actors can be sequenced such that each one conducts a small part of an overall computation, allowing the programmer to compose multiple actors into one actor. Last, actors are inherently concurrent, able to compute results in parallel independently of each other.

Over time, the concept of actors was integrated into object oriented (OO) programming, and many of the aspects of actors are still present in languages like C++, Objective-C, and Cocoa in addition to ABM. Several aspects of Actors greatly influenced the development of ABM even independent of OO programming. For instance, OO lacks an emphasis on concurrent computation but that was a key element of Actors. Though almost all ABM languages are by necessity serial (since current affordable computers are all serial), many of them still attempt to simulate concurrent computation. In addition, even when the language does not support concurrency, model builders often design their models to operate concurrently, either through interweaving of actions or through asynchronous updating.[2]

---

2. These techniques will be discussed in the following vignette. It is sufficient to know that they emulate parallel computation on a serial machine.

Since the real world, whether it is particles bouncing around, sheep and wolves moving in a meadow, or voters deciding how to vote, operates in parallel, both ABM and Actors have emphasized parallel computation.

Another feature present in Actors that is shared with ABM is the notion of local interactions. Actors can only communicate with actors they already know about; there is no global directory of mailing addresses. Again, this echoes the "real world" as it can be difficult to find an address for a random name: you often have to reach out to people you already know to be put in touch with people you do not know. After all, it is rare that a single agent in the real world has the ability to access any resource it wants; instead, it often has a list of resources it has access to, and then must decide how to access those resources. ABM likewise relies on local interactions, as they are the mechanisms by which the real world typically works.

Besides having a local topology of interaction, the Actors topology is also dynamic: that is, actors can learn new addresses and forget old ones, much as agents moving around a landscape often interact with different agents at different time steps. Not only does this conserve memory, since agents and actors do not have to remember everyone they have ever met, but it also allows them to change and adapt to fluctuating environments.

Many of the properties that agents possess are also properties of actors. For instance, agents are described as having behaviors, and so are actors. Agents are described as passing messages to other agents and this idea has influenced many ABM platforms to adopt this same metaphor. Many of the core constructs of OOP and the Actors language have long influenced or directly migrated into the major ABM platforms.

Data Parallelism

In the mid-1980s, Danny Hillis completed his doctoral thesis at MIT on the architecture of a parallel computer he dubbed a "connection machine." Unlike the classic von Neumann architecture of most other computers at that time, the connection machine (or CM) did not handle all its calculations through a single central processing unit (Hillis, 1989). Instead it made use of thousands of low-cost, low-capacity processors connected to each other in a "hypercube" so each processor could communicate with any other processor with just a few intermediate processors in between. The CM employed an architecture that was called, "Single Instruction, Multiple Data," usually abbreviated SIMD, which would give the same instruction to each of the thousands of processors, each of which held data elements. Hillis founded a company, Thinking Machines, to manufacture and sell the computer.

At first, the machine was perceived as hard to program, since standard serial processing languages did not work efficiently with the machine. By the end of the 1980s, special parallel languages such as StarLisp (a parallel version of Lisp) and C-Star were created for programming the CM. The CM-2 had 65,536 processors, and to use them efficiently it was important not to have some processors waiting for others. The easiest way to do this was to use "data-parallel" methods, in which the data was spread evenly across the processors, each of which simultaneously executed the same instruction on its data. (In contrast, most parallel machines at the time used control-parallel methods whereby there were multiple parallel execution threads.) Scientists at Thinking Machines came up with some novel powerful applications for the CM. One of the first of these was an improved form of document retrieval (Stanfill & Kahle, 1986). Suppose one had an example of a document that was relevant and wanted to find others. You could encode the known document as a query of search terms. Each processor was loaded with a document from the database, and each responded to the query by scoring its document's proximity in term-space to the query document. One could then retrieve the highest scoring document(s) and repeat.

Another application that was developed to take advantage of the parallel architecture revolved around object recognition. In the object recognition application, a collection of two-dimensional objects from a large known objects database was placed on a table and the task for the machine was to produce a labeled picture with each object recognized. A Thinking Machine scientist, Lew Tucker, devised an algorithm that generated hypotheses that were loaded to each processor, and then, similarly to the document retrieval application, each hypothesis was scored by comparing it to the 2D array of pixels captured by the camera (Tucker, Feynman & Fritzsche, 1988).

The data parallel approach was well suited to quickly computing cellular automata, as described earlier. The physicist Richard Feynman, along with Stephen Wolfram, developed a fluid flow application based on a cellular automaton (Tucker & Robertson, 1988). Feynman had shown that almost all fluid flows could be modeled independently of the type of particle, using a hexagonal lattice. So Feynman and Wolfram chose spherical particles and computed the change in each hexagon of the lattice in data parallel style. The result was a beautiful visualization of turbulent fluids.

Both examples above have been taken up by agent-based modelers and can be run on serial hardware using ABM methods. The SIMD data parallel paradigm did not ultimately succeed in the hardware marketplace and was eclipsed by faster, more sophisticated, but less parallel, processors. But, its methods of giving the same instruction to multiple processors influenced ABM languages, which were also giving single instructions to multiple distributed agents. In essence, the data parallel model was taken up by ABM, but primarily enacted on serial machines. In fact, one early ABM language, StarLogo, was written in StarLisp and originally implemented on a Connection Machine.

Computer Graphics, Particle Systems, and Boids

Computer graphics has advanced markedly with the rest of computer science over time. As computers have become faster and faster, computer displays have improved to render more and more realistic visualizations and computer-based images. Since computer graphics has as its goal taking an image inside the author's head and translating it into a visual representation, it bears a lot of similarity to computer modeling. In computer modeling, the goal is to take a conceptual model and translate it into a computational artifact. Thus, it is no surprise that computer graphics has influenced agent-based modeling.

Early on in computer graphics, many developers used a large combination of flat surfaces to represent objects. This proved a good first approximation: after all, the vast majority of our visual range is usually occupied by surfaces, like walls and ceilings, the sky or a road before us. However, surfaces are not adequate representation for less sharply defined phenomena such as smoke, stars, or light (Blinn, 1982). To model these phenomena, computer graphics developers turned to point representations. Points could be given size, position, and velocity and made for more natural representation for these phenomena than surfaces. In addition, points were easier to work with (and their rules of movement, when described procedurally) were easier to deal with than surfaces. The point-based approach to computer graphics became known as particle systems (Reeves, 1983). Such systems have much in common with agent-based modeling because they can simulate visually salient emergent phenomenon, such as smoke coming out of a smokestack, by modeling the individual particles of smoke and writing simple rules of how they interact to visualize the resultant global pattern. Agent-based models likewise use simple rules of agent-based interaction and then let you observe the global phenomenon.

Inspired by the use of particle systems and the aforementioned work on turtles and Logo programming language, Craig Reynolds moved beyond the concept of particles as small, indistinct objects to using particle systems to describe the motion of birds flocking (Reynolds, 1987), which we described in chapter 7. Reynolds called these generic flocking creatures "boids" and used three simple rules to describe their behavior:

Separation Boids should not get too close to any other object in the environment
Alignment Boids should steer toward the same heading as their local flockmates
Cohesion Boids should move toward the center of their local group

Despite the simplicity of these three rules, Reynolds was able to achieve realistic flocking simulations. In fact, the local interaction of these rules not only enabled Reynolds develop a model that looked like flocking at the global level, but also rendered each of the smaller parts to look like flocks. Thus, if an obstacle were introduced in the path of the flock, it could quite easily break in to two flocks, move around the object, and then reassemble on the other side of the object. All of this was accomplished without any special coding to handle object avoidance.

The "Boids" model was in many ways an agent-based model, though this term had not yet come into use. The individual boids kept track of their own attributes yet contributed to a global phenomenon that emerged from their own local interactions. The fact that the flocks were able to adapt to novel situations (e.g., the introduction of a foreign object) without disrupting the emergent pattern is a classic example of how a well-written ABM is generalizable beyond the conditions for which it was originally conceived. Since ABMs do not require a global description of the system, they do not need to anticipate all possible events that might happen.

Shortly after Reynolds's presentation of the Boids model at SIGGRAPH '87, Chris Langton organized the first workshop on Artificial Life, where Reynolds's model was also presented. Artificial Life has developed into a community that embraces many of these different methods of computation where computers are being used to emulate human and biological systems. Artificial Life, therefore, began to use systems like Reynolds's Boids, von Neumann's cellular automata, and Holland's genetic algorithms. Though Artificial Life is distinct from agent-based modeling in that its goal is to build systems that reflect lifelike objects within a computer, many of the methods and techniques of ABM and Artificial Life are quite similar.

Conclusion

ABM has come a long way from the days of Thomas Schelling (1971) flipping coins on a checkerboard. These six vignettes have attempted to shed some light on the roots of this field. Nonetheless, the field is still quite young. There is considerable research that has yet to be carried out on how to best implement ABM, what tools are most useful for supporting ABM, and where to best apply ABM. It is clear that ABM has become a primary methodology and set of tools for understanding complex systems from natural science, social science, and engineering. We hope that in this book, we have provided a sufficient introduction for you to effectively use ABM. It is also our hope that agent-based models become a core literacy for citizens and scientists so that everyone can use models to reason, and so that public media can use models to support arguments and to inform policy.

References

Abrahamson, D., & Wilensky, U. (2004). SAMPLER: Collaborative interactive computer-based statistics learning environment. Proceedings of the 10th International Congress on Mathematical Education, Copenhagen, July 4–11, 2004.

Aktipis, A. (2004). Know when to walk away: Contingent movement and the evolution of cooperation. *Journal of Theoretical Biology, 231*(2), 249–260.

An, G., & Wilensky, U. (2009). From artificial life to in silico medicine: NetLogo as a means of translational knowledge representation in biomedical research. In A. Adamatzky & M. Komosinski (Eds.), *Artificial Life Models in Software* (2nd ed., pp. 183–214). Berlin: Springer-Verlag.

Anas, A. (2002). Prejudice, exclusion, and compensating transfers: The economics of ethnic segregation. *Journal of Urban Economics, 52*(3), 409–432.

Anderson, P. (1972). More is different. *Science, 177*, 393–396.

Arthur, W. B. (1994). Inductive reasoning and bounded rationality. *American Economic Review, 84*(2), 406–411.

Arthur, W. B., Holland, J. H., LeBaron, B., Palmer, R., & Taylor, P. (1997). Asset pricing under endogenous expectations in an artificial stock market. In W. Arthur, D. Lane, & S. Durlauf (Eds.), *The Economy as an Evolving Complex System: II* (pp. 15–44). Redwood City, CA: Addison-Wesley.

Ashlock, D. (2006). *Evolutionary Computation for Modeling and Optimization*. New York: Springer-Verlag.

Axelrod, R. (1984). *The Evolution of Cooperation*. New York: Basic Books.

Axelrod, R. (1997). Advancing the art of simulation in the social sciences. In R. Conte, R. Hegelsmann, & P. Terna (Eds.), *Simulating Social Phenomena* (pp. 21–40). Berlin: Springer-Verlag.

Axtell, R., Axelrod, R., Epstein, J. M., & Cohen, M. D. (1996). Aligning simulation models: A case study and results. *Computational & Mathematical Organization Theory, 1*, 123–141.

Axtell, R., Epstein, J., Dean, J., Gumerman, G., Swedlund, A., Harburger, J., et al. (2002). Population growth and collapse in a multiagent model of the Kayenta Anasazi in Long House Valley. *Proceedings of the National Academy of Sciences of the United States of America, 99*(suppl. 3), 7275–7279.

Ayres, I. (2007). *Super Crunchers: Why Thinking-By-Numbers Is the New Way To Be Smart*. New York: Bantam Books.

Bak, P. (1996). *How Nature Works: The Science of Self-Organized Criticality*. New York: Springer.

Bak, P., Chen, K., & Tang, C. (1990). A forest-fire model and some thoughts on turbulence. [Part A]. *Physics Letters, 147*, 297–300.

Bak, P., Tang, C., & Wiesenfeld, K. (1987). Self-organized criticality: An explanation of 1/f noise. *Physical Review Letters, 59*, 381–384.

Bakshy, E., & Wilensky, U. (2007a). NetLogo-Mathematica Link. http://ccl.northwestern.edu/netlogo/mathematica.html. Center for Connected Learning and Computer-Based Modeling, Northwestern University, Evanston, IL.

Bakshy, E., & Wilensky, U. (2007b). Turtle histories and alternate universes: Exploratory modeling with NetLogo and Mathematica. Proceedings of the Agent2007 Conference, Chicago, November 15–17.

Barabási, A.-L. (2002). *Linked: The New Science of Networks*. Cambridge, MA: Perseus.

Barabási, A. L., & Albert, R. (1999). Emergence of scaling in random networks. *Science, 286*(5439), 509–512.

Batty, M. (2005). *Cities and Complexity: Understanding Cities with Cellular Automata, Agent-Based Models, and Fractals*. Cambridge, MA: MIT Press.

Batty, M., & Longley, P. (1994). *Fractal Cities: A Geometry of Form and Function*. San Diego: Academic Press.

Bauer, B., Muller, J. P., & Odell, J. (2000). Agent UML: A Formalism for Specifying Multiagent Interaction. *Lecture Notes in Computer Science, 1957*, 109–120.

Belding, T. C. (2000). *Numerical Replication of Computer Simulations: Some Pitfalls and How to Avoid Them*. University of Michigan's Center for the Study of Complex Systems, Technical Report.

Bentley, W. A., & Humphreys, W. J. (1962). *Snow Crystals*. New York: Dover.

Berland, M., & Rand, W. (2009). Participatory simulation as a tool for agent-based simulation. Proceedings of the International Conference on Agents and Artificial Intelligence (ICAART-09), Porto, Portugal, 553–557.

Berland, M., & Wilensky, U. (2006). Constructionist collaborative engineering: Results from an implementation of PVBOT. Paper presented at the annual meeting of the American Educational Research Association, San Francisco, CA.

Berlekamp, E., Conway, J. H., & Guy, R. (1982). *Winning Ways for Your Mathematical Plays*. London: Academic.

Bertin, J. (1967). *Semiologie graphique*. The Hague: Mouton.

Bertin, J. (1983). *Semiology of Graphics*. Madison: University of Wisconsin Press.

Blikstein, P., Rand, W., & Wilensky, U. (2007). Examining group behavior and collaboration using ABM and robots. Proceedings of the Agent2007 Conference, Chicago, November 15–17.

Blikstein, P., & Wilensky, U. (2006). A case study of multi-agent-based simulation in undergraduate materials science education. Proceedings of the Annual Conference of the American Society for Engineering Education, Chicago, IL, June 18–21.

Blikstein, P., & Wilensky, U. (2007). Bifocal modeling: A framework for combining computer modeling, robotics and real-world sensing. Paper presented at the 2007 annual meeting of the American Educational Research Association, Chicago, IL, April 9–13. http://ccl.northwestern.edu/papers/2007/09-bifocal_modeling.pdf.

Blikstein, P., & Wilensky, U. (2009). An atom is known by the company it keeps: A constructionist learning environment for materials science using multi-agent simulation. *International Journal of Computers for Mathematical Learning, 14*(1), 81–119.

Blinn, J. (1982). Light reflection functions for simulation of clouds and dusty surfaces. *Computer Graphics, 16*(3), 21–29.

Bonabeau, E. (2012). http://www.icosystem.com/labsdemos/the-game/.

Bonabeau, E., Dorigo, M., & Théraulaz, G. (1999). *Swarm Intelligence: From Natural to Artificial Systems*. London: Oxford University Press.

Bonabeau, E., Funes, P., & Orme, B. (2003). Exploratory design of swarms. 2nd International Workshop on the Mathematics and Algorithms of Social Insects. Georgia Institute of Technology, Atlanta.

Bonabeau, E., & Meyer, C. (2001). Swarm intelligence: A whole new way to think about business. *Harvard Business Review, 5*, 107–114.

Booch, G., Rumbaugh, J., & Jacobson, I. (2005). *The Unified Modeling Language User's Guide*. New York: Addison-Wesley.

Borges, J. L. (1946). On exactitude in science. *Los Anales de Buenos Aires, 1*.

Box, G. (1979). Robustness in the strategy of scientific model building. In R. L. Launer & G. N. Wilkinson (Eds.), *Robustness in Statistics*. New York: Academic Press.

Box, G., & Draper, N. (1987). *Empirical Model-Building and Response Surfaces*. New York: Wiley.

Box, G., Jenkins, G., & Reinsel, G. (1994). *Time Series Analysis: Forecasting and Control* (3rd ed.). Englewood Cliffs, NJ: Prentice-Hall.

Branko, G., & Shephard, G. C. (1987). *Tilings and Patterns*. New York: W. H. Freeman.

Broadbent, S. R., & Hammersley, J. M. (1957). Percolation processes I. Crystals and mazes. *Proceedings of the Cambridge Philosophical Society, 53*, 629–641.

Brown, D. G., Page, S. E., Riolo, R., Zellner, M., & Rand, W. (2005). Path dependence and the validation of agent-based spatial models of land use. *International Journal of Geographical Information Science, 19*(2), 153–174.

Brown, D., Riolo, R., Robinson, D. T., North, M., & Rand, W. (2005). Spatial process and data models: Toward integration of agent-based models and GIS. *Journal of Geographical Systems, 7*(1), 25–47.

Brown, D. G., Robinson, D. T., Nassauer, J. I., An, L., Page, S. E., Low, B., et al. (2008). Exurbia from the bottom-up: Agent-based modeling and empirical requirements. *Geoforum, 39*(2), 805–818.

Burks, A. (1970). *Essays on Cellular Automata*. Urbana: University of Illinois Press.

Card, S. K., Newell, A., & Moran, T. P. (1983). *The Psychology of Human-Computer Interaction*. Hillsdale, NJ: Erlbaum.

Carley, K. (2002). Simulating society: The tension between transparency and veridicality. Proceedings of Agents 2002, Chicago IL.

Cassandras, C., & Lafortune, S. (1999). *Introduction to Discrete Event Systems*. Boston: Kluwer Academic.

Casti, J. L. (1995). Seeing the light at El Farol: A look at the most important problem in complex systems theory. *Complexity, 1*(5), 7–10.

Centola, D., Wilensky, U., & McKenzie, E. (2000). A hands-on modeling approach to evolution: Learning about the evolution of cooperation and altruism through multi-agent modeling—The EACH Project. Proceedings of the Fourth Annual International Conference of the Learning Sciences, Ann Arbor, MI.

Challet, D., Marsili, M., & Zhang, Y.-C. (2004). *Minority Games*. Oxford: Oxford University Press.

Church, A. (1932). A set of postulates for the foundation of logic. *Annals of Mathematics* 2nd ser., 346–66.

Cohen, M. D., March, J. G., & Olsen, J. P. (1972). A garbage can model of organizational choice. *Administrative Science Quarterly, 17*(1), 1–25.

Colella, V. (2000). Participatory simulations: Building collaborative understanding through immersive dynamic modeling. *Journal of the Learning Sciences, 9*(4), 471–500.

Collier, N., Howe, T., & North, M. (2003). Onward and upward: The transition to Repast 2.0. Proceedings of the First Annual North American Association for Computational Social and Organizational Science Conference, Pittsburgh, PA.

Conway, J. (1976). *On Numbers and Games*. Waltham, MA: Academic Press.

Cook, M. (2004). Universality in elementary cellular automata. *Complex Systems, 15*, 1–40.

Dawkins, R. (1986). *The Blind Watchmaker*. New York: Norton.

Dean, J. S., Gumerman, G. J., Epstein, J. M., Axtell, R. L., Swedlund, A. C., Parker, M. T., et al. (2000). Understanding Anasazi culture change through agent-based modeling. In T. A. Kohler & G. J. Gumerman (Eds.), *Dynamics in Human and Primate Societies: Agent-Based Modeling of Social and Spatial Processes* (pp. 179–205). New York: Oxford University Press.

DeAngelis, D. L., & Gross, L. J. (1992). *Individual-Based Models and Approaches in Ecology: Populations, Communities and Ecosystems*. New York: Chapman & Hall.

DeAngelis, D., & Mooij, W. (2005). Individual-based modeling of ecological and evolutionary processes. *Annual Review of Ecology Evolution and Systematics, 36*(1), 147–168.

Deneubourg, J. L., & Goss, S. (1989). Collective patterns and decision-making. *Ethology Ecology and Evolution, 1*, 295–311.

Deneubourg, J. L., Goss, S., Sandini, G., Ferrari, F., & Dario, P. (1990). Self-organizing collection and transport of objects in unpredictable environments. *Proc. of Japan—USA Symposium on Flexible Automation, Kyoto, Japan, ISCIE*.

Dewdney, A. K. (1987). Diverse personalities search for social equilibrium at a computer party, Computer Recreations. *Scientific American*, (Sept): 112–117.

Dewdney, A. K. (1990). *The Magic Machine*. San Francisco: Freeman.

DiSessa, A. A. (2000). *Changing Minds: Computers, Learning, and Literacy*. Cambridge, MA: MIT Press.

Dix, A., Finlay, J., Abowd, J., & Beale, R. (2004). *Human-Computer Interaction*. Englewood Cliffs, NJ: Prentice Hall.

Dorigo, M., & Stützle, T. (2004). *Ant Colony Optimization*. Cambridge, MA: MIT Press.

Dragulescu, A. & Yakovenko, V.M. (2000). Statistical mechanics of money. *European Physical Journal B*, *17*, 723–729.

Dubins, L. E., & Savage, L. J. (1965). *How to Gamble if You Must: Inequalities for Stochastic Processes*. New York: Dover.

Edelson, D. (2004). My world: a case study in adapting scientists' tools for learners. Proceedings of the 6th international conference on the Learning sciences.

Edmonds, B., & Hales, D. (2003). Replication, replication and replication: Some hard lessons from model alignment. *Journal of Artificial Societies and Social Simulation*, *6*(4).

Einstein, A. (1933). "On the Method of Theoretical Physics." The Herbert Spencer Lecture, delivered at Oxford (10 June 1933); also published in *Philosophy of Science, 1*(2), 163–169, 1934.

Enfield, N. J. (2003). *Linguistic Epidemiology: Semantics and Grammar of Language Contact in Mainland Southeast Asia*. New York: Routledge.

Epstein, J. (1999). Agent-based computational models and generative social science. *Complexity*, *4*(5), 41–60.

Epstein, J. (2006). *Generative Social Science: Studies in Agent-Based Computational Modeling*. Princeton: Princeton University Press.

Epstein, J., & Axtell, R. (1996). *Growing Artificial Societies*. Cambridge, MA: MIT Press.

Erdös, P., & Renyi, A. (1959). On random graphs. *Publicationes Mathematicae (Debrecen)*, *6*, 290–297.

Erdös, P., & Renyi, A. (1960). On the evolution of random graphs. *Publications of the Mathematical Institute of the Hungarian Academy of Sciences*, *5*, 17–61.

Feurzeig, W., Papert, S., Bloom, M., Grant, R., & Solomon, C. (1969). *Programming languages as a conceptual framework for teaching mathematics* (Tech. Rep. No. 1899). Cambridge, MA: Bolt, Beranek, & Newman.

Flach, P. (2012). *Machine Learning: The Art and Science of Algorithms That Make Sense of Data*. Cambridge: Cambridge University Press.

Fogel, D. B., Chellapilla, K., & Angeline, P. J. (1999). Inductive reasoning and bounded rationality reconsidered. *IEEE Transactions on Evolutionary Computation*, *3*(2), 142–146.

Forrester, J. (1961). *Industrial Dynamics*. Cambridge, MA: MIT Press.

Forrester, J. W. (1968). *Principles of Systems*. Norwalk, CT: Productivity Press.

Fredkin, E. (1990). An informational process based on reversible cellular automata. *Physica D. Nonlinear Phenomena*, *45*(1–3), 254–270.

Frey, S., & Goldstone, R. (2013). Cyclic game dynamics driven by iterated reasoning. *PLoS ONE*, *8*(2), e56416. doi:10.1371/journal.pone.0056416.

Galilei, G. (1638) *Discorsi e dimostrazioni matematiche, intorno à due nuove scienze* 213 (Leiden: Louis Elsevier), or *Mathematical discourses and demonstrations, relating to Two New Sciences*, English translation by Henry Crew and Alfonso de Salvio (1914).

Garcia-Ruiz, J. M., Louis, E., Meakin, P., & Sander, L. (Eds.). (1993). *Growth Patterns in Physical Sciences and Biology (Nato Science Series B)*. New York: Springer.

Gardner, M. (1970). Mathematical games: The fantastic combinations of John Conway's new solitaire game, "Life. *Scientific American, 223*, 120–123.

Gause, G. F. (1936). *The Struggle for Existence*. New York: Dover.

Giancoli, D. (1984). *General Physics*. Englewood Cliffs, NJ: Prentice Hall.

Gladwell, M. (2000). *The Tipping Point*. New York: Little, Brown.

Gluckmann, G. M., & Bryson, J. (2011). An agent-based model of the effects of a primate social structure on the speed of natural selection. Evolutionary Computation and Multi-Agent Systems and Simulation (ECoMASS) at GECCO 2011, Dublin.

Goldberg, A., & Kay, A. (1976). *Smalltalk-72: Instruction Manual* (pp. 749–750). Palo Alto, CA: Xerox Corporation.

Gould, J. L., & Gould, C. G. (1988). *The Honey Bee*. W. H. Freeman.

Grasse, P. P. (1959). La reconstruction du nid et les coordinations inter-individuelles chez *Bellicositermes natalensis* et *Cubitermes* sp. La theorie de la stigmergie: Essai d'interpretation du comportement des termites constructeurs. *Insectes Sociaux, 6*, 41–81.

Grimm, V., Berger, U., Bastianen, F., Eliassen, S., Ginot, V., Giske, J., et al. (2006). A standard protocol for describing individual-based and agent-based models. *Ecological Modelling, 198*, 115–126.

Grimm, V., & Railsback, S. (2005). *Individual-Based Modeling and Ecology*. Princeton: Princeton University Press.

Grimm, V., Revilla, E., Berger, E., Jeltsch, F., Mooij, W., Railsback, S., et al. (2005). Pattern-oriented modeling of agent-based complex systems: Lessons from ecology. *Science, 310*, 987–991.

Grimmett, G. (1999). *Percolation*. Berlin: Springer Verlag.

Hammersley, J. M., & Handscomb, D. C. (1964). *Monte Carlo Methods*. New York: Chapman and Hall.

Hammond, R. A., & Axelrod, R. (2006). The evolution of ethnocentrism. *Journal of Conflict Resolution, 50*(6), 926.

Harel, I., & Papert, S. (1990). Software design as a learning environment. *Interactive Environments Journal, 1*(1), 41–84.

Hartmann, G., & Wehner, R. (1995). The ant's path integration system: A neural architecture. *Biological Cybernetics, 73*(6), 483–497.

Hawking, S. (2001). *The Universe in a Nutshell*. New York: Bantam Books.

Hebb, D. O. (1949). *The Organization of Behavior: A Neuropsychological Theory*. New York: John Wiley & Sons.

Hewitt, C., & Baker, H. (1977). Actors and continuous functionals. *MIT Working Papers* (1977).

Hewitt, C., Bishop, P., & Steiger, R. (1973). A universal modular actor formalism for artificial intelligence. *Proc. of International Joint Conference on Artificial Intelligence*, 1973.

Hillis, W. D. (1991). Co-evolving parasites improve simulated evolution as an optimization procedure. In C. Langton, C. Taylor, D. Farmer, & S. Rasmussen (Eds.), *Artificial Life II, SFI Studies in the Sciences of Complexity* (pp. 313–324). Boulder, CO: Westview Press.

Hillis, W. D. (1989). *The Connection Machine*. Cambridge, MA: MIT Press.

Hofmeyr, S. A., & Forrest, S. (2000). Architecture for an artificial immune system. *Evolutionary Computation, 8*(4), 443–473.

Holland, J. (1975). *Adaptation in Natural and Artificial Systems*. Ann Arbor: University of Michigan Press.

Holland, J. H. (1993). Echoing emergence. *SFI Working Papers* 93.04–23.

Holland, J. H. (1994). Echoing emergence: Objectives, rough definitions, and speculations for Echo-class models. In G. A. Cowan, D. Pines, & D. Meltzer (Eds.), *Complexity: Metaphors, Models and Reality* (pp. 309–342). Reading, MA: Addison-Wesley.

Holland, J. H. (1996). *Hidden Order: How Adaptation Builds Complexity*. Reading, MA: Addison-Wesley.

Holland, J. H. (1998). *Emergence: From Chaos to Order*. Reading, MA: Addison-Wesley.

Hölldobler, B., & Wilson, E. O. (1998). *The Ants*. Berlin: Springer.

Holmevik, J. R. (1994). Compiling simula: A historical study of technological genesis. *IEEE Annals of the History of Computing, 16*(4), 25–37.

Hutton, T. (2010). Codd's self-replicating computer. *Artificial Life, 16*(2), 99–117.

Izquierdo, L. R., & Polhill, J. G. (2006). Is your model susceptible to floating point errors? *Journal of Artificial Societies and Social Simulation, 9*(4).

Jackson, D. E., Holcombe, M., & Ratnieks, F. (2004). Trail geometry gives polarity to ant foraging networks. *Nature, 432,* 907–909.

Janis, I. L. (1982). *Groupthink: Psychological Studies of Policy Decisions and Fiascoes.* Boston: Houghton Mifflin.

Janson, S., Knuth, D. E., Luczak, T., & Pittel, B. (1993). The birth of the giant component. *Random Structures and Algorithms, 4*(3), 233–358.

Kalos, M. H., & Whitlock, P. A. (1986). Monte Carlo Methods (Vol. I). *Basics.* New York: Wiley-Interscience.

Kay, A. (1993). The early history of Smalltalk. *ACM SIGPLAN Notices, 28*(3), 69–95.

Keller, E. F. (1985). *Reflections on Gender and Science.* New Haven, CT: Yale University Press.

Keller, E. F., & Segel, L. (1970). Initiation of slime mold aggregation viewed as an instability. *Journal of Theoretical Biology, 26,* 399–415.

Klopfer, E. (2003). Technologies to support the creation of complex systems models—Using StarLogo software with students. *Bio Systems, 71,* 111–123.

Klopfer, E., Yoon, S., & Perry, J. (2005). Using Palm technology in participatory simulations of complex systems: A new take on ubiquitous and accessible mobile computing. *Journal of Science Education and Technology, 14*(3), 285–297.

Kornhauser, D., Rand, W., & Wilensky, U. (2007). Visualization tools for agent-based modeling in NetLogo. Proceedings of the Agent 2007 Conference on Complex Interaction and Social Emergence, Evanston.

Kornhauser, D., Rand, W., & Wilensky, U. (2009). Design guidelines for agent-based model visualization. *Journal of Artificial Societies and Social Simulation, 12*(2), 1.

Korzybski, A. (1990). *Collected Writings 1920–1950.* Forest Hills, NY: Institute of General Semantics.

Kretzschmar, M., van den Hof, S., Wallinga, J., & van Wijngaarden, J. (2004). Ring vaccination and smallpox control. http://www.cdc.gov/ncidod/EID/vol10no5/03-0419.htm

Labov, W. (2001). *Principles of Linguistic Change: Social Factors* (Vol. 3). New York: Wiley-Blackwell.

Landau, L. D., Lifshitz, E., & Mikhailovich, E. (1976). *Statistical Physics* (3rd ed.). Oxford: Pergamon Press.

Langley, P., & Simon, H. A. (1995). Applications of machine learning and rule induction. *Communications of the ACM, 38*(11), 54–64.

Lansing, J. S. (2006). *Perfect Order: Recognizing Complexity in Bali.* Princeton: Princeton University Press.

Lansing, J. S., & Kremer, J. N. (1993). Emergent properties of Balinese water temples. *American Anthropologist, 95*(1), 97–114.

Latour, B., & Woolgar, S. (1979). *Laboratory Life: The Social Construction of Scientific Facts.* Beverly Hills, CA: Sage Publications.

Lave, C. A., & March, J. (1975). *An Introduction to Models in the Social Sciences.* New York: Harper & Row.

LeBaron, B. & Tesfatsion, L. (2008). Modeling macroeconomies as open-ended dynamic systems of interacting agents. *American Economic Review (Papers & Proceedings), 98*(2), 246–250.

Lechner, T., Ren, P., Watson, B., Brozefsky, C., & Wilensky, U. (2006). Procedural Modeling of Urban Land Use. Proceedings of the 33rd International Conference and Exhibition on Computer Graphics and Interactive Technologies (ACM SIGGRAPH 2006). Boston, MA.

Lent, D., Graham, P., & Collett, T. (2010). Image-matching during ant navigation occurs through saccade-like body turns controlled by learned visual features. *Proceedings of the National Academy of Sciences of the United States of America, 107*(37), 16348–16353.

Lerner, R., Levy, S. T., & Wilensky, U. (2010). Encouraging collaborative constructionism: Principles behind the modeling commons. Proceedings of Constructionism 2010. Paris.

Levy, S. T., Novak, M., & Wilensky, U. (2006). Students' foraging through the complexities of the particulate world: Scaffolding for independent inquiry in the connected chemistry (MAC) curriculum. Paper presented at the annual meeting of the American Educational Research Association, San Francisco, CA.

Levy, S. T., & Wilensky, U. (2009). Students' learning with the Connected Chemistry (CC1) curriculum: Navigating the complexities of the particulate world. *Journal of Science Education and Technology*, *18*(3), 243–254.

Lewes, G. H. (1875). *Problems of Life and Mind (First Series)*, 2. London: Trübner.

Li, H., & Tesfatsion, L. (2009). Development of open source software for power market research: The AMES test bed. *Journal of Energy Markets*, *2*(2), 111–128.

Longley, P., Goodchild, M. F., Maguire, D., & Rhind, D. (2005). *Geographic Information Systems and Science*. New York: Wiley.

Lotka, A. J. (1925). *Elements of Physical Biology*. New York: Dover.

Luke, S., Cioffi-Revilla, C., et al. (2004). MASON: A multiagent simulation environment. *Simulation*, *81*(7), 517–527.

Macy, M., & Willer, R. (2002). From factors to actors: Computational sociology and agent-based modeling. *Annual Review of Sociology*, *28*, 143–166.

Maroulis, S., Guimera, R., Petry, H., Stringer, M. J., Gomez, L. M., Amaral, L. A. N., et al. (2010). Complex systems view of educational policy research. *Science*, *330*(6000), 38. doi:10.1126/science.1195153.

McCarthy, J. (1960). Recursive functions of symbolic expressions and their computation by machine. *Communications of the ACM*, *3*(4), 184–195.

McGarigal, K., & Marks, B. J. (1995). *FRAGSTATS: Spatial Pattern Analysis Program for Quantifying Landscape Structure*. Washington, DC: US Forest Service.

Meadows, D. (1972). *The Limits to Growth: A Report for the Club of Rome's Project on the Predicament of Mankind*. New York: Universe.

Metropolis, N., & Ulam, S. (1949). The Monte Carlo method. *Journal of the American Statistical Association*, *44*(247), 335–341.

Michie, D. (1989). Problems of computer-aided concept formation. In J. R. Quinlan (Ed.), *Applications of Expert Systems* (Vol. 2, pp. 310–333). Wokingham, UK: Addison-Wesley.

Milgram, S. (1967). The small world problem. *Psychology Today*, *2*, 60–67.

Miller, J. (1998). Active nonlinear tests (ANTs) of complex simulation models. *Management Science*, *44*(6), 820–830.

Minar, N., & Burkhart, B. Langton, C. & Askenazi, M. (1996). The swarm simulation system: A toolkit for building multi-agent simulations. *Santa Fe Working Papers*.

Mitchell, M. (1998). *An Introduction to Genetic Algorithms*. Cambridge, MA: MIT Press.

Mitchell, M. (2009). *Complexity: A Guided Tour*. New York: Oxford University Press.

Mitchell, M., & Forrest, S. (1994). Genetic algorithms and artificial life. *Artificial Life*, *1*(3), 267–289.

Mitchell, T. (1997). *Machine Learning*. New York: McGraw-Hill.

Moore, C., & Newman, M. E. J. (2000). Epidemics and percolation in small-world networks. *Physical Review E: Statistical Physics, Plasmas, Fluids, and Related Interdisciplinary Topics*, *61*(5), 5678–5682.

Morris, M. (1993). Epidemiology and social networks: Modeling structured diffusion. *Sociological Methods & Research*, *22*, 99–126.

Mort, J. (1991). Perspective: The applicability of percolation theory to innovation. *Journal of Product Innovation Management*, *8*(1), 32–38.

Nash, J. F. (1950). Equilibrium points in N-person games. *Proceedings of the National Academy of Sciences of the United States of America*, *36*(1), 48–49.

Newman, M. E. (2005). A measure of betweenness centrality based on random walks. *Social Networks*, *27*(1), 39–54.

Newman, M. (2010). *Networks: An Introduction*. Oxford: Oxford University Press.

Newman, M., Girvan, M., & Farmer, J. D. (2002). Optimal design, robustness, and risk aversion. *Physical Review Letters*, *89*(2), 028301-1-4.

Newman, M., Watts, D. J., & Strogatz, S. (2006). *The Structure and Dynamics of Networks*. Princeton: Princeton University Press.

Niazi, M. O. S., Hussain, A., & Kolberg, M. (2010). Verification & validation of an agent-based forest fire simulation model. Proceedings of the Agent Directed Simulation Symposium 2010, as part of the ACM SCS Spring Simulation Multiconference, pp. 142–149, Orlando, FL, April 11–15.

North, M. J., Collier, N., & Vos, J. (2006). Experiences creating three implementations of the repast agent modeling toolkit. *ACM Transactions on Modeling and Computer Simulation*, *16*(1), 1–25.

Opper, M., & Saad, D. (Eds.). (2001). *Advanced Mean Field Methods: Theory and Practice—Neural Information Processing*. Cambridge, MA: MIT Press.

Papadimitriou, C. H. (1994). *Computational Complexity*. Reading, MA: Addison-Wesley.

Papert, S. (1980). *Mindstorms: Children, Computers, and Powerful Ideas*. New York: Basic Books.

Papert, S. (1987). Computer criticism vs. technocentric thinking. *Educational Researcher*, *16*(1), 22–30.

Papert, S. (1991). Situating constructionism. In I. Harel & S. Papert (Eds.), *Constructionism* (pp. 1–12). Norwood, NJ: Ablex Publishing.

Pareto, V. (1964). *Cours d'économie politique: Nouvelle édition par G. H. Bousquet et G. Busino*. Geneva: Librairie Droz.

Parker, D. C., Manson, S. M., Janssen, M. A., Hoffman, M. J., & Deadman, P. (2003). Multi-agent systems for the simulation of land-use and land-cover change: A review. *Annals of the Association of American Geographers*, *93*(2), 314–337.

Parunak, H. V. D., Savit, R., & Riolo, R. (1998). Agent-based modeling vs. equation-based modeling: A case study and users' guide. Workshop on Multi-Agent Systems and Agent-Based Simulation (MABS '98). Springer.

Patton, R. (2005). *Software Testing* (2nd ed.). New York: Sams.

Polhill, J. G., & Izquierdo, L. R. (2005). Lessons learned from converting the artificial stock market to interval arithmetic. *Journal of Artificial Societies and Social Simulation*, *8*(2).

Polhill, J. G., Izquierdo, L. R., & Gotts, N. M. (2005). The ghost in the model (and other effects of floating point arithmetic). *Journal of Artificial Societies and Social Simulation*, *8*(1).

Polhill, J. G., Izquierdo, L. R., & Gotts, N. M. (2006). What every agent-based modeller should know about floating point arithmetic. *Environmental Modelling & Software*, *21*(3), 283–309.

Quinlan, J. R. (1986). Induction of decision trees. *Machine Learning*, *1*(1), 81–106.

Rand, W. (2006). Machine learning meets agent-based modeling: When not to go to a bar. In C. M. Macal, D. L. Sallach, & M. J. North (Eds.), *Proceedings of the Agent 2006 Conference on Social Agents: Results and Prospects* (pp. 51–59). Chicago, IL: Argonne National Laboratory and the University of Chicago.

Rand, W., Blikstein, P., & Wilensky, U. (2008). *GoGoBot: Group Collaboration, Multi-Agent Modeling, and Robots. AAMAS 2008*. Lisbon: Estoril.

Rand, W., Brown, D. G., Page, S. E., Riolo, R., & Fernandez, L. E. (2003). Statistical validation of spatial patterns in agent-based models. In *Proceedings of Agent-Based Simulation 4*, Montpellier, France.

Rand, W., & Rust, R. T. (2011). Agent-based modeling in marketing: Guidelines for rigor. *International Journal of Research in Marketing*, *28*(3), 181–193.

Rand, W., & Stonedahl, F. (2007). The El Farol Bar problem and computational effort: Why people fail to use bars efficiently. In *Proceedings of Agent 2007 on Complex Interaction and Social Emergence*, Chicago, IL.

Rand, W., & Wilensky, U. (2007). Full-spectrum modeling: From simplicity to elaboration and realism in urban pattern formation. Proceedings of the North American Association Computational Social and Organization Sciences conference (NAACSOS), Atlanta, GA.

Reeves, W. T. (1983). Particle systems: A technique for modeling a class of fuzzy objects. *ACM Transactions on Graphics*, *2*(2), 91–108.

Rendell, P. (2002). Turing universality of the game of life. In *Collision-Based Computing* (pp. 513–539). London: Springer.

Resnick, M. (1994a). Changing the centralized mind. *Technology Review, 97*(5), 32–40.

Resnick, M. (1994b). *Turtles, Termites, and Traffic Jams: Explorations in Massively Parallel Microworlds.* Cambridge, MA: MIT Press.

Resnick, M. (1996). Beyond the centralized mindset. *Journal of the Learning Sciences, 5*(1), 1–22.

Resnick, M., & Wilensky, U. (1993). Beyond the deterministic, centralized mindsets: A new thinking for new science. Paper presented at the Annual meeting of the American Educational Research Association, Atlanta, GA.

Resnick, M., & Wilensky, U. (1998). Diving into complexity: Developing probabilistic decentralized thinking through role-playing activities. *Journal of the Learning Sciences, 7*(2), 153–171.

Reynolds, C. W. (1987). Flocks, herds and schools: A distributed behavioral model. *SIGGRAPH Computer Graphics, 21*(4), 25–34.

Richmond, B., Peterson, S., & Vescuso, P. (1989). An academic user's guide to Stella. *System Dynamics Review, 5*(2), 217–220.

Rogers, E. M. (2003). *Diffusion of Innovations* (5th ed.). New York: Free Press.

Rosenblatt, F. (1962). *Principles of Neurodynamics: Perceptrons and the Theory of Brain Mechanisms.* Washington, DC: Spartan.

Rubinstein, A. (2012). *Economic Fables.* New York: Open Book.

Russell, E., & Wilensky, U. (2008) Consuming spatial data in NetLogo using the GIS extension. Proceedings of Swarmfest, Chicago, IL.

Russell, S. J., & Norvig, P. (1995). *Artificial Intelligence: A Modern Approach.* Upper Saddle River, NJ: Prentice-Hall.

Sahimi, M. (1994). *Applications of Percolation Theory.* New York: Taylor & Francis.

Samuel, A. L. (1959). Some studies in machine learning using the game of checkers. *IBM Journal of Research and Development, 44*(1), 206–226.

Schelling, T. C. (1971). Dynamic models of segregation. *Journal of Mathematical Sociology, 1*, 143–186.

Schelling, T. (1978). *Micromotives and Macrobehavior.* New York: Norton.

Schmitz, O. J., & Booth, G. (1997). Modelling food web complexity: The consequences of individual-based, spatially explicit behavioural ecology on trophic interactions. *Evolutionary Ecology, 11*(4), 379–398.

Schoonderwoerd, R., Holland, O., Bruten, J., & Rothkrantz, L. (1996). Ant-based load balancing in telecommunications networks. *Adaptive Behavior, 5*(2), 169–207.

Sengupta, P., & Wilensky, U. (2005). NIELS Curriculum. http://ccl.northwestern.edu/NIELS. Center for Connected Learning and Computer-Based Modeling, Northwestern University, Evanston, IL.

Sengupta, P., & Wilensky, U. (2008). On learning electricity with multi-agent based computational models (NIELS). In G. Kanselaar, J. van Merri'nboer, P. Kirschner, & T. de Jong, Proceedings of the International Conference of the Learning Sciences (ICLS). Utrecht, The Netherlands: ICLS.

Sengupta, P., & Wilensky, U. (2009). Learning electricity with NIELS: Thinking with electrons and thinking in levels. *International Journal of Computers for Mathematical Learning, 14*(1), 21–50.

Shneiderman, B., & Plaisant, C. (2004). *Designing the User Interface: Strategies for Effective Human-Computer Interaction* (4th ed.). New York: Pearson Addison Wesley.

Simon, H. (1982). *Models of Bounded Rationality.* Cambridge, MA: MIT Press.

Simon, H. (1991). Bounded rationality and organizational learning. *Organization Science, 2*(1), 125–134.

Sipitakiat, A., Blikstein, P., & Cavallo, D. (2004). Gogo board: Augmenting programmable bricks for economically challenged audiences. Proceedings of the International Conference of the Learning Sciences, Los Angeles, CA.

Smith, E. R., & Conrey, F. R. (2007). Agent-based modeling: A new approach for theory building in social psychology. *Personality and Social Psychology Review, 11*(1), 87.

Stanfill, C., & Kahle, B. (1986). Parallel free-text search on the connection machine system. *Communications of the ACM, 29*(12), 1229–1239.

Stanley, M. H. R., Amaral, L. A. N., Buldyrev, S. V., Havlin, S., Leschhorn, H., Maass, P., et al. (1996). Scaling behaviour in the growth of companies. *Nature*, *379*(6568), 804.

Stanley, H. E. (1971). *Introduction to Phase Transitions and Critical Phenomena*. New York: Oxford University Press.

Sterman, J. (2000). *Business Dynamics: Systems Thinking for a Complex World*. New York: Irwin/McGraw-Hill.

Stauffer, D., & Aharony, A. (1994). *Introduction to Percolation Theory*. London: Taylor & Francis.

Stieff, M., & Wilensky, U. (2003). Connected chemistry: Incorporating interactive simulations into the chemistry classroom. *Journal of Science Education and Technology*, *12*(3), 285–302.

Stonedahl, F., Rand, W., & Wilensky, U. (2010). Evolving viral marketing strategies. Proceedings of the 12th Annual Conference on Genetic and Evolutionary Computation. Portland, OR.

Stonedahl, F., & Wilensky, U. (2010a). Finding forms of flocking: Evolutionary search in ABM parameter-spaces. Proceedings of the MABS Workshop at the Ninth International Conference on Autonomous Agents and Multi-Agent Systems. Toronto, Canada.

Stonedahl, F., & Wilensky, U. (2010b). Evolutionary robustness checking in the artificial Anasazi model. Proceedings of the AAAI Fall Symposium on Complex Adaptive Systems: Resilience, Robustness, and Evolvability. November 11–13, 2010. Arlington, VA.

Strogatz, S. H. (1994). *Nonlinear Dynamics and Chaos: With Applications to Physics, Biology, Chemistry, and Engineering*. Cambridge, MA: Westview Press.

Sun, J., & Tesfatsion, L. (2007). Dynamic testing of wholesale power market designs: An open-source agent-based framework. *Computational Economics*, *30*(3), 291–327.

Sussman, G., & Steele, G. (1998). The first report on scheme revisited. *Higher-Order and Symbolic Computation*, *11*(4), 399–404.

Sweeney, L. B., & Meadows, D. (2010). *The Systems Thinking Playbook: Exercises to Stretch and Build Learning and Systems Thinking Capabilities*. White River Junction, VT: Chelsea Green Publishing.

Tan, P. N., Steinbach, M., & Kumar, V. (2005). *Introduction to Data Mining*. Boston: Addison-Wesley Longman.

Taylor, C. A. (1996). *Defining Science: A Rhetoric of Demarcation*. Madison: University of Wisconsin Press.

Tesfatsion, L., & Judd, K. L. (2006). *Handbook of Computational Economics* (Vol. 13). Amsterdam: Elsevier.

Theraulaz, G., & Bonabeau, E. (1999). A brief history of stigmergy. *Artificial Life*, *5*(2), 97–116.

Tisue, S., & Wilensky, U. (2004). NetLogo: Design and implementation of a multi-agent modeling environment. Proceedings of the Agent 2004 conference, Chicago, IL, October 2004.

Troutman, C., Clark, B., & Goldrick, M. (2008). Social networks and intraspeaker variation during periods of language change. University of Pennsylvania Working Papers in Linguistics, Vol. 14. http://repository.upenn.edu/pwpl/vol14/iss1/25.

Troutman, C., Clark, B., & Goldrick, M. (2008). Social networks and intraspeaker variation during periods of language change. University of Pennsylvania Working Papers in Linguistics, Vol. 14. http://repository.upenn.edu/pwpl/vol14/iss1/25.

Tseng, P. (2009). Effects of performance schedules on event ticket sales. Ph.D. dissertation, University of Maryland.

Tucker, L., Feynman, C., & Fritzsche, D. (1988). Object recognition using the Connection Machine. Computer Vision and Pattern Recognition, 1988. Proceedings CVPR '88, Computer Society Conference on Computer Vision and Pattern Recognition. IEEE, 1988.

Tucker, L., & Robertson, G. (1988). Architecture and applications of the connection machine. *Computer*, *21*(8), 26–38.

Tufte, E. (1983). *The Visual Display of Quantitative Information*. Cheshire, CT: Graphics Press.

Tufte, E. (1996). *Visual Explanation*. Cheshire, CT: Graphics Press.

Turing, A. (1950). Computing machinery and intelligence. *Mind LIX*, *236*, 433–460.

Valente, T. W. (1995). *Networks Models of the Diffusion of Innovations*. New York: Hampton Press.

Vohra, R. V., & Wellman, M. P. (2007). Foundations of multi-agent learning: Introduction to the special issue. *Artificial Intelligence*, *171*(7), 363–364.

Volterra, V. (1926). Fluctuations in the abundance of a species considered mathematically. *Nature*, *188*, 558–560.

Von Neumann, J., Aspray, W., & Burks, A. (1987). *Papers of John Von Neumann on Computing and Computer Theory*. Cambridge, MA: MIT Press.

Von Neumann, J., & Burks, A. (1966). *Theory of Self-Reproducing Automata*. Urbana: University of Illinois Press.

Wagh, A., & Wilensky, U. (2013). Leveling the playing field: Making multi-level evolutionary processes accessible through participatory simulations. Proceedings of the Biannual Conference of Computer-Supported Collaborative Learning (CSCL), Madison, Wisconsin.

Walter, G. (1950). An electromechanical animal. *Dialectica*, *4*, 42–49.

Watts, D. J. (1999). A simple model of global cascades on random networks. *Proceedings of the National Academy of Sciences of the United States of America*, *99*(9), 5766–5771.

Watts, D. J. (2003). *Six Degrees*. New York: Norton.

Watts, D. J., & Strogatz, S. H. (1998). Collective dynamics of "small-world" networks. *Nature*, *393*, 440–442.

Weber, L. J., Goodwin, R. A., Li, S., Nestler, J. M., & Anderson, J. J. (2006). Application of an Eulerian-Lagrangian-Agent method (ELAM) to rank alternative designs of a juvenile fish passage facility. *Journal of Hydroinformatics*, *8*(4), 271–295.

Weiss, G. (2000). *Multiagent Systems: A Modern Approach to Distributed Artificial Intelligence*. Cambridge, MA: MIT Press.

Westerveldt, J., & Cohen, G. L. (2012). *Ecologist-Developed Spatially-Explicit Dynamic Landscape Models (Modeling Dynamic Systems)*. New York: Springer.

Wiener, N. (1961). *Cybernetics: Or, Control and Communication in the Animal and the Machine*. Cambridge, MA: MIT Press.

Wilensky, U. (1999b). GasLab: An extensible modeling toolkit for exploring micro-and-macro-views of gases. In N. Roberts, W. Feurzeig, & B. Hunter (Eds.), *Computer Modeling and Simulation in Science Education* (pp. 151–178). Berlin: Springer Verlag.

Wilensky, U. (2001, updated 2013). Modeling nature's emergent patterns with multi-agent languages. Proceedings of the EuroLogo 2001 Conference, Linz, Austria. http://ccl.northwestern.edu/papers/2013/mnep9.pdf.

Wilensky, U. (2003). Statistical mechanics for secondary school: The GasLab Modeling Toolkit. *International Journal of Computers for Mathematical Learning*, *8*(1), 1–41.

Wilensky, U., & Centola, D. (2007). Simulated evolution: Facilitating students' understanding of the multiple levels of fitness through multi-agent modeling. Paper presented at the Evolution Challenges conference, Phoenix, AZ, November 1–4. http://ccl.northwestern.edu/papers/2007/SimulatedEvolution-clean.pdf.

Wilensky, U., Levy, S., & Novak, M. (2004). NetLogo Connected Chemistry Curriculum. http://ccl.northwestern.edu/curriculum/ConnectedChemistry. Center for Connected Learning and Computer-Based Modeling, Northwestern University, Evanston, IL.

Wilensky, U., & Novak, M. (2010). Teaching and Learning Evolution as an Emergent Process—The BEAGLE project. In R. S. Taylor & M. Ferrari (Eds.), *Epistemology and Science Education: Understanding the Evolution vs. Intelligent Design Controversy* (pp. 213–243). New York: Routledge.

Wilensky, U., & Papert, S. (2010). Restructurations: Reformulations of knowledge disciplines through new representational forms. Proceedings of the Constructionism 2010 Conference, Paris, France.

Wilensky, U., Papert, S., Sherin, B., diSessa, A., Kay, A., & Turkle, S. (2005). *Center for learning and computation-based knowledge (CLICK)*. Proposal to the National Science Foundation—Science of Learning Center.

Wilensky, U., & Rand, W. (2007). Making models match: Replicating agent-based models. *Journal of Artificial Societies and Social Simulation*, *10*, 42.

Wilensky, U., & Reisman, K. (1998). Learning biology through constructing and testing computational theories—An embodied modeling approach. Proceedings of the Second International Conference on Complex Systems, Nashua, NH.

Wilensky, U., & Reisman, K. (2006). Thinking like a wolf, a sheep or a firefly: Learning biology through constructing and testing computational theories. *Cognition and Instruction, 24*(2), 171–209.

Wilensky, U., & Resnick, M. (1999). Thinking in levels: A dynamic systems approach to making sense of the world. *Journal of Science Education and Technology, 8*(1), 3–19.

Wilensky, U., & Stroup, W. (2000). Networked gridlock: Students enacting complex dynamic phenomena with the HubNet architecture. Proceedings of the Fourth Annual International Conference of the Learning Sciences, Ann Arbor, MI, June 14–17.

Wilensky, U., & Stroup, W. (2002). *Participatory Simulations guide for HubNet*. Evanston, IL: Center for Connected Learning and Computer Based Modeling, Northwestern University; http://ccl.northwestern.edu/ps/guide.

Wilkerson-Jerde, M. H., & Wilensky, U. (2010). Restructuring change, interpreting changes: The deltatick modeling and analysis toolkit. *Proceedings of Constructionism 2010*, Paris.

Wilkerson-Jerde, M., & Wilensky, U. (in press). From probabilistic birth to exponential population: Making sense of the calculus of complex systems. *Journal of the Learning Sciences*.

Wilson, E. O. (1974). *The Insect Societies*. Cambridge, MA: Belknap Press.

Wilson, W., de Roos, A., & McCauley, E. (1993). Spatial instabilities within the diffusive Lotka-Volterra system: Individual-based simulation results. *Theoretical Population Biology, 43*(1), 91–127.

Wilson, W. G. (1998). Resolving discrepancies between deterministic population models and individual-based simulations. *American Naturalist, 151*(2), 116–134.

Witten, T. A., Jr., & Sander, L. M. (1981). Diffusion limited aggregation. *Physical Review Letters, 47*, 1400–1403.

Witten, T. A., Jr., & Sander, L. M. (1983). Diffusion limited aggregation. *Physical Review B: Condensed Matter and Materials Physics, 27*(9), 5686–5697.

Wittlinger, M., Wehner, R., & Wolf, H. (2006). The ant odometer: Stepping on stilts and stumps. *Science, 312*(5782), 1965–1967.

Wolfram, S. (1983). Statistical mechanics of cellular automata. *Reviews of Modern Physics, 5*(3), 601–644.

Wolfram, S. (2002). *A New Kind of Science*. Champaign, IL: Wolfram Media.

Yoon, I., Williams, R. J., Levine, E., Yoon, S., Dunne, J. A., & Martinez, N. D. (2004). Webs on the Web (WoW): 3D visualization of ecological networks on the WWW for collaborative research and education. Proceedings of the IS&T/SPIE Symposium on Electronic Imaging, Visualization and Data Analysis 5295:124–132.

Zuse, K. (1969). *Rechnender Raum*. Brunswick: Vieweg & Sohn.

Software and Models

Chapter 0

Wilensky, U. (1999). NetLogo (computer software). Center for Connected Learning and Computer-Based Modeling, Northwestern University, Evanston, IL.

Wilensky, U. (1997a). NetLogo Traffic Basic model. Center for Connected Learning and Computer-Based Modeling, Northwestern University, Evanston, IL. http://ccl.northwestern.edu/netlogo/models/TrafficBasic.

Wilensky, U. (1997b). NetLogo Fire model. Center for Connected Learning and Computer-Based Modeling, Northwestern University, Evanston, IL. http://ccl.northwestern.edu/netlogo/models/Fire.

Wilensky, U. (1997c). NetLogo Wolf Sheep Predation model. Center for Connected Learning and Computer-Based Modeling, Northwestern University, Evanston, IL. http://ccl.northwestern.edu/netlogo/models/WolfSheepPredation.

Wilensky, U. (1998). NetLogo Flocking model. Center for Connected Learning and Computer-Based Modeling, Northwestern University, Evanston, IL. http://ccl.northwestern.edu/netlogo/models/Flocking.

Chapter 1

Richmond, B., & Peterson, S. (1990). *STELLA II* (computer software). Hanover, NH: High Performance Systems Inc.

Wilensky, U. (1997). *NetLogo Ants model*. Center for Connected Learning and Computer-Based Modeling, Northwestern University, Evanston, IL.

Chapter 2

Wilensky, U. (1998). *NetLogo CA 1D Elementary*. http://ccl.northwestern.edu/netlogo/models/CA1DElementary/. Center for Connected Learning and Computer-Based Modeling, Northwestern University, Evanston, IL.

Chapter 3

Maroulis, S., & Wilensky, U. (2004). NetLogo HubNet Oil Cartel model. http://ccl.northwestern.edu/netlogo/models/HubNetOilCartel. Center for Connected Learning and Computer-Based Modeling, Northwestern University, Evanston, IL.

Rand, W., & Wilensky, U. (2007). NetLogo El Farol model. http://ccl.northwestern.edu/netlogo/models/ElFarol. Center for Connected Learning and Computer-Based Modeling, Northwestern University, Evanston, IL.

Wilensky, U. (1997a). NetLogo Fire model. http://ccl.northwestern.edu/netlogo/models/Fire. Center for Connected Learning and Computer-Based Modeling, Northwestern University, Evanston, IL.

Wilensky, U. (1997b). NetLogo DLA model. http://ccl.northwestern.edu/netlogo/models/DLA. Center for Connected Learning and Computer-Based Modeling, Northwestern University, Evanston, IL.

Wilensky, U. (1997c). NetLogo Mandelbrot model. http://ccl.northwestern.edu/netlogo/models/Mandelbrot. Center for Connected Learning and Computer-Based Modeling, Northwestern University, Evanston, IL.

Wilensky, U. (1997d). NetLogo Segregation model. http://ccl.northwestern.edu/netlogo/models/Segregation. Center for Connected Learning and Computer-Based Modeling, Northwestern University, Evanston, IL.

Wilensky, U. (1998). NetLogo Percolation model. http://ccl.northwestern.edu/netlogo/models/Percolation. Center for Connected Learning and Computer-Based Modeling, Northwestern University, Evanston, IL.

Wilensky, U., & Stroup, W. (2003). NetLogo HubNet Root Beer Game model. http://ccl.northwestern.edu/netlogo/models/HubNetRootBeerGame. Center for Connected Learning and Computer-Based Modeling, Northwestern University, Evanston, IL.

Chapter 4

Novak, M. & Wilensky, U. (2005). NetLogo Bug Hunt Camouflage model. http://ccl.northwestern.edu/netlogo/models/BugHuntCamouflage. Center for Connected Learning and Computer-Based Modeling, Northwestern University, Evanston, IL.

Nichols, N. & Wilensky, U. (2006). NetLogo Sunflower Biomorphs model. http://ccl.northwestern.edu/netlogo/models/SunflowerBiomorphs. Center for Connected Learning and Computer-Based Modeling, Northwestern University, Evanston, IL.

Wilensky, U. (2005). NetLogo Wolf Sheep Predation (System Dynamics) model. http://ccl.northwestern.edu/netlogo/models/WolfSheepPredation(SystemDynamics). Center for Connected Learning and Computer-Based Modeling, Northwestern University, Evanston, IL.

Wilensky, U., & Shargel, B. (2002). BehaviorSpace (computer software). Center for Connected Learning and Computer Based Modeling, Northwestern University, Evanston, IL. http://ccl.northwestern.edu/netlogo/docs/behaviorspace.html.

Chapter 5

Tinker, R., & Wilensky, U. (2007). NetLogo climate change model. Center for Connected Learning and Computer-Based Modeling, Northwestern University, Evanston, IL. http://ccl.northwestern.edu/netlogo/models/ClimateChange

Wilensky, U. (1997a). NetLogo AIDS model. Center for Connected Learning and Computer-Based Modeling, Northwestern University, Evanston, IL. http://ccl.northwestern.edu/netlogo/models/AIDS.

Wilensky, U. (1997b). NetLogo termites model. Center for Connected Learning and Computer-Based Modeling, Northwestern University, Evanston, IL. http://ccl.northwestern.edu/netlogo/models/termites.

Wilensky, U. (1997b). NetLogo traffic basic model. Center for Connected Learning and Computer-Based Modeling, Northwestern University, Evanston, IL. http://ccl.northwestern.edu/netlogo/models/TrafficBasic.

Wilensky, U. (1998b). NetLogo tumor model. Center for Connected Learning and Computer-Based Modeling, Northwestern University, Evanston, IL. http://ccl.northwestern.edu/netlogo/models/Tumor.

Wilensky, U. (2000). *NetLogo 3DModels Library*. Center for Connected Learning and Computer-Based Modeling, Northwestern University, Evanston, IL.

Wilensky, U. (2002). NetLogo Traffic Grid model. Center for Connected Learning and Computer-Based Modeling, Northwestern University, Evanston, IL. http://ccl.northwestern.edu/netlogo/models/TrafficGrid.

Wilensky, U. (2003). NetLogo ethnocentrism model. Center for Connected Learning and Computer-Based Modeling, Northwestern University, Evanston, IL. http://ccl.northwestern.edu/netlogo/models/ethnocentrism.

Wilensky, U. (2005a). NetLogo small worlds model. Center for Connected Learning and Computer-Based Modeling, Northwestern University, Evanston, IL. http://ccl.northwestern.edu/netlogo/models/SmallWorlds.

Wilensky, U. (2005b). NetLogo Flocking 3D Alternate model. Center for Connected Learning and Computer-Based Modeling, Northwestern University, Evanston, IL. http://ccl.northwestern.edu/netlogo/models/Flocking3DAlternate.

Wilensky, U. (2006). NetLogo Grand Canyon model. Center for Connected Learning and Computer-Based Modeling, Northwestern University, Evanston, IL. http://ccl.northwestern.edu/netlogo/models/GrandCanyon.

Wilensky, U., & Rand, W. (2006). NetLogo 3DPercolation model. Center for Connected Learning and Computer-Based Modeling, Northwestern University, Evanston, IL. http://ccl.northwestern.edu/netlogo/models/Percolation3D.

Chapter 6

Troutman, C., & Wilensky, U. (2007). NetLogo Language Change model. http://ccl.northwestern.edu/netlogo/models/LanguageChange. Center for Connected Learning and Computer-Based Modeling, Northwestern University, Evanston, IL.

Wilensky, U. (2006). NetLogo Grand Canyon model. http://ccl.northwestern.edu/netlogo/models/GrandCanyon. Center for Connected Learning and Computer-Based Modeling, Northwestern University, Evanston, IL.

Wilensky, U., & Shargel, B. (2001). *BehaviorSpace* (computer software). Center for Connected Learning and Computer Based Modeling, Northwestern University, Evanston, IL:

Chapter 7

Parker, M. (2000). *Ascape* (computer software). Brookings Institution, Washington, DC.

Stonedahl & Wilensky. U. (2007). NetLogo Artificial Anasazi model. http://ccl.northwestern.edu/netlogo/models/ArtificialAnasazi. Center for Connected Learning and Computer-Based Modeling, Northwestern University, Evanston, IL.

Stonedahl, F., & Wilensky, U. (2010c). BehaviorSearch (computer software). Center for Connected Learning and Computer-Based Modeling, Northwestern University, Evanston, IL.

Wilensky, U. (1998a). NetLogo Flocking model. Center for Connected Learning and Computer-Based Modeling, Northwestern University, Evanston, IL. Retrieved from http://ccl.northwestern.edu/netlogo/models/Flocking.

Wilensky, U. (1998b). NetLogo Voting model. Center for Connected Learning and Computer-Based Modeling, Northwestern University, Evanston, IL. Retrieved from http://ccl.northwestern.edu/netlogo/models/Voting.

Wilensky, U. (2003). NetLogo Ethnocentrism model. http://ccl.northwestern.edu/netlogo/models/Ethnocentrism. Center for Connected Learning and Computer-Based Modeling, Northwestern University, Evanston, IL.

Chapter 8

Brady, C. (2013). Arduino extension link. https://github.com/cbradyatinquire/arduino-extension.

Bakshy, E., & Wilensky, U. (2007a). NetLogo-Mathematica Link. http://ccl.northwestern.edu/netlogo/mathematica.html. Center for Connected Learning and Computer-Based Modeling, Northwestern University, Evanston, IL.

Blikstein, P., & Wilensky, U. (2005). NetLogoLab (computer software and hardware). http://ccl.northwestern.edu/netlogolab. Center for Connected Learning and Computer Based Modeling, Northwestern University, Evanston, IL.

Densmore, O., Guerin, S., McKenna, S., & Jung, D. (2004). NetLogo Cruising Model. http://www.gisagents.org/2006/02/car-cruising-model-gis-example.html.

Densmore, O. & Guerin, S. (2007). NetLogo Venice model.

Kim, D., Sun, W., Stonedahl, F., & Wilensky, U. (2010). NetLogo hydrogen diffusion 3D model. http://ccl.northwestern.edu/netlogo/models/hydrogendiffusion3D. Center for Connected Learning and Computer-Based Modeling, Northwestern University, Evanston, IL.

Mitchell, M., Tisue, S., & Wilensky, U. (2012). NetLogo Robby the Robot model. http://ccl.northwestern.edu/netlogo/models/RobbytheRobot. Center for Connected Learning and Computer-Based Modeling, Northwestern University, Evanston, IL.

Stonedahl, F. (2012). NetLogo Raytracing extension. https://github.com/fstonedahl/RayTracing-Extension.

Stonedahl, F., & Wilensky, U. (2010c). BehaviorSearch (computer software). http://behaviorsearch.org. Center for Connected Learning and Computer-Based Modeling, Northwestern University, Evanston, IL.

Wilensky, U. (2002). NetLogo Mousetraps 3D model. http://ccl.northwestern.edu/netlogo/models/Mousetraps3D. Center for Connected Learning and Computer-Based Modeling, Northwestern University, Evanston, IL.

Wilensky, U. (2003). NetLogo Honeycomb model. http://ccl.northwestern.edu/netlogo/models/honeycomb. Center for Connected Learning and Computer-Based Modeling, Northwestern University, Evanston, IL.

Wilensky, U. (2005a). NetLogo Flocking 3D Alternate model. http://ccl.northwestern.edu/netlogo/models/Flocking3DAlternate. Center for Connected Learning and Computer-Based Modeling, Northwestern University, Evanston, IL.

Wilensky, U. (2005b). NetLogo Wolf Sheep predation (docked) model. http://ccl.northwestern.edu/netlogo/models/WolfSheepPredation(docked). Center for Connected Learning and Computer-Based Modeling, Northwestern University, Evanston, IL.

Wilensky, U. (2006a). NetLogo DLA 3D model. http://ccl.northwestern.edu/netlogo/models/DLA3D. Center for Connected Learning and Computer-Based Modeling, Northwestern University, Evanston, IL.

Wilensky, U. (2006b). NetLogo Grand Canyon model. http://ccl.northwestern.edu/netlogo/models/GrandCanyon. Center for Connected Learning and Computer-Based Modeling, Northwestern University, Evanston, IL.

Wilensky, U. (2006c). NetLogo Percolation 3D model. http://ccl.northwestern.edu/netlogo/models/Percolation3D. Center for Connected Learning and Computer-Based Modeling, Northwestern University, Evanston, IL.

Wilensky, U. (2006d). NetLogo Sandpile 3D model. http://ccl.northwestern.edu/netlogo/models/Sandpile3D. Center for Connected Learning and Computer-Based Modeling, Northwestern University, Evanston, IL.

Wilensky, U. (2006e). http://ccl.northwestern.edu/netlogo/models/TabonucoYagrumo. NetLogo Tabonuco Yagrumo model. Center for Connected Learning and Computer-Based Modeling, Northwestern University, Evanston, IL.

Wilensky, U. (2006f). NetLogo Tabonuco Yagrumo Hybrid model. http://ccl.northwestern.edu/netlogo/models/TabonucoYagrumoHybrid. Center for Connected Learning and Computer-Based Modeling, Northwestern University, Evanston, IL.

Wilensky, U., & Maroulis, S. (2005). System Dynamics Modeler (computer software). http://ccl.northwestern.edu/netlogo/docs/systemdynamics.html. Center for Connected Learning and Computer Based Modeling, Northwestern University, Evanston, IL.

Wilensky, U., & Stroup, W. (1999b). NetLogo HubNet Disease model. http://ccl.northwestern.edu/netlogo/models/HubNetDisease. Center for Connected Learning and Computer-Based Modeling, Northwestern University, Evanston, IL.

Wilensky, U., & Stroup, W. (1999c). HubNet. Evanston, IL: Center for Connected Learning and Computer-Based Modeling, Northwestern University. Retrieved from http://ccl.northwestern.edu/netlogo

Chapter 9

Collier, N. (2001). Repast (Computer software). Chicago: University of Chicago. Retrieved from http://repast.sourceforge.net.

Index